praise for

Ritual at World's End

Carvalhaes here scribes a *lex naturae* whose law is sap, whose court is soil, whose sanction is water, wept by the oppressed, danced by the Indigenous, seeping liberation beyond grammar. Like the river he now consults, his text loves the lowest place, pushing politics into the ground like a seed. He ranges wide across theory, North and South, but keeps all such intelligence accountable to the talk of weeds, of birds, of the poor. A *liturgos* of the people, indeed--hosted by a tree called Wonder! But be prepared, all who read here, while your toes may begin sprouting flowers, your heart will bleed martyrs and may cost you everything.

James W. Perkinson
Professor of Social Ethics
Ecumenical Theological Seminary
Detroit, Michigan

This book explores a new eco-liturgical liberation theology that is truly inspiring and hope-filled in the context of the seemingly endless Covid19 pandemic. The earth has been pulled into a vortex of ennui — of helplessness and despondency. I live in a country literally gasping for breath under the impact of the pandemic. Lock downs exposed deep structural injustices and interrupted all aspects of our lives, including the traditional worship life of the churches. Should this not be a moment to pause; to look critically at the life and ministry of the church; and take new directions? A eco-liturgical liberation theology is a creative earth-centred theology that offers some answers — will we grasp the moment?

Aruna Gnanadason
Author of *With Courage and Compassion: Women and the Ecumenical Movement*
And Former Director
Women in Church and Society and Justice, Peace, and Creative Programs
World Council of Churches
Geneva, Switzerland

In this earth-shattering, earth-reorienting book, Cláudio Carvalhaes, the most creative and revolutionary liturgical scholar today, invites us to awaken from "our slumber" and envision every facet of worship as deeply connected to a planet on fire. Radical earth-grounded liturgy just might convert worshippers to see and respond to the most vulnerable among us—trees, birds, lands, seas, mountains, rocks, animals, seeds, bugs, minerals. A crucial book destined to become the most essential classic in contemporary liturgical studies.

Bonnie J. Miller-McLemore
E. Rhodes and Leona B. Carpenter Professor, *Emerita*
Vanderbilt University
Nashville, Tennessee

Ritual at World's End maps Cláudio's conversion to an ecological approach to liturgy. It also manifests his ever-confident eschewal of the usual authorities in liturgical theology. Instead, he is looking to liberation theologians, and listening to the poor. So, these are the field notes of a man on a journey—to the land, to his past, with his children, for the overlooked—as he wrestles with his questions, privilege, and responsibilities. Passion and urgency, truth-telling and testimony, combine with great force in Cláudio's thinking, and this remarkable book will be well-read, gather companions, and muster more justice in the life of believers. Read it for it's challenge, gift, provocation, blessing, agenda-setting, summons…

Stephen Burns
Professor of Liturgical and Practical Theology
Pilgrim Theological College, University of Divinity
Melbourne, Australia

In his groundbreaking eco-liturgical liberation theology, Claudio Carvalhaes provokes and challenges us to live, love, and flourish in a relational sense by recognizing that our lives are intrinsically interwoven with one another and the earth. As a Dalit comparative liberation theologian, I am deeply moved by Claudio's passionate call to listen to, worship with, and live for the dal, the broken and crushed peoples of the world and our planet herself. This provocative book will make you cry, laugh, and learn.

Joshua Samuel
United Theological College
Bangalore, India

Dr. Carvalhaes is the prophet of our time, who is relentlessly reminding and reprimanding us for neglecting the painful cry of the earth. In his ground-breaking book, Ritual at World's End: An Eco-Liturgical Liberation Theology he proposes to reforest our minds, reimagine green faith, reread the stories of the gospel, and the Christian tradition using a new principle, lex naturae. This book disrupts our theologies, thinking, theories, practices, liturgies, rituals, the ordo, and traditions. It is a call to pay attention to the voice of the earth, and learn a new grammar of faith.

Moses Shanthi Kumar Bollam
Ph.D. Student, *Union Theological Seminary*
New York City

Soaked in the spirituality of Jesus, infected by a Franciscan radicalism, committed to this earth and the Kingdom that is coming – all this is true of this book, which I read with enthusiasm and consternation. We have never needed an eco-liberation theology more than we do today. This book will be obligatory reading for my students!

Prof. Ralph Kunz
Theological Seminary, University of Zürich
Switzerland

In this sharp, critical and path breaking book, Cláudio Carvalhaes invites us to re-imagine worship as rituals of defiance and alternatives. He encourages us to recognize the power of Liturgy as our political engagement to overthrow and ruin the pyramids of injustice. It is an invitation to resist the temptation to be co-opted by the Empire, and the nerve to come out of the Empire, creating counter-imperial alternatives. This prophetic volume of an eco-liturgical liberation theology is a paradigm shift in Liturgical Studies and a must read for all.

Sudipta Singh
former Mission Secretary for Research and Capacity Development
Council of World Mission

A fresh sacramental drip of ruach that will breathe, blow, and bless any liturgical community desiring to re-align, re-connect, and re-member the ecology of creation and community to which they belong. Thank you dear Cláudio!

Derek Elmi-Buursma
Pastor
Loop Church Chicago, Illinois

Once again, prolific scholar, theologian, and liturgist Cláudio Carvalhaes brings a pastoral heart and a prophetic fire to the work of critically engaging, lovingly deconstructing, and passionately reimagining a space of worship and a manner of prayer that will not only bear witness to the trees clapping their hands, but will also run into the fields and dance along with them. This collection of essays on eco-liturgical liberation theology is not only paradigm-shifting and genre-bending (a hallmark of Carvalhaes' work) but it also shakes our piety, inviting us to embrace the earth and to sing the songs of stars and birds.

Scholarly and mystical, medicinal and liberative in its thrust, this book will be an indispensable addition to the library of anyone who wishes to delve into a faith that is grounded in the earth.

Rev. Thomas R. Gaulke, Ph.D.
Pastor and author of *An Unpromising Hope*

RITUAL AT WORLD'S END

Essays on
Eco-Liturgical Liberation Theology

Cláudio Carvalhaes

Ritual at World's End

Essays on Eco-Liturgical Liberation Theology

Cláudio Carvalhaes

Barber's Son Press

York, Pennsylvania

BARBER'S SON PRESS

York, Pennsylvania

© 2021 Cláudio Carvalhaes.

Foreword © 2021 Ivone Gebara.

All artwork and photography © the artists; other contributions © the contributors. *Permissions listed individually at the end of the book.*

Photography: Rafael Carvalhaes Ortiz, front cover; and Katie Deveney Perella Carvalhaes, back cover.

Artwork: Olivia Maia Victoriano Pacheco da Silva, Mabel Bastos Chiavegatti, Sarah Grinaboldi Ortiz, Isaque Grinaboldi Ortiz, Nicolas Chiavegatti Scaff, Luíza Carvalhaes Rocha, Carine Shresta Bollam, Davi Chiavegatti Scaff, Marshall Jacob Frantz, Avery Leigh Frantz, Samuel Bastos Chiavegatti, Chris Immanuel Bollam, Peter Isaac Lindsey Perella Carvalhaes, George Emerson Vander Tuig, Cecilia Anne Perella Carvalhaes, and Elizabeth Kathryn Perella Carvalhaes.

ISBN: 978-1-7347188-2-9 (hardcover), 978-1-7347188-3-6 (softcover); LCCN: 2021943530.

10   9   8   7   6   5   4   3   2   1

Dedication

To

Ivone Gebara,

Nancy Cardoso,

Leonardo Boff,

Jaci C. Maraschin,

Rubem Alves

and

Odair Pedroso Mateus

They gave me a place in the world,

they gave me language to live by,

they filled my heart with justice and wonder.

TABLE OF CONTENTS

Original Artwork in this Book   *ii*

Publisher's Note   *iii*
Who Do You Say "Whom" Is?

Foreword   1
 by Ivone Gebara

Introduction   7

 Wonder and Me, Rooted   21

 The Ecological Lord's Prayer   22

Chapter One   23
Eco-Liturgical Liberation Theology

Chapter Two   79
Lex Naturae: A New Way into
a Liturgical Political Theology

Chapter Three   108
Rituals and Performances in the
Anthropocene: Eco-Liturgical
Liberation Pantheologies

 Appendix to Chapter Three   135

Chapter Four   139
Worship, Liturgy and Public Witness

Chapter Five   **157**
From Multiculturalisms to
Multinaturalisms: Liturgical
Theological Shifts

Chapter Six   **171**
The Christian as Humus: Virtual/Real
Earthly Rituals of Ourselves

Chapter Seven   **185**
Class, Interreligious Borders, and Ways
of Living with Pachamama

Chapter Eight   **207**
Birds, People, Then Religion: An
Eco-Liberation Theological and
Pedagogical Approach to Interreligious
Rituals

Chapter Nine   **219**
White Reasoning and Worship
Methodology

    An Example: Let it Burn!   **336**

Chapter Ten   **243**
Queering Christian Worship Services
    with Janet Walton

Chapter Eleven   **263**
God´s Petticoat and Capitalism—
Full Fashion
    with Nancy Cardoso Pereira

Chapter Twelve   277
Ecclesiologies as Foreign
Ecclesiologies: Worshiping with
the Homeless

Chapter Thirteen   293
Praying from the Ends of the World

Chapter Fourteen   317
African-Indigenous Jurema:
The Greatest Common Divisor
of the Brazilian Minimum Religion
with Nancy Cardoso Pereira

Conclusion   333

    A Blessing to You All   338

Notes   345

Permissions   383

Bibliography   385

Index   399

Author   401

Original Artwork in This Book

Olivia Maia Victoriano Pacheco da Silva, 1 year old

Mabel Bastos Chiavegatti, 2 years old

Sarah Grinaboldi Ortiz, 3 years old

Isaque Grinaboldi Ortiz, 3 years old

Nicolas Chiavegatti Scaff, 4 years old

Luíza Carvalhaes Rocha, 6 years old

Carine Shresta Bollam, 7 years old

Davi Chiavegatti Scaff, 7 years old

Marshall Jacob Frantz, 7 years old

Avery Leigh Frantz, 8 years old

Samuel Bastos-Chiavegatti, 9 years old

Chris Immanuel Bollam, 9 years old

Peter Isaac Lindsey Perella Carvalhaes, 9 years old

George Emerson Vander Tuig, 11 years old

Cecilia Anne Perella Carvalhaes, 13 years old

Elizabeth Kathryn Perella Carvalhaes, 15 years old

PUBLISHER'S NOTE

Who Do We Say 'Whom' Is?

No one would assume it unusual for a prolific and active scholar to collect essays and papers delivered at conferences and initially published in journals into a monograph, and that is exactly what *Ritual at World's End* is. What makes this book different, however, is its relentless commitment to a particular spiritual journey, an active presence of a cloud of witnesses who are a community of readers, and its urgent contribution to *this* moment.

Theology can be many things in any myriad of expressions, but theology is autobiography; in this book Cláudio Carvalhaes leads us through a unique expedition and is willing to deviate from a map—for if the map were certain, the journey would simply be a formality. Many theologians, like Cláudio, do not differentiate their simultaneous roles of being scholar and pastor, and we ought to celebrate those willing to take intellectual or spiritual risks: risks which are ultimately vocational proclamations of identity and context, forging genuinely new ways of being and doing the Christian faith.

This book is such a passage, showing us the twists and turns which do not change its pervasive, opening desire—to follow the Christ and worship God—disclosing, expanding, and deepening our approach to the very practical question of how to live out the Beatitudes. Seeking to do this more faithfully, Cláudio does not simply point to the emperor who has no clothes, and not just to colonialism and racism, but offers us a deep look into the mirror of the theologian himself.

The cultural critique which runs throughout this book, then, is not just pointed, but is *self-implicating*. As such we are invited to shed skins with the author, leaving them behind along the path for others to discover, understand, and continue the journey. The nature of theology and its "publics"; our relationship to the land; the *polis* and the political; the multiplicity of our sexualities; and our ontologies of "being together" are genuinely challenged, stretched, and in some cases shattered. Gathering those remaining fragments, we realize how ignorant—often, how *willfully* ignorant—we have been in our approach to the world as a whole.

The fellow traveler is left to ask for themselves "What is worship if it is *not* self-implicating?" and "How is that self-implication liberating?"

Adding, then, "—*liberative* Good News…*for whom?*"
And finally: "Who do we say that *whom* is?"

Just as the reader is emphatically invited as a valued theological agent through Cláudio's work, this book also represents a community of readers. As a true scholarly project, these essays have been presented, discussed, debated, initially published, peer-reviewed, rewritten, revised, taught, and lived. The product before you is the result of dialogue with many and numerous contexts.

But what haunts me exigently is Cláudio's commitment to the physical product of this book to be a canvas which celebrates his communities, relationships, families, close colleagues, and children—all contributing to the project as both an event and a testament to community and cloud of witnesses.

The artwork throughout this haunting book, in its final presentation, is for me a deliberate editorial spooking of Paul Tillich's *My Search for Absolutes,* an "intellectual autobiography" exhibiting the theologian's main ideas—paired with bold drawings by the Jewish modernist Saul Steinberg. Published posthumously in October, 1967, the book was unintentionally *in media res*: a few days before its release the "Stop the Draft Week" protests and demonstrations ended with a standoff between U.S. Marshalls and the Army defending the Pentagon in an event that began with 100,000 rallying against the Vietnam War at the Lincoln Memorial. The day the book was published saw a mass shooting in Lock Haven, Pennsylvania, and two days later, a mass murder of children in Arcadia, Florida. The following day the "Baltimore Four," which included a Catholic priest and United Church of Christ pastor, broke into a federal building in Baltimore and performed a ritual protest. After desecrating sixteen drawers of draft records with their own and animal blood the Four gifted Bibles to the police who arrested them.

Ritual at World's End arrives to us similarly *in media res*—in the middle of things—to urgent ecological, hoplological, geo-political crises in need of ritual, protest, and evangelism to the corpse of Christendom. Cláudio does not in any way saccharine this moment or need. Yet the reader will experience his joy for the journey and hope for the future, enacting a subversive, liturgical festival celebrating the community and especially the heirs of this world.

"This is," Cláudio will proclaim on page 77, "the collective work of an eco-liturgical liberation theologian."

Christopher D. Rodkey

FOREWORD

Ivone Gebara

Nicolas Chiavegatti Scaff, 4 years old

> *My God, my God, why have you forsaken me?*
> *Why are you so far from helping me, from the words of my groaning?*
> *O my God, I cry by day, but you do not answer;*
> *and by night, but find no rest.*

Psalm 22:1-2 NRSV

The painful cry expressed by the psalmist represents the sentiment of most marginalized people who have experienced injustice. The feelings of abandonment, helplessness and orphanhood, seem to inhabit innumerous hearts, regardless of different times and cultures. They seem to renew themselves in different situations and cause us to ask questions about the meaning of our lives. Why is there so much pain and suffering? Why is one born in a fragile boat at sea, unable to reach the 'promised land'? Why is one born in the prison of the body of a young woman who has been taken prisoner?

The immediate answer, both spoken and unspoken, is simply this: to live with dignity on this planet! To enjoy the beauty that surrounds us. To eat and drink without tears. To have a house to shelter us on cold nights. To make our hearts more tender and sensitive. So many beautiful answers, but none of them seem useful or effective throughout human history. Few savor the answers. Many die without them, even after constantly seeking them.

The abandonment of women and men who are victims of cruelty and the irresponsibility of others seems to continue incessantly throughout the world. Likewise, the cry of the poor and the cry of those who hear the voices of the poor in solidarity, continue to accompany the new faces of violence in our history. Violence born of you and me. Violence that creates a multitude of executioners and victims.

How long will you forget me, O God? How long will my enemies triumph? How long will we remain wandering for shelter?

Yesterday and today, here and there, greed is still fertile, prejudice abounds, and the weapons of death acquire unmatched power. Extermination camps still abound today. Children continue to be separated from their parents at the borders invented by the shrewd who appropriate the land. Hunger continues on large plantations and thirst-quenching water is a plasticized mirage.

Can we still pray? Who do we pray to? Who really listens to us? What words do we use to pray? Pray! What does it really mean to pray?

Praying is a wonderful human invention that helps sustain life. It's like singing and making poetry for a living. It is a symbolic sustenance that springs forth almost unintentionally. We pray in thoughts, words and deeds. We pray by dancing, singing, crying and being silent. Anything and everything to maintain life, to defend life, to respect life, to love life, life that is as fragile as a breath.

To many, someone hears them, to many others their screams become only whispers that are lost in the great noises of the world. But everyone finds a way to pray! They pray for themselves, for others ... They pray to try to get out of the immediate situation that is oppressing them, far from the presence of cruelty that tears their lives away from them, they pray to ward off fear and anguish.

In this book, *Liturgical Liberation Theology*, Cláudio Carvalhaes sharpens our sensibility by inviting us to rethink an important part of Christian theology which is the Liturgy. Liturgy as a cry, praise, thanksgiving!

Centered on the figure of Jesus, liturgy wants to include as a part of this figure all the men and women who suffer and are wronged in this world. Liturgy is both historical memory and historical imagination! Liturgy uses the past to reframe the present!

> *"By the rivers of Babylon—there we sat down and there we wept when we remembered Zion. On the willows there we hung up our harps.*

> Psalm 137:1-2

Multiple variations of this old lament are born in numerous groups and speak of stolen forests, homeless lands and premeditated death. Local poetry becomes both a memory and a nourishing force for hope.

However, often times, by reading the same texts, repeating the same words and gestures, liturgies lose their strength and leave aside the necessary newness of their meaning. This meaning touches on a constant of human life expressed in both suffering and small resurrections, as if we were able and needed to feed ourselves on our lives being transformed into symbol, narrative, song and music. Liturgy is an expression of the dynamics of life and not just the memory of mysteries expressed through hermetic words born in other cultural contexts and in the offices of scholars.

This book invites us to rethink the place of our celebrations. It underlines the faith in liberation, a fragile, temporal liberation, mixed with the history of those who seek to affirm human and planetary dignity every day. It is not liberation as an end of the story or as a romantic happy ending that moves us or alienates or deludes us. It is liberation as a renewable, daily, personal and collective process. Liberation as little lights amid the immense difficulties and darkness of life, liberation as a welcome of the provisional happiness translated into a thousand and one forms of our daily life.

Liberation for a poor child who wanted an ice cream and someone offered them one. Liberation for a worker who received a bicycle. Liberation for a woman who got medicine for her sick child. Liberation of having land to plant. Everything so small, out of the spotlight of televisions and big newspapers!

Liturgy of memory and imagination that live together in the diversity of people, places and situations. Silence and word depending on what you are living. Sometimes the pain is so great that it drowns out words, singing and poetry. Tears blur one's vision and sobs interrupt the voices. Only silence and tears have room to manifest. Drowned in the immense pain as if "the waters of the sea of life would drown us" only silence is appropriate in this space.

Liturgy has to make room for silence. You have to allow for the pain to take over almost completely so that slowly the healing movement can take place and the poetry of prayer and community singing can also assume its place. As we mourn for the crucified and the hungry, tears and wailing are our mad prayer, our hoarse cry, our plea for relief, our only breath. This means being able to welcome the states of the soul and emotions as ingredients to express our liturgies.

We live in such a plural world, embroidered with such plural pain, plural joy and plural memory, that the challenge of a common language to express pain and hope becomes difficult. This is why friend Cláudio Carvalhaes invites us to think about our traditions based on creative ruptures. These ruptures break the homogeneity of the established liturgical order and combine it with the inevitable memories and pains of the present. Liturgy thus becomes hybrid, mixed, polyphonic, polyhedral--just like life itself. It loses its traditional rigor, it loses its character of fixed anamnesis, it loses the formal sacredness, it loses the hierarchies. Only in this way can the heart mourn its sorrows and breath in the salvific encounter in the continuity of life mixed with its many deaths, both great and small, as well as its small and minimal hopes.

A liberating theological liturgy opens itself to a critical and historical political awareness of the use of liturgy as a political control of bodies. It especially reveals the misuse of liturgical memory in service to the growth of power and wealth of those who think themselves closest to the power of divinity. A deity hovering above the visible heavens, above the ends of the earth, far from the margins. Divinity dominating many faces and present on many altars.

Even before colonization began, great Christian liturgies consecrated kings and emperors who dominated empires and sang victories against enemies. Celebrations in the name of God that revealed the commitment of the ministers of religion to the powers of this world. In the colonization process, especially since the 16th century, the liturgy and in particular the sacraments, became services submissive to spiritual powers and in turn submissive to temporal ones. The sacraments were weapons of domination, sensitive liturgical signs that indicated the extent of the empires and indicated who was part of them. Through baptism one entered into the Kingdom of God and the kings who ruled the earth. By marriage you controlled birth and the education of the members of these kingdoms. Control over bodies, especially women's sexuality to maintain the order of the world, the order of God, the order of those who recognize themselves as superior legislators of the world. Control over cultures and beliefs as if the rulers held the key to salvation from around the world. For the world to be truly theirs, they must kill everything that is different in the world!

Forms of colonial Christianity that are still very present in our midst legitimize a hierarchical world where the rich and wise dominate for their alleged holiness. At the same time the consciousness of many begins to awaken in different ways. How can we get out of this millennial habit that has become so ingrained in our bodies and makes us love the idea of heavenly perfection more than the suffering bodies we find on the streets and corners of the world? How do we stop the misuse of the Bible to justify unlimited dictatorships and authoritarianisms? What then would be a liturgy for liberation theology?

Liberation theologian Cláudio lists some of the many efforts that have been made over the past few years to rethink liturgies, but more than that, he invites us to realize the diversity in the bodies that erupt in our midst with their stories, their questions, their struggles for survival, their contradictions and limits, their hopes both big and small. It is to them that the specialists, theologians and servants of the people should turn their eyes and create spaces for those who hunger and thirst for bread and justice to be the true artisans of their celebrations.

A lot of new things have taken shape in our current history and each has its own specific cry and its own response. Their memory makes us realize the great mutation at work in our world...

- *The impressive mobility of people from all over the earth in search of the promised land, land where milk and honey flow, in search of decent housing, land to plant and a harvest that seems to grow.*

- *The immense number of organized women who say NO to the many forms of domination and use their voices to shout throughout the world, waving their flag in an impressive and growing march that reaches around the globe.*

• *The numerous organizations against the emission of gases that causes climate change and the devastation of forests. And much more...*

The world is no longer the same, especially over the last forty years. Theologians have to hear more ... Learn from many stories ... From new and old parables, from the plural food that is the characteristic nourishment of each group. They must leave the imperial hierarchical metaphysics that have dominated liturgies for so long.

In this present school, they may lose the established liturgical order, but life will go on with perhaps more flavor and solidarity.

Cláudio's book invites us to perceive the power of liturgical art as in need of renewal, an ongoing renewal from the many productions of authors who carry in their hearts the burning flame of justice and love of neighbor. Liturgy as necessary poetry, as gratuitousness, as dialogue, as gesture and word born from the ground of life.

I recommend reading and reflecting on this book by Cláudio Carvalhaes and thank Life for having given us this artist and theologian who invites us to think about the things we rarely think about and sing with him, "I believe the world will be better when the least of these who suffer begin to believe in the power of the wretched of the earth."[1]

Ivone Gebara
July, 2019*

---

*This book has shifted and twisted through time and space as I have, as Dr. Gebara wrote, reflected on "Liturgy as necessary poetry, as gratuitousness, as dialogue, as gesture and word born from the ground of life." As I have sunk deeper into the ground of life through the writing process, the work of liturgical liberation theology has birthed an eco-liturgical liberation theology, realizing that the wretched of the earth is Pachamama too. Graciously, Dr. Gebara reminded me, "Deep down what I wrote can also adjust to the progression of your thinking. The earth is in us, and we are in the earth."

--Cláudio Carvalhaes, July, 2021

INTRODUCTION

Samuel Bastos-Chiavegatti, 9 years old

The struggle for land is the mother of all struggles.[1]

The cycle of liberation theology is not complete, from the lights of the manger and the poverty of Bethlehem to the crucified, emerges the depth of life. The challenge remains and is outlined in the theology from the poor. The chants born of this theological unveiling, of this courage to see the Christological truth bear our life of faith. Day by day Jesus pulls us from death so that we may joyfully live with our neighbor, poor and devoid of life in our Latin America. In Latin American lands, one cannot live without being a militant of a faith centered on the poor.

Milton Schwantes[2]

The end of the world must be postponed to tell more stories.

Ailton Krenak[3]

Trees, Conversion, and This Book

Glicéria Tupinambá, a leader of the Tupinambá Indigenous nation in Brazil is a writer and an important voice for the Indigenous peoples throughout Brazil. In 2010 she and her little baby were incarcerated for fighting for her people, a police action that was condemned all over the world. Glicéria Tupinambá is the co-author of the book "Os Donos da Terra"[4] (The Owners of The Land). Julie Dorrico, when commenting on this book, mentions Glicéria Tupinambá in an interview she gave elsewhere:

> *The Tupinambá people have their origins in the tree, and she makes a point of proving that point by comparing the human fingerprint to the tree's rings when cut from the trunk; both bodies decompose in the same way; both when burned turn to ashes; and when we're inside the tree we breathe better, she tells me sublimely. Glicéria ends the parallel stating that trees are the oldest enchanted beings that live on Earth, that take care of humans and animals, which are sacred... The message is not just about ecology, it's also about the end of the enchanted world.*[5]

When Indigenous people fight for their territories, they are fighting for their land, their bodies, their ancestry, their spirits, different levels of existences, the homes of the animals and the more than human beings who live there. That is why they say, *"The struggle for land is the mother of all struggles."* The land is inhabited by much more complex forms of cosmologies, cosmopolitics, and cosmogonies.

If the Tupinambás are the people of the tree, we are the people of merchandise, as shaman and leader of the Yanomami people, Davi Kopenawa, says in his book, *The Falling Sky.*[6] In a recent talk he gave at a university, he said this:

> *You live here on the other side, you can't see it from here... the non-indigenous authorities have a word they always use: "important." For those of you who live in the city, the most important thing is the merchandise. Despite having many goods, non-indigenous people don't share. They are stingy. Making a lot of merchandise is bad for the forest. For us, it is the animals, the forest, fertility, that are important. What is important is to share food among our people, our survival, our growth, our way of living, and our existence as a people.*[7]

This distinction--the people of the forest and the people of the merchandise--is at first the unsurmountable difference between the worlds we live in on earth. One people lives in relationality and tries to take care of their homes, while the other consumes everything and does not have the slightest clue of what the natural world is.

I am clearly located in the second group. When I think of us, I can see how detached and far away from the land we are. I never had anything close to a deep identity with animals, forests, and trees. In fact, I know almost nothing of the land I was born on or the land I live on now. It is clear that I fully depend on everything that comes out of the land, but I live as if I am floating above the land with no need for any relation with it unless I go for a walk "in nature."

However, I have been changing--slowly. When I married Katie in 2016, she gave me a huge gift and I cannot thank her enough: I adopted our three kids and became a father. That has changed me in ways that I am still figuring out. One of them is the awareness of my responsibility to the earth I will leave to them. I have learned from Indigenous people that we are responsible for seven generations: three before us, our own, and three ahead of us. I received a world that was hurting, but I am leaving one on the brink of unimaginable disasters. The loss of the critical zone (the space between the top of the trees and the few miles above where complex interactions between air, rocks, water, soil, and living organisms, control and keep the equilibrium of life on earth), the warming of temperatures, the death of oceans, the melting of glaciers, the extinction of animals, the drastic impoverishing of people--all of it happening right now--have filled me with dread and affected my inner life. For the inner life is never separate from the outside life we live. The more I have read, the more I have dreaded. I became anxious and fearful. But instead of running away, I went the other way around: I entered fully into the earth's troubles, so I could try to have a better understanding and figure out what we can do to change them. While our situation is one of desperation, there are so many things we can do.

With this book, I propose that through rituals, we can attend to the poor, deepen our relationship with the earth, and through communal living and working together, find ways to expand our sense of neighborliness with the poor and beyond the humankind. I feel as if I was in a deep slumber, unaware of the natural world around me. When I started to gain awareness, I did not know where to begin or what to do. My change has been an awakening and an engagement with the earth in a very different way than before.

One day, I was walking with my kids,
and I said, "Stop! Listen!"
And they said, "What?"
"Listen!" I said, "Listen to the birds, they are chirping and
singing so beautifully. Isn't this amazing?"

And at night we would pray for those going hungry.

Weeks later I was walking with my youngest son, Ike.
And he said, "Dad, stop! Listen!"
And I said, "Listen to what?"
"Listen to the birds, they are chirping and singing so
beautifully!"

This awakening is what changes everything, and that is what I want to
do with this book.
I want to say, "Stop! Listen! The birds are chirping and singing
so beautifully!"
And then add: "So many people are going hungry."

This awareness and perception can help us create new worlds to live.

In this process of paying attention to the natural world and listening to the birds, I also found a tree who became my companion for prayer, meditation, and friendship. I met Wonder at the Conodoguinet Creek where I visited daily. I approached her and started talking to her. I had learned with Robin Kimmerer that we should talk to more than human people through names or she/he/they pronouns. With Wonder, I learned to pace myself differently and to pay attention to presences I never did before. In February, 2019, Robin Kimmerer, a botanist, and citizen of the Potawatomi Nation, gave a lecture at Union Seminary. I was on sabbatical but watched it online. At the end of her lecture, she said, we need new rituals to deal with our times.

I was shaken and had a call from the earth…to the earth. At that moment I decided to change everything. I decided the earth would literally be the ground of my thinking and, hopefully, my living. From the time of my youth, I had always been concerned with land ownership, or the lack thereof, and I had been involved with the *Landless Movement* in Brazil. However, my involvement was focused more on agrarian reform and the problem of latifundia, or land ownership. I was never entangled into the pulsing life of the earth and all its inhabitants. My theology was fundamentally an anthropocentric project, done by humans, about humans, and to humans. What else to do, if only God and humans have agency? Ms. Kimmerer's lecture, along with the birds, my friend the tree, and climate disaster changed me. I had to start reading more Indigenous people, biologists, geochemists, botanists, cosmologists, and anthropologists, and I had to start thinking of religion differently. I changed all the courses I was teaching and my bibliographies. The focus of my attention changed, and my rituals started to take on different forms of perception and attentiveness.

This book shows precisely this divide in my thinking. Half of this book was done before this conversion and the other half illustrates the process of this change. Chapter one started only as liturgical liberation theology, without the ecological underpinning. I presented this work in several places around the world. It was only later, after my conversion, that I had to change the chapter and change the proposal of this book. The project became eco-liturgical liberation theology. Chapter one carries the methodological center of the book, from which everything flows, even though other chapters came before the systematization of this proposal. Chapter two was my first attempt to explore the earth as the ground of my thinking. The other chapters are fundamental liturgical changes that I believe that Christian churches need to adopt. Chapter 3 is the most recent place of my scholarship and thinking: eco-liturgical liberation theology and rituals. I wrote this chapter while teaching the course *Natural Theology: Perspectivism & Performance Theory* at Union seminary during the Summer of 2021.[8]

As you go through this book, you will vividly see how my writing is like a performance, trying to connect different movements and thinkers, in order to find a cohesive way of thinking/feeling/doing theology and rituals. The language moves, shifts, jumps, and changes, as it searches for a path and pattern. The book carries contradictions. Sometimes I stay too long on some topics and not long enough on others. The book tries to combine many forms of wisdom that resist cohesion. In this book, I think with Ivone Gebara, James Cone, and Winona LaDuke; Mary-Jane Rubenstein, Leonardo Boff, and Davi Kopenawa; Eduardo Viveiros de Castro with Nancy Cardoso and Tyson Yunkaporta; Donna Haraway with Isabel Stengers and Gustavo Gutierrez; Anna Tsing with Tissa Balasuriya and Ronald Grimes; Jonathan Z. Smith with Jaci Maraschin and Ailton Krenak; Bruno Latour, Marcella Althaus-Reid and Marc Ellis; Thich Nhat Hanh, Achille Mbembe and Judith Butler, as well as many other movements from the ground.

But that is not enough. Now I am more aware that I need to bring the rivers to speak in me and with me. If the forests do not offer to you a call in this book, then the book is not worth it. If the trees, the animals, the rivers, the birds, and the oceans do not come to the forefront, at least with a call for us to stop everything and go be with them and consider them as persons and establish connections, then this book did not find its purpose. If attention to the poor and the wretched of the earth is not fully vivid here as a demand to change our world, then it is better for this book to rest somewhere where no one will read it.

I am learning that God lives in the little chipmunk under my house, and I honor him as my neighbor. God lives within the universe, between gravity and dark matter, working with and against each other. God produces and sustains, and is produced and sustained, by the multiverses. God is everywhere in life, growing with cells and bacteria, seedlings, caterpillars, ants, dolphins, wolves, jaguars, the trees and rivers near my house, the clouds, my dog Amora, my spouse, and our kids. The God of the natural world is my natural theology. No more is my God made of a singular, male, anthropomorphic, one, disembodied, humanoid. Now I love a God of new myths and stories, making and shaping the universe in endless new divinities. God is among the poor, as the poor, resisting and re-existing everyday. God is a collective desire to see all we used to call sacred and has always been in the natural world. No more a God as an idea of divinity, as a human comfort, and as a control above everything else. No more control. Instead, the agency of God is in the plurality of the agencies of the universes and each animal, each vegetable, each mineral, each cell, and each process of symbiosis. A God of endless relationalities. A God of reciprocity and mutuality. A God of a thousand forms of liberation.

This God can carry a deep love for the earth and all who suffer. This deep love requires values where actions (and rituals) create moral developments, and in turn propitiate and protect spaces for a multitude of worlds to co-exist.

The proposal of an eco-liturgical liberation theology is to affect a change in the field of liturgical studies. In its diversity, liturgical theology has been a field of predominantly white male thinkers from the global North. Very little liturgical theology comes from the global South unless we are used as illustrations in the predominant thought of Europe and the United States. With this book, I initiate a distinctive way of thinking about liturgical theologies. I mark terms, surface the history of coloniality in concepts, localize universal claims, and pay attention to the ways a modern structural code of thinking liturgically has always been the norm. There is very little known or considered about liturgical theologies and liturgies done with people who are suffering. Feminist liturgical theology has been successful in showing the patriarchal ways in which this field has been erected and has tried to keep its erection. Feminist liturgical theologies unmasked the histories of a male formation of the field and gave us possibilities to think otherwise. This book aims to show how a colonial system of thinking has not allowed us to consider other forms of thinking and living. The reason is always the same: the protection of a tradition.

Liturgy is a field that only allows itself to understand itself. When liturgy has a conversation with other fields, it often engages the terms of dialogue only to quickly bend back into itself, folding in its own structure of thinking. I want us to think liturgical theology without coming back to the same place, and instead, opening liturgy up to what these conversations will entail, ask, and demand. Any dialogue involves deep changes in all who engage in the conversation. I go into this dialogue without fear of losing myself in other forms of thinking and ritualizing. In this process I might lose what some call faithfulness, but I feel very faithful, since the making of tradition is a process of changes, transitions, and transformations. I want to escape the anthropocentric centrality of thinking, and--as much as I have not succeeded--I want to think with other beings and other creatures. I can begin by saying it out loud, so I can eventually hear it. To start, the earth and the law of the land are my guides from and to God. If the fact that we are killing so many people and so many animals and other beings and parts of the earth is not enough reason for me to change what I believe and what I ritualize, then I better call myself an idolater and stick to my tradition and to the God I always knew.

Somebody told me that churches are not ready to do this and that, even if they were, it would take 20 years for this to start happening. I thought, that is exactly what this book is about: a way to help us think of a time to come, but that is built now, where we learn to tend the land and contemplate fields of imagination where seedlings of life are already inside of the land, perhaps even sprouting here and there. Perhaps all this book can do is to help us practice the future that is coming now and shift the past so our future will come from elsewhere. If we cannot imagine a future for all beings now, we will not be able to do it in the future. This book is both wishful thinking and a demand to action while we still have a chance.

I have heard the same thing about my first book *Eucharist in Globalization*. The church is not ready yet. My second book *What's Worship Got to Do with It?: Interpreting Life Liturgically* was also about dreaming and imagining new ways of thinking liturgical theology and doing rituals. What we have now is a mimicry of the possibility of the gospel, a bad joke of a revolutionary ministry. We have impoverished the gospel of Jesus so much. We have turned God into our likeness. But there is something in the gospel of Jesus that is bigger than we have become and what we can take. On the one hand, the message of Jesus is in solidarity with the poor, but we found a way around that. On the other hand, we have made this gospel center exclusively on humans. Like the call to engage with the poor that we must continue to stress, we must also engage with a God that is beyond humankind and attend to the natural world. This book, along with the others, is a path to wonder and wander, being expanded by the endless possibilities of God in the magnitude of the multiverses and the tiny unseen worlds of mycelium and symbioses. If we let this new world percolate in our minds and bodies, we can find grammar and gestures and rituals to live with the natural world and find spaces for different worlds to live together. Paraphrasing Hector Babenco's movie, I want us to all be at play in the fields of God.

An Itinerary to The Book

This book is a map of 10 years of writing, showing the ways in which I was caught by places I lived and visited, invitations that I received, and my ways of making sense of the myself, the world I live and the teachings I do. The book's line of coherence lays in the zigzags of life, its inconstancies, the intensities of moments, the desperation of situations and now, in moving away from speed and exasperation to perhaps a slower space where I might ponder about things just a little longer.

Please do not expect a typical manuscript.

This book is a collection of essays, each of them standing on itself and yet, begging for the imagination to stretch it beyond its limits. Hopefully, the reader will read what is important and take it elsewhere. The lineup of chapters does not carry any sense of progression of thought but rather, moves us from here to there as to show the breath of the possibilities in the liturgical and theological thinking/doing. So here is the limited map and a certain itinerary…

Chapter One, "Eco-Liturgical Liberation Theology" began as a full book seeking an eco-liturgical liberation theology. However, as it stands now, it shows where it starts, how it can move and where it can go. In this chapter, liberation theology encounters liturgy that encounters the earth. And possibilities abound!

Even while the first chapter was intended to be the foundation for a book project, my writing led me into new directions which follow throughout the rest of this book. Chapter Two, *Lex Naturae: A New Way into a Liturgical Political Theology,*" holds the key from which everything in liturgy should be oriented, namely, *Lex Naturae*, the law of land. The law of land carries the central wisdom within which we must move. The law of prayer and the law of life, which combined compose our political life, must be subsumed to the law of the land and we should move with the land and not move the land according to our own desires or faith beliefs. Every political move is also an ecological move and the Christian politics should be grounded on the liturgy of the land.

The third chapter, "Rituals and Performances in the Anthropocene: Eco-Liturgical Liberation Pantheologies," carries the ritual theory necessary to start engaging liturgy and the land. Chapter four—"Worship, Liturgy and Public Witness"—presents itself first as a primer in public theology primer, but I quickly re-orient my position in contestation to public theology. My initial editors were very open to my criticisms and published it. The essay shows that public theology lacks a real engagement with injustice; I demonstrate how public theology must be done *liturgically*.

Chapter Five, "From Multiculturalisms to Multinaturalisms: Liturgical Theological Shifts," is a criticism to culture as a central aspect of theology and multiculturalism as a form of inclusion in churches. Taking from Eduardo Viveiros de Castro's notion of perspectivism, the primary thrust of this chapter is to think more in terms of multinaturalisms rather than the binary culture/nature.

"The Christian as Humus: Virtual/Real Earthly Rituals of Ourselves," enters into a discussion of the offering of eucharist during the COVID-19 pandemic and pushes forcefully into the liturgical dilemma of whether celebrating the sacrament is done on behalf of God or as a representation of something else. Rather, I argue that the doing of the sacraments is the doing of ourselves.

Chapter Seven, "Class, Interreligious Borders, and Ways of Living with Pachamama," shows the battle of worlds which we have today. The essay combines economic analysis, class struggles, interreligious limits and how our common affiliation with the earth is a way into many different worlds living together. To this end, the eighth chapter, "Birds, People, Then Religion: An Eco-Liberation Theological and Pedagogical Approach to Interreligious Rituals," responds to the crisis of the 2016 presidential election in the United States as a significant cultural event which discloses the truth of our present condition. It brings forth how some religions care for the poor and then shows how a ritual done in James Chapel at Union Seminary in New York can signal ways of connecting our very different religious selves together and with those suffering.

Following this, "White Reasoning and Worship Methodology," is an attempt to analyze how white culture is deeply settled in the creation and making of the liturgical orders of Christianity. Taking an example from the Presbyterian church, I show how we need to change the core of the liturgical production rather than only adding multicultural prayers or small actions in worship here and there.

Chapter ten, "Queering Christian Worship Services," shows how to start thinking about worship with a LGBTQIA+ perspective. It sets us an itinerary to help us start thinking about worship by breaking heteronormativity and change the ways we create and do worship. In this way, this chapter is very limited. While it shows a way of starting to change our ways of thinking/doing worship, it also shows the limitations in doing so.

"God's Petticoat and Capitalism—Full Fashion," chapter eleven, is an essay written with Brazilian Biblicist and theologian Nancy Cardoso in honor of Marcella Althaus-Reid. It brings Althaus-Reid's queer theology, economy, fashion and Brazilian poetry to give an account of God in our world today.

Chapter twelve, "Ecclesiologies as Foreign Ecclesiologies: Worshiping with the Homeless," manifests the demand of the Christian churches to care for homeless people and help end this disastrous situation. What if ecclesiology is thought from the perspective of the homeless? What would that change to our ecclesiological, liturgical theologies? Is there any other way to think about it? The thirteenth chapter, "Praying from the Ends of the World," then shows a methodological way of being in the world with those suffering. By way of being with those who are destitute and in pain, listening to their own voices, we create a new vocabulary of prayer, thus hopefully changing our theological thinking and our missional action.   Also written with Nancy Cardoso, "African-Indigenous Jurema: The Greatest Common Divisor of The Brazilian Minimum Religion," points us into new ways of thinking religion from elsewhere, a crossroads of religions and forms of being together.

Finally, the conclusion of this book offers my journeyed reader a blessing for following this path with me in a multitude of ways—for it is my reader who carries this work which I initiate collegially with you. As my incredible editor Christopher Rodkey said so poignantly, this is a work of a community. *Yes!* So many people (human and more-than human) made this book possible. And I am so grateful!

The Front and Back Covers of the Book

The front and back covers of this book are very special to me. Doing this book with *Barber's Son Press* was a joy since Chris, the editor, was so open to create the design with me. The cover is Dona Esther's, my 90-year-old mother's, hands holding many seeds, easy to find in local supermarkets where she lives and where I was born. My brother-in-law Reginaldo bought the seeds, and my nephew Rafael took the pictures.

In this picture, whole worlds are placed together. My mother worked on the land and her parents too. Her grandmother might have been an Indigenous shaman who was turned into a nurse in the stories because of colonization and the "proper terms" of civilization. But colonization is so brutal that I do not know anything about her besides that she was a nurse, and I cannot know anything else for certain. The three generations before me were land workers (Indigenous people?) and Gypsies uprooted from their own lands and turned into *colonos*, paid workers of the new landowners. This is what civilization has always done. My mom had to move to the city, as she was forced to care for wealthy families. She later married my father Waldemar, a man of so many talents. He loved movies, theater, and music. He played guitar, violin, harmonica, and was my favorite clown. We grew up as 4 children: Mércia, Jose, Ana Maria, and after 10 years, me.

I grew up in a neighborhood called Mooca in the East side of São Paulo, near downtown. The Tamanduatei River (river of true anteaters) had mighty waters that ran into the Tiete River. Sadly, the Tamanduatei River was always polluted and smelled bad. Our house was flooded many times with big rains. We had to cross the river over a bridge, and I was always scared of falling. I had several nightmares with me falling into the river. This patch of land was first the home of the Guaiana Indigenous people from the Tupi-Guarani Nation. I heard that this area was once home to one of the most populated Indigenous peoples in the whole state of São Paulo. The Guaianas were flourishing, but colonization, wiped out all of the Indigenous people from that part of the land. I want to honor the Guaianas, their lives and forms of living. Throughout my life I never heard about them, and I had to research to find out, when the Portuguese arrived, who were the people who lived where I spent so many years of my life.

Our tiny house had a tiny backyard, and one day my mom got me a seed, and I planted a lemon tree. I remember vividly that day on that 10x10 inch piece of land. The tree grew up so strongly and beautifully that she started to crack everything around it. She had to be cut down and I cried. My mother always had all kinds of plants and used to talk and sing to them. That memory is in my bones. Our poor neighborhood had empty barren land where we used to play soccer. We also played soccer on the streets and under a big bridge. My parents grew up with many immigrants around the neighborhood and I played with their children. I do not remember many trees or parks, only dogs, cats, mice, rats, little lizards, and cockroaches. Sometimes crickets. Besides cats and dogs, I was absolutely afraid of everything else. We had dogs and I loved them. Everyone was a hard worker in that hood. There was some stealing here and there, and one murder in the street by my house, which horrified me! At 8 years old, I started shining shoes at a public square every afternoon after school, and when I was 13 years old, I started working full time. When I go back, I can barely see my old friends, because they are mostly all gone. My relationship with that patch of land was one of joy, but also fear, and not connected to the earth. In that way I lived in a place where I never landed fully. The picture on the front cover shows me where I came from and from whom I came from. I thank God for my mother's hands and the earth who fed me.

The back cover has a picture of me holding the waters of Conodoguinet Creek, near my family's home in Central Pennsylvania. The creek was named by the Indigenous people as a river with many bends. It is a shallow creek where kids play, and the creek goes through farms, villages, and towns, giving life everywhere. The creek makes amazing zigzags through the land, going up and down, which, for some Indigenous people, carries mighty power. That patch of land was the land of the Susquehannock, Lenni Lenape, and Iroquois. The Conodoguinet Creek runs into the Susquehanna River, which is a mighty river deeply shaped by the Appalachian Mountains. The Europeans arrived in the 1600s and killed all the Indigenous people either by guns or disease.

I am trying to relate to the Conodoguinet Creek in more personal ways. I am trying to learn more about the river, I go listen to the waters, and I try to hear the sounds of ancestry and what, perhaps, they are trying to tell me. At the part of the creek where I linger, there is this jewel of a tree. I named her *Wonder*. I am learning to listen and talk to Wonder. She always shelters me and listen to my cries. She lives right at the side of the river. It is a place where I have been learning to perceive the earth differently, and it is such a different way of relating that I am mostly lost.

Nonetheless, I have already changed my heart and my relationship with the land through these precious people. I am on my way to become Wonder. I am also on a path, through deep relationship, to become the birds near my home. I do not want to replicate the ways I grew up. I want to learn how to care for that patch of land and help my children to relate to it as well. Central Pennsylvania was the place where my wife Katie, her first husband Peter, and their parents and grandparents lived for generations. I hope that from that patch of land they will care for any other place they might go live.

These two pictures convey the seven generations that I belong to and the lands they represent. It is a call to me to land in these places and relate to their people: humans and more than humans. I must land there, where I lived/live, and from there try to figure out how to live. So much to learn and to do.

Gratitude

I have so many people to thank. To Paul Galbreath who always reads what I write, and to Mary-Jane Rubenstein who was so gracious to read chapter 3. So many people helped me along the way through each chapter, it is impossible to name them all. Katie Mulligan was my most dedicated editor. Katie is a pastor and a mother, a cat lover and a great scholar. She edited this work while being a pastor in New York, doing worship services and preaching, funerals and animal blessings, taking care of kids, cats, and herself. All amidst COVID-19. She is a fascinating person and I learn so much with her. She can see the whole forest and pay attention to each tree. If you see mistakes in this book, itis because I pressed her to finish quicker than she would like to because I had deadlines to fulfill. Nonetheless, she did miracles! Also, I want to thank Chris Rodkey who agreed to publish this book with his Press. He is indeed the son of a barber and that is the name of the publisher: Barbers Son Press. He gave so much wisdom to this book. Chris is also a fantastic pastor in Central Pennsylvania, and a father, and an amazing scholar. He also did this work while taking care of his family, wife, 4 kids and cats, pastoring a church, running for democrat positions in central Pennsylvania, teaching religion at Penn State and leading a boy scout chapter. These two amazing pastors, I tell you, I do not know how they do it all. But I know their hearts and I could not feel more blessed to have had them with me during this journey. To them, my love and gratitude.

I want to thank my students whom I love and learn from all the time. I want to thank Union Theological Seminary in New York City who gives me all the conditions and freedom to do my scholarship and my rituals.

To my family in Brazil who sustain me even if from a distance. And to my family here in the United States. My wife, Katie, is a wonder and I am so grateful to her. She always supports me and helps me in so many ways. Without her I would not have been able to do this book or do what I do. She is the love of my life. And to my precious children Libby, Cici and Ike. I never know what to say about them because they are like wonder: the more you see the more you wonder. Libby is a fantastic singer, musician and theater actress. Cici is also a theater actress and an amazing artist. She is always creating something. Ike is a wonderer, a creative mind and a wonderful storyteller. He is also becoming a theater actor. They all carry a compassionate heart. They have been the joy of my life.

Throughout the book you will see drawings of children from Brazil, India and the USA. This book is fundamentally an attempt to keep the earth livable for their generation and the generations after them.

Cláudio Carvalhaes
June, 2021

Wonder and Me, Rooted.

THE ECOLOGICAL LORD'S PRAYER

Our God who art in pluriverses, the skies and the earth,

Blessed be your name: life. May your pulsing life come to be seen, heard, touched and felt through the oceans, the forests, in the rocks, in the life of plants and in the sounds of animals and singing birds.

May the atmosphere of the sky that carries our ability to breathe stay balanced as fossils are kept under the earth.

Give us this day our daily bread through a variety of seeds and grains and leaves without pesticides, without monocultures, from local farms and agro-biodiverse-cultures.

Forgive our plundering of the earth, our total lack of relation and reciprocity with the earth and more than human beings; as cells, mycelium, fungi and infinite processes of symbiosis forgive us daily by giving life back when we destroy it.

And lead us not into consumerism and devouring the earth but deliver us from the apathy that says nothing can be changed.

For life is kinship, relationally and reciprocity. Now and forever.

Amen.

CHAPTER ONE

Eco-Liturgical Liberation Theology[1]

George Emerson Vander Tuig, 11 years old

Thank God, it rained in the wilderness. Thank goodness the corn sprouted. Thank God, the cattle did not die. Thank God, I'm healed. God, like rain, corn, living cattle, healing... God, as alms, help, bread. God, as asking in me, beggar in others. God, like food. God, as a need, without omnipotence and science... God, as work, house, companion ... breaks my solitude, screams with me, sighs with me, seeks with me.

Ivone Gebara[2]

True Christian liberation is discovered and promoted in liturgy, and only in liturgy...

Ignacio Ellacuría[3]

Introduction

I was the pastor of a small congregation of undocumented people for five years in Massachusetts, U.S.A. One day, I was in the parking lot of my small town waiting for a spot to go to the post office. After a while, a spot became vacant, and I was the first to park. However, the car behind me went ahead and parked before me. I was furious. I left my car and went to talk to that driver. I asked her if she had not seen that I was in front of her and that she was supposed to park after me.

She did not say a thing.

I asked again if she had not seen that there was a line, and I said that we should respect the line. She turned to me and said, "The first places are for citizens of this country. You and your people get the spots available after us." I went into such an angered state that I felt a white cloud take over me. I did not know how long I was standing there, but when I finally recovered my senses, she was not there anymore. I went to my car and stayed there for about two hours.

The days passed, and I had to decide what to do during worship. When worship came, I put away the liturgy and said, "Turn off the video and close the doors. I have a story to tell you." I told them what had happened to me, and tears started to roll down form the faces of some of my people. I asked if anyone there had a story like that, and literally everyone raised their hands. We listened to all the stories, and everybody wept.

At the end, we were exhausted, and I could not let the worship finish only with those stories. I then said, "Now let us say a story of love, when someone loved you in this country." We were there for three hours telling stories, and at the end of worship, it was as if our death and life was condensed in those three hours. We left better. Not with any resolution but knowing that at least we had each other.

From Where do we Speak?

Black Liberation theologian James Cone reminds us that theology starts where it hurts, and this has impacted me deeply. I add that liturgy also starts where it hurts. Having been a shoeshining boy at the age of eight, I have lived under the shadows of society. It was a little Presbyterian congregation in São Paulo that supported my family and gave me food, shelter, stories, songs, strength, and imagination to keep going. They shed a light on my life! Later, it was liberation theology that became not only a choice within theologies' vast menu, but also a way of survival. It was a theology that spoke to my situation and to many of the excluded people in Latin America. Now, having come this far by grace, I have learned that unless I continue to hear the suffering of those who are hurting from the worst places of our world, I cannot do theology, I cannot sing a new song to God, I cannot partake the meal, and I cannot praise or pray.

To continue on this liberation path, we must follow people and movements that feed love for the poor. We must continue to follow Jesus Christ, who lived his life as an immigrant and refugee and who said, "For I was hungry and you gave me food, I was thirsty and you gave me something to drink, I was a stranger and you welcomed me, I was naked and you gave me clothing, I was sick and you took care of me, I was in prison and you visited me" (Matt. 25:35-36).
We must follow the Hebrew Bible, or Tanakh:

> *Speak out for those who cannot speak,*
> *for the rights of all the destitute...*
> *defend the rights of the poor and needy.*
>
> Proverbs 31:8-9

We must follow Dietrich Bonhoeffer, who said "We have for once learnt to see the great events of world history from below, from the perspective of the outcast, the suspects, the maltreated, the powerless, the oppressed, the reviled – in short, from the perspective of those who suffer."[4]

We must follow Edward Said, whose work was associated with "the memory of forgotten voices... of the poor, the disadvantaged, the voiceless, the unrepresented, the powerless."[5] We must continue learning with Martin Luther King Jr. and must follow the work of women such as Angela Davis, Nancy Cardoso and Ivone Gebara whose work intersects ecofeminist theology, economic justice, the lives of campesinos, and small rural farmers with agribusiness, race, prison complex systems, and womanist thought. We must be constantly reminded of the lives and work of Camilo Torres, Oscar Romero, Elder Camera, Dorothy Stang, and all the rural workers and the poor killed by the systems of power. They are the seeds of our revolution. We must remember Dorothy Soelle and Pedro Casaldáliga and their work with the forgotten people. More than ever, we need to hear the voices of Indigenous people and nations like Ailton Krenak, Davi Kopenawa, Robin Wall Kimmerer, Nick Estes, the Zapatistas, and so many others. And now we must also fully listen to other people who we do not consider as people: animals, rivers, trees, plants, environments, eco-systems, mountains, rocks, birds, and the sea.

We cannot afford to do any work that is not in the flow of social movements and thinkers engaging the intersectionality of ecology, race, class, gender, anthropology, Indigenous thinking, biology, cosmology, geology, economy, and sexuality. This intersectionality demands us liturgical theologians--or any theologian--to engage in many dialogues that go beyond our field and to venture into other fundamental sources for new forms of liberation and liberation theologies, pushing us toward a much more ample eco-liturgical liberation theology. I have just started.

Within the liturgical field, which is small, I begin by placing myself in what Don Saliers calls the "liberationist moral and political critiques of Christian liturgy," and the "ambiguity of liturgical formation," continuing to press what he affirmed when he said that "liturgical theology suffers when it fails to acknowledge 'hidden' power issues and the malformative histories of practice."[6] The hidden and not so hidden power structures within the liturgical field have taken us into our current situation. Now more than ever, we need a reorientation to the earth and the law of the land.

Who and Whose Histories? A quest for methodology

Liberation Theologian and Biblicist José Comblin tells a story about a peasant in Brazil who went to church every Sunday and complained that all the Biblical and liturgical texts had nothing to do with the people, but instead, supported the priest.[7]

His complaint includes us. Do the texts we use serve tradition or the poor? Do they serve the middle upper-class church or the poor? What do our supposedly neutral choices reveal about our social markers and public interests in race, sex, gender, and culture?

The quest for liturgy includes how we see the field and how we see, feel, and think the world. The way we see/feel the world shapes our intellectual work, agendas, interests, and commitments. The writing of our liturgical history today reflects the commitments we have with the field and what we want from it. Brazilian Catholic liturgical theologian Ione Buyst says that the very question of our scholarship defines our path, our *meta-hodos.* Our research and methodologies reveal where we are positioned. Jonathan Z. Smith orients ritual towards attention to place:

> *Ritual is, first and foremost, a mode of paying attention. It is a process for marking interest. It is the recognition of this fundamental characteristic of ritual that most sharply distinguishes our understanding from that of the Reformers, with their all too easy equation of ritual with blind and thoroughness habit. It is this characteristic, as well, that explains the role of place as a fundamental component of ritual: place directs attention.*[8]

Every liturgical work is a way of paying attention, or of marking interest. For any liberation liturgical theology, our ritual orientation must be grounded in a space, or as Michel de Certeau calls it, "practiced place." To do liturgy is to follow the law of the land and to take *lex naturae* as its guiding rule to attend to the land and it inhabits.[9] To ritualize is to pay attention to the life of the land, its people, its humans and its more-than-humans who are suffering.

Prof. Bryan D. Spinks writes, "…we imagine the past is mediated to a certain degree by our own present views, needs, and concerns, both conscious and unconscious… the past is always reconstructed through the lenses of the present."[10] If the past is "reconstructed through the lenses of the present," then it does matter how we see the world today. The liturgical field often has its nose turned to the inside of the discipline--liturgy explains liturgy and can only be juxtaposed by liturgical things.

Fidelity to Christian denominations plays a fundamental role in current liturgical historical research, and allegiances to institutions and official authority are a guiding principle in liturgical scholarship. This is why it is so difficult to deal with intellectual differences within our fields. We have fences erected in all places, and when somebody or something steps out of our denominational silo of liturgical scholarship, we feel attacked as if our personal beliefs are in danger. One is either in or out of the circle of truth, reflecting not only the passive-aggressive forms of behavior we sometimes have in the field, but fundamentally how our liturgical "enterprise" is a business oriented by modernity and its need for exclusionary belief systems.

Perhaps the worst aspect of theological legalism is the liturgical legalism. Ritual actions uphold the foundation upon which everything in the Christian building stands upon. Religious rituals are held to high standards so they will not be challenged or put to historical, social, economic, gender, sexual, ecological, racial and class tests. In the liturgical field, the stakes are always extremely high, and the consequences of dissent can be ruthless.

Nonetheless, we must continue engaging tradition through ruptures and continuations, since faithfulness and betrayal are both parts of what tradition entails. Perhaps we need to see tradition as something we aspire to and not only what we are holding on to from the past. As Graham Harvey says:

> The possibility of 'becoming tradition' may seem contradictory, but even prior to contact with Europeans (sometimes taken as the temporal location of definitive traditional authenticity) tradition was always something aimed for and lived towards rather than simply inherited.[11]

Betraying a tradition for the sake of our present and our future sometimes can be the only way to be truly faithful to the past. That is to say that betrayal is at the heart of the methodological concern for the survival of liturgical theology. Some small and some big changes are already occurring in the field but so much more must change. For example, Nathan Mitchell says in his book *Meeting Mystery* that "Christian worship is worldly by definition,"[12] thus betraying the notion that liturgy, understood as divine, can only be explained by divine liturgy. Ronald Grimes writes,

> Liturgy is essentially cultural as it is religious. Consequently, it ought to be subjected not just to t11he theological criticism but to ritual, ethical, and other sorts of criticism that proceed on anthropological, ecological and psychological grounds.[14]

Eco-liturgical liberation theology must embrace other community knowledges, both their thinking and practices: Indigenous knowledges, peasant and local farmers' knowledges, women's knowledges, children's knowledges, Black communities' knowledges, LGBTQIA+ communities' knowledges. They carry the past and the future with them, with the capacity to illuminate our past and our future.

By bringing the future into our present, our past changes. The book *Liturgy's Imagined Past/s*, out of a conference at Yale in 2014 offers a window into the changes happening in the historical approach of the field. Martin D. Jean says that in regards to methodology, the conference "probed the impact of important shifts in historiography (for example, the turns to social history and gender history) on the work of historians of liturgy and on how they imagine and display the past."[14] This is an important turn but this move will only engage our real past if the shifts in historiography are extended towards the histories of Indigenous genocide, racism, homophobia, economic oppression, class divisions, the absence of the earth, and the colonizing powers' theft of land. So far, the mirror of this historiography, as Martin D. Jean mentioned, reflects a certain subject, that is, a white heterosexual, patriarchal, middle-upper class church. It is time for us to show the poor, the Black, the Latinx, the queer, the disabled, the Indigenous, all of them included in our liturgical histories as a fundamental part of our "own" mirror.

With an expansive notion of subjectivity in our histories, our task is now to understand the history of Christianity and its ritual expressions as a colonial project of land theft, economic oppression, and exploitation of the poor. The movie *The Mission* is a great example of the contradictory nature of the Christian mission as it narrates how the Jesuits make "savages" into docile Christians. The Portuguese and Spaniard colonial project extracts all they desire from the land and from the Indigenous people and justifies itself by denying that Indigenous people are humans. Even singing beautifully in Latin was not enough for the colonial project to keep them alive. The devouring appetite for plundering always outstrips a religious belief in humanity.

The absence of colonized people in liturgical histories makes the Christian faith an imperial faith only, just as the absence of women turns Christianity into a patriarchal project. Mary Collins, Teresa Berger, Kathleen E. Corley, Janet Walton, Marjorie Proctor-Smith and many others have clearly showed us this truth. Christianity, as a white supremacy project, omits the histories of Black people and erases the history of slavery in our liturgical theologies. Our ignorance of the historical participation of marginalized groups in our history, and the emphasis on the golden path of the global North, reveals the class structure of our liturgies. In the same way, not knowing the rituals of marginalized groups leads us to think that the only pattern within liturgical history is the somewhat fixed ordo that originated with the early church.

For the last 500 years, the North of the globe has rendered theological assessments of liturgical theology subsumed to the rules and practices of prayer-belief-being of particular local contexts. Those contextual histories were then imposed as universal laws onto the whole world. The whole South of the globe is screaming to be heard, and we cannot grapple with or accept this different voice. We must continue the liturgical turn I have proposed in *Liturgy and Postcolonialism* in 2015 to expand the theoretical possibilities of the liturgical field, and to engage sources and writers and people who are not part of the self-enclosed global North pantheon that shapes the field.

Reading from the margins entails a commitment to and conversation with the margins and different voices. When teaching courses on liturgical theology, finding sustained voices from the South that do not serve as illustrations or tokens is almost impossible--small articles must contend with huge volumes. We need new eyes and new ears to see and to listen to the poor.[15] We need new connections and relations with the earth. We need strange (to us) partners to ritually think differently. The way we feel/think our present matters, not only in how we feel/think our past, but also how we are already feeling/thinking our future. Can we feel/think the signs of our present and future in the face of climate change? Can we feel/think of a past when we hear the cries of Black people being brutalized, or Indigenous people being ripped apart? Can we feel/think those who are going hungry and devastated even more by this pandemic? Ritual, the act of paying attention, easily reveals where our attention is focused, with whom and where we are thinking/feeling, the and the historical, ecological, theological, and liturgical sources and interpretations we choose.

Beyond Inclusion/Exclusion

Notions of inclusion and exclusion still dominate our forms of thinking. Our illusions of identity and nostalgia for a certain form of Christian faith upholds theoretical and practical forms of white supremacy--not as an individual belief but as a whole system of beliefs and thoughts that fosters ecclesiologies, theologies, and liturgies enclosed in identities that hide behind tradition. The white supremacy here is not only a mark of white people but a project of hierarchical structures of power and maintenance of wealth. It does not matter the color of the individual running the institutions. To add people of color in white institutions will do little to change the ways of feeling/thinking of these institutions. We must stop pleading for inclusion into the white project of church. Instead, we must create other forms of churches as we create other forms of organizing communities, societies, and forms of ritualizing life.

We start by identifying ourselves as part of the nobodies, with those who are living in poverty, cut off from basic forms of living. We must find ways to belong with those who are without a home, those who cannot risk being gay in a patriarchal society, those who are Black and without a way to survive in a white supremacist society, and the trees living in forests decimated by economic powers of extractivism. Our allegiance cannot be clear cut from the pigmentation of our skin but instead must lie with the places and rivers, and birds, and fishes and cells and mycelium who came before us and prepared the way for us. Rituals can help us practice cultivating love and solidarity with more than human ancestralities!

Our identities in the human world along with animal, vegetal, and mineral worlds are fundamental to a sense of mutuality and belonging that is necessary to find the common strength to fight against that which is killing us all: the economic elite and its extractivist projects, white supremacy, hierarchical patriarchalism, heterosexuality, capitalism and many forms of fascism. Instead of letting this one world define all our worlds, we can engage in the multiplication of worlds and eco-systems to open the way for new forms of life to emerge. Again, rituals done with poor people and earthlings, can help us foster and invent a new future to be lived now.

If we continue entrenched into our own atomized forms of identity siloes, we will be doing exactly what the empire did and still does: conquer and divide. As we continue divided, the empire will easily continue to crush us all. Theology, theological education, church, and ritualization of life must all be an endeavor toward mutual belonging with multiple centers. Willie Jennings writes in *After Whiteness: An Education in Belonging*:

> *Theological education is supposed to open up sites where we enter the struggle to rethink our people. We think them again, but now with others who must rethink their people. And in this thinking together we begin to see what we had not seen before: we belong to each other, we belong together. Belonging must become the hermeneutic starting point from which we think the social, the political, the individual, the ecclesial, and most crucial for this work, the educational. Western education (and theological education) as it now exists works against a pedagogy of belonging. Theological education must capture its central work—to form us in the art of cultivating belonging.*"[16]

This work on belonging is the *ubuntu* work, the work of a collectivity, of people allowing themselves to be affected by others so that we can expand our horizons by a thousand other horizons, our thinking pluralized by a plethora of other forms of thinking/living, our sense of self entangled with other forms of life, theologies that honor birds and trees and bees, liturgies that help us pay attention to forms of life we have never seen or been aware of before…all so we can start to think/feel the many other fundamental forms of belonging and being together.

Poor and Poverty

Since we all start where it hurts, we must engage with the poor and poverty. Surely there are many forms of pain and hurt but here we are We must triage and attend to those near who are dying: the hungry, abandoned people and the more than human people: forests, seas, rivers, soil. The bodies of many living creatures located into a territory, in a certain patch of land, wrapped in colonial, social, historical, sexual, gender, and ability help define where the pain comes from, the ways the pain is produced, and how we can collectively address that pain. Gustavo Gutierrez reminds us that poverty is everywhere in the Bible:

> *Poverty is a central theme both in the Old and the New Testaments It is treated both briefly and profoundly; it describes social situations and expresses spiritual experiences communicated only with difficulty; it defines personal attitudes, a whole people's attitude before God, and the relationships of persons with each other.*[18]

Gutierrez also told us that "Material poverty is a scandalous condition. Spiritual poverty is an attitude of openness to God and spiritual childhood."[18] 50 years after the publication of his book, we must hold on to the fundamental theme of poverty in the Bible but complexify the notion of poverty to our days. If God means life, or forms of life, then desecrated people and places are the only places from which we can speak of God, to God, or about God.

We must ponder the ways in which governments have used the notion of the poor or barren people or areas to justify exploitation. Any green area is a poor area since it does not produce some form of profit. People and places that do not offer something for consumption, they are all poor. The poor is everyone outside of the economic system of production of wealth; they are those whose resources have been taken away and placed at the margins of economic and symbolic means. "The poor" is an abstraction used by those who want to satisfy their production of thinking.

Anthropologist Eduardo Viveiros de Castro gives us a correction to a capitalist understanding of the poor and identifies the danger of homogenizing the poor in the leftist movement and some sectors of traditional liberation theology. Castro says:

> *The problem is that the political left middle-class, the leftist intellectual, sees his Other essentially as a poor. Poor here is a negative category, right? Poor is someone who defines oneself by what s/he does not have. The poor*

has no money, no education, no opportunity. So the natural attitude towards the poor, and this is not a criticism, is the natural view, is that the poor have to stop being that. For the poor to be something, he has to stop being poor. So the natural attitude is for you to free the poor, to emancipate the poor from their conditions. Get him out of slave labor, give him education, decent housing. However, and invariably, this movement has the middle-class person as the standard. You do not change yourself, you change the poor. You bring the poor to your height, since you are suggesting that you are above the poor. At the same time, you make the poor homogeneous. Yes, because if the poor are defined by someone who does not have something, then everyone is equal…

And he continues defining the poor in Brazil:

If you look at the ethnic, cultural, and Brazilian composition of poverty, you will see who the poor are. Basically Indians, black people. What I call Indians includes Africans. It includes the immigrants who did not work. These people are this mixture: he is indigenous, he is black, he is poor immigrant, he is Brazilian free, he is the caboclo, he is the half-breed, he is the son of the maid with the boss, son of the slave with the boss. The cultural unconscious of these poor Brazilians is largely Indigenous. It has a non-white component. It's that phrase that I invented: in Brazil everyone is Indigenous except who is not. So instead of making the poor look more like you, you have to help the poor become more like himself. What is the poor as a positive? No more transformed into something like me, but transformed into something that he has always being but are prevented from being when they are turned poor. What were they? Indigenous. We need to help them fight for themselves to set their own course and destiny instead of putting ourselves in the government position of "Look, I'm going to get you out of poverty." And doing what? Giving them consumption, consumption, consumption.[19]

We must listen to De Castro's harsh criticisms. The system creates the poor while the assistant machines (states, churches, charity places, NGO's and so on) continue with the cycle of helping the poor, and the wealth of the rich remains intact. Poverty as negative condition allows those who are on the positive side of life to feel a necessary distance, maintaining class hierarchies softened by the good will of those who want to work for the poor. Welfare and assistance programs are created without eliminating the positive/negative signs of wealth and poverty. The system of injustice is thus kept. De Castro asserts that looking at the poor as an outsider keeps our gaze towards the transformation of the poor, who we believe are the ones who need to be changed. Those on the positive side never consider interior transformations and change to their own lives necessary to pursue.

Relationalities, policy changes, and redistribution of wealth are never considered as part of our work with the poor. What can we say of a single church in New York with an endowment of 5 billion dollars? Surely this church helps the poor. Yet churches maintain and reflect the economic system of neoliberalism with some tall steeple churches possessing so much money while the vast majority of the churches are dying. Liturgy becomes a vehicle for injustice when we ask for forgiveness and cannot even see our sins. Worship is thus a cave where we flee to say our prayers, thank God for God's mercy, and be happy that we are helping someone, while no radical collective change is proposed--perhaps where every pastor is honored, and each community lives with the resources of the whole people.

In a nutshell, liturgy is the place where the lives of the people happen in words and action. If liturgy is the work of the people and a mode of being together, the liturgical space and its rituals must do and talk about the ways we live together, organize society, and care for each other, humans and more than humans. The liturgical work can be the communal life of monks in a monastery, or it can be the daily activities of a person and how they are entangled in larger schemes of political economic symbolic structures. Thus, it should not be a surprise that the liturgical gatherings would point to a need for universal income as the world of work is rapidly changing and creating precarious jobs without any benefits. In order to live the fulness of a love unknown and beyond ourselves, a hierarchical structure of job positions must be dismantled, and everyone should get the same salary, adjusted for cost of living. If we are to build a social structure where everyone is protected, the liturgical space is a privileged place of praise and work, *ora et labora*.

In the same way, when hunger is growing exponentially with the pandemic, the Eucharist should be a shared meal of the day. When rivers are polluted, baptisms should be put on hold until the waters are clean, and fish can swim in it. If the fish die, our faith dies too.

Against the Cartesian Self – Autonomy and Symbiosis

The condition of our time is anxiety as democracies become structures without the *demos*, people, and where popular sovereignty is erased. Liturgies must address how the notion of the subject is composed, organized, activated, and enacted by power. We own land, identity, religion, work, and our own selves, and so we become separate individuals and societies. As Safatle says:

For we are deeply colonized by the notion that labor produces the right to possession. What I work on is mine. A people, as a collective political subject, as a collective worker, should also appear as the owner of objects in which he works. Following this scheme, social emancipation is usually understood as taking possession of objects whose source of existence are my work or the work of the people of which I am a part.[20]

If we are dominated by all forms of possession, what can we propose that will create the conditions of possibility for some form of agency? Safatle argues that the relation of people as *Kratos* to emancipated objects can create a condition of emancipation of subjects. He says:

For if we accept that emancipation of objects is the first condition for the emancipation of subjects, then we will be obliged to accept the existence of a kratos that comes from things, which is the affection of things in subjects in an involuntary and external dimension.... On the other hand, to speak about the emancipation of objects means that, far from being instruments or possessions, things can appear as what cause us and what act in us without being linked to the will of a person, to the deliberation of a conscience, like these works of art that affect us without being the expression of a person's deliberation. They are not only the sedimentation of the circuits of stories that composed it, but also the force of their bodies, of their matter, of the path of their own materiality, of their "own life." A kratos liberated from the metaphysics of property would be the recognition of the force of things in us, in our action. The exercise of this kratos would be the condition for a society in which objects would affect us in their impropriety and inappropriateness. That is to say, we are talking about a society in which objects would be inappropriate, in which they would neither be individual property nor collective property, but would be the expression that we live inside circuits of objects that affect us and of which we do not own. A democratic society would be a society where things no longer exist in the form of what can be possessed. This interferes in the very notion of what we mean by "subjects." For subjects will have the marks of the objects that affect them and which they carry.[21]

Thus, subjects of eco-liturgical liberation theologies must move away from the modern notion of emancipation and autonomy. The pretense of autonomy and emancipation created a notion of self that is divided, centered on an illusion of individual indivisibility and fulness that is marked by economic historical developments. This atomized sense of self dismantled intertwined notions of life and self that are related to the land and all its living beings.

The self in liberation theologies did not see sex or earth or race as fundamental parts of the self of the poor. The emancipation of the poor was mostly understood as economic, but without a much larger cosmology we were fighting a fight that happens outside, without the harsh work within. With a pulverized sense of self, we get stuck in concepts of modernity and a sense that we are betraying the struggle. We must reach out for forms of the self that are not based on autonomy but on deep relationality, as we subvert categories of modernity and establish new forms of thinking/action.

In Latin America, these two words are fundamental: emancipation and autonomy. We can still use them to clarify where we stand and with whom, but we must get rid of the notion of autonomy that comes from the individual of liberalism in the 18th century. The enlightenment development of the notion of autonomy through individual freedom, as Kant showed us, proved to be a path towards the freedom of our own histories without the control of the church. Freedom as citizens meant autonomy as individuals not subjected to labor and with material independency, where the worker is not attached to anything. This modern notion of freedom is costly as we abandon any form of subjugation, living an autonomous life without any coercion or need. We are without care from or for anyone; we own our own life.

Perhaps if we can rethink our notion of autonomy as collective agency, we can continue to use this term. We are never individuals; we are a composition of organisms. We have entire communities within our bodies. We, as individuals, only come after. The constitution of our bodies is billions of cells and "foreign agents." This notion calls us into the consideration that we are and have always been a collective project and never an individual one. It is biologically impossible to live alone only by ourselves! What liberalism did, and does, is to use a Darwinist notion of competition between creatures to claim that the economic world is for the strong. Liberalism creates an ideology, a fake news, where reality is like human survival: the survival of the fittest, of the individual. However, the fittest must build on the collective in order to champion its own success and to become a winner by "pulling oneself up by one's bootstraps", That notion of independent liberal autonomy has been shaped and sold by the illusion of the American dream, along with the necessary erasure of the fact that the American Dream depends on the work and defeat of so many others. This lie encourages us to struggle for better jobs, better churches, and better positions as pastors.

Isabelle Stengers writes about autonomy as something collectively created, a multi-species autonomy, in which I cannot survive without the survival of other species in me and around me. Everything is interdependency: She says:

> *I tried to link autonomy with artifact, a fact of the art. This art could be characterized as turning interdependency, which is always the case, whether we like it or not, into an active constraint, a constraint that activates feeling, thinking, and imagining.*[22]

Against the Cartesian notion of the self as an individual and discrete agent, we understand the self and its autonomous ways as symbiosis, as a collective living between organisms/people who are not the same but live together for the betterment of all. It is this symbiotic living that allows us to create a plurality of worlds and communities where individuals are sustained, not for the sake of their own lives but for the life of the community. I sustain you so I can be sustained. Love and selfishness together, and together we can activate, perhaps through rituals too, a series of constraints of desire, demolishing narcissism, and developing *active feeling, thinking, imagining,* and living so we can form and shape *A World of Many Worlds.*[23]

The Decolonial Self/Subject

We search for a decolonial subject where the sources of knowledge and even the constitution of our realities can reclaim what coloniality stole, killed, and destroyed[24] in our lands, within our people, and within ourselves. In his book *Orientalism,* Edward Said writes of doing an inventory of our history, citing the Italian political philosopher Antonio Gramsci and his *Prison Notebooks.*[25] This inventory is the search for what was lost during coloniality and modernity in the lands where our people lived: the forms of self that constituted stories and relations. A decolonial self entails a wound--a devastating work of mourning. This inventory has to do with the rediscovery of knowledges that were killed, something Boaventura de Sousa Santos calls 'cognitive injustice,' and epistemicide.[26] It is to go after the subject/object ignorance produced by coloniality. This inventory is an excavation, digging into the lands where we were born and made foreigners and enemies of our own people, figuring out where and with whom we belong. This inventory discovers catalogues and archives burnt over the last 500 years. This inventory engenders forms of life, of self, of cosmologies, and living with the earth that can transform our faith and our ways of living.

Epistemicide is grounded in the Cartesian formula "I think, therefore I am." Enrique Dussel's vast work is a meditation in the ways modernity has erased the entire world just to show its own specificities.[27] Grassfoguel builds on Dussel's work to say that "the condition of possibility for the mid-17th century Cartesian "I think, therefore I am" (*ego cogito*) is the 150 years of "I conquer, therefore I am" (*ego conquiro*) is historically mediated by the genocide/epistemicide of the "I exterminate, therefore I am" (*ego extermino*)."[28]

It is this form of *cogito* on which theology was based, even liberation theologies. An inventory of the history of oppressed people will change our perspective regarding with whom we should be aligned. We must excavate a different sense of self from the debris of the extractivist zones of plundering, the historical deposits of exclusion, negation, denial, massacre, genocide, and murder. We must excavate the sources of faith, local knowledge, and practices that came from our grandmothers and great grandmothers as they inhabited the land.

We must understand poverty itself as the center of the poor's condition and subjectivity as a decolonial subject so that other forms of knowledges and resistances can be sought. Gloria Anzaldúa tells us that we must live in the borderland, a place between what is and isn't ours, a place of full cosmologies and the debris of coloniality, where we belong and do not, living with an open decolonial wound in our histories and bodies; for the wound will both make us remember and to heal.[29] The self is not based on a detached notion of the mind and the body, but rather a self that comes to its awareness from the wound of coloniality in the body. That notion of self is not limited by experience but finds modes of being, its very source of life, in the signifiers that float and overflow within and around the borderland.

Another way to understand the notion of a symbiotic self is through the African notion of *ubuntu*. Desmond Tutu tells us what *ubuntu* is against the Cartesian notion of the self:

> *Ubuntu is very difficult to render into a Western language. It speaks of the very essence of being human. When we want to give high praise to someone we say, "Yu, u nobuntu"; "Hey, so-and-so has ubuntu." Then you are generous, you are hospitable, you are friendly and caring and compassionate. You share what you have. It is to say, "My humanity is caught up, is inextricably bound up, in yours." We belong in a bundle of life. We say, "A person is a person through other persons." It is not, "I think therefore I am." It says rather: "I am human because I belong. I participate, I share."*[30]

It is in the expansiveness of the relationality with the land and others that we find a sense of self. Ripped apart from community the self loses its essence, bearings, sustenance, and modes of being.

Another form of understanding of self comes from anthropologist Eduardo Viveiros de Castro called Perspectivism.[30] Briefly, the structure of myths in Indigenous communities shares a notion of the cosmos that includes local environments and a multitude of persons (human and non-human) where multiple entities live in communities forming common and different worlds. Everything is human, says Castro.

> *If Western relativism has multiculturalism as its public politics, Amerindian shamanic perspectivism has multinaturalism as its cosmic politics.... Thus if a subject is an insufficiently analyzed object in the modern naturalist world, the Amerindian epistemological convention follows the inverse principle, which is that an object is an insufficiently interpreted subject... "In Amerindian cosmologies, the real world of different species depends on their point of view, for the 'world in general' consists only of different species, being the abstract space of divergence between them as points of view.[31]*

Perspectivism does not provide any form of an atomized self as Castro puts it, "When everything is human, the human becomes a wholly other thing."[32] That form of complexity calls our sense of self to exist in forms unknown to 0us. What does perspectivism do to our theological sense of self? Our relations with animals and the earth will be "natural," our relations with spirits and forests and rivers will be a continuation of our arms and legs, and priests will help us relate safely with other energies.

In Brazil, the Jurema religion offers another sense of self that combines the natural and human worlds.[33] Jurema, a hybridization of African and local Indigenous religions,[34] is not like Homi Bhabba's third space--as if one loses one part to be in relation with the other--but rather, it is the fulness of two cosmologies coming together into a new one. The self lives in the enactment of the ritual in relationship with nature, with place, and with ancestors.

> *Jurema is a typical religious expression of northeastern Brazil. It is both a rural and urban religion, but scholars have only recently become interested in the urban Jurema that involves the confluence of other religious expressions such as umbanda, Catholicism, candomblé and voodoo from Maranhão. Its name, of Tupi origin, is linked to some species of trees found in the dry region of the northeast: Mimosa hostilis (recently reclassified as Mimosa tenuiflora), Mimosa verrucosa and Vitexagnus-*

castus, respectively known as black, gentle, and white juremas. The black jurema is used to make the beverage that gives the name to this religious world. It probably originated in pajelança and toré, religious systems that are at the base of indigenous sacred understanding.[35]

This notion of self does not rely on racial identities even though it does not deny them; it welcomes anyone who wants to be under a tree and honor it. Jurema brings elements of several religions and brings together people often pulled apart from each other. The smoke of Jurema is the strength of resistance now elaborated into a notion of self that is far more complex than the Cartesian self.

Thus, the notion of the subject for eco-liturgical liberation theologies is not based on the atomized and detached sense of Cartesian self; the self can only be lived and understood if in relation with others, humans and more than human beings. The self is crossed by other forms of relationality without binaries of body versus mind, earth versus heaven, a transcendent and immanent God with its natural and special forms of revelations.

Instead of turning the poor into our likeness, eco-liturgical liberation theology facilitates relations with others so that the construct of God is created, molded, shaped, reshaped transformed, embraced, or avoided. Christians who understand the freedom Jesus gave us will not be afraid to delve into the knowledges of the oppressed and be transformed by them. Let us follow Paul's admonition to the Romans (12:1-2):

> *I appeal to you therefore, brothers and sisters, by the mercies of God, to present your bodies as a living sacrifice, holy and acceptable to God, which is your spiritual worship. Do not be conformed to this world, but be transformed by the renewing of your minds, so that you may discern what is the will of God—what is good and acceptable and perfect.*

The spiritual worship of Christians insists that we not conform to this world. When Christianity becomes a mirror of capitalism and a weapon of white supremacy, we must not be conformed with Christianity either. To be renewed in our minds means to unlearn the ways in which we are formed, rejecting what we have learned, take an inventory of our history, and move into other forms of knowledges and beliefs. Surely, a new form of subject must be part of this change of the mind.

Liturgical spaces are privileged places for things to appear—not to be possessed, but to be brought, to be shared, and to be symbolized. Going against the tide of religious commerce and mercantilism of liturgical objects is the first move towards the allowing objects to affect us into dispossession. It is there where the order of things can be subverted, other circuits of stories can be created, other forms of relations can be inaugurated, and other systems of affections can appear, as we learn to be dispossessed by things we cannot control or own.

Perhaps our task of liberation theology is to inhabit spaces to create relationship with the land, where local objects and other subjects can join to ritualized forms of life and protection and healing. At the heart of a decolonial liturgical theology is the search back to the earth. We have been uprooted and forced into forms of living that do not consider the earth as our place of most profound belonging. Thus, to talk about liturgies of theologies we must engage everything that pertains to the earth, and most fundamentally, the patch of land we inhabit.[36]

We can create a place, not to help the poor, but for Christians to inhabit and subvert the place of dispossession where the fascist states continuously desecrate the poor and extract all forms of life, power and energy from people and the earth. Only by being deprived of our belongings we can figure out what sharing everything means, drawing closer to those in situations of exclusion and understanding what it means to not have shelter or to know where our next meal will come from. The task is not then to include the poor into our way of living but rather to disrupt our religions from any economic security to create networks of life together where capitalism has desecrated everything. That means turning our church buildings into shelters, parking lots into gardens and small farms, our office budgets into support for collective forms of living. The task is to transform "the means of production into the production of means."[37]

Don Pedro Casaldáliga says it all in his poem *Evangelical Poverty*. Perhaps a liturgical gathering would be the place to say this poem together one hundred times, until we learn it by heart.

> *Have nothing.*
> *Take nothing.*
> *Can't do anything.*
> *Don't ask for anything.*
> *And, in passing,*
> *do not kill anything;*
> *don't shut up.*
> *Only the Gospel, like a sharp knife.*
> *And weeping and laughter in the eyes.*
> *And the hand extended and clasped.*
> *And life, on horseback, given.*
> *And this sun and these rivers and this purchased land,*

as witnesses of the revolution already broken.
And nothing else![38]

A Decolonial History of Liturgy

In the histories of the South of the globe over the last 500 years, liturgy was indeed a "weapon of mass destruction," used to sustain the colonial power of European centers. The liturgical field has not grappled enough with the massacres of colonization and the harm done by and through our liturgies. We wonder with Aimé Cesaire's shocking notes,

> *Christian bourgeois of the twentieth century… cannot forgive Hitler not for the crime in itself, the crime against man, it is not the humiliation of man as such, it is the crime against the white man, the humiliation of the white man, and the fact that he applied to Europe colonialist procedures which until then had been reserved exclusively for the Arabs of Algeria, the coolies of India, and the blacks of Africa.*[39]

Cesaire's commentary pushes us to consider how the flagellation and genocide of entire populations in the South of the world is never mentioned in liturgical studies.

We have learned that we must engage the Shoah in liturgies, and now we must also engage other sorrows too. Cesaire's quote reminds us of the conscious or unconscious ways we do not deal with the south of the globe or the marginalized--those living below the line of Ecuador and their disasters and catastrophes are never in the imagination of *liturgy's past.* There is a demand for us liturgists to do more with the liturgy of Kristallnacht in relation to the colonization of other people's lands, the defacing of other people's identities, the enslavement of Africans and the mass killings of Indigenous people. Following Cesaire's thinking, the Holocaust cannot be interpreted just within European history, and therefore, every liturgical move that touches the Holocaust should also touch what preceded and followed it in the global South.

From an eco-liturgical liberation theology perspective, there is no good liturgical theology that does not address the power dynamics and disasters of coloniality in both colonialism and neo-colonialism within our Christian faith. Unless these many histories are told--from the violent destruction of Christianity to the ways in which some forms of Christianity have now become the only organizing space of protection for Indigenous and Quilombolas (slave descendants)--we will continue to limit ourselves to obscure historical moments in Euro-American history as our liturgy's sole and sufficient past.

Instead, accessing these many histories we can understand our present better and see how neocolonialism continues to hold sway over people's lands, natural and religious resources, governments, and imaginaries. By assessing colonial histories, we can understand that coloniality is at present in our present day, and we can see how liturgy continues to be a colonial project that serves as an "apparatus of the state" that serves only a certain class of people.

As I mentioned in *Liturgy and Postcolonialism*, one of the key considerations for us liturgical theologians is Brazilian Alfredo Bosi's discussion of the angle of the practices and universalizing discourses of religion, the idea of totality and daily life cut by economic division and oppressive hierarchies of power marked by our *cultum*, the supine models of our liturgical being. Bosi writes about the notion of colony as the intersection of *colo-cultus*, culture:[40]

Colo is to occupy the land, work and cultivate the land. It is to live and cultivate the land. That is why colonization means taking people's homes and obliging others to work. It is the colonization of the land.

Cultus - In this relationship, the land is linked to the cult of the dead, which are our ancestral ways of relating to our community. Colonization uproots people from the land and breaks the cult relationship with their ancestry. The root, the deepest axis of belonging, is lost. The particularity of place is removed, and the universal is imposed. Cultus is the colonization of the body and its relations.

Culture is what you will work on the land, the cultivation of the deepest and most important work for this group and society. When we attack artists, for instance, we are saying that we do not want to cultivate this freer, more generous form of life; we want a culture of limits, of policing, of clear ideological standards. Culture is the colonization of the mind.

Every liturgy is an intersection of *colo*, *cultus* and culture. Most churches occupy lands that belong to others. Due to our illusion of purity, we erase the knowledge from that land, from the communities that belonged to that ground. The uprootedness created by Christianity also detached Christians from the land we occupy now as private property. Christians cultivate a series of beliefs, feelings, and actions that are often foreign to the Indigenous people that used to live in the land. Every gathering and every ritual repeat and enact our whole cosmologies and modes of being.

Thus, our *cultus* is a result of dialectic processes as colonization also entails a dialectic process of power differentiators in complex compositions of religious, economic, and racial figures. For instance, the worship space where we offer our worship to God is always already a private space owned by a religious group, a certain class, which, in some ways, is already trumping God's ownership of the land. If we are to take the eschatological aspect of our faith seriously, space is as fundamental as time. Who owns the land? Who has access to it? Who makes the decisions? Who is in the hierarchical structure? Can the homeless sleep in these premises if needed? Can these religious places become a shelter, a home?

Is the worship a place for univocity, of one voice and the voices of those who are with us, and what about those voices who are by shifting, altering, transforming, and changing our stable sense of identity? Whose voice can speak in our liturgies? Can the poor/subaltern speak or is it a Pentecostal place with a plethora of voices that makes a cacophony and even unintelligible theology? Are the voices as plural as we are plural, with voices from those who came before us to speak? Is the worship space a place that demands racial justice? How do we undo those structures? Jewish Liberation theologian Marc Ellis proposes: "[t]here shouldn't be any religious ritual until there is justice."[41] And then he asks: What would that do to our religious communities?[42]

These questions are questions asked by eco-liturgical liberation theologies. Everything, literally the whole life, is at stake in religious worship spaces. The worship space is a privileged space as it engages identities, struggles, and our ways of being. In the worship space, we open a small window into what life is and what life should be. But to understand the inside of the worship space we need to understand the outside of this cultic space. The liturgical field has repeatedly said that liturgy can only be understood by liturgy, and that the Eucharist is explained by the church and the church by the Eucharist. The theology of Christian rites can only be explained by the tradition shaped by our willingness to accept its authority. Its own symbols are only juxtaposed with each other: bath with gathering, word with meal and so on.

This is key for our understanding of an eco-liturgical liberation theology. Because what is proposed here, is the bringing of the world, especially the patch of land we inhabit, into the very space of worship. The idea is to understand the worship space as the world of God and the land we live in, not only the inner world of the church. In this way, it is important to ask what is in our culture/nature that determines who we are, what we make of this world, of this land, so that we can know what, but even more importantly, how and with whom we worship. In this way, our historical work and the inventory of our land and struggle matter, since they shed light and shadows on our ways of living and the kind of people, human and more than human, with whom we are concerned.

In the background of this eco-liturgical liberation theology, I hope we will hear the voices of more than humans speaking to us, calling us, trying to get in relation with us. I hope we will also make an attempt to juxtapose race with word, immigration with bath, nation-state with gathering, health care with sending forth, earth with God.

Liturgical Liberation Theology

Influences

An eco-liturgical liberation theology should not come as a shock. There are plenty of sources in the early Christian churches that demand for us to care for the poor and to challenge richness and gold. And yet, somehow some churches have cared more to embellish the altar with gold than to attend to the poor.

The key work of Tissa Balasuriya, *The Eucharist and Human Liberation* was perhaps the first liturgical liberation theology *avant-la-letre*. In Brazil, Jaci C. Maraschin and his vast liturgical and theological production was the primary thinker relating liturgy and liberation theology. His own *Community of Liberation* was an experiment on Liturgical Liberation theology with an emphasis on the aesthetics of liberation.[43] Júlio de Santa Ana wrote a small but important book called *Pão Vinho e Amizade*,[44] which is a liturgical liberation theological account on life.

The work of Rubem Alves was fundamental for theology to gain a new language, with other frequencies, symbols, sounds and colors, which helped liturgy to think of itself in a variety of representations, rituals, and bodily relations. Nelson Kirst expanded the field with a solid traditional reading on liturgy, and Brazilian feminist liturgist Ione Buyst developed much more what I am calling a liturgical liberation theology. Other names that helped us get us here are Odair Pedroso Mateus, Simei Monteiro, Carlos Eduardo B. Calvani, José Rubens Jardilino and the late Ernesto Cardoso and Marcos Antonio Gianelli.[45]

Figuring out the present theologically

Nathan Mitchell says: "Liturgical discourse must inevitably give way to the body, to the embodied action of ethical performance… the human body is the basic site of liturgy… liturgy's first and most obvious language is the body."[46] We begin with hungry bodies, empty bellies, bodies exploited in every way, economically, socially, politically, sexually, racially.

Bodies turned into disposable things, objects. Bodies whose value is not in simple existence but rather, in consumeristic qualities.

Bodies excluded from the common good, living under bridges or old cars, or scattered along highways with no real shelter.

Sick bodies without care or assistance. Bodies whose mental health is diminished and whose conditions of possibilities are abandonment and carelessness.

Bodies of people living in desperate conditions. Black bodies lynched at midday and Black bodies locked in public jails. Indigenous bodies burnt in public squares. Queer bodies killed everywhere. Women's bodies abused and exploited. Poor bodies going hungry. Bodies of affliction, bodies of pain. Bodies whose only value lies in the exchange of sexual goods. Bodies of families trying to make it with very little, under the pressure of economic loss, living increasingly with the barebones of what is left to keep breathing. Bodies used by the state, violated by the state.

Bodies between necropolitics and biopower, with the state determining those who are to live and who are to die.

How are we to respond to these realities?

Gathering — Bodies in Worship

This is a not a simple quest to respond to this reality by using the field of liturgical studies. Surely the gathering on Sundays or any other day of the week is not enough to respond to the complexities of this all. In fact, there is very little that can be done there. However, in all its exaggerations, overstatements, and over determined expectations, worship is still an important event done throughout the world where the poor can find a place to rest their bodies, find sustenance, and be honored. During worship, those who are deemed garbage of the world, can reclaim their dignity. Hovering around death every day, the poor can fill with life, if the liturgy is life!

Worship is fundamentally a place of response where people respond to God's love and for the world. In worship the poor and excluded come hungry and wounded. Bodies marked by death go through worship by thinking, feeling, singing and talking about death--the death of hunger, of homelessness, of unemployment, of not having healthcare, of mental illness, of broken bodies. Like the disciples who went through the fullness of Jesus' death, we are surprised by Jesus' resurrection. It is this surprise in worship that we hope to find every time we meet, that the Holy Spirit will take our spirit of sorrow and will give us a heart filled with gladness. By the sustenance of the Spirit, through death and all the disasters of the world, we can receive and create together possibilities for new life. That creation is the celebratory moment of worship. Worship is the repetition of the circular movements of death and life. The fullness of Holy Friday and Easter Sunday enacted every time we worship.

Worship is the Christian way of understanding religion, *religare*, that which binds people and all realities back together,[47] the movement of the spirit with the body, the awakening of our condition and possibilities, the ungrasping of our mind from ideas and concepts, fears, anger and disconnection. Worship is the undoing of binaries such as knowledge of God and the knowledge of ourselves, immanence and transcendence, the sacred and profane, human and nature, us and them. Worship can be fundamentally a link that helps us connect with people, every people, the earth, the animals, the cosmos, sentient, and non-sentient beings, all there is.

Worship is an exercise in justice, where we learn the alienation of people from their sources and the ideologies that keep them in emotional, spiritual, and material chains. In this way, worship and liberation are paramount and so we can understand Ignacio Ellacuría's saying: "True Christian liberation is discovered and promoted in liturgy and only in liturgy."[48] At worship, a deep solidarity arises, care and honoring is relentlessly pursued, peace and justice kiss each other. As Catherine Bell says: through rituals people can "make and remake their worlds."[49]

Worship and Liturgy: Theologia Prima

Let us expand that a bit. Taking this understanding of worship, I will now rely on Aidan Kavanagh's notion of *Theologia Prima* and *Theologia Secunda* in his book *On Liturgical Theology*. In that book he says:

> 'Theology' is not the very first result of an assembly's being brought by liturgical experience to the edge of chaos. rather, it seems that what results in the first instance from such an experience is deep change in the very lives of those who participate in the liturgical act... I hold that it is theology being born, theology in the first instance. It is what tradition has called theology prima. To argue with minds accustomed to thinking of theology in such a manner that theology at its genesis is communitarian, even proletarian; that it is aboriginally liturgical in context, partly conscious and partly unconscious, that it stems from an experience of near chaos, that it is long term and dialectical; and that its agents are more likely to be charwomen and shopkeepers than pontiffs and professors - all this is to argue against the grain. It is to argue that the theology which we most readily recognize and practice is in fact neither primary nor seminal but secondary and derivative: theology secunda. It is also to argue that doing

liturgical theology comes closer to doing theology prima than theology secunda.[50]

Primary liturgical theology is the common work of the community when worshiping God. The worship, the praise of God, and the *liturgia*, are the ways the community praises God. Worship is both the doing of a showing and, using words from Richard Schechner, the "showing-doing."[51] The doing of the liturgy is the living, its praxis, the reasoning of bodies in movement, life in fullness as it happens with what we bring and what is brought to us. The showing is the manifestation of this doing, it is the ritualized forms that shows how life is done.

In other words, worship is the doing of life by showing how life happens through rituals. Secondary liturgical theology is, on the other hand, following Schechner, the showing of this doing, i.e., the thinking and reasoning of that life as liturgically lived. It is the thinking, writing, describing, telling, showing of such an event through the rationality of bodies in movements through words, gestures, speeches, and actions. The whole of the worship service: prayer, singing, preaching, sacrament, "everything in worship is, in its fullest sense," according to Wannenwetsch "a form of life."[52] However worship is also expressed in various forms of liturgies—feasts, rituals, performances, theater, etc.—that entail other forms of life.

Thus, *liturgia secunda*, is the theory of these forms of life, the thinking of a praxis, the showing of a doing, an attempt to gain a certain awareness of what happened during the worship. Primary theology is praxis, the doing of life in its performances and rituals, and second theology is theory, the attempt to elucidate the event and what happened during that event.

In some ways, this relation can be compared with Liberation theology's methodology. For liberation theologians, the theology is the second step since the first step is life lived by the poor. The analogy that I would use here is the worship space—whatever space that is—as a case in point of a larger community's life, a privileged space to understand the world from that local context. In primary theology lies the bodies and experiences of the people worshiping God to illuminate both the primary and the secondary theology.

Communities pulse their environment, their struggles, and their desires in worship. Brazilian liberation liturgical theologian Júlio Cesar Adam analyzed the *Romaria da Terra*, a liturgy done by campesinos and the landless movements in Brazil and wrote a book about their liturgy. Adam's book can be said to be the first contemporary book on eco-liturgical liberation theology. It is worth this long quote from Adam:

Liturgy's first impulse is in the search for what moves people in the daily lives of the people, in moving ourselves in search of something that is lacking, Liturgy entails social action within its own contexts: each worship denounces and celebrates its world. Worship celebration and liberation cannot work separately. No service will change the world if the celebrants don't let one flow into the other, worship in the daily life and daily life into the service... liturgy is not something that is done only with the head, with ideas, with liturgical agendas, with musical notes, with tradition. Liturgy is done with all this, but its first impulse is in the search for what moves people in their daily lives, in moving ourselves in search of something that that is lacking, in the feet that dance the victory for the things that God did and does among the poor, the least and the last... Liturgy entails social action within its own contexts: each worship denounces and celebrates its world. When life is more agitated, the worship will be more agitated which can be even more aggressive and provocative. If life happens in a provisory way, searching for a fixed place to stay. Liturgy will be a pilgrimage... The world expressed in that liturgy is not an abstracted reality imagined by its members but constitutes what people live and fight in their daily lives. If they celebrate resistance and liberation is because they are living in resistance and searching for liberation. Worship celebration and liberation cannot work separately. No service will change the world if the celebrants don't let one flow into the other, worship in the daily life and daily life into the service.[53]

We cannot isolate the worship space only as a performance of one's "holy" things. The holy things are the outcast, the broken, the disenfranchised, the unbeautiful, and the poor. The primary theology includes what Nathan Michel calls "the three distinct--yet essentially interdependent--liturgy of the world, liturgy of the church, and the liturgy of the neighbor. That is one reason why a sacramental rite such as the eucharist can never be understood apart from economics and ethics."[54]

The trinomial of *lex: orandi, credendi and vivendi* (prayer, belief and ethics/life) must be now expanded by another *lex*, a law I am calling the *lex ecologicus* or *lex naturae*, which is the full relation of living organisms to one another and to their physical surroundings. We must learn with Indigenous people and consider humanity to include more than human beings--animals as living other shades of humanity, the whole ecology, with the flora and fauna, plants, flowers and animals, spirits and all the rivers and forests and seas of the whole geographical world--as full of God's glory just as any human being.

Thus, what is proposed here is for liturgical theologians to see the whole world/earth as a worship space, as a *locus theologicus*, without the dichotomy of the in and the out of worship. Worship is a collective doing of the liturgy of life that presses in on the liturgical borders of the church and which calls all liturgists to cross borders. Liturgy cannot be explained by liturgy alone anymore but must be challenged by the real experiences of the people and the life of the earth. What does each patch of the earth say about the law of the land that we must follow? What does immigration tell of the liturgy? How do we understand the reasons of poverty in worship so we can start to act to overcome it? How do we honor those defaced by the world? Engaged in this circular movement of mutual teachings, where reality checks tradition to its validity and tradition helps sustain a much stronger sense of reality, we worship as an action. An action born in God's love.

We always start with God's love. There is no other place to start. The love that still visits us from the past, that is fully present to us now, and is always coming from the future to visit us. Grounded in that eternal love, we are drenched with compassion for others and then we act. Grounded in love, we can affirm the agency of God's emergence and earth's symbiosis. The church is a patch of the earth to multiply by means of grace the lives of the world and to call upon the name of God to remember what was forgotten, to pray with those who are hurting, and to be in solidarity with them, be it people or polluted rivers. This praying with the poor and animals being mercilessly killed is what is an eco-liturgical liberation theology might mean. Salvation is existing in mutuality and reciprocity with the earth, standing in solidarity with somebody else wherever they are, being fully there, giving, receiving, learning, and being transformed.

Praying with those suffering, we have access to the whole world inside/outside of the liturgical space, and we start praying from where it hurts. The ritual performance of our worship would then be a way of attending to human suffering with God's love, offering and receiving, in a deeper mutuality and inner circularity, multiple expressions of all our dignity. In each place, we realize a new form of who we are in God and with the earth, at each place we live. In this in/out practice, we can begin to understand liturgy as the real encounter with what is dying and how to work with the earth and each other to open ways for what is emerging to fully appear and give us direction.

Worship is the gathering of a people living at the edge of the chaos of oppression and poverty that is always ready to devour them. All at once we discover prayers and gestures that no theology has ever thought. At the edge of the chaos of racism, class struggles, sexism and patriarchy, broken immigration systems, pungent militarism, state violence, state owned private sectors, extractivism, and plundering, communities gather to make sense of their lives, to share in solidarity with each other's sufferings, to feed each other with the holy meal, and to sing their spirituals and praise songs just to make it to another week in a fascist white supremacist world. At the edge of chaos, the Dalits are kept in utter humiliation, but a community gathers to undo the homogeneity of caste and social humiliation with rites of moral responsibility.[55] At the edge of the chaos, Indigenous people continue to fight to survive the violence of more than 500 years of brutal oppression by colonizers, now seen through the presence of agribusiness and state sanctified violence.

Liturgy then becomes what the meaning of the word should have become, that is, the full work of the people with God and a billion species. Liturgy's etymological sense, the work of few people on behalf of many, does not have space anymore.

Worship and Liturgy: Theologia Secunda

The work of the eco-liturgical liberation theologian is to give an account of those actions. For instance, she goes to a Black Lives Matter manifestation, or to a struggle of the landless movement, and comes back to her community. At worship, she shares the strategies, the songs, the words, and the symbols. Now the community gains a sense of how racism, economic power, and politics work in intertwined ways, and they see how a community is responding. They see how the struggle for the land becomes a way of collective symbiotic autonomy. They then add their religious sources and expand their liturgies. Eco-liturgical liberation theology is then a way of incorporating these worship goals through the working of the people with more than human people in actions, songs, movements, and gestures. It is a way of processing the liberation dreamed, announced, and lived during that time. Kavanagh used to say that liturgy is "doing the world the way the world was meant to be done"[56] and that is what we do in worship: the creation of liturgies that will do the world as it is meant to be done.

Eco-liturgical liberation theology is the theory/practice of the worship practice/theory, but now we add the law of the land. The eco-liturgical liberation theologian must be present there, with the people and more than human people, to see what arises from the people and the earth, what is necessary, how people deal with their own hurts and pain, and to learn how to hear what the earth is saying. If we have lost our way to listen to the earth, worship must provide forms of relation and protocols with other subjects and more than human people near us.

Thus, at worship we can hear the cry of bees being decimated, animals being slaughtered, trees being cut, and mountains having their tops removed. At worship, people will cry with them! And they will cry out for what they hope, dream, and need. They will offer and demand, search and give, relate and reciprocate. They will sing their songs and their songs will be juxtaposed with the songs of the traditions. The birds will be an estuary of new traditional songs and hymnodies. They will bring their symbols and their symbols will be juxtaposed with the Bible, the table/altar/tree, the water/river/ocean. They will bring the earth's holy things and their earth's holy things will be juxtaposed with Biblical holy things. They will bring their prayers and their prayers will be juxtaposed with the prayers done in the last 2000 years and the new ones done by owls, tigers, skunks, bears, sealions, sharks, hummingbirds, and caterpillars.

Eco-liturgical liberation theology must take an account of the whole body/bodies of the humans and more than human peoples within communities located in certain parts of land so it can be a circular movement of whole bodies together. The *Romaria* studied by Júlio Cesar Adam shows that there is not dichotomy between liturgy and worship and land. The worship is cultus/land, it is *theologia prima* and his book *is theologia secunda.* Using Otto Maduro's title of his book *Maps for a Fiesta,*[57] I would say that *theologia prima* is the feast and *theologia secunda* is the mapping of that feast. The secondary theology of this eco-liturgical liberation theology is grounded somewhat in the methodology of liberation theology.

Some Themes for Eco-Liturgical Liberation Theology

Humus

We are soil, humus, stardust and the memory of the universes. Eco-liturgical liberation theologies must be a cosmological story of pluriversal proportions but lived locally, shared, and picked up from the place a community lives, with its own inhabitants, stories, challenges, needs and forms of relation and transformation with all peoples, human and more than humans. We hear the earth, and we honor the earth by searching for a song/rhythm/sound/dance for the times we are living in.[58] The old songs will continue with us until we learn how to sing with the birds and with rivers. We will teach restraint in the face of the fastness of our world, and we will help each other to slow down until we can move "according to the pace of the cattle that are before me and according to the pace of the children" (Genesis 33:14).

Our worship starts where we stand, in symbiosis with the earth, as humus, in love and reciprocity with the earth we inhabit. We will do away with any sense of property but will engage in forms of reciprocity and gift exchange with the earth, living through the saying: "and the dust returns to the earth as it was, and the breath returns to God who gave it"

(Ecclesiastes 12:7). However in between these moments of eternity we will live connected with the earth and will take care of the earth for the next generations, living with the wisdom of Indigenous people who tell us we need to think about seven generations: three before us, our generation and three ahead of us. Every single theology must start honoring the earth and paying attention to the elements. Every liturgy must say a word of gratitude to the surroundings and ask for forgiveness for what we have. Every liturgy must be a way to learn how to dream with trees and rivers, inventing forms of restitution to the poor, to the community, and to the earth.

Assembly

The liturgical gathering teaches us that we are not only the people gathered. COVID-19 has challenged our ways of understanding our ecclesiologies. We are not only the real/virtual community but the virtual/real communities as well. COVID-19 is causing so many local churches who cannot survive without its members to vanish. How do we create other forms of worship gathering and mutual sustenance? We are a people of God whether we are in the same place or far away. We are a people of God but also not only a people of God. We are a much larger assembly. The earth is an assembly of all its inhabitants and the Christian assembly is just a fraction of the much larger assembly.

We must learn that even our assemblies are made of people but also of the trees and rivers that surround our gathering spaces, with birds chirping, mice running around, warmth under the earth, deer and coyotes nearby, and the grasshopper jumping everywhere. We are an assembly of creatures, all of us! We shall learn how to listen to God's voice in other species' breaths, singing and living. The assembly is the cloud of witnesses that attests to the fulness of time where past, present, and future collapse into a new organization of time. In other words, we are talking about ancestries, honoring those who came before us and their places of living and dying. We walk with those who disappeared, who were taken away by all forms of violence. As the song says: *Yo te llevo dentro, hasta la raíz / I carry you within me, to its roots.*[59] Here we must remember liberation theologian Ernesto Cardenal said something like this:

> *When you have won the vote, think about those who died, when you stand up with the leaders, think about those who died, when you arrive at the airport's big cities, think of those who died, when your voice speaks to microphones or television, think of those who died, when the old lady with her problems arrives, think of those who died, when looking at the shirtless,*

the excluded, the thrown to the side, think of those who died, to think of them and to think with those who lived, for you are their representatives, and they have entrusted you to think of those who have died.[60]

Our liturgies must have litanies to sustain those living, and litanies to help those who died, to keep their history alive. To think/pray/sing/honor those who died (humans and non-humans) is a fundamental way of positioning ourselves in the trenches of the struggles of our present day. Liturgies are spiritual ways to sustain us in the struggle. We do not die, we do not let others die, and we will create conditions of living for all creatures.

There is too much at stake! As Walter Benjamin reminds us, "Even the dead will not be safe from the enemy if he wins."[61] The assembly is the encounter of heaven and earth, an opportunity to tell yet another story so we can, as Indigenous thinker Ailton Krenak says, postpone the end of the world.[62]

Liturgy as an Event[63]

Any liturgy is a full event in the lives of its people, so it carries the gifts of prayers and orders of worship from people who are wrestling with their faith in historical contexts, reimagining the life of the church as an event from below, feeling and breathing with people in their daily lives.

The church of Jesus Christ should be understood as the daily living out of a community who worships God, breathes together its prayers and songs and gestures, breaks bread around a common table, cares for each other, mends what is broken, sustains what is threatened to be ripped apart, and holds on to life as a fragile gift of God that is so often susceptible to be taken away. Church is about life together, keeping people alive, generating honor to each other and protecting one another from violence. Moreover, the church in its worship form is the manifestation of an event, a daily or weekly miracle that, when happening in the community, carries the promise that something will happen!

Church as an event happens when people gather to worship God and are transformed by the "renewal of our minds." Church as an event is the manifestation of the Holy Spirit visiting the community and bringing healing, empowerment, and sustenance to its people. Church as an event is like a signpost to the world pointing in the direction of life, avoiding the many paths of death. Church as event is a true happening in the life of a community being oriented by God to a new life, and in this relation, a life also offered to the world. Church as an event is the fulness of God's glory in the bodies of people, putting in their hearts the desire to live a life of solidarity, filling them with blessings, and marking the incarnation of

Jesus' life with the fruits of the Spirit. Church as an event takes the daily life of the people as its main sources of theological insights and from the living together that happens on the streets, we find the collective breathing that sustains each other. Thus, starting from where life happens, the event of worship becomes the highest event of faith in the life of a community.

We must experience church in ways that our whole lives are affected by the various contexts and languages created from where the struggle is happening by naming injustice and calling for God's justice. From each place, the power of life bursting into prayers and songs can be felt and will open ways for other communities to pair their own lives with each community here represented. Liturgies do not resign us to death nor to the impossibility of explaining why death looms large so intensely around our people. Instead, liturgies face the complicit reality of death, the erosion of language, the abandonment of those suffering, the pain of so many, and the growing sense that we are incapable of changing anything in the oppressive structures of the world.

Liturgies must offer us something new, either by their ancient wisdom or by their new deeply grounded prayer that was birthed in pain and desperation. Liturgies must help us excavate our lives, as said Edward Said, recovering buried forms of memories that will renew the strength that comes from the connection that people hold to their locations, creating practices that will sustain the bodies of its believers and their historical processes of transformation.

Today's world is filled with evil manifestations: fascism, patriarchy, wars, ecological destruction, prejudices, and social inequality. We are losing the already meager resources to survive. More and more we need communities to pray with others, to sing together, to share a meal, to be anointed and to heal, to prophesy, and to keep the world going. Through eco-liturgical liberation liturgies people do not deny the world's pain, avoid suffering with the earth's devastation, normalize the threats of violence, nor shrug their shoulders with apathy before forceful agents of death. Instead, people take into account the depersonalization of individuals and restore a sense of self from a collective understanding of a body, the body of Christ.

Eco-liturgical liberation liturgies tell us of the power of collective memory that can restore in us a new heart, helping us to think otherwise and live the gospel in ways that we have not yet lived. These liturgies bring joy to where there is no joy, healing where there is hurt, and an affirmation of life where there is only condemnation to death.

Each liturgical context shows the power and the ingenuity of people who, when staying together, create the conditions of possibilities of life to continue. These liturgies expand books of prayers with vibrant collections of prayers and life pulsing at every line. They show us the paradoxes of life so that we avoid the temptation of praying or singing too glibly. These prayers demand a covenant with God and one another. Liturgies push against resignation and exhaustion, fear and hopelessness. With each liturgy, we find ourselves singing with others and for those who cannot sing, praying with each other and for those who cannot pray. Together a whole powerful community is represented within these liturgies.

Liturgy is an event that brings us closer to every that thing that dies and gives life, just as every flower bulb is an event, as every rain is an event, as every cloud passing is an event, as the wind blowing is an event, as the cyclical cycles of the earth are all amazing events. Perhaps, if we can see liturgies as events, we might mirror the amazing and spectacular events of the earth and follow the wonder that is the law of the land.

Unconscious

One of the problems with theologies, including liberation liturgies, is that we work too much in the mode of our consciousness. Daughters of Aristotelian premises, liberation theologies act with the injunction of autonomy and emancipation, decision and deliberation, action and responsibility, where the fruits of deliberation are calculations of means and ends, decision and possible choices. The preferential love of God for the poor is paramount to any liturgical theology. This liturgical theological option not only honors the poor as full-fledged human beings and God's beloved children, but also, sees the poor as fundamental agents of God's love in the world. Liturgy is a celebration of Jesus and if any liturgy wants to celebrate Jesus, churches must go where the poor, naked, hungry, thirsty, and imprisoned live, where every piece of land is being killed, and learn there where God dwells and where salvation comes from as we consider the presence of God in history. Liberation theology's classic belief is that the gospel read within poor communities has the power to turn each person into the subject of his/her own history. Conscious of our call to determine history, we are the ones empowered by God to work with God to give rise to the utopia of the Kin-dom of God in our midst.

However, we will not get anywhere with only the format of consciousness, emancipation, and autonomy. Our consciousness will only sleep through its demands and stumble upon the unknown within our selves and in the struggle itself. That means that the unconscious must come to the front of the work we do, giving space to the collective analytical act, to the full living of the slip of the tongue, the unorganized forms of the self, the dispossession of identities, and mutual presence until we are able to embrace the feeling of abandonment. Not only do we have the freedom to choose and to deliberate precisely and clearly, we also must own our desires for servitude and oppression.

There, in the place where we feel abandoned by the state, or even by God, we are able to muster the strength to change things, not with God not as our rescue, but through the strength of knowing that we do not own our selves, which allows God to move through these unknown parts of ourselves. If the conscious part of ourselves establishes our relation as embracing our own histories, the unconscious part can help us perform the event of God within a community, letting go control of anything including history. The unconscious, as Professor Pamela Copper-White says,[64] is present within our conversations and our gatherings, as we project and dispute issues with other people in an interlocking dynamic where we play out our inner dramas with one another. We project our pain and anger and sorrows onto other people and God; God becomes that which we project, leaving little to imagine, believe, and hold on to. But Cooper-White offers a good definition of ritual for us: "ritual is any act which symbolically carries conscious or unconscious meaning and is repeated over a given period of time."[65]

Thus, the weekly performance of liturgy can help us see these projections and open us into something else. Liturgical performances teach us to see God in new places, to allow ourselves to be affected in new ways, and interpret our desires for freedom and servitude. Surely the cultic space is not a session with a therapist, but it is an open gathering where religious traditions and liturgical performances ask questions about ourselves, communities, and the world. Collective organization done through liturgies and rituals must also run in an organic mode so the unconscious can be a place to find our freedom. In Pentecostal churches today, instead of letting loose the unconscious to find freedom, there is a formation of the conscious that brings forth the worst part of ourselves, opening destructive spaces for fascism to reappear under 'qualities of self-righteousness, Godly fear, God's anger, and the absolute of non-contradictions.

How do we deal with our growing existential angst in our liturgies? We must reconcile the ways the capitalistic *lack of lack* engulfs us with promises of fulfillment that will never be delivered. The pleasure offered is not the distinction between law and desire, but the socialization of pleasure from all forms of illusions and fantasies. I believe we could say that traditional Christian churches work in the mode of law and desire and the neo-Pentecostal churches, and the charismatic movements work on the neoliberal key of loose fantasies without law, or the law of the necessary experience of all fantasies.

How can liturgies offer a space where we do not get caught into the normalization of fantasies and the demands for pleasures that must be fulfilled, even if the canceling of the other is necessary? Perhaps we might help each other in dealing with the angst of the unfamiliar, the strange, the lost, by increasing our capacity to deal with the unexpected, the surprise, and the mourning of people and places. Liturgies must engage in subversion which is the dissolution and establishment of a new order. The unconscious is to be dealt with extreme care, with the help of community elders, healers, shamans, organic theologians, psychologists, and psychoanalysts.

If the process of healing, with all its local forms of mediations is to be used, then we must challenge liberation theology's popular method: to see, to judge and to act. For this method is based on a limited form of social analysis. We might expand this method with psychoanalytical processes, but what if a method entails not only what we cannot see, or will not see, and there will be no place for us to fully exist? What if the proclamation of healing also entails the impossibility of being cured, and that becomes the beginning of all healing: its impossibility? God then becomes a force of life that goes beyond set binaries and dismantles the questions of suffering or evil in the world.

We must continually explode Descartes' forms of the *cogito*--I think therefore I am--and exchange them for the *ubuntu* forms of life--we are, therefore I am; I am, therefore we are--or even Lacan's famous subversion of Descartes—"I think where I am not, therefore I am where I do not think; I am not whenever I am the plaything of my thought; I think of what I am where I do not think to think."[66] Perhaps our liturgies are the forms of negativity where we find ourselves and God in that which we have not affirmed. If that is so, we must organize liturgies in unending signifiers, oneiric ways, tangential forms of sacredness, a bricolage of materialities, relationships with the spirit of things, and the commonality of breathing shared by the human, animal, vegetable, and mineral world.

But perhaps more than that, our unconscious is where cells and bacteria, fungi and mycelium constitute us. With these collective autonomous agencies, together and in difference, we might understand Buddha's response to Mara's challenges: when he is at the least of his strength, he touches the earth and all the earth powers come to his rescue. We need liturgies that teach us how to deeply touch the earth at the same time as we are touching the deepest parts of ourselves.

Major Liberation Theology Themes
re-read under an Eco-Liturgical Liberation Theology

Briefly, here are some of the major tenets for liberation theology that can be used for an eco-liturgical liberation theology. I have expanded and challenged the themes, adding the necessary movement to engage the earth.

On Jesus and a New Christian Ecological Paradigm

The place of Jesus in an eco-liturgical liberation theology is one that occupies places in relationalities with a variety of "people:" the one who talks, rather harshly, with a tree, who makes the desert part of his home, who sees God in a dove and in a hen, who sees life in the fulness of birds and flowers, and who takes water as a living being. In the death of Jesus, we see the death of our planet as well. The one who dies on the cross continues to utter a plethora of voices in our time: the voices of those who have been killed by the powers of death; the voices of those who have been placed on lynching trees;[67] the voices of women who died under the violence of men; the voices of LGBTQIA+ murdered at every corner everywhere; the voices of Indigenous people who have been killed for the last 500 years; the voices of species being extinguished, animals being slaughtered, and forests being decimated. The dead tree that carried Jesus's body is also a symbol of all the dead trees who died because of human action.

The cry of Jesus is the cry of the earth and the cry of the oppressed. Leonardo Boff writes:

> *It is not only the poor and oppressed that must be liberated; today all humans must be liberated. We are hostages to a paradigm that places us—against the thrust of the universe—over things instead of being with them in the great cosmic community. That is why I am extending the intuitions of liberation theology and demonstrating their validity and applicability for the questions enveloping the Earth...*[68]

Boff details then a new cosmology and a new ecological paradigm. As he says: "A new form of dialogue with all beings and their relationships ... new awareness of the planet as a whole."[69]

Ivone Gebara already sees this entanglement of Jesus' life with creation and the devastation of the earth and writes, "My question for the gospel has to do with the devastation of the planet, the elimination of so many species, and the destruction of so many human groups, among whom the most directly affected are the poorest of the economically poor."[70] She continues:

> *it is the earth that is both the subject and the object of salvation. We need to abandon a merely anthropocentric Christianity and open ourselves up to a more biocentric understanding of salvation. To Jesus' humanistic perspective, we need to add an ecological perspective. This new way of doing things seems to me perfectly justified, because it maintains not only the most fundamental aspects of Jesus' perspective but also the understanding that we are a living body in constant evolution.*[71]

The reading of Jesus demands a new cosmology and a more expansive notion of Jesus, both in the plural relations and *cruzos* with other religions and as a cosmic presence. One example is what Boff says of Teilhard de Chardin:

> *Everything was being managed within the cosmogenic process as more complex orders emerged, each time being internalized and interconnected with all beings. When a certain level of accumulation of this background energy occurs, then there is the emergence of historical facts and of each individual. Who saw this gestation of Christ in the cosmos was the paleontologist and mystic Teilhard de Chardin (+1955), the one who reconciled the Christian faith with the idea of expanded evolution and the new cosmology.*[72]

If the word was made flesh, now it is the flesh of the *oikos*, the *eco*, the patch of land that will bring forth the word. The word of Jesus with the flesh of the earth will bring about new forms of ritualizing where the flesh of the Spirit and the spirits of the bodies that live everywhere will orient our way into a future where our kids will be able to live.

On Method

The sources of God's revelation are expanded. Along with the documents of the church and the Bible, the lives of the poor became not only sources for the discourse of God, but a hermeneutical axis from which faith and doxa would be understood. Praxis became a complex way of engaging life, theory, tradition, and theology.

Liturgy is for people and not people for liturgy. In this way, life comes first, and liturgical theology must voice whatever is needed for people to live well. In Clodovis Boff's *Theology and Praxis: Epistemological*

Foundations,[73] an in-depth work on the method of liberation theology, he identifies the correlation between three organizing principles: socio-analytical mediation, hermeneutical mediation, and the dialectic between theory and praxis. In an eco-liturgical liberation theology, the socio-analytical mediation is only one form of mediation. Mediations are varied and enacted primarily through liturgies, performances, rituals, feasts, theater, liturgical/social movements, and daily practices. Moreover, expansive forms of hermeneutical mediations happen in the living of life or lived religion, in liturgical rituals which embrace traditions beyond what pertains to the official rites. The dialectic between theory and praxis is done between the showing of a doing and a doing of a showing. The socio-analytical method becomes very limited when it does not consider the earth, environmental studies, Indigenous knowledges, and power dynamics with land (colonialism and capitalism) as its main source to understand our lives. If liturgical liberation theologies claim that the talk about God must start where it hurts, then they must consider humans, more than humans, inter-species, the elements, and the land as their major bodies and multiple agents.

Moreover, any liturgical theology will only work if done and developed with the people (human and more than human) that live at the place where the name of God is uttered. The name of God, with the names of other people and spirits, will compose the pantheon of people to relate and correlate, depend, exchange, and reciprocate. The social analytical method must engage other cosmologies and learn to be guided by the moon and the sun, the movements of the waters, and the path of the earth. The socio-analytical method must be entangled with many other knowledges about being in the world so we can create pluriverses and open up the possibilities for emergence to flourish.

The Body

Instead of adjusting the lives of the people to the official mode of being proscribed by pre-ordered liturgies, the experiences of suffering people (human, animal, vegetal, and mineral worlds) organize the structures and tradition of rituals and liturgical orders. Whole universes of bodies--in many forms of and shapes of valences, forces, relations and symbiosis, networks of life and threads of emergencies, all forms of struggles, peoples presences and habitats, many forms of spiritualities, senses of justice, life begetting life, struggles and forms of resistance, labor and sustenance, food chains, queering sexualities, racial oppressive structures, invasive species, hunger and droughts, abusive and exploitation of land and people, hurts of communities, everything that permeates their experiences--are sources for an eco-liturgical liberation theology.

When we approach each other, we must work against the narcissism of our times, stories told only for the sake of individuals, prayers lifted only for the sake of personal support, and God personalized as a ladder for social climbing. Rituals are collective events for the sake of community and individuals. The privatization of faith and the support of narcissistic narratives can only destroy networks of symbiosis and communal agencies and turn our bodies into private resources. Rituals must become aware of conscious and unconscious forms of capitalist forms of affection, religious acts, and spiritual demands, and dispel individualized forms of "common" gatherings. In other words, when we let personal experiences be detached from larger structures of oppression and belonging, these experiences tend to become a self-enclosed cry that prevents the whole body from fully engaging these experiences.

Our sense of self through feeling, dancing, moving, breathing, and being must understand the self as a collective of agents/selves/cells. Our selves can only be fully perceived if we can hear the singing of the birds as our own singing, the flowing of the rivers as our own flowing, the movement of the clouds as our own movement. Our self is always many, multiple, linked, and connected with other forms of life and vital matter. Our self is only possible if entangled with the self of somebody else, of that which is not me/us, but is fundamentally related to me. Thus, rituals and movements are also made of many selves in a plethora of worlds in creation, movements, and transformations.

Scientist Antonio Nobrega tells us about life in the human body saying, "We have 37 trillion individual cells (besides the perhaps 50 trillion prokaryotic cells) in our body, each cell 100 trillion atoms, within a cell there are 23 thousand genes and 92 thousand proteins… the human body is a walking galaxy of cellular systems.[74] This system, like the systems within the natural world, has a deep care for within itself. Against the biological new Darwinism that claims that the cell selfishly works for its own survival, serious scientists and biologists are saying that our cells are a deep composite of care for other beings. Nobrega affirms in rather poetic ways: "the master line of nature is that there is an unconditional love within the function of the natural system: take care for your neighbor.

When there is selfishness somewhere in our body, it is a mark that something is not working well. All our cells work in absolute collaboration. When a cell decides not to work anymore is the appearance of cancer. Each cell will work on its own place and will not want to exploit or save more than necessary. Its own work is for the functioning of the whole body."[75] That means that our collective self is also organized to live collectively, caring for others. Thus, liturgies should operate with this base denominator that we are here to care for each other and alert us when we are going beyond our limits or desires.

On Difference

No European local context placed under the guise of the universal claim of God's authority will be accepted as definite anymore. Our liturgies must be based on the particularity of contexts, patches of the Anthropocene with local living beings that animate that space. As Derrida reminds us, "context, always remains open, thus fallible and insufficient," which means that we cannot rely only on private contexts since we are always a bundle of complex and diverse environments, cultural formations and global connections.

Difference in liturgical theology reminds us of the dangers of Christian singularities when they are used as appropriations, enclosing everything in the Christian theological oneness, often racializing other people, establishing its erected liturgical male authority over local, earthly forms of supine rituals. Every ritual encompasses a collective autonomy not individual rights, connections not private stories, incommensurability not self-enclosed systems, a thousand forms of fragmented knowledges not mastery of knowledge, inconceivability not dogmas, the unknowable not full understanding, complexity and deep belonging not fading differences. Rituals then must carry what Derrida calls *a heteronomy without servitude.*[76]

On decolonizing rituals, sacraments, bodies, and symbols

We must engage the work of decolonizing our rituals by thinking about liturgical theology otherwise, from an ecological perspective, and from local knowledges. In a conversation with a student who had just finished his PhD in liturgy in a very prestigious school in the United States, I asked who he had read from the South of the globe during his five years of studies. He could not name a single scholar. All his formation was centered on scholars from the U.S. and Europe, and mostly men.

Christianity has carried a whole array of colonial markers and symbols and ways of establishing systems of oppression. We have not done enough to decolonize our bodies, minds, and cosmologies from the suppression of knowledges, repression of bodies, and erasure of histories. As Sri Lankan liturgical theologian Tissa Balasuriya strongly puts it:

> *Over the centuries the spirituality of the Eucharist—of giving and not of grabbing—was obliterated. The Eucharist went side by side with the worst and the largest-scale exploitation that the world has ever seen... The tragedy of the subordination of Christianity to European power*

politics was also the tragedy of the Eucharist. As the priests and monks went hand in hand with the colonialists, the Eucharist was desecrated in the service of empire."[77]

We still need to celebrate the sacraments not as anamnesis of a certain form of theology but as forms of life that were buried by centuries of erasure.

Rituals and sacraments should revive symbols that were and are fundamental to the past and present histories of local people, from the land where they live, expanding the cosmologies of our communal remembrances. For instance, C. J. Kaunda talks about rituals of resistance and how symbols organize the ways African people mark their lives, shape their subjectivities, and orient themselves in the world. Enriching the ritual space with symbols where body and voice find a way to perform, ritual enactments "enabled the weak to break free from the cultural bounds of society as long as they remained within the spaces of the ritual."[78] Rituals can "reorder power relations."[79] Prayers can evoke spirits, shift knowledge, reorient cosmologies, rearticulate relations, and create vocabularies to imagine new worlds.

Liturgical seasons can speak in much broader ways than many of us are used to celebrating. While most of white Christianity engages Lent in a very discrete way, Mexican Americans engage the earth.[80] In *Mestizo Worship: A Pastoral Approach to Communion Missiology*, we are reminded that, "On Ash Wednesday Mexican Americans renew their cultic communion with mother earth. For them, the earth has always been sacred, and they retain a fundamental identity with it... To deprive a people of its own land is like depriving children of their mother. Mexican Americans sense that the earth belongs to them and they to it—like a mother and child. On Ash Wednesday they celebrate their personal and collective communion with their earthly basis of belonging and identity."[81]

Similarly, we can only understand African American worship if we dig deep into its history. There we learn about the *church*, the "invisible institution" that kept people alive. Giving thanks, praising God under the backdrop of the history of pain and exploitation, was a way to survive. Bodies in movement, singing, experimenting, and experiencing God in various ways "bound up in the cosmos" was a way to fight racism and slavery. A shared "sacred cosmos"[82] as a cosmology saw no distinction between sacred and profane, life and worship.[83] It is this reconnection and circularity between people, earth, and the cosmos, that eco-liturgical liberation theology must foster to break down the powers of coloniality that still pervade so much of our worship life and our liturgical theological thinking.

On salvation

As a consequence, one of the major themes of Christian theology, salvation, gained new meaning. Salvation from this world became salvation within this world and with one another. Salvation became liberation from structural social sins and was transformed by the consciousness of our place in the history of God right now. Salvation is our participation in movements of liberation like the life of Colombian Roman Catholic priest Camilo Torres Restrepo who joined the *National Liberation Army* (ELN), or like those who joined the *Zapatista Army of National Liberation*, or those fight in the trenches like the social movement *Landless Movement*, or other anarchist movements like *Indecline*, or Indigenous people gathering together to fight in *Standing Rock*, or the *Poor People's Campaign*, or Black Lives Matter. Salvation comes from deep within and it is manifested by the ways we gain awareness of self and eliminate confusion.

Salvation is engaging green movements to fight on behalf of the earth, animals, plants, forests, like *Greenpeace, Extinction Rebellion,* Earthjustice, Friends of the Earth etc. Salvation is the implosion of colonial structures built during Indigenous genocide and slavery by institutions that uphold white supremacy. Salvation is about bringing capitalism down and creating new forms of living. Salvation is about co-working with all the earthling agents, sharing forms of regeneration and mutual transformation and renewal. Salvation is thus a plural event found in the community of humans and other-than-human bodies.

Salvation can be richly empowered by the notion of interbeing described by Buddhist monk Thich Nhat Hanh for whom the body is connected to the cosmos, to God's creation, to our ancestors, and each other. He says:

> *Our human body contains both our cosmic body and the true nature of the cosmos—reality itself, beyond all words, labels, and perceptions. Our cosmic body is the universe, creation, the masterpiece of God. Looking deeply into the cosmos, we see its true nature. And we can say that the true nature of the cosmos is God. Looking deeply into creation, we see the creator.*[84]

Thus, the liturgical understanding of salvation must be broad and expansive, far beyond the limits of Christian horizons of truth, and multiple in its rituals, gestures, meditations, prayers, songs, bowing, honoring, and singing.

Preferential option for the poor

Liberation theologians read the Bible from the side of the poor and insist that from the Exodus story to the prophets, from the incarnation of God in Jesus to the life, death and resurrection of Jesus Christ, and from the life of the church through the salvific manifestations of God in History, God clearly shows a preferential option for the poor. Our task is to hear God's voice in and from the bodies of vulnerable people. As Marcella Althaus-Reid taught us,[85] God is not represented in the wretched of the earth but is the miserable outcasts and destitute.

However, the notion of the poor cannot be used as a political category or tool, or a sociological term that to be controlled and discussed. The poor must mean everything that is destitute of *imago Dei*, turned worthless, garbage. It is living with, staying with, and developing a form of what theologian Marc Ellis call "dystopic solidarity,"[86] in which we learn to be with other humans. As we enter a time when the earth must be part of this solidarity, the "dystopic solidarity" must also engage all forms of life, human and more-than-human, with full respect and equality. We must take all the necessary precautions Ellis offers which makes solidarity possible:

> *Don't trust a solidarity extended to all. Such solidarity is too rich and spread too thin. Wish every one well. Our aloneness is more honest when we clear the decks. And watch out for the blanket coverings of Other categories, old and new. They often highlight what they hide. Such categories trumpet regret. As a way of life. Which doesn't mean there isn't privilege. In every age. Privilege is like rain. It exists somewhere at every moment. Rather ask what privilege has to say - and do. What privilege is willing to give away. For others. If you've noticed, though, most who speak of giving up privilege hoard their own. The prophet(ic) is privilege. Given over. Into history. By moving deeper. Into failure.*[87]

Liturgical solidarity must find the languages that can only be found in places where the excluded live. They must become our prayer and thus engage our cosmologies and our practices. As we saw, the poor are the people who are hurting, including humans, animals, land, plants, rivers, mountains and so on.

The metaphor must the desert, not the Exodus

The Exodus is no longer the best metaphor for our collective struggle. Challenged by Indigenous people, the exodus story must be put away. We cannot claim our freedom on the demise and destitution of other people. Our metaphor must include the deserted areas, places where life is lived but in harsher ways, where water is very limited, other people are scarce, the scorching sun accompanies us during the day, and extreme cold comes at night.

The desert is the place where Hagar was thrown, abandoned by all.[88] She only had God as her witness. Climate disasters and destructive human action will turn so many places on earth into wilderness areas. It is in the desert that we will need to learn how to live in difficult places. As Richard E. Wentz says:

> *To be 'in the desert' is to want something—water, promise of exodus. But there is no replenishment of these desires. The imagination and the 'self are transfigured—given illumination—when the desert has its way. In the emptiness, the Voice says, 'stay with me; talk with me, not about me or you. This is my body, along with the echoes from yonder mountain.' This is what Belden Lane teaches us.*[89]

It is in these deserts that we will need to learn how to take care of ourselves and to clothe ourselves with a common garment of solidarity, exhibiting what Jan Patocka called the "solidarity of the shaken," mentioned at the end of this work. Thus, worship will be a way of learning how to live in the desert, sharing the little water we have, figuring out how to live in communion with the desert, being affected by all its living creatures, inhabitants and actants.[90]

On political theologies

As Karl Marx rightly says in *A Contribution to The Critique of The Political Economy*: "The mode of production in material life determines the general character of the social, political and spiritual processes of life."[91] Every theology is public, is political, is sexual, and is also economic. A historical materialist understanding of history reveals that societies must be understood through the material conditions of development, i.e., the ways in which society produces and reproduces the material means for human existence.

We must be aware of the whole process of production: from who owns the natural resources, how these sources are produced, and who uses and has access to it. Social classes are organized through the process of production, and a structure of power forces and dependency ensues. Every theology is natural, and the earth is at the heart of all these processes, yet most often through its absence. What we often call natural resources for economic development are forms of life that we do not care about and can only relate to as profit.

Liturgically, this means the reestablishing people's belonging to the earth, mapping the land's richness and the community's wealth, understanding the community's relation to the land, and comprehending the ways in which the people of that community are entangled with the means of productions. Liturgically we pray and preach about the ideologies that blind us to the structures of oppression and the necessity of turning, as said before, the means of production into production of means for life for the whole earth.

Now, what does it mean for liturgical political theologies to engage animals and plants as part of a fundamental democracy? Can the bees speak? Can the rivers cast their vote? Can the mountains tell us what we need to do?

On class struggles

Linked to historical materialism, we must consider class struggles. If Louis Althusser is right when he said, "Philosophy is, in the last instance, class struggle in the field of theory,"[92] I offer that liturgy is class struggle in the field of practice. Through the struggles of the poor, we see that the world is marked by battles for wealth. The desire for money and accumulation of wealth creates a distinction between people and establishes class struggles. Economic disparity and hierarchical division of people into classes undergird state control of the people and the law.

As we look into the concrete realities of our people, we look at the economic, the social, the political, and the cultural aspects of our lives and we see poor people eaten up by economic and political powers controlled by a very small elite. There is no way to read the Bible and understand God's love if not through the lenses of injustice and death caused by class struggles.

Thus, the brothers Boffs talk about a necessary conversion to do Latin American liberation theology: One needs to convert from their own class to the class of the poor. That also means a liturgical conversion when we enact in worship a full commitment with the poor and a liturgy done with, by, and for the poor. Otherwise, everything we do and think will still be dependent on unequal social power dynamics, which make it impossible to think and imagine and work together.

For instance, when I talk about class above, what do I need to engage when I bring in animals? Do my arguments still hold? How? Unless everything is transversed by issues of the earth and earthlings, there will be no future for any life in this planet.

On racisms of all forms

Along with class struggles, racial struggles are at the heart of the unequal structures and oppressions of our societies. White supremacy has unequally distributed resources to whites and controlled the law for their own power and dominance. Under white supremacy, reds, blacks, browns, and yellows are not considered full humans or carriers of the fullness of God's image.

As James Cone says:

In a racist society, God is never color-blind. To say God is color-blind is analogous to saying that God is blind to justice and injustice, to right and wrong, to good and evil. Certainly, this is not the picture of God revealed in the Old and New Testaments... Yahweh sides with the poor within the community of Israel against the rich and other political oppressors. In the New Testament, Jesus is not for all, but for the oppressed, the poor and unwanted of society, and against oppressors.[93]

Thus, any color-blind liturgy that tends to work for all under the banner of God's love is working for the sustenance of white supremacy, and the oppression of colored people. Liturgy is a song of liberation!

How can this song join the choir of birds? The sounds of whales? The singing of the cicadas?

On organic intellectuals

Theologians become "organic intellectuals" (Gramsci), grounded in their academic work, and living with the poor, who are well-versed in their own wisdom. Gramsci helped people gain, in the words of Paulo Freire, conscientization of their power and the possibility of enacting transformation in this world as subjects of their own history! But, as said before, the liturgical space is a place where we learn with the unconscious, and our ability to see, judge, act, and control is minimal, if any.

Liturgical theologians must know the people's arts, dances, ritualized forms of beliefs, the songs people sing, prayers people pray, spiritual practices, ways of blessing, anointing, and dreaming, special religious clothing, colors, foods and condiments, spaces and ritual/liturgical objects, their mystic, their symbols, their spiritualities, and all the movements of the spirit within the community so as to connect these local forms of spiritual wisdom with other forms of wisdom from other oppressed people around the globe. The task is to create transnational forms of solidarity, known and unknown, through liturgical forms of doing and thinking religion.

How do organic intellectuals engage with organic vegetables? How can they listen to inorganic forms of life and have them as partners in their thinking-feeling producing?

On ecumenical/inter-riting/interreligious dialogue

The Christian faith cannot be thought by itself, nor can it contain the whole world. Our ritual work is fundamentally interconnected, interrelated, and intertwined. To do interreligious dialogue through ritual is fundamental to our world! Thus, we need to be in conversation with other religious liberation theologies, from other places, sources, and hurts so that we can create mutual forms of blessings, healing, transformation, and affections. As Sri Lankan Liturgical theologian Tissa Balasuriya says, "The radical transformation of the world and of the mentalities of people is not likely to come about without the participation and cooperation of believers in the world religions."[94]

How can religions establish the earth as a common ground and engage in mutual liturgical actions of healing and regeneration of people and the earth?

On sexualities, queerness, and the necessary ways of undoing hetero supremacy

Liturgical theologians should follow Marcella Althaus-Reid's ways of doing theology and doing liturgies without underwear.[95] While we can critique her work,[96] her critique of liberation theologies is still very much needed. Unless liturgy is queer from its inception and at the core of thinking-doing, it will be heteronormative.

Liberation liturgical theologians must not only queer rituals but think of rituals from a non-binary structure. We must expand the liturgical space for queer and transgender people to be full-fledged inhabitants of a collective gathering, to think of God in queer ways, and to live a life that is beyond the binaries of gender and sexualities. Our bodies are the loci of all our interconnectedness and those loci are multiple, multifaceted, and multisensorial. Moreover, our bodies belong to the earth and the connectivity between bodies and the earth is central to living together in the world.

How much are we affected by the bodily presence of other beings, objects who are all actants? How can the sexualities of animals infuse our human sexualities with life and queer our own sensations, affections, and forms of relating and being?

On psychoanalytic analysis of the present

The modes of affections that circulate in our world today are the results of the political and economic structures of how we live. The current forms of fascism and neoliberalism are shaping new behaviors, new forms of suffering, new diseases, and new pathologies. For instance, depression and panic attacks are epidemic illnesses of our time, and resentment pervades so many of our social and familial relations. Our social feelings are structured around the ways democracy is falling apart, representation is denied, corruption is growing, and populism is on the rise. The political forms of organization organize our lives in the fields, in the cities, and give signals to our minds and our hearts of how to respond. We are mostly lost, we are getting poorer, violence is escalating, necropolitics is the law of the day, and biopolitics defines the bodies of governments and individual bodies.

In this mode of ongoing pain, violence, and disasters, liturgies must offer both a challenge to the larger forms of political structure and forms of coping for individuals to continue with their lives. Neo-pentecostal churches everywhere are replacing the once present form of the State. Local communities are offering performative responses and mechanisms to keep afloat. The problem is that these churches are entangled with a politics of death and maintain the oppression of people by preaching freedom that is based in oppression. These forms of worship spaces create an endless liturgical circle of the eternal return of death and the symptoms of death. Eco-liturgical Liberation theologies must learn how to offer cultic space for catharsis, healing, mourning, desperation, and exhaustion.

If liturgies are all about human feelings--about the ways we process our loss, our depression, our anger, and our inability to respond--then the entire array of symptoms must be considered through liturgical acts, mystical gestures, and listening processes. By dissecting power structures between culture, politics, economy, state power, militarism, nuclear weapons, and its many tentacles from a liturgical perspective, we gain a chance to be a microcosm of the world, and liturgists will see the cultic expressions of faith necessarily entangled in much broader relations and interconnectedness. This vitalism and vital matter can help us see vitality in everything that exists.[97]

On creating and associating with new forms of decolonial and postcolonial thinking

Any liturgical thinking must engage colonial histories of oppressions and present notions of coloniality that takes hold of ritual structures and traditions. These forms of thinking help us dialogue with traditions, unearth rich forms of life from buried pasts by colonization, empower our present with new possibilities of life, and see movements that can recreate a new future!

On aesthetics and spirituality

Liturgy is not only about objectivity but is about that which cannot be grasped by objective thought. Through a vast array of symbols and wonders turned liturgical as they become part of a ritual, we need to face the horrific parts of ourselves. In the same way, we search for what is beautiful and for what sustains life against the necro-politics, consumerism, and exhaustion of our society. We must search for vast forms of spirituality that originate and end with life and death, joy and sadness, miracles and suffering, horrors, and lightness, to help us turn our desires to God and to move us towards one another. Latin America, and many other places, have issued an immense challenge and a wake-up call to theologians.

If we pay attention to the religious and civil development of Latin America in the last 40 years, the religious phenomenon that is sweeping the continent has been produced within the liturgical bounds. All the new theological, religious, and political remaking of Latin America has been shaped by the liturgical transformation created and operated by neo-Pentecostal churches. By recreating liturgical sources with a mixture of Indigenous, African, and European religious sources, along with an accommodation to neo-liberal economic thinking and practices, they have established a whole new form of Christianity.

This new form of Christianity is a sociological event developed by liturgies, rituals, songs, testimonies, and an array of new and old liturgical practices that have captured the imagination, heart, and mind of the people. In this form of Christianity, liturgy has many faces that promise liberation but keep people in chains, offer dreams but leave people alone in their own nightmares, step heavily on people's desires but keep them captive to the logic of the market, thrive on people's imagination and potentialities but turn everything into the financial wealth of these churches.

The liberation movement is constantly challenged by the question of why people go in masses to these churches and say they feel filled. Again, the body is fundamental to our new aesthetics and spirituality. What is the relation of the body of a tree with my body? The body of water? Clouds?

Our notion of spiritualities must go beyond Christianity to learn from earth spiritualities, and beyond the transcendent-immanent God to see how everything composes vast complex and infinite forms of life in mutations and symbioses.

On deep ecological forms of thinking

It is about time for Christian discourse to engage other than human discourses and centrality. It is about time to feel and think faith with other-than-humans and see everything as *imago Dei*, be it animals, clouds, mountains, rivers, rocks, forests, cells, etc. It is about time for the Christian faith to do a reversal of its forms of catechumenate. We must turn to the wisdom of Indigenous people and learn from them as our necessary teachers of a new catechumenate on ecology. With Indigenous people and their mystagogies and ontologies we learn that our bodies are the earth, and the earth is our bodies.

Unless Eco-Liturgical Liberation Theologies start from ecological terms, with Pachamama and Indigenous sources, and prepare us to be converted to the earth, we will not survive. The ecological work must be the ground zero of all and any religious and social movement![98] Thus, along with the law of prayer, belief, and ethical living, Christians must start thinking about *lex naturae* as the ground from which we think everything else.[99] Every human category transformed by the breathing of the frogs. Every human sound transversed by the singing of a bird. All of life needs to be broken by the presence of birds, eagles, foxes, dolphins, whales, turtles, worms, cells, trees, leaves, and wind. Every liturgical agency must engage the agency of all the more-than-human beings.

In this way, we must *create networks of liberation, transformation, mutual care, and reciprocities.* Liturgy by itself cannot do much, but it must move us to create spaces for other communities who are struggling for justice. Liturgy must pay attention to movement of liberation and get its own people involved with the Poor People's Campaign, landless movements, local artist's movements, homeless people, the so-called white trash folks, battered mothers, single mothers, Black Lives Matter, Jews of Conscience, transgender folks, children, immigrants, Palestinians, refugees, undocumented people, climate refugees, guardians of the forest, and Indigenous populations.

Conclusion

Eco-liturgical liberation theology is a genitive theology, hearing the cry of those suffering as Gutierrez taught us, but also a theology that is modified by the flesh of the earth, the presence of more than human beings, and their cries. Since it is liturgical, it is the whole work of the people (human and more than human) moving, dancing, singing, shaping, and transforming the earth in all its many worlds. Thus, if the work of poor people truly shapes the assembly of many actors/agents and their actions, we will learn that primary theology is the movement done by the people in worship in response to God's love, with other people and hurting bodies. This kind of worship is an exercise in justice as we give glory to God.

Our notion of community is at stake when a group of people and other beings gather in worship, for everybody's liberation, freedom, protection, and care are bound together. No one will pray for oneself only or search for a miracle that is not transformational for the lives of the whole community of beings: humans, animals, vegetal, mineral. The God of the poor is a God who moves through all these relationalities, who makes the world alive as we attend to each other by ways of solidarity and reciprocity. A God of the poor is a God who will work with the disasters of capitalism and the reconstruction of communities. Putrefied bodies and the smell of life's glory will fuse in fulness and love where entanglements of life and mutual care are put together for the sustenance of small communities and entire universes in each hub of land, farm, desert, and neighborhood around the earth.

As the eco-liturgical theologian does secondary theology, she is reminded of four conceptual ways to talk about other groups of people. The first is Pierre Bourdieu and his notion of *habitus*.[100] *Habitus* is the reasoning of life from the ground, an orientation to and understanding of the world that is absorbed and shaped at the level of practice. As Craig Dykstra says, practices are "habitations of the Spirit,"[101] organizing, claiming, moving, and searching for just ways of living. The Zapatista Movement, Indigenous women's movements, Ribeirinhos and Quilombolas movements have so much to teach us about *habitus* from the perspective of the earth. We have so much to learn with Indigenous people about *habitus* and habitations.

The second thinker is Jan Patocka and his notion of the "solidarity of the shaken." The solidarity of the shaken is the *"solidarity of those who are capable of understanding what life and death are all about, and so what history is about."*[102] It is the history of the shaken that has kept us alive. Slowly we will learn that only those who have been shaken by the violence of the state, genocide, and brutality are the ones who can say what restitutes, what affirms, and what sustains people. For they are the agents of collective struggles, gathered agents of a collective history.

The third thinker is Wangari Muta Maathai from Kenya.[103] Maathai won the Nobel Peace Prize in 2004 through her environmental work combining peace and reforestation. A mother of three children, Maathai knew the power of soil and how dead soil creates war. Inspired by her work, thirty million trees were planted in thirty years.

The fourth thinker is Ailton Krenak from Brazil. Ailton is from the Krenak nation in Brazil and is leading a revolution of awareness and consciousness in Brazil. We Christians have reproduced by our liturgies, theologies, and faith an abstraction of unity, man as a measure of things:

> *We should admit nature as an immense multitude of forms, including each part of us, which is part of everything: we are 70% water and a lot of other materials that make us up. And we created this abstraction of unity, man as a measure of things, and we went around running over everything, in a general conviction until everyone accepts that there is a humanity with which they identify, acting in the world at our disposal, taking whatever people want. This contact with another possibility implies listening, feeling, smelling, inhaling, exhaling those layers of what was left out of us as "nature", and for some reason it is still confusing. There is something about these layers that is quasi-human: a layer identified by us that is disappearing, that is being exterminated from the interface of human and more than humans. But there are the quasi-humans who are thousands of people who insist on staying out of this civilized dance, of technique, of controlling the planet. And by dancing a strange choreography, they are removed from the scene, due to epidemics, poverty, hunger, directed violence.*[104]

We are invited to join the quasi-humans to dance that dance of life with the risk of death.

The question is: *Will Christian liturgy really do all this?*[105] Most probably not. But we need to imagine something else, dream of a reality that is not here yet, so that it can arrive. It just takes a little longer for the impossible to become possible. To anticipate this reality, we need to do some important things:

First, we need to accept that what people ritualize is what they live out in their communities. Whoever has the power of the ritual can empower their communities. So much of Christianity has been a self-enclosed ritual movement around itself, but theologians could do their work in ritual spaces without the dichotomy we have today. At the heart of theological education lies a huge anti-intellectualism that divides praxis and theory, liturgy, and theology.

Second, unless the earth is the ground zero of our thinking we will keep talking about religion, faith, and rituals until we have no more earth to live or to talk about. Our theologies must devote time to be with rivers and animals and trees and forests. They must become fundamental partners in our theological not only human thinking.

Third, as we are converted to the earth, we must be converted to the wretched of the earth. Without this conversion, none of what Christians do makes any sense. As Brazilian liturgical theologian Ione Buyst says, we need to be part of worship services with the poor, spend time with them, learn how and why they worship, and follow their primary and secondary theologies.

Fourth, we must work on intersectionality of the body, class, gender, race, ableism, immigration-refugees, earth, nuclear weapons, militarism, extractivism, erotics, aesthetics, economics, and so on to create trans-national, pluriverses, natural-cultural, and interreligious work. We must activate a network of corporeal gestures that turns our habits into a life of reciprocities, solidarities, and mutual care between all beings. Rituals are the flesh border crossing in open wounded events where we are bodily implicated in callings and responses, healing, and mutual regeneration. Within these rituals, we establish and/or heal violence, we set each other accountable and/or set each other apart, we learn that either our struggle is one or we maintain the divide and conquer motif of empire. Using Mayra Rivera's words, I include rituals as "Social arrangements [that] meet us in the bodies of others."[106]

Fifth, we need to learn how to live and breathe wonder and laughter. To deal with the fires of our time and the shortage of breath, I have wandered around with clowns, in awe with those who can make us laugh. The way to go through the fires of our times is through laughter. During this pandemic, I realized I have a clown voice--still mostly in silent mode within me--that is slowly coming out. I started playing with my 9-year-old son and we created *Lettuce and Tomato*.[107]

Liturgy is life expanded! Liturgy is resistance! Liturgy is re-existence! Of everyone! But we must go first to those suffering and trying to re-exist again, even against all the intermittent attempts of nonexistence, abandonment, and death! Existence comes with a voice and every voice matters. As Amos Yong says, for every tongue a different practice. And tongues of animals and plants too. How do we make this cacophony of tongues/voices/practices sing together in solidarity? I hope the wisdom of our shared liturgical earthly imagination can help us move towards God's full glory and a flourishing humanity, especially the poor and the earthly ecological system.[108]

I finish with the words of Nancy Cardoso, a theologian thinking about a liberation liturgical theology in the midst of the people:

I watch the Quilombos Mass,[109] *because life gave me the Quilombolas (descendants of slaves in Brazil) to work with and I tremble with the beauty of this mass and fear that the struggle will crush me! So I pray the prayer of singing... I listen in order to be better, I see the video to connect the meaning between history, memory, commitment and - God help me - action. In that video, liturgy has the performance that joins it all... this theatrical event that re-do the pain that happens in life and place it before us... the Mass is like this Quilombo that I approach and it reaches me back... I learned from you that the liturgy is this: re-live the pains and pleasures of this life that give meaning to the community... and because it's art, it also brings the scare. I think that those who works with the liturgy − the good liturgies! − they have to know how to make these mixtures: create the collective performance that helps the community to make their way ... in my case: I anticipate the quilombo praying the quilombo. It's almost a lie because now it's only desire.*

Then I see you mention so many people but it is not because of them that you do the prayer: it is the performance of their theology, the commitments, the people that come together in their texts that makes you pray... I was thinking that every text of theology - if it is not a frigid academic text - it has this hope of being prayed! Of being able to be read as a loaf of a prayer..."[110]

This is the collective work of an eco-liturgical liberation theologian.

CHAPTER TWO

Lex Naturae:
A New Way into a Liturgical Political Theology[1]

Luíza Carvalhaes Rocha, 6 years old

We know that the whole creation has been groaning in labor pains until now;
and not only the creation, but we ourselves,
who have the first fruits of the Spirit,
groan inwardly while we wait for adoption, the redemption of our bodies.
For in hope we were saved. Now hope that is seen is not hope.
For who hopes for what is seen?

Romans 8:22-24

Introduction

The little Baptist Church of Santo Antonio in the Desert of Sonora in Mexico gathers to celebrate a feast of baptism. On the back of the church, there is a water reservoir. From that reservoir, plants are watered, animals drink, and people boil water to drink and to cook. On baptismal day, the water reservoir becomes the baptismal font. All those who are going to be baptized get dunked there while the congregation sings a hymn. The cleansing of life comes from the clean water of their water reservoir. After the worship ends, the water reservoir/baptismal font now becomes a pool party for the kids. For the rest of the day the kids play in the pool and rejoice in the 110° F weather.

In the forgotten lands of São Feliz do Araguaia in the Mato Grosso state in Brazil, Don Pedro Casaldáliga chose to live and work with the forgotten people of the land: small farmers and Indigenous people. Casaldáliga was regarded as a "subversive and extremist", an "impertinent and troublesome "bishop whose teaching "was dangerous because it was so much embedded in liberation theology."[2] With his life threatened by agribusiness, he persisted, preaching and living a gospel fully enmeshed with the life of God through honoring and protecting the earth, the poor and the memory of the martyrs who were made along the way. The prayers of the people, their sacraments and all their worship always provided sustenance and orientation to the people. Together, they survived. Now, at 90-years-old and very debilitated, he still lives there among his own people. Surely Don Pedro Casaldáliga is a mixture of Saint Francis and Oscar Romero for our times

Somewhere near East London in South Africa, a Christian community orients their lives: worship, seeds, and animals in three circles united by a center. At the center of these three circles there is a baptismal font. Earth, animals and worship have equal standing in equal community. They pray, they eat, they plant, they live their lives in a circle of mutualities that defies the Christian dualisms of immanence and transcendence, culture and nature, human and animals.

These three examples serve to tell us that the most important political gesture the field of liturgy can offer to a Christian praxis of praying-believing-acting is to initiate, or rather persist, in more radical ways, to pray-believe-act under the orientation of Gaia. The evolution of Western liturgical theology shows us how Christians have become completely detached from the earth, its bio-ecological diversities, and its processes of relation. We have elevated and removed the altar from the earth; we have perverted sacraments into limited and exclusionary means of grace instead of the ends of grace; we have separated earthly sources of faith from spiritual practices; we have denied materiality for the spirit; we have turned our attention from place to time.

We must recover the earth as central and fundamental to our lives as Christians from the perspective of liturgy. Liturgical spaces are indeed political spaces, and they are a fundamental part of environmental politics and bio power--power over the bodies of people, animals, plants, seeds, and societies.

Let us here engage *lex naturae*, the orienting ground from which we can learn how to pray, to believe and to act. In this time of the Anthropocene, liturgical political theology, oriented by *lex naturae* and centered on Gaia, opens us to engage public spaces by placing our history of time and places into the deeper context of the millions of years of the earth. *Lex naturae* can orient us in renewing the earth and transforming our rituals, our religious vows, our sacred things, our beliefs, our symbols, our gestures, our actions, and our songs.

Thus, the liturgical movement of this essay offers first the development of what I am calling *lex naturae*. The next movement connects *lex naturae* to the other *leges* (*lexes*, laws) of the Christian faith: *orandi-credendi-vivendi* (prayer-belief-ethics), assuming that every other *lex* must be oriented by *lex naturae*. The heart moves to the disruptions necessary to a recovery of liturgical political theology by developing the relationship between theology, liturgy, time, place and space. The movement finishes with a proposal of how to read the liturgical calendar from the signs of place.

Lex naturae

In order for the Christian religion to reconnect us to God we need to *religare* (bind together) with the earth. The current cultural emphasis toward a multicultural worship reifies the existing form of dominance politics. Depending on a plurality of cultures to repair our broken liturgical practices is insufficient as the Marxist notion of class struggle can not fully engage the struggle until animals are brought into equal consideration., If we consider an Indigenous perspective that animals are forms of humans, then the wrestling of class struggles between different shades of humanity becomes much more complex as Viveiros de Castro explains.[3]

The ontological liturgical, political, and always economical notion of the sacred, fundamentally based on a movement between cultures, is a production of economies of desire that creates mechanisms to neutralize any form of connection with the earth and prevents transformation. We are not cut off from nature, since we are never not deeply connected with the earth, but rather, liturgical work created from forms of thinking that do not consider or are not grounded in the earth, renders that work incomplete and ineffective. Thus, when a sustained theological discussion is not organized around the main law of nature, our faith, prayers, and actions continue to be under the grasp of anthropocentric patriarchal political economies that privilege human desires and consumerism through the exploitation of natural resources we assume will always be there to fulfil our needs.

In order to respond to our political moment, liturgical theologies must engage *lex naturae*, the law of nature that relates to *colōnus* and *colōnia*, a place where culture, land, economy, and power are always intertwined. As Nancy Cardoso Pereira poignantly says:

> *Three neighboring words clash here: economics, ecology, ecumenism. The three share the oikos: basic social unit (home, but also world). Simplifying: economy → oikos + nomos (law / norm); ecology → oikos + logos (understanding / study); ecumenismo → oikos + form of the passive participle feminine (inhabited / inhabitants). These are three ways of being in the world and of organizing life in the world. While the economy disposes, it regulates the way of production of life in relation to the world, ecology is concerned with understanding these relations their logics and implications and ecumenism asks about the (objective and subjective) forms of occupation / experience of the world.[4]*

The liturgical space has, for the most part, forgotten its material relation. The material that composes our life in fullness and all its power dynamics is often not addressed fully. Thus, what do we have in our liturgies: ecumenism? Perhaps Yes and often No. Ecology? Most often No and sometimes, superficially Yes. Economy? Absolutely Not! We need more than this: there is something fundamentally lacking in our political liturgies.

The most urgent political turn in liturgical studies is the creation and organization of a desperately necessary *lex naturae*. If, in the Christian communities what was at stake was the relation between prayers and beliefs and ways of living, this foundation now needs to be guided and reorganized by *lex naturae*. Without this law, no other brilliant theological concept will survive the Anthropocene. *Lex naturae* is not about the protection of religions or traditions but mainly, and most importantly, the protection and restitution of the well-being of the entire world.

We are at a point where no book of common worship or new liturgical practices can be created without the guidance and needs of the earth. No belief is more important than the biodiversity of the earth and the centrality of Gaia in the Anthropocene. This centrality is based on relationalities and not hierarchies. We must urgently grieve what has been lost so that we can move toward a more ethically and morally sound relationship with creation. We must attune our bodies, our communities, and our worship to a deeper and more robust understanding of what it means to be citizens in the Anthropocene.[5]

In the timeline of the earth, we humans are living only in the last 0.1% of the total time of earth's existence, which some people are calling the Anthropocene or the age of humans (more precisely, the geological age in which human intervention has devastated and depleted the earth). During this time, we have negatively affected the whole earth immensely. Since the Industrial Revolution, created to fulfill the desires of European countries, colonization has taken, and is still taking, the majority of resources from the poor and feeding the rich. Much of this exploitation and damage cannot be reversed. Our form of humanity has killed too many other humans and killed vertiginous numbers of species of animals, plants, and ocean life. The industrialization of agriculture has displaced thousands of people and urbanization became the escape for those expelled from the rural areas. If we are to think about *lex naturae*, we must attend to the ways we have damaged, changed, and oppressed the earth's landscape, animal and vegetal lives, the climate, and our daily life. A new Latina theology of the *cotidiano*, for instance, or the grandmothers' kitchens of womanist theologians would have to include the Anthropocene in order to consider Gaia.

Gaia is, as Bruno Latour articulates, "the occasion for a return to Earth that allows for a differentiated version of the respective qualities that can be required of sciences, politics, and religions, as these are finally reduced to more modest and more earthbound definitions of their former vocations."[6] Gaia, Pachamama, is the place of uncountable living organisms and various forms of humans, including animals and humus, who are interdependently living. Gaia is the site of constant struggle, survival, and flourishing of all that lives and occupies the earth. With Gaia, we must pay attention to the ways the earth changes and moves, and to how humans change and move the earth through their nation-state boundaries, territories, and geopolitical decisions.

In *Staying with the Trouble: Making Kin in the Chthulucene*, Donna Haraway calls into question the ways in which our time is wrapped up in capital and proposes a new *Chthulucene*:

> The scandals of times called the Anthropocene and the Capitalocene are the latest and most dangerous of these exterminating forces. Living-with and dying-with each other potently in the Chthulucene can be a fierce reply to the dictates of both Anthropos and Capital... Chthulucene is a simple word. It is a compound of two Greek roots (khthôn and kainos) that together name a kind of timeplace for learning to stay with the trouble of living and dying in response-ability on a damaged earth. Kainos means now, a time of beginnings, a time for on-going, for freshness. Nothing in kainos must mean conventional pasts, presents, or futures. There is nothing in times of beginnings that insists on wiping out what has come before, or, indeed, wiping out what comes after. Kainos can be full of inheritances, of remembering, and full of comings, of nurturing what might still be. I hear kainos in the sense of thick, ongoing presence, with hyphae infusing all sorts of temporalities and materialities...[7]

Gaia, in this Chthulucene time, must be our ground, horizon and orientation, delineating our speed, imposing our limits and organizing our desires. Chthulucene in its current history, conditions and demands must be the orienting rhizome axes from which we orient our prayers, our theologies, beliefs, and the daily lives of individuals, communities, the so-called nations, and all production. Chthulucene is the call for our response-ability to nurture and change. Our main questions come from Larry L. Rasmussen:

> How, then, do we hymn the Earth differently? How do we write and sing a new song for a strange land, even though it be our own? How do we do it with our neighbors, all our neighbors— human and other-than-human— when Earth is "hot, flat and crowded" and borders and walls no longer protect? Where do we turn when we discover that the religion we have lived by since the industrial-technological era emerged— eternal and exponential economic growth— is an illusion, dogma masquerading as common sense and kept alive by willpower and little else?[8]

This set of questions is all about a necessary *lex naturae* that poses serious challenges for us all to consider.

(1) First, it challenges the ways in which we, the humankind, inscribe the very notion of nature and how we understand nature. Since nature cannot speak and we do not know what nature is really like, any understanding of nature is therefore a human idea, a self-inscribed notion of nature on nature, by the ways we see and know and engage the earth. Moreover, any look at nature is already an interpretation, the transformation of nature into the subject of our objective lenses. Thus, *lex naturae* is a construction that is not natural. This caution, however, should not prevent us from working with and from nature, but rather should challenge the very categories--such as supernaturalism and naïve realism--as well as the values we impose on nature and our own personal worldviews--i.e., beliefs (cosmology), prayers (ritual actions) and ethics (notions of good and bad).

(2) Second, and as an extension of the first challenge, *lex naturae* challenges our naïve understanding of nature as only harmonious forms of living and sharing as well as our colonial view of nature as a resource that is at our service. We can learn with Indigenous communities to establish a circularity of life around many forms of humanities, animals, vegetables and trees to live on the earth—to embrace *lex naturae.* In this way, *lex naturae* highlights the "species struggle" and how the humankind heteronomous patriarchal forms of Christianities and their hierarchical structures, white supremacist discourses, racial compositions, sexual prejudices, disembodied faith, fear of matter, and liturgies detached from the earth are damaging for our future.

(3) Earthly liturgies will have a preferential option for the poor and the oppressed, including people, earth and animals--liturgies that deepen Christ's incarnation in our Adamic humus and becoming what we have always already been: soil, matter, water. As *imago Dei* we are made of what God is made. In Christ, immanence and transcendence are undone and transcendence is but a way into deeper forms of immanence and matter. Thus, Christological liturgies are essentially liturgies of the land, reminding us not only of our origin and destiny but also that the soil we walk in is filled with power dynamics where every private land is stolen land, and every nation-state land is also stolen land. As Larry Rasmussen reminds us by citing Bonhoeffer: "the constructive work of faith and the experience of Jesus Christ will be this-worldly and earth-honoring. Transcendence, which is indeed God, is 'the beyond in the midst of life,' experienced in an ethic of human responsibility for 'the whole of earthly life.'"[9] With *lex naturae*, our bodies gain a much more expansive notion of life and death where soil, notions of class, race, sex, gender, and social conditions are all understood together. With *lex naturae*, bodies will be considered in their many forms of vulnerability and resilience, and with Sojourner Truth we will "speak upon the ashes," and also from the ashes.

(4) *Lex naturae* then challenges the sole use of the Bible in our communities, the limitations of our creeds, the sources of our revelation, the structures of our theologies, the power dynamics of our communities, the cosmologies of our denominations, the thinking of the sacraments, the limits of Christian holy things, the self-enclosed juxtapositions of our liturgies. While challenging the inside of the Christian faith, *lex orandi-credendi-vivendi*, now oriented by *lex naturae*, will call attention to *res*, matter, natural things, rivers, oceans, phytoplankton, seeds, soil, biodiversity, fauna, flora, birds, and animals, calling attention to the internal unbalance and oppressive power dynamics of nature with capitalism and consumerism.

(5) *Lex naturae* creates and is the source of our prophetic voices, it sounds an end-of-the-world siren against the global mass production of products and energies, the absurd forms of consumerism, all forms of new sustainable development, racist environment policies, the domination of business over the pace of the earth, the poisoning of all the soil, the *acidization* of all the oceans, the ongoing land grabbing from Indigenous communities, and the destitution of regular life cycles.

(6) We are all living in a fold, where we all belong to the same earth. *Lex naturae* fosters, in a new natural key, what Martin Luther King Jr. said in his *Letter from Birmingham Jail*: "We are caught in an inescapable network of mutuality, tied in a single garment of destiny. Whatever affects one directly affects all indirectly."[10] This mutuality is also found in the voices and movements of the Spirit/spirits and their different relations of life to matter, moving in and through us, balancing our lives with a variety of energies in leaves, plants, and soil. Our mutuality comes from the earth, from our shared beginning and end, our communitarian/cosmopolitan forms of living and our common mortality. From dust we come, and to dust we shall return. As Robin Kimmerer asks us: "How can we begin to move toward ecological and cultural sustainability if we cannot even imagine what the path feels like? If we can't imagine the generosity of geese?"[11] *Lex naturae* turns our eyes to see anew the geese, the seeds, the turtles and so on.

(7) *Lex naturae* teaches us to turn our discerning eyes and ears to the signs of places and spaces instead of discerning the signs of time. Pedro Casaldáliga, a prophetic voice in Latin America calls us into this discernment: "This is our task: to discern the signs of places in which we do not yet belong but in which we will belong – 'no places' that will become concrete utopias."[12] The concrete utopia to be thought now is somewhat paradoxical: If we are to "discern the signs of places in which we do not yet belong but in which we will belong," then we must begin to think of the earth not only as the place we inhabit now, but also as a place already gone

in parts of the world, and soon to be fully gone and become a no place, at least for our kind of humans. The earth has been deprived of its basic forms of living, destroyed in violent forms, shapes and speeds. Mountaintop removals are one among thousands of examples of the unbalanced structures of power, threatening not only the earth but the entirety of our common living. Human over-fishing and the disposal of plastic garbage in the oceans, shows disrespect for the basic sources and structures of life, prioritizes consumption over the earth's regenerative pace, and sets the tone and the speed of our lives. We cannot deny or necessarily reverse the damage, yet we are called to discern these signs of the earth so that we can one day fully belong to it.

(8) *Lex naturae* helps us in our task as liturgists and theologians to debunk interpretations of the earth as God's gift to us as an object given to us, its subjects, for the commodification of our desires. *Lex naturae* proposes something else than the theological understanding that God has an exclusive preference for us, the one kind of human, as an exclusive being to be differentiated from other species, the fauna, and the flora. In this matter, *lex naturae* goes against the traditional interpretation of the Bible in Genesis 1:26: "Then God said, 'Let us make humankind in our image, according to our likeness; and let them have dominion over the fish of the sea, and over the birds of the air, and over the cattle, and over all the wild animals of the earth, and over every creeping thing that creeps upon the earth'" (Genesis 1:26). *Lex naturae* pleads for an intertwined correlation of values and relationality where dominium will be no more but a sharing of forces and dynamics that will fight the unbalanced forms of consideration and treatment of other human kinds. Moreover, God's promise to Noah must be reconsidered as ocean water levels are growing and many parts of the earth are already flooding. Bruno Latour calls our attention to those who deny flooding based on Scriptures:

> "Some of them don't even hesitate to stand up in a political meeting and invoke the covenant in Genesis where God promises Noah that He will send no more floods: 'Never again will I curse the ground because of man, even though every inclination of his heart is evil from childhood, and never again will I destroy all living creatures, as I have done' (Gen. 8: 21). With such solid assurance, it would be wrong indeed to worry!"[13]

To overcome such denial, new theological frameworks must be proposed and complicated, beyond the duality of God's immanence/transcendence, Jesus' humanity and divine nature, and the eschatological discourse of time as separate from space.

(9) The theological narrative of *lex naturae* must join other narratives of peoples who embody cosmologies where the earth is the axis of life and animals, spirits, and the whole biosphere live together.

(10) *Lex naturae* opens itself to wonder and to the wonder-full ways of Gaia in all its existence. It orients people to go beyond the established, thought through narratives, and opens up worlds of wonder and awe. This is fundamentally the work of *lex naturae*: to wonder and see how the wonderings unfold in each place.

(11) *Lex naturae* pushes against the fallacy of economic sustainable development. The narratives of *lex naturae* begin with the Paris agreement then radicalizes these agreements with its political and economic possibilities. *Lex naturae* helps us pray and believe in ways that create historical agendas and local manifestations that break actual forms of domination and oppression. For instance, it joins those who fight to extinguish fossil fuel and coal energy, putting limits to global movement and local electronic usages. We learn with Augustine that prayer orients our desire and Christian prayer can help especially people in the developed worlds to diminish our sense of entitlement. The ethics of *lex naturae* reworks the workers' market, reducing work hours and increasing pay and time for leisure. The belief of *lex naturae* puts a halt on companies that pollute rivers, turns private lands into common lands, blocks transgenic products, abolishes pesticides, shuts down all of the agri-business companies, and places in recovery centers all their CEOS until they are treated from their lust and greed and detachment from the earth. Every business that owns natural resources will lose its dominance, and natural resources will be for all. The beliefs generated by *lex naturae* will close banks, create alternative economies of solidarity, and erase debt.

(12) *Lex naturae* goes against any religiosity that understands nature as something detached from the core of our living or the earth as a subjugated being to a certain Cartesian scientific ontological notion of human kind where humans are the most fundamental beings. If we learn to listen to the earth and to the spirits, as we learn to listen to God, then we will understand that nothing in our lives exist away from the earth! We breathe, we drink, we eat, we shit, we sleep because of natural resources and eco-systems in our bodies and in the earth.

(13) The theological narrative of *lex naturae* is interreligious par excellence, and joins the Pope's Encyclical Letter *Laudato si'*, the Buddhist cosmologies of immanence, Buddha's relation with the earth, the Muslim prayers that honor the earth with people's foreheads, the earth festivities of Judaism, the balancing energies by Voduns and Orixas of African religiosities, and so on. Surely *lex naturae* must be aware of supernaturalism and otherworldly realities beyond Christianity!

(14) There is much more beyond thinking in Cartesian ways! As Amitav Ghosh said in a recent lecture at Union Theological Seminary "In every culture of all time, there have been people who have been able to give voice to nature… If one does not allow for that we are trapped in the world of cognition – that what we see and touch is all there is."[14] We need different forms of thinking and feeling and living and praying and believing! But we are all trapped in schemes of political thinking, otherworldly beliefs not connected with the earth, and worldviews that reify the illusion and the realities of this lie of separation.

(15) With *lex naturae*, we are thrown into realms of strangeness, disorientation, weirdness, loss, disaster and ruin. We cannot deal with issues properly; we get lost on our way; we propose pacts that are not enough; we deal with contradictions and with forms of politics that do not offer us the space to think in new ways. Our Anthropocene reasoning is not enough. We need a plurality of knowledges. A political liturgical theology offers us not only rational discourse but also a place for feelings and emotions to be engaged, expanded, learned and dealt with. Art, rituals, stories, and songs all inhabit a place in our bodies that is not necessarily the objectivity of our minds, providing ways to resist, and for new liturgical and life-giving imaginaries. We need this space to think, to feel, to touch, to hear, to listen, to taste, to see, and to perceive living and non-living actants, together, creating new forms of assemblages and assemblies, solidarities and fluidarities, composing and performing Gaia in new possible ways. We do not need another world as if we need another Gaia. What we need is to say: another kind of human being is possible!

(16) To create a political liturgical theology, we must engage other sources of imagination. Under the immense responsibility to care for the earth, *lex naturae* must be woven and engaged through new rituals necessary for new awarenesses, and companions--species, living and not living creatures, for the new time called Anthropocene, and for new relations and understandings with the spaces/places we live. We cannot create this theology by pure European forms of reasoning, old-religion rituals, or writing books and articles. We need other forms of, wonder, artistry, and expansive forms of re-imagining the earth, with correlations and juxtapositions not yet known. It is time for us to pay attention to artists engaging *Gaia* through art.[15] Very recently, Larry Rasmussen taught in my class Thinking Worship Theologically and he offered five steps for local congregations to engage in this re-imagining:

> *Lose themselves in wonder, telling and retelling of stories, do and create new rituals, resist and renew and sing a song, asking God and each other to 'give us the courage to enter the song.'*[16]

Thus, the combination of all the *leges, orandi-credendi-vivendi,* now organized by *lex naturae,* is a new liturgical political theology as it reorganizes the whole *polis,* including the public, private, external, internal, objective, and subjective spaces of religion.

The Liturgical Laws,
the Sacred, and the Earth

The liturgical space is fundamentally a political space. When liturgy evolved from the Greek civil notion of work on behalf of the people to the work of the church, the meaning of liturgy gained a communal and political perspective. Thus, when the church started to define liturgy as ways of understanding faith and prayer, the church was defining not only its own space as public space but also its place in relation to the larger public space. This was the time when the connection of two "laws," *lex orandi* and *lex credendi* (law of prayer and law of belief), organized and defined both the forms and content of beliefs and prayer. These new forms of prayers and beliefs were dangerous acts for the early Christians. Their prayers and beliefs were done under the shadow and threat of the Roman empire. Hiding their worship places, prayers, and liturgical actions through communion and baptism was a way of preparing themselves to die in case they would be caught by the empire. Liturgy was the way the church prayed and believed, and in another word, lived (*lex vivendi*), that shaped their public witness.

As we see through the New Testament, the early Christian churches were taught to care for each other in distinctive ways. The Book of Acts shows the rise and fall of a full commitment to each other's needs, and the letters to the churches admonish them to help those in need (Ephesians 4:28), carry each other's burdens (Galatians 6:2), provide and share with others (Hebrews 13:16), give clothes and daily food (James 2:14-17), care for the interests of others (Philippians 2:4), welcome people (Romans 12:13), care for the weak (Romans 15:1), etc.

Their *lex orandi-credendi-vivendi* was known and had supporters and opponents. Since we know best about someone by their opponents, here is a testimony:

> *The Christians are a gang… of discredited and proscribed desperadoes who band themselves against the gods. Fellows who gather together illiterates from the dregs of the populace and credulous women with the instability natural to their sex, and so organize a rabble of profane conspirators, leagued together by meetings at night and ritual fasts and*

unnatural repasts… a secret tribe that shuns the light, silent in the open,
but talkative in hid corners… Root and branch it must be exterminated
and accursed. They (the Christians) recognize one another by secret signs
and marks: They fall in love almost before they are acquainted, everywhere
they introduce a kind of religion of lust, a promiscuous "brotherhood" and
"sisterhood" by which ordinary fornication, under the cover of a hallowed
name, is converted to incest.[17]

The law of prayer and belief was fully connected with *lex vivendi*, the way
of living/witnessing. When the church was coopted by Constantine,
however, the law of living had to be now ruled by the *lex* of the empire,
which determined new ways of praying and believing. There was an
attempt to homogenize beliefs and prayers. The movement from houses to
basilicas sharply redefined what it was to be a Christian. For instance, the
ritual of baptism that summoned the three *leges*--prayer, faith and life--was
once the entrance to the Christian family, but now it was a required to
enter into the Empire, where the pledge of faith to God now rested under
the *lex* of the emperor.

If in the New Testament there are theological and liturgical
gestures against the empire, such as Paul calling God "father" to
undermine the fatherhood of the Emperor, the new life of the churches
under the Constantinian empire now lived under a new political zone.[18]
Since Constantine, the *leges* of Christianity have been used both in favor of
and against the empire. The bishops who were friends of the poor,
Christian resistance to the Roman calendar, critique of blood sports so
popular with the Romans all utilized the *leges* to move against the empire.
At the same time, the *leges* were used to justify baptism to be used as more
a civilian code of belonging to the Empire than a mode of entering the
Christian family and the grandiose liturgical spaces where prominent
bishops and their pointy hats, golden rings and fashionable dress assumed
all the hierarchy of the empire. *Lex orandi-credendi-vivendi* moved away
from the people and was used to maintain, support and foster the forms of
another *lex*: Caesar's *lex*.

Caesar's *lex* over Christianity quickly but not entirely
overshadowed the *leges* of the church. *Lex orandi-credendi-vivendi* has
always shaped political theologies. Liturgical moves were both theological
causes and consequences of political movements, shifting and moving the
whole body of Christ in certain directions, orienting and reorienting a faith
that often moved itself away from the poor and closer to those in power.

Over time, the focal point of liturgical theologies in their ritual
expressions was aimed to protect those in power, now proclaimed the
sacred. The who and the what of God is intrinsically related to the how of

the sacred, or in other words, the ways we liturgize God are the ways we organize the places of our local communities, public spaces filled with tension, earthly grounds fertile to life and possibilities, places prone to the topographies of God's grace, and the manifestations of space. Questions like: Who is God? And how does this God show up? Where were and are the means of salvation? And what are we to do with it all? were and are often channeled to certain political theologies in order to keep power and authority. *Lex ecclesia* or the law of the church subverted the other *leges*. Through the liturgical frames of content and forms, the church determines the ruling of God. They cannot allow God not to be what God must (not) be. Thus, the work of liturgists was to be watch dogs of the ways of God or the sacred that needed to be protected. In Christianity, the fear of having the sacred run amuck, be disrespected or be taken away led the church to build complicated laws to compose proper liturgies so God was always protected. In this way, the sacred was turned into the sacraments and in this way the church could control the means of grace where one finds God. What remained available of the sacred to the people were sacramentalities: things that point to the sacraments, that are related somewhat to the sacraments, but are not sacred as the sacraments. In this way our sacramentality was scattered and dis-placed into discrete rituals.

In this form of the constitution of the sacred, the earth has only been a backdrop for human and Godly actions. In such a disembodied form, it is at the altars/tables of the liturgical places where the sacred is to be celebrated and shared. The sacraments, which carry the very presence of God, with a life of their own, do not depend on the geographical spaces where the altars/tables are grounded. As a result, liturgical spaces can be settled in stolen lands, they can be built on private land, they can be structured anywhere the church declares sacred. The discontinuity of the sacraments and the earth is such that the materiality of its holy things, the economic aspects of the sacred transactions and the expansive relations of the elements of the sacraments are never hinged by any other marker beyond Godself who is understood as the essence of all things. For example, the waters of baptism are never related to rivers near or far, grapes and wheat are never juxtaposed to non-documented immigrants who harvest them for people in the United States to celebrate their most holy meal. The sacramental laws, *lex credendi-orandi* are detached from *lex vivendi*, the law of living.

For most Protestants, whose theological sense of the sacred resides in the pulpit or the proclamation of the word, the duality of the profane and the sacred is never truly resolved since it moves and turns and twists according to the interpretation of the word of God. The sacraments offer a temporary resolution as the sacred is carried and manifested in sacramental moments of time and place (as in a worship service) where the duality is finally diffused...only to return to its tension after the sacraments are presided. A further resolution may be found in the moral claims of political theologies which are consequences of liturgical political theologies, still dependent on a certain interpretation of what is sacred.

These political liturgical theologies only consider their aesthetic composition, with contemporary or traditional objects, with or without the cross and so on, but never consider their ethical, economic and exclusionary forms of public spaces and their means of production. In order to maintain such a disembodied liturgical theology, the sacred must be attached to time, to actions and thoughts that honor tradition, and disconnected from the earth and the places they are grounded. The geographical location serves only as an outlet for the sacred to appear. The "natural world" as God's natural revelation must never be a main site for God's salvation. Scriptures and tradition trump nature in revelation ranks.

The presence of the three liturgical *leges* are pulled into these complex relations with spaces and places but are never fundamentally connected to the earth. Prayers, beliefs, and ethics/daily life all take for granted the existence of the earth--it can indeed all be blessed by natural revelation, but the earth can never be considered as central to its most fundamental existence. As such, prayers, beliefs, and ethics/daily life are never to be held accountable or called to "sit with the trouble" or address the scandalous ecological destruction we continue to carry out. In sum, I am trying to get to Wendell Berry's definition of the sacred, very much akin to Indigenous knowledges:

> *There are no unsacred places;*
> *there are only sacred places*
> *and desecrated places.*[19]

Liturgies, Time, and Space

Growing up in a conservative church I kept hearing in worship that Jesus was coming, and the world was going to end. I always thought that the world would end because, at some point, time would come and God would put an end to the world, as we knew it. The end of times, I learned later, would bring about a millennial in which Jesus ruled it all. After that, I was taught that the earth was only a temporary receptacle that was bound to be destroyed, a necessary object of transition to the real life that was waiting for us. In my evangelistic zeal, I remember battling the Jehovah's Witnesses for their heresy that the earth would be a place for many of us to live eternity. I could not understand how they had such an attachment to the earth when we were going to be in heaven.

This detachment from the earth is also shown by the absence of space/place in Christian theologies and liturgies, which have created an abyss between faith and matter, where faith elevates matter to the point of its dissipation. The problematic biblical interpretation of a war between flesh and spirit in the apostle Paul's thinking created an aversion to matter, including body, earth, things, women, etc. Christian spirituality was thus fully organized around time and spirit, heaven and men. As Brazilian theologian Vitor Westhelle puts it so well in his superb book *Eschatology and Space. The Lost Dimension in Theology Past and Present*:

> *The finitude of time and space is set in such radical opposition to eternity that transcendence is sequestered from the world we see and experience. Time is the only compass to guide us to the world to come. Space is at best a diversion, and at worst the very cause of our errings. Creation and consummation are absolute limits set by the span of time.*[20]

In worship this is clear. Christian liturgies are ways of ordering life and faith through time. In many churches, life/faith is ordered through the liturgical calendar, which sets up a clear division of theological emphases in a circular time, in an elliptic way where all of life is explained and lived year-round. Through the year calendar, we eternally return, not to the earth, but to the same event, always temporal, but rarely spatial.

Our sacraments are a reification of time, not matter. In Baptism we learn that we have belonged to God since time immemorial. In the Eucharist, we remember Jesus coming in the fullness of time, whose death is often detached from its political underpinnings and location. Both sacraments orient us to an eschatological time, detached from an earthly space. *Kairos*, without embodiment in space, is an idea with dangerous consequences. *Topos*, however, presupposes space, matter, density, weight, presences, sentience, cosmologies, orientation, and time.

Space, Place, and Worship

As a consequence, the eschatological liturgies of Christianity are too often like revolving doors around their own concerns and doctrines. The worship of the church does its round work, supposedly speaking back to itself, itself being God, and on its way, it does the work of showing/offering God to the world. The real space of worship is the altar, for God is required to show up there, in the tabernacle space of the holy of the holies. Worship happens in a social value-free environment, where the presence of God is its value meaning. We need to rethink and reclaim the liturgical space.

Let us briefly see how Yi-Fu Tuan and Edward Relph see space and place. Tuan says: "space is freedom, place is security,"[21] and Relph says "… space and place are dialectically structured in human environmental experience, since our understanding of space is related to the places we inhabit, which in turn derive meaning from their spatial context."[22] Both authors note that space and place are often detached from economic practices. While they understand its powers phonemically, they do not attend to its commodification of codes and practices. Thus, from these frameworks, we could say that liturgical space offers both freedom in its openness to welcome people, and security in its ritual offerings. Meaning is not made there but the space offers meaning to be learnt and engaged.

We need to understand space differently in all its layers of complexities. This is David Harvey's definition of space:

> space is neither absolute, relative or relational in itself, but it can become one or all simultaneously depending on the circumstances. The problem of the proper conceptualization of space is resolved through human practice with respect to it. In other words, there are no philosophical answers to philosophical questions that arise over the nature of space - the answers lie in human practice. The question "what is space?" is therefore replaced by the question "how is it that different human practices create and make use of different conceptualizations of space?" The property relationship, for example, creates absolute spaces within which monopoly control can operate. The movement of people, goods, services, and information takes place in a relative space because it takes money, time, energy, and the like to overcome the friction of distance. Parcels of land also capture benefits because they contain relationships with other parcels….in the form of rent relational space comes into its own as an important aspect of human social practice.[23]

Within this understanding of space, we can circulate objects, people, goods, structures, modes of production, economic developments and class struggle. We can count the history of colonial power and show that no space is value-free. Spaces are indeed places of official and contested meanings. That means that the whole structure of religious buildings is grounded in more than religious meanings, including the commodification and the economic values sustained by private spaces. Churches have been fundamentally erected on portions of land stolen from Indigenous communities, making every owner of private space a carrier of injustice and oppression, re-inscribing violence as the land carries markers of the injustice, and the owner actively partakes in the perpetuation of violence when the history of the space is not brought to light or acknowledged. The question that lingers with us then is: how can holy liturgies speak of sacred things when the very space/ground they inhabit is marked by injustice? What is the political attestation of its message?

The *place* of worship is also marked by those who inhabit that *space*, with boundaries and markers that show who are invited, or not, to that space. Let us not forget that during slavery in the United States, Christian churches had the balcony reserved for Black people, and pews closer to the altar/pulpit were bought and secured by rich white families.

Let us move even beyond that notion of space, towards Indigenous people's forms of thinking and relating to land and space. Winona LaDuke from the Dakota nation gives us an expansive notion of space:

> *We have a word in our language which describes the practice of living in harmony with natural law: minocimaatisiiwin. This word describes how you behave as an individual in a relationship with other individuals and in relationship with the land and all things. We have tried to retain this way of living and this way of thinking in spite of all that has happened to us over the centuries. I believe we do retain most of these practices in our community, even if they are overshadowed at times by individualism... Our traditional forms of land use and ownership are similar to those found in community land trusts being established today. The land is owned collectively, and each family has traditional areas where it fishes and hunts. We call our concept of land ownership Anishinaabeg akiing: "the land of the people," which doesn't imply that we own our land, but that we belong on it. Unfortunately, our definition doesn't stand up well in court because this country's legal system upholds the concept of private property.*[24]

This expansive notion of space, land, living and believing, holds a circularity of relations that are based on the natural law--not the natural law of Hobbes, Locke, and Rousseau--but that of the earth ruling and orienting our lives, our desires, and limiting our ways of living. Lakota people see space as more than a grid of abstract or independent notions, or independent meanings but rather, a place with a plethora of relations, a place of multi-naturalisms and human kinds, making the *ecos-oikos* a place where the fauna and flora worlds co-exist in horizontal commonality and gnarly entanglement.

Unfortunately, liturgical theologies are far from helping us engage the earth as space in either Harvey or LaDuke's way. Instead, it quickly reminds us that our life is made of a spiritual relation to God who seems to be always above and beyond us. In a recent interreligious dialogue, religious leaders were lamenting the lack of vertical connections with God, showing a clear detachment from the earth. The love of others, which is the other/same side of the love of God, often does not reach down to the land/earth and does not proliferate horizontally, like the grapevines or the rhizomes. The ritual services of Christian churches tend to keep us detached from the earth. Our spiritualities, springing from our ritual services, tend not to look to the lilies or the birds for comfort and security, as Jesus said, but rather, to look at a higher spiritual space which we actually do not know where or how to find it.

In our worship services, we sing glory to a placeless One who is the same yesterday, today and forever more, who lives somewhere, this somewhere being understood as somewhen. A placeless god who, by not being rooted in place, does not need to extend care for the place. This God lives in eternity (somewhen), not somewhere (paradise?), that does not have an ecological address, a physical place to be attached/ accountable to and in relationship with. While we confess our sins in specific times, we ask God to get rid of them geographically, distancing our sins like the West is far from the East. Our sermons organize our lives through distinctions between the secular *Chronos* and the sacred *Kairos* overlooking the *topos* of the God of time. Our baptism is a testimony to a new time, where the old time is put behind and we become "new creatures" in a new time. Our Eucharist/Communion liturgies name God's salvific acts in history, moments in time when (with not the fully where) God has come to rescue God's people and manifested Godself in the fullness of time in Jesus Christ. The elements of the eucharist are holders of this Kairos time when God is manifested fully in our midst and that is why many churches will call the sacraments the means of grace. Our offerings are to be expressions of our gratitude for the bounty of God in our lives. This bounty was at first related to the harvest of God's gifts, but now it is related to our separation from places of production. The charge and benediction announce that the Lord is coming in an eschatological promise wrapped in a new time. Through our liturgical actions and words, the church is called to be a witness in our time, announcing the now and not-yet presence of the Kingdom of God. And thus, detaching us from our response-ability to respond to the urgencies of our common home, we need not be stewards of this home, for our eschatological promise has to do with *chronos*, not *topos*.

The political theology of our liturgies is condensed, expressed and structured fundamentally around time. However, the very "ground" of liturgical theologies, time itself, is organized in a way that makes liturgies both timeless and placeless, which frees us from being accountable to the destruction of place and to the environmental racism and ecological injustices we continue to perpetrate. There is a hope and a belief that what we do in worship is and should be timeless, just as God is not bound by time. The hope, belief, and illusion that the church continues to foster with the same timeless liturgical ordo throughout history attest to the timelessness of the liturgical enterprise. In this logical way, the grounding of liturgy in time by its timelessness is also the negation that liturgies are marked by time. It is thus through this affirmation and negation that time is at the center of the Christian liturgical theologies.

Denominational worship books are full expressions of this relation between eschatological theology and timeless liturgical orders. Worship books are celebrated as carriers of a timeless wisdom from some other time that is not ours. In actuality, every worship book is written locally by a certain group of people at a certain time, but after this 'event," every other church is called to forget the time, place and people that created the books of common worship. The church is called to repeat that disembodied wisdom the same way everywhere else, rendering the where of its ritual performance completely unnecessary. The genius of liturgical books is to turn a local story into a universal understanding of the sacredness of a placeless God. By surreptitiously suppressing the spaces/places of the locations and cultures where they were written, the writers of these books can hide behind their timeless faithfulness to the gospel. Instead of being expressions of specific cultures, the liturgies are placeless expressions of faith. The meaning of faith created is not what the people wrote but what the communities repeat, oriented by the timelessness of the liturgical ordos and its non-negotiable truths. The language of Christian liturgies in worship books attests to the eternal God who is the same God anywhere in the world since, again, the where does not really matter. The universality of such liturgies is not different from many other religions whose liturgical truth is timeless and detached from cultural, social, economic, and spatial realities. Westhelle says:

> *Space indeed became illusory. What modernity then finally accomplished is a recombination of time and space in which space is no longer even linked to place. The words of Anthony Giddens, reading into utopian imagination the omens announcing the disappearance of real spaces, aptly states: The severance of time from space does not mean that these henceforth become mutually alien aspects of human social organization. On the contrary: it provides the very basis for the recombination in ways that coordinate social activities without necessary reference to particularities of place.*[25]

YES!!!

Since Vatican II, liturgical renewal has been marked by concern with cultures and contexts.[26] The question of culture has always been a question of authenticity that pertains both to the culture and the gospel. These studies start by honoring cultures and highly praising the cultural diversity in the liturgical *ordo*. Liturgy then serves as the criteria and evaluation of what is good or bad in each culture. The end result repeats a certain embellishment of the English forms of timeless (and spaceless) liturgical ordo with some local words included, even "*Navajo*" or vests or dance, that serve to both conceal and reveal the timelessness of liturgy by setting aside real contexts, spaces, and local beings (humans and more than human) and experiences. Even in this effort to renew and diversify liturgies, the timelessness of the liturgical ordo takes precedence over the particularity of any culture and the spaces where they are celebrated.

When we relate the liturgical ordo, which is the theological framing of the liturgical practice, to cultures, spaces and contextuality we are often talking about the material ways in which liturgies are to be enacted. For instance, "sacred spaces" often refers to the architectural planning of inner concrete spaces in churches that must be conducive to the relation with God through the doing of our timeless liturgies. Sacred space is intended to separate the believer from the world and help her focus only on God. Any material attachment or any distraction must be left outside.

From that liturgical space, be it enacted with short or expansive liturgies, Christian communities learn how to think, to relate, to act and to live. In other words, in worship, Christian communities learn how to organize their moral and ethical lives and how to understand what being human is all about. What is silenced in the liturgy, including space and place, also engages and shapes Christian communities, for what is not said is also a form of saying it. For instance, the rivers, the mountains, the voices of animals who live around the churches where liturgical rites happen, are rarely considered, listened to, voiced, celebrated with and cared for…and their absence is present in the liturgy. These absences shape the very notion of what it is to be human, creating an exceptional notion of humanity where all of these other beings are less than human, lower than human, without forms of agency and sentience, "outside" of the world we live in. Just like our notion of nature, these other than human beings are understood in our liturgies as something out there, away from us.

Thus, the politics of liturgical spaces and how we understand these spaces is central to how we live the Christian faith. Our history shows that the very political core of Christian liturgical theology is to rule the space by denying its spatial location. We deny it in twofold ways: first, by developing a placeless theology that aims the message of Christ to the spirit and the heart of an individual human being and avoiding all the political structures that form the very ways that individual lives in places; second, by evolving a contextual theology that, while dealing with some of the concrete situations of the church environment such as homelessness and/or the artistic community, still avoids the power dynamics of class, and racialized environments. Through both theological forms of escapisms that avoid material constructions of reality, Christian churches perform political actions intended to either implement or uphold clear, dominant political agendas or maintain neutrality. In both ways, Christian churches continue to shape reality by electing presidents, avoiding racial struggles, and supporting economic views.

To truly create sacred space and a political liturgical theology that is guided and organized by *lex naturae*, we must tackle economic inequality, class struggle, racial conflicts, means of production and its relation to the earth.

Conclusion

The power of rituals in religious communities cannot be dismissed. The existence of rituals is political to its core and influences the politics of both small local communities and entire countries. Our proposal here is thus to see how a liturgical move to orient us to think, pray, relate and live into spaces, places, earth and Gaia can be a full incarnation of God in our midst.

I offer this way of discerning places through the liturgical calendar that most Christians celebrate:

All Saints Day

The earth is our main saint and Wendel Berry, Cesar Chavez, Dolores Huerta and all the small farmers and workers are the patrons of the United States. Through them we create movements of solidarity-fluidarity with and from the earth, in each patch of world we live in, bound to an ethics of response-ability and care, "taking stock," in Bonhoeffer's words, of Gaia today.

Christ the King

Christ's kingship holds a king without reign, with transversalities of many human kinds and spiritualities on the earth. Christ as king/transcendent only if existing in fully immanent forms of cells, fungus, and mycelium, fulfilled in the lives of animals, trees, mountains, and air. A kingship of service and reciprocity, through an oath of honor (sacrament) to the neighbor, both human beings and more than human neighbors. As Bonhoeffer says: "The transcendent is not the infinite, unattainable tasks, but the neighbor within reach in any given situation. God in human form."[27]

Advent

The preparation of the coming of Jesus is the daily tending of the earth, being healed by the earth, and healing the earth from our destruction, announcing that the earth (and us) will be restituted once again. In each location, a different restitution; in each patch of land, a different care.

Christmastide

Jesus is the resolution of God's transcendence and immanence, where transcendence loses its "out there" nature and becomes fully immanent in a billion ways, everything springing from the earth and through the pluriverses that constantly fill us with wonder. Life abundant beginning, once again!

Transfiguration

We become clouds and God abides with us. Mountaintops are sacred meeting places, as are valleys and forests and rivers. Every place can be a sacred meeting place if we are attuned to God and the awareness of life already within us. Baptism then carries a full circularity of life through water in us. We are water, becoming water, and returning back to water. Grapes and wheat are soil, turning into the body of Christ, thus also carrying a circularity of life from humus to humus. We are soil, we are water, always becoming a symbiotic Christ, becoming humus, and returning to humus.

Lent

We put our ears to the floor. We listen to the earth. We fast. We thank God for the bounty of life. We do not eat meat. We only eat what is in season where we live. Through Lent we rehearse a life fully lived with the earth all year long.

Eastertide

We weep with the earth, and we groan with the earth. We clean the rivers and the oceans. The resurrection of Jesus is the resurrection of the earth. We plant new trees, we learn about biodiversity, we care for the insects, we celebrate new life springing forth.

Pentecost

The celebration of the harvest everywhere. The spirit of life springing forth and showing us its renewal, renovation and restoration. We feast on the bountiful gifts of the earth and on the generous givenness of the Spirit. We abandon pesticides, plastic, and fossil fuels. With and through the Spirit, we correct injustices, our lust and greed diminish, our desires are reoriented, and we give back what we have taken beyond our measure.

Trinity Sunday

The triune God is a society made of a quaternity: God the earth, God the water, God the air, God the fire. Trinity as the thousand combinations and forms of symbiosis. With this trinity, *lex naturae* goes against the trinity of our time, composed, in the words of Eduardo Viveiros de Castro, by "State the Father, Market the Son and Reason/Science the Holy Spirit."[28]

Ordinary time

We learn with Indigenous people about cyclical time and relinquish any need for a *telos*, a certain end. Everything is in God and God is everything. Life in its billion ways of living. Everyday we learn a little more about the patch of land we inhabit, and we see everything as ourselves, everything as sacred, as we live fully in the radical immanence of God everywhere. Even as we desecrate the earth, we restitute what we can restore. We rest, we work in our gardens, we share our harvest, we support local farmers, we develop house economies, we care for the worms and the bees and the trees and the birds, we drink the water of our rivers, we pray the prayers of our communities and the communities across the world, our baptisms are in the local rivers, the eucharist is the food harvested in our gardens. We share with the poor, and we live as a community--not as individuals in pursuit of personal happiness.

Let us discern for ourselves a liturgical political theology grounded in our places and the law of nature in each place. For *lex naturae* is nothing else than the law of nature, its complexities, its movements, and its emergencies.

CHAPTER THREE

Rituals and Performances in the Anthropocene: Eco-Liturgical Liberation Pantheologies

Peter Isaac Lindsey Perella Carvalhaes, 9 years old

All important ideas must include the trees,
the mountains, and the rivers.

Mary Oliver
Leaves and Blossoms Along the Way

For a colonized people the most essential value,
because the most concrete, is first and foremost the land:
the land which will bring them bread and, above all, dignity.

Frantz Fanon
The Wretched of the Earth

Honeyeaters

We ritualize to not forget. We have already forgotten so many things--silenced so many things—that we have lost our ability to hear. So, we need rituals, performances, and ceremonies to help us to listen and remember who we were, who we are, and who we are becoming. In Australia, the birds called Honeyeaters are disappearing because they are so few in number and they cannot hear their elders singing. Since the males do not know their own songs, the females have no interest in them. They try to learn other birds' songs but that does not help them; they are dying. Like the honeyeaters, we forgot we ever had songs to sing. Robin Wall Kimmerer, botanist, and member of the of the Potawatomi Nation, reminds us of why we need ceremonies:

> *Our elders say that ceremony is the way we can remember to remember. In the dance of the giveaway, remember that the earth is a gift that we must pass on, just as it came to us. When we forget, the dances we'll need will be for mourning. For the passing of polar bears, the silence of cranes, for the death of rivers and the memory of snow"*[1]

After I read the story of the Honeyeaters, I had to make sense of this loss and wrote this poem to them. It was way of ritualizing the loss of the honeyeaters and keep them in my memory. Rituals are ways to help us go through many losses in this time of the Anthropocene:[2]

Dear Honeyeaters,
By the maple tree near my house I sat down and wept.
I have heard about you. How beautiful you all are!
Far away from you, I heard about your condition
Your struggle to survive
Your home being desecrated
Your refugia being erased
Your people dwindling down…

I heard you can't find your own singing
The young ones can't find your elders to teach you your own songs
For they are all almost gone
But the few young ones are trying to learn your own songs
So, you can mate and prosper and continue living

Your singing comes from learning with your own people
How wonderful is that!
You are literally the songs of your fathers, mothers, great fathers,
         great mothers, great grandmothers and great grandfathers.

But how tragic it is:
They are not there anymore, and they cannot teach you the songs you
         so desperately need to sing
And without your own songs, you go on mimicking the songs of
         other birds.

In different places, we hear you sing different songs
You are trying to survive by learning whatever song you hear
But those songs are not your songs

And without your songs, your "warbly noises," you can't court
         the females
They are not attracted to the unrecognizable songs you sing.
You sound metallic, too loud, off of your own tune.

You are there but at the same time… you are not.
You exist yes, but for whom?

Your own people cannot come close to you
For your songs are not recognizable
You are losing your own self because your own self is not your own!

You are not a lone ranger singer
Your self is collective because your song is collective.
Your song belongs to generations past, made by ways of listening
　　　　that only your people know

But now… now you are losing your self.
Your song doesn't fulfill you
As much as you try
As much as you listen
As much as you are eager and perhaps even desperate to sing any songs

Your song now is a foreign song
You are becoming a foreign to yourself
The songs you sing are not yours, are not you
You live in a diaspora of songs

Yes, I can utterly relate to you when
You don't understand how, after a whole day singing
Nobody cares
Nobody approaches
Nobody listens

Your songs are becoming less complex!
And without your song you are losing your strength!
Through the regular battles of your day with other species, you
　　　　easily lose your fights,
especially against the "noisy miners," other Honeyeaters who
　　　　are more aggressive.

I don't know much about you. And I don't know what to say. I don't know
what will happen to the very few of you. What I hope the people who live
you in Australia will help you to continue and re-exist. All I really know
is that my heart fell to the ground, and I feel that there is very little singing
in me. With your loss I also die. What I will do is to sing to you every day.
And listen to your songs in my computer so I can keep you in my heart.

All my love to you.

There is already too much mourning in our world with the passing of so many people to COVID-19, and so many species going extinct. We have no other choice but to dance with and for the people (human and more than human) and gifts we still have, but also, we must dance to mourn what we lose everyday. To ritualize is to compose ourselves with those still living and those who are dying. When I mourn both the death of my friend's mother and the vanishing bees, I compose an assemblage of human kinds who will always be a part of me, in life and in death.

Church of the Forest

The church forests in Ethiopia are more than a metaphor for our time, they are a living reality. Please watch the video[3] before you continue reading. The video shows a patch of land in Ethiopia that still holds a tiny forest in a region devastated by agriculture and cattle grazing. It looks now like everything is dead around this forest. But this circular forest space was saved by the church and still carries the wisdom and the presence of ancestor trees and life blooming in fullness. In the middle of this tiny forest, there is a church: a church of the forest. In a wonderful visible manifestation of a wonderful symbiosis, the church keeps the forest as the forest keeps the church. This patch of land still carries the joy and the spirit(s) of life of the whole forest. The church's definition of ecclesiology is amazing. Here are some of the sayings of the people of the church forests:

> *Ethiopian Orthodox teachings a church to be a church should be enveloped by a forest. It should resemble the garden of Eden... We are taught that God gives mercy when you pray here. So, the spiritual connectivity is so strong. The more I studied them, the more I understand them, the more I see their importance, their significance and then I end up being hooked with these forests... Every plant contains the power of God, the Treasure of God, the Blessing of God... Every time someone plants a tree, the tree prays for the person to live longer... We need to cultivate the life of the youth as we need to cultivate the lives of the forests, or we will; not have future. That is why we need a wall around the forest... if the church loses the forest, it will lose itself... The idea of making a wall to protect the forest came from the church itself. Every rural church has a wall to protect the inner circle which people think is the most sacred place. So, let's move that wall outside and include the forest as part of the church itself. We are making a barrier... against cattle grazing so that regeneration and the health of the forest can be sustained. The church has protecting the forests for centuries and the forests have been a guardian, it was a kind of mutual*

benefiting. The church itself was built from these forests. The inner wall of the church has been painted and all those pictures, scripture and murals were made out of barks, trees, leaves roods, barks and flowers... they are embedded into one another. The church is within the forest the forest is inside of the church... In ecological culture, the whole is greater than the sum of its parts. There are millions of other creatures. It is so complicated, sophisticated interaction you cannot explain. Because of the coexistence there is what you call emergent property. It is a new hybrid character. The mystery is to think beyond what you see. There is a problem always, a misperception that these forests will stay forever. We don't have any other back up. To safeguard the Ethiopian biodiversity is only the church forests. If we lose that, then that's all.... So, if you really care, we have to respect trees, we have to learn to live with forests.[4]

The forest churches of Ethiopia teach us to read Genesis 8:22 from the perspective of the forest: "As long as the *forest* endures, seedtime and harvest, cold and heat, summer and winter, day and night will never cease." There is no discontinuity between the life of faith of the people of the church and the life of the forest of the people of the forest. The forest is the prayer of the church, and the church is the ground of the forest. Spirituality is a process of mutual regeneration, restoration, symbiotic entanglements, and healing between the church and the forest and between the people of the church and the people of the forest. There is no God without the trees and there are no trees without God. The deep forms of relationalities formed by these sophisticated interactions are the source of life within these natural communities.

The same cry for the life of the forests in this tiny patch of land in Ethiopia finds its resonant thunder in the Amazon Forest where the shaman Davi Kopenawa talks about the forest:

The forest is alive. It can only die if the white people persist in destroying it. If they succeed, the rivers will disappear underground, the soil will crumble, the trees will shrivel up, and the stones will crack in the heat. The dried-up earth will become empty and silent. The xapiri spirits who come down from the mountains to play on their mirrors in the forest will escape far away. Their shaman fathers will no longer be able to call them and make them dance to protect us. They will be powerless to repel the epidemic fumes which devour us. They will no longer be able to hold back the evil beings who will turn the forest to chaos. We will die one after the other, the white people as well as us. All the shamans will finally perish. Then, if none of them survive to hold it up, the sky will fall.[5]

We must become the church of the forests, the church of the rivers, the church of the plants, the church of the coral reefs, the church of the hummingbirds, the church of the mountains, the church of the rocks, the church of the mycelium, the church of the cells, the church of the oceans, the church of the agriculture and food, the church of the clouds, the church of the animals, the church of the plants and so on. But we can only do that if our rituals perform life together with them.

Liberation Theologies, Rituals and the Environment

We are living amid the ruins of earth, devoured mercilessly by modernity, colonization, and capitalism. Uprooted from the land, we talk as if we are from nowhere, as if we belong to cities but not to the land. We desperately need eco-theologies and liturgies that incorporate the earth and that wrestle with the many inhabitants of each particular patch of land. Our liturgies must begin where the liturgical theologian lives and include the small farmers, parks, trees, rivers, rocks, and animals that surround us. We speak from the context of people and power dynamics in social, racial, cultural, economic sexual structures, but we neglect the land. Land and earthly space are the forgotten places in our theological work.[6] Alister McGrath in *Re-Imagining nature: The Promise of a Christian Natural Theology* illustrates a modernist colonizing European point of view that draws on the concept of nature as an abstract notion:

> *Natural theology cannot be undertaken apart from actual knowledge of the living God as a prior conceptual system of its own… Rather must it be undertaken in an integrated unity with positive theology in which it plays an indispensable part in our inquiry and understanding God.*[7]

McGrath's "prior conceptual system" is simply the modern European understanding of God. "Nature," as the frame of this conceptual system, is outside God and ourselves and can only partially point to God, reifying the divide of natural/special revelation of God in most Christian theology. The positivism and unity McGrath proposes is nothing but a white moral philosophical European demand where nature must be subsumed by God and the conceptual system.

McGrath mentions Plato's "synoptikon, a 'view from somewhere,'"[8] but the location of this somewhere is never mentioned. Working from the illusory--even if sublime--notion of nature as a monolithic thing out there, McGrath's somewhere can be anywhere, which can be everywhere, and thus it is actually nowhere. Nature as an idealized concept resides solely in the mind, encrypted in the conceptual system that he insists organizes both

God and nature. This claim is a typical modern project where the affirmation of God is performed in a local place, a clear somewhere, in this case Great Britain, but stripped of its particularity and spoken with the authority of a male European theologian, the project claims a universal affirmation. A local theology of Great Britain is declared the world's faithful point of view. Surely McGrath writes from a context the same way liberation theologians write from a context too. We are always from a place, an illustration of context. However, as Eduardo Viveiros de Castro ironically says: "All of us are context-bound, but some are so much more context-bound than others."[9]

People of the south do not have the luxury of claiming the particular as universal. Liberation theologies instead, claim that God starts from a people, located somewhere and marked by that location. Poor folks, Black people, women, LGBTQIA+ people, from a specific location--Latin America, North America, Africa, Asia and so on—speak of God from people's daily lives and suffering in their contexts. Every theology has a location and a context. While liberation theologies offer a correction to McGrath's understanding of nature and God as a thing out there, detached from us, a conceptual system, they have also forgotten the soil, the spaces, the patches of land where these theologies are lived. The land and place define peoples' suffering and oppression, but it is often absent from our theologies. The somewhere of liberation theologies includes:

> In Latin America, the somewhere of theology is in the lives of the poor and class struggle.[10]
> In Black theology, the somewhere of theology is in the Black community.
> In Womanist theology, the somewhere of theology is in lives and bodies of Black women.
> In Feminist theology the somewhere of theology is in the gender of white women.
> In African theology, the somewhere of theology is in the culture of people.
> In Hispanic theology, the somewhere of theology is in the family and ways of doing things together.
> In Queer theology, the somewhere of theology is in the sexual lives and the bodies of people.
> In Minjung theology the somewhere of theology is in the poor people of Korea.
> In Dalit theology, the somewhere of theology is in the caste systems of India.

It is important to say that Palestinian liberation theologies are fully grounded in the earth and in the dispute over land. Dalit theologies are embedded in the very notion that Dalits are people of the earth. My pamphletarian critique of these liberation theologies, however, does not take into account the nuances and the ways in which all these theologies do deal with the land in one way of another. My general critique is that the whole project of liberation theology is done mostly through an ethnocentric, anthropocentric, and utilitarian structure.[11]

The body is at the heart of liberation theologies just as the incarnation of Jesus is at the heart of Christianity. In our theologies, however, these bodies seem to float above the earth separate from the land and the means of production that define the ways people live. God might, we say, be with the poor, their contexts, and their bodies but not in the land where people live, struggle, and relate. Rarely can we find the soil, water, animals, seeds, and the dynamics of private property in these theologies. We theologians are so colonized and so entrenched in the process of thinking that we cannot actually think of the land and its inhabitants when we do theology. This is not because we simply "forget." We were trained not to pay attention to the land, to understand the earth as a partial revelator of God, so that the land cannot take away from the full revelation of Christ. The simple binary that says God is above (lift up your hearts) and the devil, or dirt is below and under our feet, profoundly impacts our cosmologies and how we understand God and the earth.

In the same way, the liturgies of the Christian faith are often self-enclosed rituals where liturgy is explained by liturgy itself. The most expressive sign of this trouble with the earth can be seen in the celebration of communion/eucharist/Lord's Supper. The table/altar is elevated above the earth as a sign of holiness. The ground is dirt-y, as we say it in English. The celebrant must be very careful not to let any element fall to the ground or it will shatter God's holiness and profane the ritual.

Since an altar on the ground becomes profane with the already profane ground, I once put soil on the altar/table and spread it around the elements. Horrified, people said I had completely disrespected tradition, the sacrament, and God. Just a little soil on the table! In the same way we use bottled mineral water in our baptismal rituals because the rivers near us are polluted. But while we seem to care intensely about our ritual practices, we have simultaneously desecrated the earth with the practices of our holy sacraments! Wendell Berry put it brilliantly: "There are no unsacred places; there are only sacred places and desecrated places."[12] Shame on us!

Eco-liturgical liberation theologies, as well as liberation theologies, must begin where it hurts, and our rituals must respond to those in pain. To realize a "showing of a doing,"[13] we must amplify our ears and listen to the cry of the people and the cry of the earth.[14] The trees and rivers and animals are people, and love of God and neighbor demands for us to care for God's creation through solidarity and reciprocity.

At each place, where we live, we are called to engage in connections, relations, restoration, and mutual healing. The question then becomes how to expand our liturgies for the sake of the natural world and for the people and the earth to live in dignity. Liberation theologies begin with understanding the condition and situation of our contexts. Liturgy, as a first step of theology, will engage our conditions and situations through the creation of rituals: gestures, metaphors, symbols, time, space, and words to include all forms of relationalities in our local communities.

The risk for most of Christianity in United States is that we live in protected places and safe environments. It would be easy to engage with nice trees and mostly clean rivers, but our task, for those of us living with such privilege, is to gain awareness of the broader contexts in which we live and connect with the earth where we are. Those who are living in harsher places have more difficult challenges, but all churches can work toward forms of caring for the earth and solidarity with the poor. We can engage with local small farmers and ecological groups to demand public policies for environmental protection, push industries to curb their gas emissions, check the systems of food distribution, research pesticide use, create sanctuaries for bees and birds , protest deforestation and initiate reforestations, clean and restore the rivers, pressure politicians, move in solidarity with Indigenous people in the protection of their lands, reconnect people with the earth, rewrite school curricula to include ecological education, fight for worker's rights and well-being, and demand universal health care. We can turn our buildings into community agencies and worship outside in parks, in the wilderness, with just a single tree, or by a river. We know also that we must continue to create and enact new rituals for to simply repeat what we have always done often results in tragedy.

Catherine Bell offers the useful concept of ritualization to describe ways of creating and cultivating ritual practices according to the needs of a chosen group and a place.[15] She writes, "[r]itualization is fundamentally a way of doing things to trigger the perception that these practices are distinct and the associations that they engender are special."[16] For our times now marked by climate change and global warming, we must create rituals that can "trigger perception" to a vaster, more complex and richer form of relationality with the earth, moving us from a humanistic exceptionality to a more bounded and deep belonging with the earth and space we inhabit. We start by hearing the birds singing our songs and treating the trees as our elders, the mountains as our ancestors, the rivers as our grandparents, the mycelium as the sustainer of our lives,[17] and the cells as our symbiotic partners.

Perception is also a work of point of view, of a perspectivism as Eduardo Viveiros de Castro says. My perception of others affects my view of the world but also the world that I view. As Deleuze said: "... Others, from my point of view, introduce the sign of the unseen in what I do see, making me grasp what I do not perceive as perceptible to an Other."[18] Performance then, is an incessant work of perception translated into bodily gestures, actions, and movements. As I perceive another person--human or more than human--near me, on the patch of land where I live, I must draw near through a performance of greetings and small actions that allow me view what I could not see before. Until the unseen becomes a part of my breathing. Ronald Grimes pushes our perspective to action by making ritual an action:

> *The gerund form is to call attention to the activity of deliberately cultivating rites. Ritualizing is not often socially supported. Rather, it happens in the margins, on the threshold; so it is alternatively stigmatized and eulogized... The result of sustained ritualizing and revised theory of ritual to account for it is likely to be the bleeding of genres – the fuzzing of boundary lines that separate ritual from art, theater, politics and therapy – but this bleeding of boundaries may not be a loss. It might represent instead ritual's connection with some of its vital sources and tributaries.[19]*

We must ritualize in ways that are naturally supportive, based on reciprocity Rituals that can be done in places where bio-systems were destroyed and we are left with the remains of capitalist disaster by creating new rituals that bleed genres, blurring the boundaries of biology, chemistry, geochemistry, cosmology, botanic studies and so on. These new rituals can help us connect with our vital sources and tributaries: gas and the atmosphere, rivers, trees and soil, rocks, birds and multispecies, animal, vegetable, and mineral worlds.

The cultivation of new rites and performances will move us away from religious excessive textualism so that we can live in the body no longer held captive by the words, so central to theologies and doctrines. As Manuel Vasquez says: "The flight from the body and its situated practice in religious studies results from failing to take seriously our embeddedness in the life-world in the social and natural worlds as they mediated through our historical practices... The result has been a suffocating textualism..."[20]

Through deep relationship with the earth, we are led inevitably to create Eco-Liturgies of Pantheologies. Pantheologies entail a relation between divinity more than humans--other matters including cosmological material, bacteria and cells, animals, elements and a whole new plethora of assemblages and symbioses of a thousand kinds. Mary-Jane Rubenstein proposes pantheologies in this way:

> *Put otherwise, if divinity loses its association with humanity and takes on more pantheological proportions—so that everything in the cosmos is in some sense and from some perspective an expression of divinity—then the scope of personhood widens considerably. Pantheologically, we are not only surrounded but also constituted by nonhuman persons who can feel, hurt, rejoice, and who for those reasons deserve our respect and care—or at the very least our thoughtful deliberation whenever we decide to override the intentions of some assemblages (say, those of termites, their nests, mounds, shelter tubes, and gut bacteria) with others (say, those of a concrete foundation for a wood-frame house; its feline, canine, and human inhabitants; and their gut bacteria). And again, if all these persons are in some sense divine, then divinity becomes not impersonal but rather omni-personal—as operative in and irreducible to a bed of reeds as it is in and to a mustard seed, a coyote, your insufferable neighbor, Hegel's snuffbox, or Poliinio's dressing gown.*[21]

Oh, the wonders and the breath of life that are possible in these eco-liturgical liberation pantheologies! But for Christians, perhaps with a smaller question from Ronald Grimes to get to the bigger possibilities of pantheologies: "What might it look like to turn serving liturgies into earth-serving ones?"[22]

The Anthropocene

We are living in the era of the Anthropocene, an era where a very small portion of humankind has literally taken life away from every part of the world. Climate change is already with us and if we do not change our ways, we will have to learn to live in the midst of disasters and ruined and lifeless land. COVID-19 is just one example of the consequences we are facing; droughts, desertification of land, acidity of oceans, constant hurricanes, and "natural disasters" will all increase as more people become refugees, experience hunger, and contract diseases. Smaller forms of subsistence will disappear, and the icecaps will melt completely causing water flood and cover entire coastal cities. The warming of the earth will be unstoppable and fewer areas on earth will be appropriate for life.

We treat our food with pesticides and our current agricultural methods rape the earth. Wall Street purchases entire aquifers and companies fight over the gold of our time: water. Eco-biomes struggle to survive, eliminating refuges as humans encroach upon wildlife habitat. If we could only perceive what is happening...Small farmers everywhere are fighting big agribusiness gobbling up rich lands for plantations. In India, the government crushes thousands of small farmers while in Indonesia, the production of rice declines, affecting about 4 million small farmers. The land suffers day by day while the rivers dry out.

The statistics are staggering, and it seems impossible to stem the voracious appetite for profit and development. I n the U.S., whether Republicans or Democrats, the growth of the economy takes precedence over the health of natural landscapes. In Alaska, for example, both the Trump and Biden administrations share the same goal: produce oil![23] Governments everywhere are oriented to development and profit for a few people. Extractivist practices are everywhere![24] Overfishing depletes our oceans, deforestation for cattle grazing and logging disappears the Amazon Forest, mining removes mountaintops for coal and minerals and producing consumer goods destroys entire eco-systems. Our situation is calamitous!

What we have learned with the anthropocene/capitolocene/ plantationocene is that there is no distinction between political acts, economic decisions, earth plundering, and climate change; they are all deeply connected to Capitalism and its vicious modes of production fuel desire, consumption, and destruction but we know something must change! The creation of an overly entitled life for a few people results in a very limited and harsh life for most people around the world.

For what? At the end, everything becomes garbage. we cannot get rid of garbage on our planet, so we just move it around as Lynn Margulis said.[25] We treat the earth as we treat other humans, and. there is a growing uneasiness that we are at the end of our strength. Politics in the Anthropocene is simply the management of disasters and chaos--merciless politicians catering to those who give money, responding to the catastrophes they help create.

Extractivism is the metaphor for our time: everything and everybody is mined for profit, and we are not in relationship with nature. The brutal extraction of life from the planet, and the depletion of all forms of life on earth are bringing us consequences that we cannot reverse in the future. People work more work hours for less money and without benefits. The gap between the rich and the poor only grows making jobs and income more precarious. Welfare, pensions, and health care for all fade into a previous era as personal responsibility becomes the rule: fend for yourself! If you can make it, then good for you! If not, the fault lies with you! Neo liberalism, based on the rights of individuals, destroys community and safety nets. As Ronald Reagan said, "the nine most terrifying words in the English language are 'I'm from the government and I'm here to help.'"[26] Take care of yourself! The government is not for the people!

Stretched thin, alone, insecure, and fearful, we work subsistence jobs and lack the capacity to cope crises alone. Meanwhile, the rich have all the support they need to live, using personally what should be communally available and protecting themselves from suffering. They tell us communism is not the answer and that it is the poor who always abuse the system.

Religious communities, who claim a communitarian form of life are deceptively based on individual rights and individual freedom. If somebody cannot make it in our communities, we say, then what can we do? We leave individuals and families in our churches to figure out something by themselves. Religious gatherings are communities without communion in the stronger sense of the word, lacking mutual care and material reciprocity.

The narcissism of our stories, images, conquests, and pain spreads everywhere. Everything is about us. The resonances of collective rituals that spark commitments and care are often trapped into personal needs and attention. "Pay attention to me!" we exclaim, while refusing to care about anybody else. We have our private houses, our own religious traditions, our own ways of living. Our narcissism disconnects us from the earth, and with the loss of the earth we also lose our sense of time. We live in abstractions--everything we buy is an abstraction that fades away. Even our phones, the holiest object of our time, fades away, becomes obsolete. We imbue our phones with our sense of place and--if we have our phones then we have a place in the world. Without our phones, we lose our sense of direction, time, and space. We count our time by our phones. We can be anywhere in the world if we have our phones. The router is my shepherd! Connection! Our phones are our source of trust and pleasure, and we check them over and over and over again to see if there is something new and good waiting for us. On the run with our phones, we can't stop, won't stop! We are so lost and confused! This is the world we have created and allowed to be created.

Sinking into the earth we might find other sources of belonging; we might find out we are not alone after all, and that new kinships and a different pace in life—not based on production--might be available to us.

Shifting, Changing, Reorienting

No need to demonize phones! We can change the world we live and belong differently by entering into other forms of relationship. Let us wonder how our phones were made and marvel at the amazing assemblage of actants within them More than 40 minerals compose that little thing we hold in our hands--that tiny device which holds so many of our feelings! We carry a whole mountain in our hands—our entire lives--brought to us by the exploitation of the natural world through entailed child labor, civil strife, and natural extraction by Apple, Samsung, and many others. The phone, in a nutshell, represents who we are and how deeply we are connected to the earth through a whole industry of wealth and exploitation. Perhaps, as we use our smart phones, we can say a prayer thanking those minerals for giving themselves to us. Perhaps we can see that actually everything we wear, or use, comes from the natural world: our glasses, the soap we use for our showers, our shoes, our underwear…

If we begin to see that all these parts come from a sum that pulses with infinities and wonders, life and vibrancies, matter, and molecular movements, then perhaps we might draw near to the earth and see God in all of it. We might see that the universe sustains us daily, for an eternity before us and for an eternity after us, offering us life in fullness that reciprocates and recycles through various forms of life.

We must detach ourselves from a barren life miserably located in prayer to a mighty God with whom we bargain for a good life. We must disentangle ourselves from metaphysical forms of good and evil, blaming this or that in order to find a solution to our inexplicable misery. We can draw near to the natural world and refrain from our narcissism and self-enclosed attention; we can draw near to a more expansive and attentive notion of life and relation--even if it starts from our phones.

Let us call these small movements eco-liturgical liberation Pantheologies--movements, gestures, and rituals where our connection to the natural world is always present in some way or another. We begin by freeing time and space for rituals, making the abstract concrete. Time is not a neutral space where vague things might occur, we are not under the control of an unmovable mover without agency, only waiting for his arrival! No, time marks the earth's life, and we are a fundamental part of it. With the arrival of the anthropocene, we are affecting time in various ways. To free time from its abstraction, we need to move away from the swallowing machine of capitalism that turns everything into the same and attend to the earth's time and how many forms of lives are affected by time. The earth has a pace, the timing patterns of the universes and their relation with planets also mark and change our lives too.

Marcia Bjornerud calls us time illiterate but asks for a sense of timefulness. She says:

> *Like inexperienced but overconfident drivers, we accelerate into landscapes and ecosystems with no sense of their long-established traffic patterns, and then react with surprise and indignation when we face the penalties for ignoring natural laws. Timefulness includes a feeling for distances and proximities in the geography of deep time. Focusing simply on the age of the Earth is like describing a symphony in terms of its total measure count. Without time, a symphony is a heap of sounds; the durations of notes and recurrence of themes give it shape. Similarly, the grandeur of Earth's story lies in the gradually unfolding, interwoven rhythms of its many movements, with short motifs scampering over tones that resonate across the entire span of the planet's history.*[27]

Along with the wonder of the planet's history and its relationship with time in the place of the Milky Way, inside other universes, we must see time, not only through the lens of God's salvation history, but also through the lenses of colonialism and capitalism which have uprooted us and placed us in a system of competition where we devour each other. In a form of mutual destruction, we desecrate what was sacred, betraying the very creation of the earth, the constitution of our bodies and our relations to other beings. When we look at our future, we must see the inexorable movement toward climate change, global warming, and the destruction of all life. Knowing this, we must locate ourselves in our time, the time of the Anthropocene, paying attention to its past and future. If we can do this, what does it do to our religions, our history and religious practices, and our sacred texts and commitments?

Along with time, we must recommit to space--to the earth--and retake the control of space against all abstraction: the abstraction of a transcendent God without place who is not committed to the wellbeing of the earth; the abstraction of a faith that lies in wait for the end times and signs of the great *parousia*; the abstraction of theology without land as if we don't touch the earth when we write or speak or worship God; the abstraction of the earth as a blue dot in the sky; the abstraction of sacraments and the elements without relation to the earth and to the rhythms of so many other more than human beings who participate in the assemblages of the Christian assemblies; the abstraction of worship that denies the full embodiment of God out of fear of a collapsed immanence; the abstraction of living as if our homes are above the earth and only constructed of neighborhoods, cities and countries, connecting to any real patch of land; the abstraction of religious buildings on private property that forget and deny the land; the abstraction of prayers that are fancy illusions of transcendence; the abstraction of the earth as an endless resources for our consumption, tourism, and fulfillment; the abstraction of Indigenous territories and sovereignty in order to signify national values, patriotic symbols and control over the land.

Dona Haraway suggests that the concept of nature/natural is always something produced, so that the notion of space is also produced.[28] Thus, our task is how to ecologize thinking, not to just keep modernizing it. Modernity divides everything, but this is a false understanding! Instead, the concatenations of things at different places with so many distinctions and differences come from the vastness of the universe as webs and flows of energies, forms, connection, and affections.

Abstractions of time and space must give way to a life that is oriented and guided by the law of the land which comes before and after religious beliefs and commandments. We will have to decolonize our bodies, minds, religious beliefs, and practices, but it can happen if we return to the natural world--the earth that we never actually left. We return to the earth, not as a single living organism, but rather vast immensities with many forms of life, breathing and creating more life in different and unexpected ways. Just look at the diversity of species and plants and flowers, and birds and trees--and ourselves--it is life booming in endless ways!

Bruno Latour offers three questions to help us think about space, time, and identity in order to reconsider our rituals, gestures, words, and ceremonies of remembrance.

Space: Where are we located?

Time: In which period do we find ourselves?

Identity: Who are we? What sort of agency do we possess? How do we cope with such novelty? How do we make sure we do not behave too badly in this existential crisis, one that is a matter of life and death?[29]

These questions are fundamental to us if we are to respond to the disasters and catastrophes of our time. If we are to answer these questions from our traditional Christian theologies, that is easy:

Time: We are in a time of here and not yet. We live under God's grace hoping for the day of resurrection. The history has a *telos*, Jesus is coming, and we are going to live in heaven.

Space: Wait, space? What for? What does space have to do with my faith?

Identity: In baptism I gain a new identity, I am a Christian.

With climate collapse, we need a different theological language to answer these questions.

Time: We are now living in the Anthropocene, capitolocene, plantationocene, *Chthulucene*.[30] The eschatology we learned emphasizing the end times only contributes to worsen climate collapse. The end times are not signs of God's coming; they are signs of our negligence, uprootedness, and irresponsibility.

Space: we have been detached from land. The only space we are aware of is the sacredness of the sanctuary of our churches or the private lands of our homes and public squares. Every place we go, we need to remind ourselves that we live in Gaia, Pachamama, a system capable of action and reaction. On the patches of land where we live, we must make common space for humans and more than humans together. Space, deeply marked by capitalism and colonialism, is open for new stories, creations, and possibilities for new worlds.

Identity: Fundamentally, we are stardust, the memory of the pluriverses, complex beings encompassing many other foreign species living within us, wonderfully making us who we are. Our identity is weirdly made of symbiosis, and we must know the forms of agencies of other species giving us identity as human. We attest to the formation of our racial, sexual and class exploitations that keep trying to rip apart the deeper tissues of mutuality and belonging with each other and earthlings. Our liberation is the liberation of everything around us! Our identity is about the kinships we make with other species around us. From these biological, racial, cosmological, and cultural *cruzos*, we fight for the plethora of identities that we stand with, in solidarity and reciprocity.

All of this to help us land! For to land as religious creatures, is to land with the divinity in our bodies, in all of these *cruzos*, with a bag of pantheologies in our eyes. Mary-Jane Rubenstein who coined the term *pantheologies* and suggests pluralistic pantheisms, defines pantheologies and asks: "Pantheologies attend not to a deity, but rather to unending sites of divinity that reveal and conceal themselves from an infinite number of perspectives. But the spirit of the question remains: however single or multiple, why appeal to divinity at all?" And she responds:

> *The first would be to claim an affective difference between ascribing agency to intra-connected world-making assemblages and ascribing divinity to them. To call all things divine, one might argue, is to profess a certain humility and awe in relation to them, and thereby to mark them as worthy of reverence.... to recognize all things as divine—not by virtue of some "essence" they share, but in their material particularities—intensifies our sense of relatedness to all things, and this sense can open onto responsibility on the one hand or disavowal on the other.*[31]

As liberation pantheologies must also be attuned to the suffering of other people, human and more than human, we can also quote Rubenstein in her work with Octavia Butler's *Parable of the Sower and Parable of the Talents* and the ways Laurel the main character feels:

> *This extraordinary responsiveness to suffering, which Lauren often simply calls "sharing," provides the visceral basis of the theology around which she eventually gathers the "Earthseed" community she helps deliver northward from the ravaged Los Angeles suburbs: "God is change," she writes, which is to say God is that which makes, unmakes, and remakes all things.*[32]

To understand that God is change, we must also understand that everything has agency! We do not worship a living God while everything else is dead matter. Biologists, cosmologists, geochemists, and botanists tell us time and again: everything has agency! Not just God or us humans! Everything acts and reacts, lives and pulses, and makes decisions! There! There is where we can start regaining our sense of space, time, and identity.

Now we can ask ourselves these questions as they pertain to ritual making and performing ceremony:

> *What does ritual and ceremony mean to you and your community?*

> *Taking into consideration time, space, identity, our relation with the life of the earth, and the suffering of so many people (human and non-*

human), what role can ritual and performances play in making visible the connection of our lives and bodies with the larger earth body and our other-than-human kin?

How can ritual that is earth-based help communities grow and heal in order to dismantle and transform oppressive and unhealthy systems and structures?

Rituals

Rituals are technologies of attention. They are about gestures, performances, and movements in which our bodies tune to what is present and orient themselves to a world to come, even while welcoming the past. Rituals are ways to imagine new worlds through our connection to this world, feel what we fear to feel, catch ourselves by surprise, dig deeper, look out, and remember. Rituals are less about the reification of beliefs and more about discoveries, awareness, and mutuality between persons, humans, trees, plants, rocks, fire, water, earth, wind, water, lizards, frogs, honeyeaters. Rituals are not about production but about relations. Rituals do not produce results; they produce the means to live. Rituals are more related to the order of wonder than the order of accomplishments. Rituals are worlds in action, circumvolving about creation and destruction. Rituals are about attention, about paying attention. I mentioned Jonathan Smith in chapter one:

> *Ritual is, first and foremost, a mode of paying attention. It is a process for marking interest. It is the recognition of this fundamental characteristic of ritual that most sharply distinguishes our understanding from that of the Reformers, with their all too easy equation of ritual with blind and thoroughness habit. It is this characteristic, as well, that explains the role of place as a fundamental component of ritual: place directs attention.*[33]

As our churches flee to suburbia and abandon downtown cities, we reveal who we were hoping to relate with in our spiritual lives. As our urban areas enter decay, churches could not tolerate poor and homeless people so close. The move to suburbia showed that churches do have a clear sense of their space and surrounding areas. However, neither downtown or suburban churches paid attention to the soil as a human kind or to other inhabitants like trees, animals, or refugia. The power dynamics of private property concern churches. Cutting 50 trees for a parking lot did not matter because we were creating a sanctuary to worship God. Everything is permitted for the worship of God, we think! As long as we leave behind a few beautiful trees for beauty, that is good enough.

We need to regain a deep connection with the land, and for that we must think and act in practical ways, acknowledging that everything is alive and has subjectivity. We must develop a new grammar of faith within the living world, a grammar that carries new possibilities that are experimental, creative, and still connected to traditions. This grammar of faith for the living world must listen to more than human relatives and offer provisional answers to what is heard. If faith "comes from what is heard, and what is heard comes through the word of Christ" (Romans 10:17), then we must start listening to the word of Christ in every living thing on earth and every living person that is more than human. As we embody this grammar, we change ourselves daily through rituals that challenge and reshape us by repetition. From this reshaping of our language/body/actions, a new multi-species moral development and ethics are created and formed, where trees and rivers and all living creatures must have a say in the ways we co-inhabit the earth and live together.

This connection might start by being more aware of our food chain. Kimmerer plainly tells us: "Don't buy it. When food has been wrenched from the Earth, depleting the soil and poisoning our relatives in the name of higher yields, don't buy it."[34] As much as possible, we can choose not to buy food that comes from big corporations, that is made with pesticides, that is brought from Peru, that is out of season, or that does not come from small farmers where we live. As we choose to engage in a ritual gesture of contention, avoiding strawberries or asparagus all year long, we then create other modes of being with other assemblages of people and more than human people. We must attend to what the land can or will produce where we live. We need to know what kinds of bees we need, what forms of manure we can use, what kind of composting is necessary, how much water we need, and what to save for the winter. In sum, we must learn to eat and to live what our patch of land gives to us.[35]

With these forms of eating and living how do we compose/compost people and vibrant matter with notions of God, divinities, and sacredness through various forms of hierophanies. For all that that we need new languages, be apophatic, cataphatic and see how these languages affects feelings, movements, thoughts, gestures, and ways of living that expands and connects us with the living natural world.

Rituals connect us with the natural world right here where we are, even if where we are is a concrete floor. Rituals take us beyond the building to feel and touch and see the ways in which the environments we inhabit together are part of symbionts, sharing time, space, and identity together.

Rituals help us to land, to arrive on the ground, inhabiting and cultivating the soil we live. We must make Pierre Bourdieu's notion of *habitus* further to mean dirt, something that Indigenous people have always done. Our *habitus* must mirror the *habitus* of the earth so that our culture--natural world, with all the species and the human world--will be a circular movement, just like the cycles of the moon or the orbit of the earth around the sun. We must connect our habituations with those who are inhabiting the patch of land we are living with, and that takes practice, attention, pause, and learning—or in a word, ritual.

How can nature be here at the city with me? Ritual! Ritual moves us beyond understanding nature as an idealized form of "natural resources" that we use for beauty, and for the contemplation of the sublime. Modernity tells us that nature exists "out there" to help us cope with real life happening "right here". This modern understand of nature, carried deep in our bones and in our faith, has kept us from landing on the earth and from being a full participant with other human kinds. We only use the land as if we do not live or belong in the world. Bruno Latour says it more clearly:

> *It would actually be a fairly good definition of 'modern' people to say that they live off a land that they don't inhabit. At least, they live in between two worlds: one is where they have their habits, the protection of law, their deeds of property, the support of their state, what we could call the world they live in; and then, in addiction, a second world, a ghostly one, often far remote in time and space that benefits from no legal protection, no clear delineation of properties, and no state to defend its rights: let's call it the world they live from. It is out of this second world that modernizers have always extracted the resources necessary to maintain their illusion that they live only in the first, in benign ignorance of the second one. Moderns have always behaved like absentee landlords.*[36]

Latour reminds us of how we relate to the land as a resource we use for living without paying attention to it. The naturalization of the system that Latour describes is what makes us live *from* and *in* the worlds we create. We have created illusions to cope with the immense system of injustices we have built for our comfort.

Rituals as practices can help us understand our positionality in the world and our distance from the earth. Through ritual we can attend to injustices created by our confusion about what we are made of and with whom we embody symbioses and assemblages. Rituals move us into what Haraway calls, *response-ability*.[37] We are *responsible* for the disasters of the Anthropocene and must create *abilities* to change it. We are responsible for other beings and have abilities to sustain human and more than human worlds of living.

Our response-ability to engage with other forms of economy and the law of the land leads to practicing an earthly economy made of gratitude, restoration, and reciprocity. To undo the capitalistic economy of production of means that never ends, has no limits, serves only a few, and is based on the ripping apart and plundering of the earth, Robin Kimmerer suggests the economy of the gift. For her, gratitude plants the seed for abundance. "Gratitude is a powerful antidote to Windigoo psychosis... A deep awareness of the gifts of the earth and of each other is medicine."[38] Harvesting and sharing is fundamental for her people:

> *... they distribute what the earth has graciously given and they dance celebrating the offerings of the earth. Generosity is simultaneously a moral and a material imperative, especially among people who live close to the land and know its waves of plenty and scarcity. Where the well-being of one is linked to the wellbeing of all. Wealth among traditional people is measured by having enough to give away. Hoarding the gift, we become constipated with wealth, bloated with possessions, too heavy to join the dance... We need the berries and the berries need us. Their gifts multiply by our care for them, and dwindle from our neglect. We are bound in a covenant of reciprocity, a pact of mutual responsibility to sustain those who sustain us. And so the empty bowl is filled.*[39]

And this process of economy of gift also entails restoration and healing. She says:

> *How we approach restoration of land depends, of course, on what we believe that "land" means. If land is just real estate, then restoration looks very different than if land is the source of a subsistence economy and a spiritual home. Restoring land for production of natural resources is not the same as renewal of land as cultural identity. We have to think about what land means.*[40]

These forms of relation can change the world and deepen our relation to the places we live.[41] The ways Indigenous people love the land is what we need to learn. Love of the land must be more than a love of liturgies, hymnals, or beliefs! Ritualization can help us learn how to love the earth when we do not know where to start. In recent classes I taught at Union Seminary, I asked students to go around and meet more than human people and greet them. Then I asked them to repeat and change their greetings-- to do better. With that, they were paying attention to somebody else other them themselves and remaking their identity in partnership with other human kinds. None of them were used to these forms of greetings to more than human people. What they showed in class, the practical ways they were relating to the earth, was absolutely fascinating!

Small performances can help us connect. In rituals we remember, create, sing, dance, and live stories. Haraway uses the term Sympoiesis, to refer to a symbiotic way of creating ourselves through theory and storytelling:

> *Science fiction, speculative fabulation, string figures, speculative feminism, science fact, so far.... String figures with the threads of reciprocating energies of biologies, arts, and activisms for multispecies resurgence.... String figures are like stories; they propose and enact patterns for participants to inhabit, somehow, on a vulnerable and wounded earth. My multispecies storytelling is about recuperation in complex histories that are as full of dying as living, as full of endings, even genocides, as beginnings... Refiguring connections.*[42]

String figures can be the juxtaposition of our sacred texts with biological learnings, our songs with the birds' songs, eucharist done on the ground or in a garden, baptisms done at a creek nearby where we care for its cleanliness and for the fishes, rocks, and life. Refiguring connections between the Christian faith and the earth we will build no more church buildings; they will be turned into shelter and local gardens. Our new mission will be how to join people who are fighting for poor people, animals, mountains, and farms. Perhaps our baptism catechumenate could be to learn with Winona LaDuke how to be a water protector.[43]

Perhaps we can learn with Indigenous thinker Tyson Yunkaporta how to inhabit our cosmologies with other stories, other forms of thinking and knowing.[44] As he says, "Indigenous knowledge is not about the what but the how. It is about process not content. Your culture is not what your hands touch or make – it's what moves your hands." He gives instructions: "Now choose four elements from that system to represent the protocols of a complexity agent – connectedness, diversity, interaction and adaptation." He demonstrates it by the fingers of one hand. And it means:

> *Connectedness involves forming pairs with multiple other agents who also pairs with others. The next step is creating or expanding networks of these connections. The final step is making sure these networks are interacting with the networks of other agents, both within your systems and in others.*

Recall the diversity protocol that has three parts – similar to you, different from you and systems beyond you… The interaction protocol is about continuously transferring knowledge, energy, and resources.

The adaptation protocol is about transformation, feedback loops and strange attractors. You must allow yourself to beg transformed through your interaction with other agents…

Put it in other way, these are the main questions to be asked:

What can we know?

What do we know?

How do we know it?

How do we work with that?

The answers we found were as follows:

What we can know is determined by our obligations and relationships to people, Ancestors, land, Law, and creation.

What we know is that the role of custodial species is to sustain creation, which is formed from complexity and connectedness.

The way we know this is through our cultural metaphors.

The way we work with this knowledge is by positioning, sharing, and adapting our cultural metaphors.[45]

One of the many distinct differences between Indigenous knowledges and religious knowledges is that Indigenous knowledges are based on practices and religious knowledges are based on belief. That is one of the hardest shifts for Christian liturgical theologians if we are to engage in eco-liturgical liberation pantheologies. That is, to engage practices not from *a priori* beliefs, but practices created from the attention and perception in meeting and living with other beings in different places.

How can these practices with rivers, trees, mountains, and birds help create a cosmology that will entail so other forms of life where God will be found? Will it shake the Christians faith as we know it? Perhaps. But if Christians believe God is life, then there is nothing to fear. In liturgies that honor the earth, or as Larry Rasmussen says, "earth honoring faith,"[46] we will give up too many words for enfleshment in movement! Instead of sermons proposing an ethical life, forms of relation that ensure ethical relationship with animals and other beings will be done.

Instead of endless theological propositions we will have greetings, gift-exchanges, stories, metaphors, dances. Baptism will honor the rivers and we will promise to be water warriors. The doing of the eucharist will acknowledge a deep correlation with agricultural practices and our ways of tending the land and producing food for all so no one goes hungry. The food chain that produces food for our celebrations will be known--from when the seeds go into the soil and all the way until it arrives in our hands. Perhaps, we will be able to think of theology the way anthropologist Eduardo Viveiros de Castro thinks of anthropology: "The peoples of the world live through practice, in practice and for practice."[47]

To learn such a *different* kind of knowledge is to change things in us, around us and allow ourselves to be changed for the love of God and for the love of the land. The wealth of wisdom and practice of Yunkaporta suggests how rituals (cosmological practices) can orient theology (cosmological stories). There are so many *string figures* we can work with and juxtapose to the Christian faith. For Haraway, it matters with whom and what we use to know *how* things work. Haraway says:

> *It matters what ideas we use to think other ideas (with)… It matters what matters we use to think other matters with; it matters what stories we tell to tell other stories with; it matters what knots knot knots, what thoughts think thoughts, what descriptions describe descriptions, what ties tie ties. It matters what stories make worlds, what worlds make stories.*[48]

One of our joys in ritualizing is to name things. Naming can shift and change and move and transform ourselves and our patch of land around us. Naming calls upon people and memories, actions, and thoughts to evoke feelings and awareness. Naming our relations can make us start thinking and believe differently. As Haraway says. "Like all offspring of colonizing and imperial histories, I—we—have to relearn how to conjugate worlds with partial connections and not universals and particulars."[49]

We must learn how to survive in the debris of capitalism and colonization as Indigenous people, Black people, and Palestinians have showed us. In the fundamental action of gift exchange, we sustain life in places where it can be developed, keep the light on where there is need for light, keep the darkness where darkness is needed, protect worlds threatened by destruction, caring for environments as we care for people.

Rituals can be a privileged place for new cosmologies to be enacted and generate heterogeneities, involving spaces and time, identities, the social conditions of more than humans with us, rituals create new cosmologies where symbiotic actants from a patch of land are a part of the assembly of all beings. As Ronald Grimes says:

> *Religious ritual is the predication of identities and differences (metaphors) son profoundly enacted that they suffuse bone and blood, thereby generating a cosmos of metaphor. Ritually, people do not dance merely to exercise limbs or to impress ticket-buyers with their skills or even to illustrate sacredly help belief. Ritualists dance, rather, to discover ways of inhabiting a place. This is the noetic, or the divinatory, function of the ritual: ritual helps people figure out, divine, even construct a cosmos. A cosmos is not merely an empty everywhere. It is everywhere as perceived from somewhere, a universe as construed from a locale. A cosmos is a topocosm, a universe in this place, an oriented, 'cosmolosized' place, a this-place which is also an ever-where. Cosmologies are important for what they tell ritualists not to perform as for what they tell them to perform.*[50]

In this process of ritualizing, we learn through Indigenous people how to live with more than human people, creating new boundaries and protocols and diplomacies. Indigenous cosmologies are part of a thick place where the people live in environments inhabited by different people and more than human people in mutual relation. As Christians begin to do this, we should pause and stop performing until we gain trust of local actants and can expand our contacts with proper protocol.

Last Lent I enacted the stations of the cross with the earth with a group of 40 pastors. We started by approaching a tree near each one's house and started to develop a relationship, learning how to greet, how to communicate, what to offer, and how to listen. As we continued, we were able to expand our relationship to other beings around and above the tree. With that small gesture our cosmologies started to grow, and abundant relationships started to appear! A new and deeply moving grammar of faith was composed! We became companions to the trees as the trees became companions to us. As our relationships continue, perhaps we will sing with the birds and feed them, dance at the river, care for the trees in the whole neighborhood, prohibit business that would destroy the environment, work against industries that are poisoning the rivers, run in zigzags with the squirrels, hear the sound of an owl, pay attention to the moisture of the soil, and care for the worms. Our new companions, whose friendship expands the circle of relationship and companionship—*God abounds! Alleluia!*

Let us delve into becoming with other species and do away with our human exceptionalism. As Haraway says; "Companion species are relentlessly becoming-with. The category companion species helps me refuse human exceptionalism without invoking posthumanism."[51] Haraway says this of Isabelle Stengers that should be at the core of our ritual ethical work: "[Isabelle Stengers] maintains that decisions must take place somehow in the presence of those who will bear their consequences. That is what she means by cosmopolitics."[52]

In this way, rituals move us to pay attention and to open space for the creation of pluriverses and the collective compositions of many strange and funny new stories, new and strange knowledges, unknown songs and unexpected gestures weaving lives together with symbiotic gatherings, breathing together with all the different species in entangled worlds.

Emergent Strategy

I first heard of emergent strategy from the forest church in Ethiopia. Emergent strategy is a way to engage the pluriverses through small actions, which is akin to rituals. We start small, in small relations, small utterances, small naming, and evoking new worlds to inhabit our worlds. Adrienne Maree Brown writes of how emergent strategy can help us, "for building complex patterns and systems of change through relatively small interactions, is to me—the potential scale of transformation that could come from movements intentionally practicing this adaptive, relational way of being, on our own and with others."[53] Brown defines emergent strategy in this way:

> Emergence is the way complex systems and patterns arise out of a multiplicity of relatively simple interactions"—I will repeat these words from Nick Obolenksy throughout this book because they are the clearest articulation of emergence that I have come across. In the framework of emergence, the whole is a mirror of the parts. Existence is fractal—the health of the cell is the health of the species and the planet. There are examples of emergence everywhere. Birds don't make a plan to migrate, raising resources to fund their way, packing for scarce times, mapping out their pit stops. They feel a call in their bodies that they must go, and they follow it, responding to each other, each bringing their adaptations.[54]

If we are to live the incarnation of Christianity in its fullness we must recognize the body in relation with other bodies, skin rubbing against other skins, and turn these encounters into rituals in which we participate.

If we are to answer the call of the earth to respond to the pain and hurt of our time, we must listen to the natural world and respond by learning how people in the natural world live and adapting to a fuller life together.

This strategic emergence must also be a form of laughter, moving through climate disasters and losses and extinction with a sense of humor and irony. It was amidst my deepest fears of climate change that a clown was reborn within me. My Clown Pachamama is now learning about the natural world and this book is my way of finding language for it. I feel like a clumsy clown walking through the world as I write--I need to lose my heightened sense of awareness so I can clown around here. I must learn how to tell this disastrous news to my kids and make them laugh as they hear it. They will live in a much more devastating world than I have.

I must tell them to keep laughing because laugher is the only way out. Joy is what keeps us standing. To be silly is to create a form of resistance that looks weak but carries intensity and resilience in it. I have to tell them to wonder so they can keep the world going around. Again, and again, I must tell them to laugh for laughter is a way transgress the world of seriousness and terrible news. Laughter is to refuse to give up! They must search for the people, human and more than human, who can make them laugh, for they are the ones we need the most. We can surely live without theologians, but we cannot live without clowns, the fun of cubs and animals chasing each other, the joy of little birds dancing in the air, the amusement of rain falling in our heads, the beauty of trees dancing with the wind. They all bring us joy and help us laugh. They are the real transgressors, and they are our most fundamental prophets. I talk to the little boy inside of me often. He is the reason I am still alive and continue to smile. Every time the adult shakes, my little boy holds my hand.[55]

As a good clown, this book is an exaggeration. This chapter is an exaggeration. Who can even think of all this silliness? It is neither academic nor non-academic. It is half baked ideas contorted in unspecified language. Take and laugh! Do it in memory of us all, including the natural world. But what I propose resonates with what Ronald Grimes writes of performances in the world's gift economy. He says:

> *Too grandiose, you say? Too full of bilgewater and balderdash? Well, ok. For the likes of us who've made it to the next millennium, it may be that ritual is possible only in a ludic-ironic-metaphoric, clowny-subjunctive-disjunctive fiddledeedee mode. But embraced-to-the-point-of-embodiment, metaphoric-ironic ritualizing, however, perverse and silly, is a way in.[56]*

Emergent strategy will help us ritualize until we are able to find laugher in our belly, connecting our bodies in this deep way to the winds, seasons, needs, wisdom, and funny parrots. Perhaps when our body is so deeply rooted in the places we live, then we can share our mourning, laughter, worries, and dreams with other people, human and more than human. We can laugh and dream with bees, birds, pigs, dolphins, mountains, flowers, creeks, and clouds. Any religion that makes us dream and laugh only about humans is still lacking.

Shaman Yanomami Davi Kopenawa in his book *The Falling Sky: Words of a Yanomami Shaman*, writes about dreaming to everyone who is not Indigenous:

> *Whites only treat us as ignorant because we are different from them. But their thought is short and obscure; it cannot go far and elevate itself, because they want to ignore death. (...) Whites do not dream far like we do. They sleep a lot, but they only dream about themselves.*[57]

Perhaps, to dream we need to pay attention to where we live, learn to ask questions, and perform something new with our bodies and attentiveness. I finish with another question from Ronald Grimes:

> *So again I put it to you: what gesture, rightly performed, might be so compelling that the creatures would be entertained and, thus, the planet saved? We can put it in other, more local ways: what does the south shore of Lake Erie ask of men on Tuesdays? Women on Thursdays? Why is the Rio Grande weeping? Where on Highway Seven should the northbound tundra swans land during the rush hour? I am sure you have your own environmental koans, conundrums in need of direct action but also of divination and contemplation. Just remember that the point is not to turn cute phrases or to moralize but to identity yourself bodily and attitudinally with the questions.*"[58]

Let us just start and learn along the way, and then we will see where we will go.

Appendix

This text was written after we celebrated a worship service at Union Theological Seminary in New York where we confessed to plants. It was the beginning of a transformation for me and my students. This was seen as outrageous and non-Christian for many. However, this is one example of how to live out this chapter in our life together.

Why I Created a Chapel Service
Where People Confess to Plants[59]

Humans are slowly waking up to what seems like a very bad dream. We are in the middle of an expanding climate catastrophe with intense disasters of increasing frequency, glaciers melting, an unimaginable rate of species extinction, and the unprecedented phenomena of forced migration as climate refugees seek new habitats. The situation is desperate and alarming. For the first time, non-Indigenous people confront what Indigenous people experienced when colonizers reached their shores: the imminent end of the known world. As we wake to this hard reality, we are at a loss about how to respond, but we know we must respond.

I am teaching two classes this fall at Union Theological Seminary in New York City — *Creating Rituals in Community: The Work of Mourning the Earth* and *Extractivism: Ripping Earth Apart: A Ritual/Liturgical Response*. These classes are small attempts to respond to our ongoing environmental trauma. In these classes, students create rituals that attend creatively to the end of our lives and respond to our feelings. We are rehearsing the impossible.

Last week our chapel service was called Temple of Confessions. As we gathered in the narthex of James Chapel, I gave an introduction that included these words:

> *Many of us have a disconnected relationship with nature and relate to nature as outside things, as "it." Today we will try to create new connections by talking to the plants, soil, and rocks and confess how we have related with them. Confessions are also forms of mending relations, healing, and changing our ways. We are all manifestations of the sacredness of life and the "we" of God's love is way beyond the human, so let us confess to "each other" including plants, soil, rocks, rivers, forests.*

We processed into the chapel carrying plants and placed them on soil. Immediately people started to come to the plants, to confess their forms of relation or non-relation. One student said something that stuck with me: "I don't know how to relate to you in this subjective way. I am afraid that if I do, I might discover a level of pain that I don't know whether I can bear."

Her reaction sums up the beauty of the ritual. By confessing, we perceive something new. We experience what were once objects of nature – animals, plants, trees, forests — as subjects, with their own full life and experience. They become to us what many sacred scriptures have claimed: a full part of creation, just as we are. And for Christians, who are called to confess their sins, we may take seriously what Jesus said: Therefore, if you are offering your gift at the altar and there remember that your brother or sister has something against you, leave your gift there in front of the altar. First go and be reconciled to them; then come and offer your gift. (Matthew 5: 23-24)

Confession is a basic practice in Christian tradition. It involves vulnerability and requires openness. It invites a response of kindness, empathy, and support. Our confession in the ritual aspired to what all Christian confession promises: healing and transformation. We looked to a new relationship with the earth, and thus with God. Ritual confession involves pausing, listening, and a new way of being. Confession can run the risk of a naïve and sentimental idealizing of the earth and of nature, but this practice sought something deeper — to expand faith as we recognize the interdependence of life and relinquish the death-dealing habits of our human autonomy in relation to our mastery over the natural world.

For some Christians, the message of this confession is a bitter pill to swallow. Christianity, as it formed in the West, too often took on the mantle of Empire, allied itself with a succession of projects of world-mastery and dominium through colonization, the slave trade, industrialization, capitalism, extraction, and imprisonment.

From the point of view of dominant forms of modern Christian practices, the material world must be dominated and explored solely to fulfill our desires. The sources of our disembodied spirituality were drawn from a spiritualized God who resided most often within our confused sense of selves. In this self-referential way, the "exteriority" of the earth could be excluded as a spiritual source of wisdom and strength. Religions that fostered a connection to the earth were labeled pagan or pantheistic and anathematized.

But if Christians were to turn to their Bibles and some of their saints, they might find that confessing to plants is not quite as obscene as one might think. The Bible is filled with stories and images of the elements of nature as persons, who speak and who are spoken to.

Psalm 19 tells us, "The heavens are telling the glory of God; and the firmament proclaims God's handiwork."

Psalm 148 summons the extremes of the inhabited world to sing forth: "Praise God, sun and moon … all you shining stars! Praise the Lord from the earth, you sea monsters, and all deeps, fire and hail, snow and frost, stormy wind fulfilling his command! Mountains and all hills, fruit trees and all cedars! Wild animals and all cattle, creeping things and flying birds!"

The Bible resists the idea that non-human life is extraneous to our deepest religious experience. Instead, it helps open us up to a more complex understanding of who we are. As creatures in and of the earth, we are all inextricably bound together in a web of life, as organisms deeply entangled in ecological community, composing, and composting the immensity of who we are, together.

From this point of view, I gain a spiritual appreciation of interdependence, of a mutual otherness. Without coral reefs, I cannot breathe. Without seeds I starve. Without rocks stable under my feet, I collapse. Without trees I cannot have water. Without the miraculous balance of the interconnection of life, I cannot survive. Body and spirit together come together with the earth.

To be reconciled is the only way not to be penalized by the fire of hell or the fire of this global warming. Romans 8:22 says "We know that the whole creation has been groaning in labor pains until now." This pain has been increased exponentially. to the point of our death.

When we confess to plants, to forests, to each tree, every meadow, to birds, fish, rocks, animals, rivers, and mountains, we repent, mourn, and reconnect ourselves to a much larger web of life, made of people, animals, creatures, and ecosystems that we have lost and stripped away from our common home. Understanding this demands a reinterpretation of democracy. When are we going to consider the seeds and the panther and the zebras and the cows and horses as part of our democracy?

Christianity's primary allegiance in the Anthropocene is with racialized capitalism and its financial markets under the sign of an exceptional patriotism. The fierce sense of coloniality within Christianity as dominion continues to give shape to our present forms of perception and of being that encompass extraction, development, richness, and the nation-state. At its best, our worship challenges such allegiance and is a manifestation of God's love that goes deep and wide, transcending ourselves until we are fully embodied in the complex and diverse ecosystems of the earth and the cosmos.

Then, perhaps, we will start living, and dreaming, with the earth.

CHAPTER FOUR

Worship, Liturgy and Public Witness[1]

Chris Immanuel Bollam, 9 years old

Do not build on the good old days, but on the bad new ones.

Walter Benjamin

Introduction

The liturgical/worship aspect of the Christian faith is fundamental for any public theology. Christian worship entails a certain posture in society, one that organizes, produces and disseminates a collective form of living. Rituals mirror societal structures myriad ways, but many theologies do not engage the liturgical space as a fundamental part of their theological doing--the *quehacer teológico*--because theology is usually related to thinking and not doing. As an important liberation theologian in the United States said: when theologians attend church, they should sit on the back seat.

The liturgical space reveals dichotomies and division in much of our theological and liturgical thinking: praxis does not belong to the doxa; liturgy is a self-enclosed event; mission is what the church does outside; the inside of the church shows how to live outside but the inside of the worship space should be protected from the outside by stained glass. For many in the liturgical field, liturgy can only be understood by liturgical things, one next to the other. The preaching is explained by the eucharist, confession by baptism and so on. J.M.R. Tillard illustrates this self-referential logic perfectly: "The eucharist is explained by the church and the church is explained by the eucharist."[2] In other words, the church can be explained only by its own internal logic and holy things, and that is perhaps one of the reasons we need public theology.

The definition of *liturgy*, the work of the people, has become the work of specialists who define what, when and how the people are supposed to engage in that work. Liturgical meaning is a circular movement, with the ritual organized around interior symbols and traditions. Gordon W. Lathrop, one of the most brilliant liturgical theologians of our time, uses notions of juxtapositions and maps to claim that meaning and structure are all inside of the liturgical grounds. He says:

The thesis operative here is this: Meaning occurs through structure, by one thing set next to another. The scheduling of the ordo [i.e., written directions about what service to schedule at what time or what specific rite, scripture readings, or prayers to use, and the suppositions which underlie those directions], the setting of one liturgical thing next to another in the shape of the liturgy, evokes and replicates the deep structure of biblical language, the use of the old to say the new by means of juxtaposition.[3]

The problem with this conception of liturgy is that it works from an already made meaning that we must only reenact when we worship. The operative assumption that underlines its structure is that meaning in worship is only constructed from within the given limits of the field.

Liturgy then is the doing of the proper liturgy already thought and defined, be it time, space, practices, words, that, if properly ritualized, will inherently bring the proper meaning of our faith. In other words, if we only name the holy things properly and do them accordingly, the gospel will surely be lived, God will surely be present, and the people of God will surely be renewed. The construction of other liturgical orders and practices, and the engagement with outside sources--political, cultural, and social-economic--runs the risk of creating alternative meaning(s), putting the church at risk of altering, shifting, or losing the proper theological meaning of liturgy and the proper way to worship God.

This constrained form of liturgical thought has consequences for theological and biblical interpretation. The liturgical calendar, biblical interpretation, the use of the lectionary, and all liturgical practices have a precise purpose. The logic of these liturgical sources takes precedence over other forms, ideas, beliefs or feelings in shaping life. The liturgical calendar, while offering Christians a path through the alternating moods and experiences of life, does not give much space to the unpredictable flow of life. The lectionary avoids some challenging texts in the Bible and does not pay attention to new readings of the Bible such as Womanist theologies and the central place of Hagar.

The historical method of reading the Bible takes precedence over other possible interpretations due to its supposedly non-ideological reading of the texts--a constructed theological read centered on universal salvation history, uncritically accepted by liturgical theologians who fail to see the ideological markers of the texts. The doctrine of the two kings still stands as a hidden liturgical politics, maintaining an uncritical posture toward the body of the king. If the historical method criticizes the king, the secular source of power, it does it in a way that its power/format does not need to be changed. Liturgical theologies are *lex credendi* shaping *lex orandi*. The universality of a certain liturgical theology fills a dogma, a (universal) *credere* that precedes feelings (as reason precedes bodies, order precedes justice, concepts precede doings), creates a private sense of public worship (meaning both the inner individual sense of faith and the inward ritualization of the faith by a group), and avoids the public demands and necessary changes required by this very faith.

Liturgies fulfill the logic of dogmatics, while liturgical theologies explain their systematic underpinning. Liturgies and theologies occur within the confines of the church walls with the assumption that public/secular powers will follow our lead. Perhaps this troublesome relationship between private/public worship and private/public politics witnesses to the fact that we must create and engage our liturgical theologies more clearly by naming, taking sides, and claiming our power.

It is redundant to call theology public, since every theology is necessarily public, even those marked "private" for the church only.

Public vs. Private Worship:
A Too Brief Historical Account

The gospel of Jesus Christ is a common good, similar to God's grace and the natural resources available to all of humanity. As the community of the Kin-dom of God, the church announces that we all carry the *imago Dei,* properly reflected when we live in a fair and equal manner, with equal chances and common limits. From the first churches we learn that it is crucial to share: anything belongs to anyone, and everything belongs to everyone. No one needs to suffer more than others since our resources belong to one another. As the church of Jesus Christ today, we live and proclaim this utopia. There is a demand upon us as the church to announce a collective gospel, a gospel that teaches us that life can only be lived fully if shared in love, the love of God, with all its limits, demands and responsibilities.

However, this aspiration of a public, common way of living has not always been realized. Every theology is necessarily public, but when we give theology a proper name, "public theology", the word "public" must be checked, developed, and defined. Also, we must engage with its pair, or opposite term, i.e., the "private" that the public is struggling against. In very broad strokes, liturgical Christian history can be divided between private and public worship and testimony. Christianity began with secret gatherings due to persecution. Using Greco-Roman banquets as ritual-cultural structures to celebrate the new faith, the Christian faith was shaped by a variety of ritual orders organized around a circular movement of public and private prayers and beliefs.[3] The *lex orandi* and *lex credendi,* the law of prayer and the law of belief, attend to the fact that the inward and outward worlds of this faith were in constant mutation and transition. With the arrival of Emperor Constantine in the 4th century, Christian gatherings moved from catacombs to public areas, from houses to basilicas, from secret to public events. This shift changed the sense of being church and the Christian faith's relationship to power. In the beginning, the

Christian faith was a threat to power; after Constantine, the church became the social structure through which the Roman Empire organized itself. The meaning of baptism transformed from a ritual to belong to the family of God to a ritual to become citizens of the Empire.

The intertwining of church and imperial leadership during this time, and the consequent expanded access to power, forever complicates the ways Christians deal with the public and private. The liturgical autonomy of local churches diminished as new centers of power reinforced relations between church and imperial leadership, and this was reflected in common forms of worship. Bishops and popes were entangled in an endless game of power with emperors and kings. Consequently, it is impossible to determine "authentic" or "original" forms of prayers and beliefs; historical power dynamics played, out through creeds and concilia, define the directions of the church and reveal its relation to the powers that be.

Liturgical space created and reflected the notion of the sacred and the hierarchy of power. When the naves of basilicas were shaped, the worship space differentiated between the sacred space, where the people stood, and the sacred of the sacred, where priests and bishops move. The altar became the high place where God manifested Godself. Whoever inhabited this space possessed religious and civil power.

During the Middle Ages, the Roman Catholic Church created private masses that excluded the people: *missa privata sine populo*. Private masses were often used to negotiate power, money, and privileges; secrecy has always been a tool of the powerful. Vatican II abolished the *missa privata/secreta* and only public masses can now be celebrated. However, another liturgical practice, the private confession, is still in use, which complicates public notion of faith. As Michel Foucault's *History of Sexuality* reminds us, Christian confession is a church apparatus of control, obedience and power that entangles the western imaginary and behavior.[4] Both mass and confession are filled with specific theologies and liturgical practices that define both the private and the public sphere of the Christian faith.

The advent of the Reformation, with Martin Luther and John Calvin, redefined the public and the private as God's "real" presence moved from the Eucharistic Altar to the inside of the believers heart.[5] Luther's doctrine of the priesthood of all believers opened up the possibility of shifting the exteriority of the faith to the interiority of the believer, thus shifting power and control.[6] The public and the private became more complex since inner faith could now only find its full meaning in the outward manifestation and celebration of the public gathering of the congregation. When that happened, countries that rejected the control or influence of the Roman Catholic Church embraced the Reformation movement.

Recent re-formations of the Christian faith have further complicated the public and the private. To name a few: a) popular Roman Catholic religiosity where poor people use their daily elements and symbols along with the authentic symbols of the Christian faith to compose a mixed expanded faith, through a new variety of personal/collective, private/public liturgical practices troubling the sense of what is public and what is private in the faith; b) some protestant churches have turned their faith, preaching, liturgical practices and hymnody into a more inward private matter detached from a political face, privatizing a faith that avoids the public while fundamentally shaping the public. In this formulation of Christianity all that matters is the feeling of God inside, where believers fully believe, feel, and spiritually engage God, whom they do not see, while they simultaneously fail to engage with the political problems that deeply affect their lives; c) other forms of Christianity, such as prosperity gospels, have been fundamentally shaped by the economic market. Preaching and liturgical practices bargain away the sacred symbols of God. Laying claim to the riches of wealthy people, pastors get rich while lay people continue to be oppressed in a circular movement that perpetuates the system of oppression in order to keep believers excluded from the economic and symbolic system.

Through this too short history, the very notion of the public and the private becomes complex. At each historical moment we see the creation of different symbols, theological narratives, a sense of the subject/faith participant, a different allegiance to God and different notions of private and public. Liturgies favor or condemn the state according to the theologies developed by their leaders and confessions. They create resistance and affirm public policies according to the necessity of their own demands. Private and public desires in a private/public faith always work in tandem, with or against, the economic order. In our present age, our challenge is to create public liturgies that engage the public illusions of neoliberal economies so that minorities can find ways to survive and thrive. To us falls the task of creating public symbols, narratives and norms that will sustain private/public hopes, limit and discipline the desires of a public/private faith and commit ourselves to those who the gospel centers: the afflicted, the naked, the prisoner, the elderly, the outcast, the poor. We must also re-create or invent liturgical practices that resist public policies that work in favor of a private religion/faith that only serves the powerful.

Public Liturgical Theologies:
(Lack of) Definition, Criticism, and Possible Alternatives

How are we to think about a public liturgical theology when the modern sense of the state is shifting rapidly? The public norms of protestant churches no longer include protest, and they fail to influence peoples lives; the pauperization of the world is growing exponentially, the ecological crisis is insurmountable, and the church does not care or notice; the idea of the modern has been detached from the light that created the possibilities of reasoning and sovereignty; democratic states have been replaced by the massive control of neo-liberal unregulated markets; individual desires are locked into lack and consumerism; the real and the virtual still remain undefined fields; the mission(s) of the church haven't been able to encompass a response to the uneven power dynamics of its own structures and the world; the massive exclusion of people from our societies leads to desperate poverty and genocide; racial and patriarchal systems remain at the heart of Christian institutions; the colonization process in the 21st century seems to be far more robust and pernicious and complicated than the colonization of the last 500 years.

How, then, do we think about a public liturgical theology? How can the private/public witness of the Christian faith engage the thousands of (dis)connections of the public/private relations of powers in our societies right now and offer a gospel that can provide hope, create resilience, provoke resistance, and engage in transformation? How can such a theology offer redemption in a world without redemption?

To answer these questions, we must understand the commitments of public liturgical theologies. If we take the meaning of our worship from the Westminster Catechism we must grapple with God's love.[7] The starting point of any public theology must be a clearer sense of what "public" means, as well as with whom and to whom we are making a commitment. In other words, the liturgical quest here is where and with whom do we pray? The answer will decide what we believe and what liturgical theology we are offering.

Public theology, a relatively new development, has to do, according to David Tracy, with "three distinct and related social realities: the wider society, the academy, and the church."[8] Expanding the realm of theology, public theology has added to the theological debate critical notions of citizenship, the place of the state and the role of law, the discussion of secularism and the dichotomy between the secular and the sacred in our societies and universities, theology as a fundamental science always in creative dialogue with other disciplines, discussion of public education, dialogue with Pentecostalism and other religions, relevant political issues of the moment, and the challenges of working within the macro and the microphysics of power simultaneously.

In places like South Africa and Brazil, public theologians work with, and also move beyond, liberation theologies to create a more engaging form of theology. Public theology rises out of liberation theologies while claiming to provide a more nuanced theological discourse. In this process, some thinkers in Latin America (fundamentally Brazil and also beginning in Argentina) criticize, sometimes naively and superficially, the rigidity of the commitments of liberation theologies. They say that liberation theologies are fossilized in one reading of reality and do not offer a larger field of knowledge for the *quehacer teológico*. Public theologians have not been attentive to the new and vast development of recent liberation theologies. Public theology has offered more possibilities to publicly engage issues of concern to the people.

Theologian Alonso Gonçalves from Brazil defines public theology this way: "the idea is to articulate theology with issues that affect people as a whole, being accessible to all in the public sphere... That's the challenge. The words involved in this project are converge, dialogue, adapt."[9]

The so-called "social democratic" proposal of Gonçalves, as is true for many public theologians, engages with an expanded view of life, citizenship and broader concerns. People as a whole and the general public square are fused into a category that is difficult to read or to define. This puts public theology at risk since its desire to include plural sources, theories, symbols, and public themes at a societal level may lose focus on specific contextual situations or the ability to develop a more sustained argument on issues that are emerging in our societies.

Moreover, the choice of key words--converge, dialogue, adapt-- raises further concerns. These words were selected by people with choice and voice, who are included in the larger society, and are able to enter societal discussions. Thus, we must ask: converge where? dialogue with whom? and adapt what and to what? It is no surprise that public theologians have made an assertion that public theology is in solidarity with the poor. However, by not taking a clear stance on the side of the poor in a more sustainable way, public theology does with the poor what it does to most other issues: it passes by them without engaging more deeply in biblical interpretation, theological thinking, public commitments, etc.

The fundamental claim of openness to difference, diversity while engaging conflict, plural spaces for all, and heterogeneities,[10] runs the risk of not creating a space for anybody except those who can afford this sense of pluralism. This creates a naïve middle-class sense of what is public and avoids the conflicts of social class and the voracious appetite of economic elites. Public theology is still problematically located primarily in universities/seminaries where theologians engage local manifestations without living the situations of the poor.

Nancy Cardoso Pereira from Brazil engages public theology and Alonso Gonçalves's definition quoted above. She says:

> *What "as a whole" means? Accessible to all? As if we were all arranged on the social fabric defined as public sphere, magically equalized by some good manners of a tired theology! To converge? Not really! The elites accumulate and expel! To dialogue? Not really! The state kills, the media lies and the market consumes us! To adapt? Ah... that is enough! There is much laziness and unwillingness in such little theology!!*[11]

Any public theology that wants to exist and expand its criticism must own its stance with regards to the poor. Solidarity at a distance is not enough. While engaging some public themes, the disconnection from the systemic conditions that create these themes and situations dilutes public theology's potency. Moreover, if public theology wants to be viable, it must engage fully the economic structures of our society. It is the elites and their economic hold that sustain oppression. If that is not named and engaged, public theology will be like navigating in a small boat across the sea, while the poor swim unprotected next to a thousand hungry sharks. Public theology must engage in public movements of resistance with the poor and propose changes to the structures of the church and its hierarchy. If public theology wants to make a difference, it must work in solidarity with the Basic Communities in Latin America, the Landless Movement in Brazil, the apartheid struggle in South Africa, the Umbrella movement in Asia, the Via Campesina and other pre-existing movements, to name and resist the racial economic patriarchal apartheid still rampant throughout the world. The neo-liberal market must be duly criticized for what it does, especially to those for whom the gospel has a preference: the least of these.

My criticism of public theology can easily be considered unfair, treating public theology as reductionist, which is exactly what public theology is trying to avoid. Any theological endeavor, including public theology, that does not have the poor as its main subject and concerns, is destined only for the academy and for middle class theologians who deal theoretically with the theological field. It will propose surface changes that will sustain access to goods and knowledge for a certain class of people, and it will only offer lip service to the poor while fundamentally maintaining the power dynamics and imbalance of our societies.

Thus, every theology, especially a public theology, must start by acknowledging where and with whom its discourse/practice starts so we know how to name the desire for God, where and how we pray, how to read the Bible, what to claim from this reading, what to sing and what to resist. Emmanuel, God at the margins, with us. If I am critical of public theology is because I want it to move toward the places where the poor live. Theology should start from where it hurts, among those who are despised in our society, those who make up the official garbage list of society: Black and Indigenous people, the poor, the unemployed, battered women, prisoners, queer people and those who cannot consume. From those places, from the refugee camp, private and public prisons, public squares with spikes everywhere so the poor cannot lay their heads, from the outskirts of society where none of us live and are scared to drive by, yes…it is from these places that we have to figure out how to pray and worship God, how to interpret the Bible, decide what songs to sing, discern what to ask for forgiveness, choose what to eat and at whose table, learn how to use the water for Baptism, and how to be sent forth into the world. From these places we can create many public liturgical theologies.

Public liturgical theology must foster necessary sustenance, conflict, and resistance, and promote social transformation by rehearsing it together every time we gather. Liturgical things may or may not converge, dialogue, adapt. The point is to get beyond that. We must converge people and resources to benefit the lives of the poor. Our dialogue must be with poor people of any religion, quasi-religion or no religion, because a dialogue with the powerful can only happen after they give up their possessions. Then, and only then, they can join the church and become disciples of Jesus Christ. We must adapt to the cries of the poor, the homeless, the abandoned, Black, Indigenous and Palestinians people until their lives matter! Instead of Gonçalves choice of words, namely "converge, dialogue, adapt," the motto of the Landless Movement (MST) in Brazil: "occupy, resist, produce." will sustain our worship to God, from beginning to end. The ways we shape our worship services locally, in autonomous ways, while in the midst of global forces, will define our testimony, public beliefs and commitments, and from there, where our feet meet the ground, with the people we decide to be with, we can create another thousand possibilities for public liturgical theologies that will address the issues at stake in each local (global) parish.

Forms of Public Liturgical Theologies

Instead of considering how we should begin to worship, we must ask where are we meeting to worship God? Our place will guide our prayers and our location will inform the shape of our faith. Each worship space is a territory, marked by social, economic and class signs.[12] Worship spaces in suburban areas or away from the poor already mark a certain mission of the church and define the identity of the group. Thus, our places will already define what kind of public theology we are offering and what kind of witnessing to Jesus we are committed to. When we gather, who owns the land where we are honoring God? Whose Indigenous people was this land stolen from? What colonial power has given the ownership of a worship space that owns a private space now? What social, class, or identity group owns this territory?

Here we find a conundrum: if the worship of God is a public event, open for all, how can some people own it? Why is this place under the ownership of a certain religious private society? If we have holy things within this space understood as Christian common goods fundamentally belonging to God (and thus to the people of God), why is the space locked away from their free use and access? If these gifts were freely given by God to the people of God, why do only some people have access to it? What is at stake in the constitution of our faith, in the confessionality of our beliefs and belongings, our creeds and major theological tenets, directed by our churches and constituting public access to religious sources and to the holy of holies? Access to holy things mirrors the access we establish in our societies, and the corresponding privatization of the common goods of God.

At the heart of the holy things, there is a clear sense of the private and the public even though these gifts are offered publicly. Every "citizen" of the Christian family lives in a territory demarcated by baptism, and by the inside space that defines the holy. If one wants to have access to holy things one must be formally trained and given permission to touch, access and distribute the holy commons.

However, at the heart of the Christian faith there is a radical criticism to any tradition or established power, to any ownership, to any privatization of the faith. Nobody owns Christianity but anyone can belong, in more than one way, and beyond the proper documentation of citizenship. Liturgy must get rid of the dogma so it can propose something to live by, even a dogma! The liturgical moment is fundamentally a critical time to decenter faith, even if it is itself a center for the faith of the believer at that moment. As Jaci Maraschin, one of the most important liturgical theologians of Latin America said:

> *The liturgical moment is always a kind of center where the memory of the divine lives in the past, faces the challenges and the exigencies of what is to happen. If the gathering emerges from tradition but does not close itself to this tradition, its very nature is to be open to what has not yet happened, and it turns tradition into a model for the future with the clear presupposition of criticism. That is why the judgment of the present proceeds from the celebration of what happened in times*

of liberation and it is animated by the hope of what might happen because of our commitment to this common decision... But what kind of gatherings do we have now? Assemblies eaten away by the commitment to the powers of this world and captive of the social, political and economic system in which we live. That is why, in general, the liturgical gatherings become tiresome, devoid of the vital element that would make them exulting in joy and interpreters of reality.[13]

Freed from the heavy weight of the past, and yet committed to the divine memory that liberated and continues to liberate us, we will be critical of our present and from that criticism we will discover the joy that comes from the Spirit!

Thus, the call to worship issued at the beginning of our worship service will announce that our love of God has to do with people more than doctrines, loving our neighbors in such a way that we will seek for justice more than anything else! We will make sure we are all alive and well, and then we will attend to and transform our beliefs as we are transformed by the gospel into people who will turn our possessions, ourselves and the common good back to each other. Nothing is ours! Neither our faith nor our hopes nor our lives and not even our God! Then God and everything else can belong to everyone!

A place where we are demanded to love

What gathers us together is God's love. We are first called by God, we were named before time immemorial, we came from the love of God who loves us all without distinction. It is this love that issues a demand on us: we must love one another. The two main commandments given by Jesus have to do with love: to love God and to love one another (Matthew 22:36-40, 1 John 4:20-21). The word "worship" means "worship, worthiness, honor." To worship is to ascribe worthiness, or honor, to somebody or something. In the same way I honor God I must honor my neighbor because of the mutuality between God and my neighbor. My public worship comes from love, and it offers love back to God. At the same time, this love/honor offered to God demands that I also love/honor those around me. It is a radical call to equality. Any private sense of this faith crumbles into a public sharing and mutual recognition and transformation. *Ubuntu!* I am because we are, we are because I am.

The fundamental sense of individual/collective, private/public love is not necessarily one of kindness since it follows the one who said that his presence would bring the sword and division.[14] This love breaks down all forms of hierarchy and injustice and demands a radical egalitarian society. As Kierkegaard puts it: "The demand to hate the beloved out of love and in love... So high - humanly speaking to a kind of madness - can Christianity press the demand of love if love is to be the fulfilling of the law."[15] The demand of love is equal honor and justice and there is a plethora of possibilities for how to meet that demand. The basic ground rule, the truth that should hold the worship space, is the demand that there will be no inequality within this nomadic community.

In order for this to happen, the liturgical space should be a foreign space, a third space, a place in between, a space always already public that belongs to a plethora of people, including those who used to live there but who were eliminated by the colonization and economic greed of those who arrived after.

Thirdspace

The worship space is fundamentally a "thirdspace," a space that is both real and imagined, a transient place that checks the formation of identities, memories, belonging, rootlessness, globalization, languages, desires, differences, placelessness and alienating aspects so marked in religious places. The worship space is fundamental to any confession of faith and to a public proposal of how Christians believe societies should be organized. The worship space is not only subject to religious interpretations but also to all of the dynamics of life, with its borders, appropriations and reappropriations, renegotiations and contestations. The worship space as a thirdspace is akin to what Edward W. Soja describes, "as an-Other way of understanding and acting to change the spatiality of human life, a distinct mode of critical spatial awareness that is appropriate to the new scope and significance being brought about in the rebalanced trialectices of spatiality–historicality–sociality."[16]

In one way or another, worship spaces produce and reproduce social dynamics, linguistic relations, governing structures, and capital production, either reiterating what is already in society or offering resistance and alternative forms of social conviviality.[17] Our religious lives are woven with understandings of law, roles of state, notions of nationality, processes of translation, negotiations of metaphors and symbols, and perceptions of mental, bodily and epistemological frameworks. In the worship (interstitial) spaces we re/create stories about ourselves and provide a hybrid space where mimicry, repetition, re-orientations, and transformations of identity thrive.[18]

Nepantla

Worship space is a very complex place. As we gather in a worship space, we claim this space as a foreign space where everybody is invited by everybody, and no one owns the keys to the public worship space. A space in between, neither mine nor yours, neither a space that belongs exclusively to one tradition nor a place that avoids this tradition. A place of continuity and rupture, creation and dismantling of dogmas, doing and undoing of identities, fostering a myriad of differences, and finding strategies to live among them.

Our worship spaces are bridges, in-between places akin to *nepantla*, a place that is on hold and home at the same time. *Nepantla* was a term used by the Nahuatl-speaking people in Mexico in the 16th century. Gloria Anzaldúa defines it so well:

> *Bridges span liminal (threshold) spaces between worlds, spaces I call nepantla, a Nahuatl word meaning tierra entre medio. Transformations occur in this in-between space, an unstable, unpredictable, precarious, always-in-transition space lacking clear boundaries. Nepantla es tierra desconocida, and living in this liminal zone means being in a constant state of displacement--an uncomfortable, even alarming feeling. Most of us dwell in nepantla so much of the time it's become a sort of "home." Though this state links us to other ideas, people, and worlds, we feel threatened by these new connections and the change they engender.*[19]

In this liminal place we create our liturgies amidst our fears, anxieties, lacks, wants and longings. From our precarious, unpredictable, and always threated life, we use our liturgical maps and draw new ones, we use traditional prayers and create new ones, we live in dialectical modes, unfolding connections and not always foreseen results.

The worship space as a state?

No. The notion of the state is very dangerous to associate with the liturgical event at the worship space. The nation state institutionalizes violence, creates states of exception, establishes nationalisms that will kill those near its borders, steals land and creates fake document to give it a sense of authenticity. The state controls citizenship and the limits of our lives. Jesus, too, was killed by the state and specifically said, "My kingdom is not from this world" (John 18:36). Moreover, the nation-state is based on a social contract that holds liberal democracy in the hands of a minority that uses militarization and force to prevent changes and transformation.

The problem with our liturgical theologies is that they have often relied on the sense of a state with centralized power to dominate over people. A very few Christian groups, such as the Quakers, have abandoned the political-country-nation-state form of organization that has structured worship. That is why most liturgies of Christian churches are never to be actually performed by the people but instead by the liberal democrats, leaders who act "on behalf of the people" while never letting the people own God's holy things.

Instead, the radical power of the people by the people should be the reference in any liturgical theology. It should be the work of holy people to redistribute the holy things and create holy ground anywhere they go. Liturgical theologies should then readjust, redistribute and resignify not only the worship space, but also all of the material goods of society: baptismal font and citizenship, housing and *oikós*, healing and health care, eucharist and food, joyful noise and circus.

Foreign space

The public space is rendered a foreign space since no one has the right to own it. The worship space redirects us all to a common place, a place in between, a place where all of us have the right to live, to eat and to have a dignified life. In this space, public theology might be a foreign space instead of a territory marked by social values and inequalities, a dis-placed place in the world where we utter to each other the words: Welcome, in the name of a loving God welcome to this place! For God's love is also here! Finally, we could get together again! And we are finally here. From many places and situations and conditions, we have arrived, some more bruised than others due to the conditions of the road, but we are here.

We are all migrants, traveling from one place to another. All of us undocumented, moving through things and moments, beliefs and doubts, fears and hopes. One thing we know: we do not belong to this world. According to Jesus, while we are sent into this world, we do not belong to this world (John 17:14). The writer of Hebrews reminds us that "here we have no lasting city, but we are looking for the city that is to come" (Hebrews 13.14). Peter challenges us to live "in reverent fear during the time of our exile" (I Peter 1:17).

This sense of being a foreigner, of walking towards somewhere else, is a mark of the early Christians, and it is present in the ancient literature. A letter to Diognetus, perhaps written in the second part of the 2nd century, describes the ways in which Christians relate themselves to place: "Christians might stay in their own countries or elsewhere, but simply as sojourners. As citizens, they share in all things with others, and yet endure all things as if foreigners. Every foreign land is to them as their native country and every land of their birth as a land of strangers."[20]

As wanderers in this world, we stop for rest, prayers, songs, and food. We bring our holy symbols. Imagine we are moving around the globe, and we found a liturgical rest area. Our task now is to worship God, and to offer help, support, care and provisions for one another to continue this journey. We set up in this frail, provisional sacred space, like the Jews who built the Tabernacle in the desert, like Bedouins stopping in deserted areas until they figure out where to go next, like Nomads making tentative shelters in urban areas and engaging with strangers all the time, or even like many immigrants crossing the desert between Mexico and the U.S., building small shrines to worship God, so we can meet our religious obligations and gain strength to make this this forbidden-cross journey.

If this worship space is a foreign space, that means it does not belong either to you or to me. It has neither a Presbyterian nor a Roman Catholic liturgy, neither a Pentecostal nor Southern Baptist worship, and for that matter, it is neither solely a Christian, nor a Muslim nor Jewish nor Hindu nor a Candomblé worship. This place will not be privatized by any denomination or religion! Like all the earth, this place belongs to God and God alone. But now, here, together, we have to figure out how to use this space and how to put together the gestures and the provisions of our faith, or lack thereof.

Thus, after hearing God's call to love God and one another, empowered by this love and this grace beyond measure, we go to work in our own locations, utilizing the wisdom of our many traditions. The task? To honor God and each other, restituting those who were stolen from, giving possession to the dispossessed, bringing life to death, and justice and peace to situations of inequality and despair.

What is the sort of public theology we shall sing? The song of the undocumented, of the queer, of Black and Indigenous communities of religions, engaging old and new resources, autochthone ritual creations and manifestations. Confused and disoriented, we engage with differences and complications. After we learn how to sing and pray somebody else's prayers and songs and eat together, we leave and go about our lives with a better idea of what the Kin-dom of God looks and feels like. Our rituals will reorient us in the world with many maps, triangulations, assemblages, and juxtapositions. At this place lies the liturgy of the church, the liturgy of the neighbor and the liturgy of the world.[21]

More than anything, the worship space should provide a full sense of what life/lives should be all about. It should be a place where other forms of civilization and resources offer new forms of existence. Perhaps we could pursue what the Brazilian anthropologist Eduardo Viveiros de Castro has said:

> *My idea for the future is not that we all should go back to live like Indigenous people, but instead, to look at them and imagine a civilization that may have a relationship with their own living conditions that is not so stupid and suicidal like ours.*

Occupy, Resist and Produce

This is the public form of a liturgical public theology: within liturgical space we learn to "occupy, resist and produce:"

Occupy – we occupy every worship space and restore what has been taken from the people. We will bring all of the poor and the beggars and the homeless inside. We will cry out: this holy place and everything that is here belongs to the poor! Rehearsed, we will mirror this movement in society and occupy places where the rich live and share what they have. We will occupy the financial buildings and multinational companies and take away their sources/structures and debunk their power. We will occupy refugee camps and bring the resources from the rich to make a home with schools, and water and seeds for harvesting, so people can begin a new life. We will occupy private and state prisons and implode their buildings. With the debris we will build new houses for immigrants and other prisoners to gather with their families. We will occupy the dumpsters of the cities and bring people out so together we can find ways to provide dignity for us all. We will occupy the lands of agri-business and distribute it to the poor. We will occupy oil companies and break down the pipelines that are putting our lives at risk.

Resist – We will resist worship services that keep power for a few leaders. We will resist worship services that make people mimic prayers and songs made by white males from Europe and the U.S. We will resist biblical readings and interpretations that are indifferent to poor contexts. We will resist monolithic forms of worship that do not engage inter-religious dialogue. Rehearsed, we will continue this resistance in society, and we will resist new laws, new tyrannies and any concentration of power and money, distributing everything. Everybody will have health care, a home, schools, and the possibility to eat 3-5 times a day! Our resistance will begin by redistributing resources to the poor.

Produce – We will produce autonomous liturgies and engage whatever worship resources any way we want in the ways that local contexts demand. We will produce new ways of engaging with each other and sing somebody else's songs and pray somebody else's prayers. We will produce a myriad of worship services that will empower people and transform social, economic, sexual, and patriarchal structures. Rehearsed within the liturgical space, we will produce ecologically sound agriculture and cooperatives. We will produce other forms of symbolic exchange, economic values and new forms of life. We will follow the campesinos across the globe and learn with them how to live this gospel of love and might.

As the lyrics of a song often sung in Latin America say:

There, we follow the Lord's receipt;
Let us all together prepare the dough with your hands,
and we will see with joy how the bread grows.
Women do not forget the salt
Men bring the yeast.
And may we have many people invited:
blind, deaf, lame, prisoners, poor.[22]

Reoriented, rehearsed and empowered, we will offer a public view of the world, thus giving God glory and honor. God's love will send us forth and God's grace will sustain us as we go beyond measures and limits to reshape territories and contexts. We will continue to work in our own locations, using the sources of our own contexts and the wisdom of our many traditions.

The task of public liturgical theology? To honor God and each other, restituting those who were stolen from, giving possession to the dispossessed, bringing life to those who are dead, and giving justice and peace to situations of inequality and despair. Let us go in peace!

CHAPTER FIVE[1]

From Multiculturalisms to Multinaturalisms: Liturgical Theological Shifts

Marshall Jacob Frantz, 7 years old

The theological turn of the twentieth century has been, among other things, the movement from universal doctrines and beliefs about God to cultural, contextual theologies. This move has helped us see that theologies have a cultural grid that defines not only the final result of the process of thinking but also thinking itself. Thinking theology is a cultural creation, dependent on the forms of knowledge that dominate that culture. Dominant cultures dominate the theological field and make universal claims. Liberation theologies, among other theologies, are critical of knowledges located in centers of power and work to restore local "subjugated knowledges."[2] A certain brand of Christian theology and liturgy centers the necessity of multicultural theologies and liturgies in order to produce justice-seeking congregations, hospitable worship services, and fair norms and forms of mutual conviviality and sharing of power.

In all of our theological and liturgical efforts, including many liberation theologies, the multicultural efforts of inclusion focused solely on particular cultures and cultural battles, forgetting and even denying the very condition of the organization of these theologies and liturgies: nature. Multicultural theologies have failed to engage the earth and the basic sustenance of our lives on earth. Introducing one aspect of the thought of Brazilian anthropologist Eduardo Viveiros de Castro namely *Amerindian Perspectivism*, can help us to expand the possibility of thinking theology in more *natural* ways and offer some challenges for theological thinking in our new twenty-first century.

Multiculturalism

When we talk about nature we are already engaging in separation. The rift between human beings and nature is the product of a cultural way of thinking prone to classification and/by separation. We human beings have always understood ourselves to be above nature. Our very identity as humans is a social construct crafted in contrast to a negative idea of "nature". For us, nature is subservient, wild, uncontrollable, and in need of being mastered, shaped, and organized. I was taught to think this way in Sunday School, as I listened to Bible studies and sermons based on Genesis 1:28: "God blessed them, and God said to them, 'Be fruitful and multiply, and fill the earth and subdue it; and have dominion over the fish of the sea and over the birds of the air and over every living thing that moves upon the earth" (NRSV).

The fundamental separation in our theologies is between God and the earth! Ever since the beginning of creation, inequality has prevailed. God versus us, us versus nature. We are taught to subdue "it"; nature has become a thing! Everything is now under our feet! "Dominion over": those magical words we love! Dominion over fish, birds and anything that moves. What the writer of Genesis could not know was that this form of relation would fit perfectly into a worldview of economic methods, financial categories, and forms of production within the developmental growth called capitalism and its agribusiness force.

The advent of modernity radicalized this theological reading of the creation story in rational, non-religious ways. Immanuel Kant's desire for human autonomy shaped new forms of being human, providing us with new ways of engaging our minds and our many forms of reasoning. God, transformed now into abstract sublimity, was also able to be grasped by reason. Our task became mastering and controlling everything with the ability and power of our mind. Over and against the darkness of religion, Kantian reason enjoined us to move onward, even and fundamentally, over nature. As Eduardo Viveiros de Castro and Déborah Danowski put it:

> *Kant's misnamed "Copernican Revolution" is, as we know, the source of the official modern conception of Man (let us keep it masculine) as consistent power, the autonomic and sovereign lawgiver of nature, the only being capable of rising above the phenomenal order or causality of which his own understanding is a condition; "human exceptionalism" is a veritable ontological state of exception, grounded on the self-grounding separation between Nature and History.*[3]

Gaining our humanity by placing ourselves over and against animal instincts, mastering the world through thinking, organizing our culture over and against an unruly nature, modernity asserted this theoretical division, imposing yet another disastrous hierarchical relationship between humans and the earth. With time, the rawness of the earth was lost to our new *oikos* in the form of a mechanized world, a rawness so deeply buried that many people are now clueless about what is entailed in processes such as water coming into our homes and out of the faucets, about who owns this resource, or where it comes from. We not only eat without knowing where our food comes from or what happens to the animals and the earth that provide it, we also could not care less.

Theologian Vitor Westhelle writes about the ways in which Christian theology was caught in that web of time over against space. In his book *Eschatology and Space, the Lost Dimension in Theology Past and Present*, he shows how historically the theological enterprise of the West was dependent on notions of time and how geographical spaces were never considered in the theological formation of doctrines, faith and general constructions. Following a theological construction of time that predates modernity and starts with Orosius and Augustine, Westhelle points to the ways in which modernity, following Hegel and his "the truth of space is time," continues this project of time against space in theologians and biblical scholars such as Paul Tillich, Karl Barth, Wolfart Pannenberg, Gerhard von Rad, Juan Luis Segundo and others. Eschatology has only been viewed as it relates to time and not to space. He writes:

> *The current crisis of eschatological thinking came through the backdoor of the historical project of the Western world with its colonial expansion and conquering enterprise. The face of the other and its truth came to the fore by a latitudinal advent. In the tradition of Hegel, the others of the Europeans were typically located either in the historical past (the Asians) or in the future (North Americans). But with the colonial backlash, thinking of the other could no longer be limited to a longitudinal and time-bound perspective. The others were "over-there." For many communities in the world, the movement of the Earth around the Sun – which registers time and is printed on the face of every analogical watch that we wear on our wrists or in clocks built into square towers – is not the dominant, or at least not the only frame to interpret reality and the experience of ultimacy. The other is definitely somewhere else and not some-when else.*[4]

The "crisis of eschatological thinking" makes us think about our present and our ends (*schata*) not in terms of geographical terms--thus geographically marked by power dynamics, race, politics and dominion, in an ecologically interdependent web--but rather, as the fulcrum of our faith disassociated with the pulsing markers of the conditions of our living. Since our theological knowledge is so bound to time, our sources are not to be taken from the earth, from the flowers, from the birds, or from the rivers. Even many of our wise prophets know very little about the processes of the earth.

If we look at the liturgical calendar that many churches use, everything is organized between *Chronos* and *Kairos* times. *Chronos* is the sequential time that moves forward in linear ways towards an eschaton where God will disclose the fullness of the Kingdom of God. *Kairos* is the fulfillment of times, or time in fullness where a moment goes beyond its limits and is filled with the past, present and future, like the coming of Jesus Christ on earth and the sacramental moments of in time when we see God's inbreaking into human history. Very little of the *schata* of life is geographical, or taken from the living cycles of microorganisms, or animals or the air, water, earth or fire. There is no Christian liturgical calendar based on earthly events.

Our liturgies and theologies cannot stop us thinking that everything that exists, sentient and non-sentient beings, live either because of us or to fulfill our needs and desires. According to our timely knowledge and assumptions, the world is only possible if we, human beings, exist; without us the world would neither be, nor have meaning nor purpose. Without our presence, we believe, the world, nature, and even some kinds of people, do not make sense, are often on the edge of living in bestial ways, and run the risk of destroying themselves. The prize of our rationality is to put proper order in the world – an order that subsumes earth to our hierarchical reasoning. We are on the side of socialization, but nature is on the side of anti-socialization; we have a culture to change things and the environment has a nature to be changed.

Moreover, modernity has made clear not only the distinction between time and space (history and nature) but also between the individual and society, nature and culture, tradition and originality, feeling and thinking, the sacred and the secular, the universal and the particular, objectivity and subjectivity, the physical and the moral, value and fact, immanence and transcendence, animal and human, body and spirit, and so on. However, reasoning according to these absolute, mythological pairings runs contrary to the wisdom and ways of so many peoples across the world.

Christianity is a religion made of these binaries. God is transcendent, we are immanent; history is where God plans God's salvation, culture is the place of God's incarnation. Nature seems to be at best a second-tier subject in the scheme of God's representation, and at worst a totally unnecessary "thing" to understanding God's love. The body is to be subsumed to the spiritual, animals are under the ruling of humans, and the sacraments, while shaped by earthly elements, must be placed in an altar above the earth. The sky has retreated too far from the earth. Theological *nomos* is marked by cultural autonomy rather than ecological relationality.

Faith in our Christian theologies is an inward gift to be lived as a testimony to the world. Faith is a cultural event that forms in relation to cultural locations. Faith in nature must be treated with caution because we fear an encounter with animism. Nature carries a natural grace of God, but we insist it needs the redemptive, special grace of God in Jesus. Jesus is also only understood through culture in our theologies. As just one example, consider what many consider a classic of Christian theology, H. Richard Niebuhr's *Christ and Culture*.[5] The book describes Jesus Christ according to five different headings: *Christ against Culture, Christ of Culture, Christ above Culture, Christ and Culture in Paradox* and *Christ the Transformer of Culture*. These five categories give Christians a sense of how to relate to, deny, oppose, or engage with culture. This sort of Christ has nothing to do with nature at all.

Liberals and minority intellectuals quickly pick up on this Christological emphasis on culture, and they criticize the notion of dominant culture that controls the means of theological knowledge production. According to this criticism, minorities were relegated to the fringes of society, to subaltern places. Cultural differences are often conflated with asymmetric power relations between the dominant culture and "the other", and a new "multiculturalism" is necessary to even the plane of cultures. Grounded in politics of identity, cultures are understood as a place of particular knowledge and power. In the U.S., for instance, theological multiculturalism attempted to engage with cultural differences by create blended forms of worship and carving spaces for various cultures to participate in predominantly white worship services.[6]

Although this scholarship helps to break the master cultural narrative, it is still grounded in the dominated culture/nature binary. Nature, ecology, environment, are all placed on the hidden spectrum of the multicultural enterprise sustaining the master and other narratives that structure life, religion and ways of living. The theological axis is autonomous, self-referential, and revolves around culture. Ecology is, and has always been, the ground that sustains and supports its ways of thinking and its ways of keeping structures of domination.

The focus on culture is fundamental for liturgy. The *Nairobi Statement of Worship and Culture* follows the same modern, humanistic assumptions we have been discussing but with a colonial hint of Christian traditions explaining what is bad in culture.[7] In order to engage with worship and culture, we are admonished to think about worship as "transcultural," "contextual," "countercultural," and "cross-cultural." In each of these realms, we learn about the "nature" of each cultural assessment, its meaning, and uniqueness that separates one from the other. What we do not hear is the way in which nature itself is intertwined with everything, organizing life, and providing the very possibility of any form of worship to exist. Contrary to what seems to be the case, Christian worship should not be understood as a form of colonialism that excludes or detaches us from the natural world. This exclusion, however, is deceptive since colonialism was deeply involved in the natural world of those it subjugated. It relies on natural resources to fuel empire--for example, the very business of colonialism made use of human and non-human resources, even if it was an evil, dysfunctional relationship. The new forms of coloniality, the power structures of colonialism, continue to be dependent on the "natural" world while claiming to be completely detached from it. In other words, multicultural enterprise maintains the homogenous metanarrative of the master oppression. The proposed diversity of multicultural liberation continues to include the subjugation of the earth and thus leaves the domination of the earth in the hands of those who control the forms of reproduction.

Multinaturalism

The dualism culture/nature continues to be maintained under the reasoning and knowledge that continue to take place "outside" of nature. This "outside," beyond nature, is the ground from which multiculturalism and the politics of difference work in an a somewhat unconscious level. In some ways, this relation can be described as an "ontological duality between nature, the domain of necessity, and culture, the domain of spontaneity, areas separated by metonymic discontinuity."[8]

The justice work intended under multiculturalism often fails to engage the complexities of the contexts of environmental relations. What is at stake are the claims of various forms of culture, experience and identity, with no connection to the larger productions of relations and the owning of natural resources. Moreover, the affirmation of identities, all kinds of identities, depends upon a radical separation from the identity of others and denies our interdependence with each other and with nature. While the professed value of multiculturalism and identity politics is centered on their goal of organizing society in a fair and just way, all the same, they reify the denial of the fact that these groups' very existence emerges from, takes place within, and depends upon nature.

Viveiros de Castro developed the notion of *Amerindian perspectivism* and *multinaturalism* in order to offer a new way of thinking, feeling and living life. It is worth the long quote:

> In sum, animals are people, or see themselves as persons. Such a notion is virtually always associated with the idea that the manifest form of each species is a mere envelope (a "clothing") which conceals an internal human form, usually only visible to the eyes of the particular species or to certain trans-specific beings such as shamans. This internal form is the "soul" or "spirit" of the animal: an intentionality or subjectivity formally identical to human consciousness, materializable, let us say, in a human bodily schema concealed behind an animal mask. At first sight then, we would have a distinction between an anthropomorphic essence of a spiritual type, common to animate beings, and a variable bodily appearance, characteristic of each individual species but which rather than being a fixed attribute is instead a changeable and removable clothing. This notion of "clothing" is one of the privileged expressions of metamorphosis

– spirits, the dead and shamans who assume animal form, beasts that turn into other beasts, humans that are inadvertently turned into animals – an omnipresent process in the "highly transformational world" proposed by Amazonian ontologies. Such an ethnographically-based reshuffling of our conceptual schemes leads me to suggest the expression, "multi-naturalism," to designate one of the contrastive features of Amerindian thought in relation to Western "multiculturalist" cosmologies. Where the latter are founded on the mutual implication of the unity of nature and the plurality of cultures – the first guaranteed by the objective universality of body and substance, the second generated by the subjective particularity of spirit and meaning – the Amerindian conception would suppose a spiritual unity and a corporeal diversity. Here, culture or the subject would be the form of the universal, whilst nature or the object would be the form of the particular.[9]

As opposed to the modern Western conception that sees one human nature within multiple cultures--meaning one human body that contains one substance and which regards all other bodies as animals without substance/soul--Indigenous thought asserts that there is instead one culture (the world) where we all live amidst multiple natures made of various forms of humanities. The human nature is one nature living among many other human natures such as animals, spirits, nature, etc. in the one culture, the world.

"Perspectivism" describes the nature of Amerindian mythology, cosmology, and daily activities. Perspectivism is a unique way in which humans view themselves and other inhabitants of the universe, the same ways that animals and spirits see themselves as humans, even if some humans do not share that understanding. Perspectivism is a view from a point that is always changeable. It is in the body that we perceive and feel ourselves, others, objects and the world. The human condition is everywhere, here and elsewhere. Each species is a center of consciousness that varies in grade and situation. There is a relation between subjects, and they dialogue about their differences. There is a unity of the spirit and a diversity of bodies. While the western modern conception of nature means one nature and multiple cultures, from the Amerindian perspective, culture is the universal and nature is the particular. Culture encompasses everything while there are many naturalisms between human forms of humans and animals. "Perspectivism is not a relativism but a multinaturalism."[10]

Multinaturalism is perspectivism. Even while living within one culture, everyone has a different nature. These different natures–of human beings, animals, spirits and so on–display forms of relationality in which many ways of being human are possible. These natures have distinct ways of seeing each other. Viveiros de Castro adds:

> *In particular, individuals of the same species see each other (and each other only) as humans see themselves, that is, as beings endowed with human figure and habits, seeing their bodily and behavioral aspects in the form of human culture. What changes when passing from one species of subject to another is the "objective correlative," the referent of these concepts: what jaguars see as "manioc beer" (the proper drink of people, jaguar-type or otherwise), humans see as "blood." Where we see a muddy salt-lick on a river bank, tapirs see their big ceremonial house, and so on. Such difference of perspective—not a plurality of views of a single world, but a single view of different worlds—cannot derive from the soul, since the latter is the common original ground of being. Rather, such difference is located in the bodily differences between species, for the body and its affections (in Spinoza's sense, the body's capacities to affect and be affected by other bodies) is the site and instrument of ontological differentiation and referential disjunction. Hence, where our modern, anthropological multiculturalist ontology is founded on the mutual implication of the unity of nature and the plurality of cultures, the Amerindian conception would suppose a spiritual unity and a corporeal diversity—or, in other words, one "culture," multiple "natures." In this sense, perspectivism is not relativism as we know it—a subjective or cultural relativism—but an objective or natural relativism—a multinaturalism.*[11]

From this perspective, multinaturalism is a way of seeing every other being as part of one same culture but different natures. Culture is where we live, and natures are the ways we inhabit this culture/world. Multiculturalism sees us all as part of many cultures with the same nature.

While multiculturalism understands humanity as detached from, or above, other forms of non-humans, multinaturalism sees everyone, humans and more than humans, as the same, depending only on the perspective of the one looking. Multiculturalism sees only humans as belonging to diversified cultural entities, with one same nature. Animals and the natural world are not only consigned to the one same nature, within an imagined sense of totalizing nature everywhere, but also are below culture. Within this hierarchical structure we position culture on top and nature down below. Culture is controllable through institutions, but nature is uncontrollable and in need of dominium. In contrast, multinaturalism recognizes both humans and animals as cultural with exchangeable nature, depending on our perspective.

Agri-culture

Eco-feminists are closer to a multinaturalist perspective as they see the earth as indistinctively connected to the living-thinking of their theologies. While still in many ways caught in the binary culture/nature, eco-feminists understand that society's means of production must engage animals, its biodiversity and the multiverses (infinite number of parallel universes). From them we learn that the materiality of life--the flesh and bones and desires of our bodies--is deeply associated with soil and seeds, animals and bio-diversities and the needs of the earth. These associations are related to the ownership of the earth and bodies, of sexualities and subjectivities, agribusiness, capitalistic exploitation and they are all intertwined. Latin American Bible scholar Nancy Cardoso proposes:

> *Economic reflection approached the field of amorous and erotic phenomena with the need to express an important perspective on property modes and forms of capital accumulation – two vital items for the understanding of the capitalist model, in a special way within capitalist agriculture – what we know as agribusiness.*[12]

This immanent, intertwined notion of life, where everything is dependent on processes and movements, challenges modern anthropocentrism that makes nature a subject of man's dominion and permanently subjugates the earth. The human prerogative seen in the theological arrangement of creation, where God's preference for the human, the final product of creation granted the ultimate blessing of dominion over everything appears to justify claiming the power to do anything required for the survival of the human species. Without multinaturalism, the earth, a subject without rights, must indeed be under the control of human need and desire. Thus, the earth is to be conquered for our own survival, and to allow for the possibility of continuously changing social constructions.

This worldview completely ignores the question of agriculture – an issue we rarely consider because most of us are not farmers. Let us pause and think about the etymology of the term "agri-culture." The word *"agri/acre"* indicates a field, land, that which is sown. The word "culture" comes from the Latin *cultura*, meaning cultivation or culture, a term that itself derives from *cultus*,[13] the past participle of *colere* (to cultivate, worship), and is also related to *colonus* and *colonia*. This cultivation of what is active is a manufacturing of what is important to honor, worth working for and ascribing honor to it.

Thus, agriculture points to a deep relation between land and people, to people living off and with the land in interdependence, cultivating each other's existence. Nonetheless, the *agri of culture*, the very land where we live and survive, has been invaded by the *culture of the agri* in our societies. We have been transformed from being people of the earth into people who own the earth. Detached by the rationalism of our humanitarian and now capitalistic ways of living-thinking, we have even let the earth be taken away from us. But since we have been detached for so long from the earth, we fail to understand that this process of the exploitation of the earth would be akin to the exploitation of people everywhere.

The colonizing and capitalist devouring of the world was, and continues to be, based upon worship of our culture, a *colos*, the bosom of empire in which society is cultivated. In this cultivation, colonizers, states, and bankers decided to get rid of our seeds and our spiritualities, our worship and our ways of living with the earth. We ended up cultivating their own worship, their own ideas. Our ontologies became their epistemologies, our faith a mere feeling that sustains the market, our thinking a way of justifying our detachment from the earth.

It is thus our work to move away from a modernist humanist perspective that denies our very connectivity with the earth and the interdependency of environmental relations and eco-systems.

Conclusion

The theological cultural paradigm has contributed to the irreversible destruction of the earth. We must shift this paradigm immediately to one that is grounded in multinaturalism. This multinaturalism can be seen in the connection and equality found between people and animals, earth and the cosmos in the myths of the Aikewara in Brazil: "When the sky was still too close to Earth, there was nothing in the world except people and tortoises." Modernity widened the separation between the sky and the earth, between people and tortoises, by creating industries, artificial products, instrumental reasoning, notions of self, and new desires to be fulfilled. Now we are all separated and far from the sky; now the earth and the sky have been colonized. With our overpopulated world, the abused earth, and our cares directed away from creation, our gods have taken flight and left us. And we can no longer live with the tortoises.

Contrary to the discourse of autonomous beings, living in separated ways, we are all intertwined, interrelated and interconnected. Christianity exemplifies this denial of interdependency. The celebration of the ritual of the Eucharist elevates the sacramental elements above the ground. What is sacred is on the table, an altar, away from the floor, which is always dirty and detached from our holy things. If, God forbid, we drop the bread on the floor, it touches the ground (is seen to be filthy) and runs a certain risk, even if we do not know exactly what this risk entails. Is it the losing of power or a lack of respect for the holy since we have desecrated the altar of God? Even though we disassociate the earth with ritual practices, the sacrament comes from the earth, the "dirt," and its elements – water, bread, and grapes – are sources of its life.

Multinaturalism call for a re-approximation to what we are: several humanities living together in this cultural universe. It is only when we can live and protect the tortoises the same way we live and protect other human beings that we become fully connected with the Spirit of God and the whole of our beings.

If we are to engage in multinaturalism and perspectivism, we must move away from our transcendental theologies, and worship a God who lives in different natures and is felt, perceived, and lived in different planes, forms, and structures. As the late Latin American theologian Jaci Maraschin said, "It is in the body that we are Spirit."[14] The culture of our times is the Spirit. The Spirit is what keeps our natures in relation. Leonardo Boff might help us think-feel, and feel-think the *ruach* of God, the Spirit that breathes in everything and in us. Using Tao, the Chinese tradition of Taoism, he expands this breath as presence in many religious traditions:

> *The Tao represents this integration, the integration of an indescribable reality and the person who seeks to unite itself with this reality. Tao means the path and the method, but it is also the mysterious and secret energy that produces all paths and projects all methods. It cannot be expressed in words, so when in front of its silence is best. It is present in all things as the immanent principle that ascribes meaning... To reach this union it is imperative to be in synchrony with the vital energy that weaves through the heavens and earth, chi. It is impossible to translate chi, but it is equivalent to the ruach of the Jewish people, to the pneuma of the Greeks, to the spiritus of the Latins, to the axé of the Yoruba/Nago; these are expressions that designate the universal breath, the supreme and cosmic energy. It is because of chi that everything changes and remains in a constant process of change...*[15]

The Spirit is working within thinking, but it is also beyond thinking! It moves within and through history, but also breaks into and causes history to move. The breathing Spirit of God is our sustenance, but this breath does not only exist in our form of humanity. God's breathing Spirit is everywhere in every sentient and non-sentient being. This leads to a godly animism, if one needs a definition, even though God's Spirit is not confined to those beings only. God's Spirit goes beyond what we know and into the multi-universes. Thus, our breathing together must entail every other being we know and do not know. Our theological thinking must gain an awareness that we can only actually breathe God's breath if we consider the oceans! Without the plants called phytoplankton, kelp, and algal plankton we simply cannot live the breath of God in us.[16]

It is this breathing together, in holy co-respiration with sentient and non-sentient beings that we can find the *schata*, the ends, and the beginnings, of our life! It is this breathing together, this holy co-respiration with other people, other humanities, other naturalisms that we can redeem not only our times but fundamentally our grounds and our spaces. The earth is the force of our times. The truth of time is space. It is this breathing together, in holy inspiration and transpiration, eco-supporting all of the endless complex systems of the earth, that we can level the plain of all sentient and non-sentient beings to actually be able to live together.

It is this eco-breathing together with God that makes the *ruach* become a force in the world! The *ruach* of God respiring in all things is what helps us see that we are not alone, that we are living together in the midst of many multinaturalisms. And we gain a new humanity, deeply connected with the earth, deeply humidified by the humus of our co-existence.

Can Christianity be a multinaturalist faith? Not in the way we know now. But since this knowledge was once invented, Christian knowledge can be reinvented under God's breath. If language is but means to receive God's Spirit, we can gain a new language to breath God's breath in Jesus. Thus, it is our task and our challenge to expand the grammar of our faith into a grammar that will have a new alphabet, new languages, new wisdoms, new ontologies, new forms, new and old prayers, new and old songs, new paradigms, new rituals and new Spirit. For the *ruach* of God is not one that is afraid. Rather, the *ruach* of God is the one who breaks into our lives with freshness of a new world possible, with challenges that can only be faced if by the grace of God.

From a Christian multinaturalism, we need liturgies that think-feel-believe in spirits incarnated in eagles and tortoises; liturgies that think-feel-believe in the long work of theory and praxis so that the Christian faith can become not only counter-cultural but also against culture when culture is detached from nature; liturgies that think-feel-hear the cries of the earth; liturgies that think-feel-believe-see what is happening to the destruction of our people and to the earth; liturgies that think-feel-listen to the birds, and learn the ways of the birds; liturgies that think-feel-believe-breath-co-inspire, respire a life lived in solidarity with sentient and non-sentient beings, striving for everyone's rights to live fully and well.

The breathing of the spirit is our multinatural possibility, the very possibility to live within and beyond natures, running against empire and for the sake of the wretched of the earth and the wretched earth.

CHAPTER SIX [1]

The Christian as Humus:
Virtual/Real Earthly Rituals of Ourselves

Isaque Grinaboldi Ortiz, 3 years old

How can we even write these days? The world is going through disasters upon disasters. COVID-19 came to change us forever and we still do not know fully how. Our lives are changing, the world is being transformed, poverty is growing exponentially, hunger affects millions, and the earth does not have what is required to continue the way we have been going. Most recently the death of George Floyd has sparked a movement for justice, freedom, and transformation that is also changing the face of this country. How do we write about performance and ritual when we are sitting on bombs about to explode?

Eric Garner's and George Floyd's dying words, "I can't breathe," carry the breath of billions of people, and also of the earth. It is a breath that has been extinguished everywhere, with the knee of human and white supremacy on the neck of the world, making us all lose our own breath. The death of George Floyd is the canary in a coal mine telling us we cannot breathe in our societies. COVID-19 is the canary telling us we will not be able to breath in the earth soon. Black folks and people of color are exhausted fighting for their own lives. James Baldwin wrote: "In America, I was free only in battle, never free to rest— and he who finds no way to rest cannot long survive the battle…"[2] People of color and the earth can never be free to rest, and we are all losing the battle.

With this as our very present context, let us think about Christian worship services, our understandings of the sacrament and our current virtual engagements. How do we think of expanded notions of the sacrament, the idea of the *real* while living in a web of interdependence between the social and the ecological? The hope of this article is to provide tools for us to expand, re-signify, and re-think the notion of the assembly in broader terms. For this to happen, the notions of the real and the virtual must be rethought. The virtual might be reconsidered—even welcomed— as deep engagement with each other. The assembly together, even if separate, is still the body of Christ at prayer. Let us re-think the assembly even more expansively from who we are: humus. The Eucharistic rite provides a quick entry into this discussion which leads us into the challenges posed by COVID-19, the climate disasters we are going through right now, and our response to these crises. The call here is to join the altars of the earth.

To Worship as We Live, and Live as We Worship

Louis–Marie Chauvet wrote that "the basic law of liturgy is 'do not say what you are doing; do what you are saying.'"[3] This injunction speaks directly to what agonizes Tissa Balasuriya about the celebration of the eucharistic ritual: "Why is it that in spite of hundreds of thousands of eucharistic celebrations, Christians continue as selfish as before? Why have the 'Christian' Mass-going peoples been the most cruel colonizers of human history?"[4]

It would seem that the Christian liturgical problem, according to Chauvet and Balasuriya, is that we do not do what we say. It seems that the doing of our rituals are not the problem but rather, that the act of doing our words does not translate into deeds. While the doing of what is said and the saying of what we are doing has never been perfect, we should question whether our saying and doing are actually changing our world. Would it be fair to say that our saying and doing have ignored racism, economic inequality, and the earth's destruction? If so, is it still worth saying and doing our rituals? Perhaps these statements are too broad and inadequate, and we should stop here. But for those who want to continue to read, let us ponder a bit further.

We cannot say our rituals have nothing to do with the larger moral and social conditions of our societies. At the same time, we cannot blame our ritual failures solely on the political, economic, and social conditions of our society. We cannot say that the prevailing inequalities in our societies are irrelevant to our ritual business because those inequalities live outside of the temple. The roots of social structures and religions and their rituals are deeply intertwined. Healing the illnesses of our societies and the ways in which we organize our ecological, political, and economic systems is directly related to "healing" our rituals. Unless we see our Christian rituals as a specific way of knowing and understanding that forms our social belonging, ethnic and racial (mis)understandings, class biases, sexual orientations and their labels, and our whole set of priorities, we will disguise the social and ecological implications of our rituals by claiming to be faithful to God and tradition. We cannot rely on the personal security of what ritual provides, or the safety of our traditions, if our world is in shambles and people are dying all around us. The saying and the doing of our rituals *properly, meaning following all of the rubrics and instructions for its proper gestures,* will not protect us from the bombs exploding all around us. Perhaps we must wrestle more deeply with the various sources or *lexes* of our faith: *orandi, vivendi, credendi, and naturae* and its relations.[5]

As we live through COVID-19 and scientists continue to recommend isolating physically, politicians—pushed by the money profiteers—insist that everything is fine. We have been thrown into a place of permanent unknowing. We live with fear, anxiety, and poverty. The specter of death looms large everywhere. In the midst of this complex context, churches now are forced to perform their rituals online. Using the Eucharist as an example, we see evidence of the divisions between those who are open to celebrating the Eucharist online and those who deny the validity of online Eucharist, which results in a eucharistic hunger or longing that is not being met. The first group maintains a clerical-centric position, where ordination is necessary for the efficacy of the eucharistic rite. Pastors and priests maintain the authority to consecrate, while the people are allowed to take bread and grape juice at home. Other less clerical traditions point to the biblical notion of the "priesthood of all believers," (1 Peter 2:5–9) in which all baptized are anointed and therefore each person can offer their own prayers--even sacraments. The second group does not recognize the authority the consecrate outside of the physical assembly of the people; they tell us we must wait to receive the Eucharist until we can gather together again.

Those in the first group are open to new possibilities of celebrating meals together online with the same traditional prayer and the same traditional minimal amount of food. What could have been unfolding as a more expansive celebration of the meal in what Leonardo Boff calls "Sacraments of Life: Life of the Sacraments," with the heightening of the holy in our homes, in small gestures, objects and presences, and even in the creation of new forms of daily rituals, of solidarity meals sharing food with the hungry, caring for the earth and praying with those in need, preserves instead a narrow understanding of the prevenient and pervasive presence of God.[6]

The second group insists that Christian assembly is not possible through digital means. For this group, the assembly, without physical proximity, cannot be constituted by digital embodiment. The longing for a "real" gathering as was experienced in their pre-COVID-19 eucharistic rites is a testament to the joy found in such gatherings, but this group also appears unwilling to risk the people's control of holy things without clerical oversight or leadership. As some would say, we could die handling it!

Liturgists should consider Walter Benjamin's observation about the epic theater: "The point at issue in the theatre today can be more accurately defined in relation to the stage than to the play. It concerns the filling-in of the orchestra pit. The abyss which separates the actors from the audience like the dead from the living…"[7] In the same way, the space between the altar and the assembly has become the distance between the altar and the world. This abyss has been made permanent by the ritual words spoken and the doings of the words at the altar, even if they affirm who we are in God. The doings-sayings are very much attached to the one saying-doing it, which keeps the abyss uncrossed. This second group insists that we wait to have the eucharist until we gather together again in person. Their longing for the people to gather in real space and time is their piety.

The Virtual Church—The Practice of Faith During COVID-19

Let us start by thinking about the present strangeness we are living in, the world of COVID-19. As we live through it, we will encounter deep questions that require both practical and theological reasoning, questions that have no simple answer. Can we as Christians adapt? Can we offer ourselves and "be transformed by the renewing of your minds, so that you may discern what is the will of God—what is good and acceptable and perfect" for our time? (Romans 12:1-2 NRSV)

Due to our current situation, should we ponder what the celebration of the Eucharist can do to us, in us, for the sake of the world, and then find ways to perform it? The question comes from reality challenging our rituals. Perhaps this is liturgical liberation theology on steroids![8] How would the sacrament, understood as either transubstantiation or consubstantiation, offer the people sacramental grace when the congregation is not "present"? If the ritual is fundamental to the transformation of the people, does physical proximity determine its efficacy? Is God somehow limited in the virtual realm? In the same way, what are the theological and pastoral understandings of grace and faith when someone is baptized, married, or buried in the midst of social distancing?

When we think about church, community, and worship in virtual spaces, sacraments and become a test case. What is a sacrament? How is God present? If a sacrament, as we learn from St. Augustine, is a visible sign of an invisible grace, perhaps we can expand the signs of grace that live within us. Jason Byassee reminds us that "In fact, as Christians, we are a sort of virtual body (this observation I owe to Graham Ward). We are members of one another with those whom we have never met through time and now through space. We long to commune with our sisters and brothers face to face, but for many we never will until the final feast. For now, we preserve our ligaments by prayer, correspondence, and mutual correction."[9]

Does one's understanding of sacraments and sacramentality in general, allow that God's grace can flow "over, under, and through" the fiberoptic and electronic cables and satellites that provide us with the internet we need to connect to each other virtually? When some Pentecostal churches ask on their radio programs for listeners to put their water glasses on top of the radio, so that the glasses will be blessed after the speaker has said a prayer, those churches are demonstrating a much stronger and broader notion of sacramental grace than most other denominations. No, grace does not depend on these prayers, but these prayers can be channels for grace to happen. Here, the listener can drink that glass of water, for it is now blessed: a visible sign of an invisible grace. For what is the difference between a cup of water on top of a radio and a loaf of bread on top of the altar, when they are both prayed over and blessed? And we could ask: why do we even need to bless the bread and the wine if they are already blessed and holy as God's own creation? As Linda Gibler says in her book *From the Beginning to Baptism*: "For at least the first two hundred years of Christian tradition water was not blessed for baptism. Clean, living water did not need to be blessed."[10] What has happened to Christians to make us think that the earth is dirty or unholy and that we need to bless the bread, the wine and the water? Why have we made the earth unholy, or partially holy? At the heart then lies a question: What is a sacrament or even sacramentality? How is God present in creation?

The ecclesia, the assembly, must now open its wings and see ourselves as who we are: living beings made of water and humus, earth's dust with the whole of humanity and all earthly creatures. We are so much more than a simple ecclesial gathering. The Christian assembly is one in fulness with all humanity reaching all the way to the stars and yet is but a breath in the world, a grain of sand on the shore of the planets. Assuming fully the physical and organic connection with each other and creation in its original blessedness, I propose that the bread and the wine are always already blessed, since it all comes from the earth, a soil already prepared and blessed by God for us all. No wonder Eucharistic prayers based on Augustine say, "Behold what you are." And the people reply, "May we become what we receive." We become what we have always been. Children of God, humus of God's creation.

Instead of finding ways to protect or guard our sacramental theologies, we should be open to listening to the Spirit talk to us in new and difficult times. Now as we experience the gift of faith and see how the sacraments can be God's presence, we could hear a voice that arises out of the earth proclaiming our common nature. Yet we hear this proclamation in the context of a racist country. To say that God's presence is already among us in a divided world, is to conceal the disrupting and provoking power of the gospel. The common humus/nature that unites all people must also be a prophetic statement against our bigoted hierarchies and division of both race and gender.

During this difficult time, it is not enough to offer only the preached word of God. Not because the preached word is not Christ himself, but because for this time we must share God's gifts by performing the word of God we hear. We must become the just, quenching water in response to a burning situation. Our rituals and our lives must intertwine as a performance of the gospel.

The notion of the assembly must be redefined. The real and the virtual must be rethought. The virtual must be reconsidered—even welcomed—as deep engagement with each other. Our almost universal experience of isolation and fear has brought our attention to our common humanity, our common humus. The real assembly must be identified by joining the struggle against racism and poverty, and by engaging deeply with the care of the earth.

The central place here is the relation within the assembly and not between the assembly and the altar. We must be committed to understanding the sound of each other's voice and the sight of each other's face as the very sacrament of God offered to each of us. There are always mediations, but the hope is to expand these mediations.

My mother once asked her pastor to visit a nursing home that she visited herself each week. But the pastor could never go. After some time without a response, she decided to take communion to her people. One night, my mother called me and said, "Son, I feel I committed a sin: I gave the Eucharist to people who were begging me for it and were about to die. They were so happy I cannot even begin to tell you. How can I be forgiven?"

I said, "Mother, I have no power to forgive anybody, but I surely believe that the gospel was made alive to those who received it."

For me, she was graced with the power of the "priesthood of all believers" and had all the authority to share the Eucharist. But was it really the Eucharist? For whom? For those of us theologians and pastors who hold ties to a certain tradition, perhaps not. But for the people who took it as God's gift to them, I believe so. Deep within me I believe that I am not called to protect any tradition; I am called instead to serve the people, the earth, and all its species and creatures. Both with and in opposition to traditions, we need to expand some meanings of our faith, re-signify beliefs, and do away with forms of communing, ministry and worship that do not attend to the moment we are living in, and the immense challenges COVID-19, Black Lives Matter movement, and climate changes are bringing to us. We are called not only to work on the inculturation of our faith but also in transignifying our beliefs, our sacramental understandings, and our metaphysics, for the time we are living demands us to change for the sake of the world God so loves.

The Intrusion of Gaia

Scientists are saying the most dramatic things about the end of the world as we know it. Some of their dire predictions require us talk about a climate crisis, not climate change. Our situation is drastic. Capitalism, with its relentless pursuit of capital and profit, makes use of extractivism as its latest asset.[11] The extraction of fossil fuels, minerals, and water to fulfill the desires of the market, results in the emission of carbon dioxide and a consequent warming of the atmosphere by possibly two or even three degrees, making it impossible for the earth to replenish itself and continue the circle of life. When added to the effects of overfishing, that same release of carbon dioxide leads to the acidification of the oceans, the death of coral reefs responsible for creating the air we breathe, the massive extinction of various forms of life, and the devastation of entire ecosystems. These developments are leading us into a place of no return. With the world's ice caps predicted to melt entirely before 2040—just a mere fifteen, twenty years! —sea levels will rise, warming the planet, flooding entire populated areas, and altering the balance of our weather patterns globally.

Mesdames et Monsieurs, we will burn! Thanks be to God?! We have seen throughout history, humankind experiencing the consequences of our choices and behaviors. We have also seen people affected by the choices and behaviors of others. People who have little to do with these changes are already seeing their effects. Africa is already feeling it, islands everywhere are feeling it, Central American and Asian farmers are feeling it. Climate change migrants already number 240 million. This situation is not an impending disaster; it is already here, unfolding on a scale that no one truly knows.

The earth, Pachamama, or Gaia, is taking the reins from us. James Lovelock describes Gaia as a living system organized in itself which acts and reacts according to its environment.[12] Bruno Latour writes of the agency of everything in Gaia,[13] something Indigenous people have always known. Gaia is not only inert matter but a live organism that continually responds to human actions. And it is precisely because Gaia has a life of its own that Isabelle Stengers tells us our time is marked by "the intrusion of Gaia deciding to interfere in our daily lives."[14] Up until this point, we believed we stood at the center of the world's stage, with the earth playing only a supporting role in our lives, making sure we had everything we needed to live the way we desired. Now Gaia is taking center stage and reclaiming her rule. Gaia has begun to make decisions about how the earth behaves and how it will change. The intrusion of Gaia means that we have receded into the background of the earth's drama. With the intrusion of the earth, our world as we know it will erupt and disappear. God's movement with the earth, the earth as the body of God, with its own reasoning, will expel us from here since we do not know reciprocity, mutual healing, and life together with other forms of life.[15] COVID-19 is a wake-up call to pay attention to the effects of our choices and behaviors— on ourselves, on others, and to ecosystems shared by all.

With this shift, Gaia is saying that our capitalistic ways of living and being are all consuming, and that there is no way that life as we know it can continue. As we ponder this new reality, we must contemplate the ways in which our religions have often been silent about the ongoing realities of appropriation, dispossession, and destruction of the earth. We must ask ourselves how our religions, especially Christianity, have sustained capitalism's deadly racist structures. The Christianity of "conquest and dominion" was a powerful idea whose structures now continue to sustain multiple forms of domination and the destruction of the earth.

Why the Earth is Fighting Back— and How We Can Still Save Humanity

The hierarchical/patriarchal structure of ecclesial norms and theological ideas that sustained and still sustain the "conquest and domination" of our time must be reconsidered. Christians are still operating in Cartesian modes of thinking as being, where the supremacy of the human mind is what orders everything, turning the complexity of entangled forms of being into discrete and isolated subjects, detached from the earth and dedicated to the pursuit of (individual) happiness. This isolated self depends on a transcendent God who is seen to be dislodged from the natural world by way of our sin. Our task now is to find both the natural revelation of God and the special revelation of God in Christ. We have grounded our thoughts in dichotomies such as body/mind, God/earth, nature/culture, natural/special revelation, heaven/earth and so on. Such grounding has sent us into modernity's detachment from the earth as a way of attaching ourselves to God and into nostalgia for a life with few consequences, to be lived fully with God in heaven and not here. That is our paradise lost: the sense of connection and belonging. We long for what we think we have lost, even though we have never actually been detached from the earth, since our bodies are made of soil, water, stars, and trees. Our paradise lost is the loss of God and thus our inability to see identities as interconnected or to perceive life deeply present in everything and everyone. Lost, we became confused and embraced the mastery of ruling everything, rather than living in reciprocity with the earth which is God's gift to us. In our attempts to fulfil our imagined destiny--to rule the earth, conquering and claim everything as rightfully ours--we are bringing upon ourselves our own demise, sealing our fate for an inevitable final self-destruction.

Our theological confusion has distanced us from the earth. The Christian God of many of our rituals has very little to do with the earth, or even the physical realm. However, with Gaia's intrusion, much is at stake. Gaia is already scrambling our beliefs and practices. The illusion of autonomy and individualism that permeates our rituals and theologies will not be enough. The faith of our contemporary Christian communities does not have the resources to stem the tide of our imminent demise. Our cosmologies are grounded in words that have little entanglement with the systems of the earth, our liturgical celebrations do not acknowledge the generosity and reciprocity of the earth. In wealthy, industrialized Christian communities, our faith is expressed in spaces that speak more of heaven than earth and more of personal piety and individual improvement than community ties and ecological bindings. Many of our altars cannot have plants or seeds or fruits because they are not considered as holy. Our songs are beautiful, but we do not try to sing with other animals or with the waters. Our prayers of confession seldom make us think about real reparations to Black and Indigenous people. Our sense of unity in Christ does not allow us to break down all the walls between Mexico and the U.S. and other borders around the world. Our sacraments are seldom rooted in the fullness of God's love within creation and nor do they see creation's living beings as fundamental parts of the body of Christ AND as means of grace. Our liturgies rarely say anything about the pollution of rivers near our communities. Our Eucharists do not acknowledge the food deserts in our cities as hunger grows the bread and the wine in our communion do not makes us fight against extractivism. We cannot confess to plants or animals for the distant way we have related to them because it would sound outrageous and sinful to our ears. Our immaterial spirituality distances itself from the earth, fearing we would be called earth-worshippers. Our God is too transcendent and fearful and cannot live in the immanent reality of both the living and inanimate parts of creation. In other words, by way of Augustine, unless we become who we are--soil/earth--and unless we gain a deep relationality and reciprocity with creation, we may never be able to relate with the earth or offer/receive ways to heal and be healed by Gaia.

The Altars of Creation

We must return to a sacramental view of the whole universe. Thomas Aquinas, Teilhard de Chardin, Matthew Fox, Sallie McFague, Rosemary Radford Ruether, Ivone Gebara, and others have called the whole universe a sacrament, the likeness of God, and a means of grace. The gratuitous excess of the heavens, stars, planets, soil, wind, water, plants, animals and fungi is the very sacrament that can transform us. Since we connect with one another by being in each other's physical presence, we must learn to connect with each other through our relationship with the earth. The earth is our sacrament. Every tree is a means of grace. Every bird sings the means of grace. Every drop of water that flows is God's means of grace to us. Nothing is outside of God's grace. Therefore, we will live in perpetual gratitude--a sort of radical immanence where our transcendent God is at the same time an immanent God of relationship, spiritual presence, and materiality.

Every day, every person will be grateful for something. The virtual gathering is just a collective reminder, both forms of sacrament discussed here might not even be the point anymore. We must hear the call of God everyday from the earth since the real sacrament occurs as we grow in love and reciprocity with the earth! One day we will listen to the birds as a sacrament, and we will sing back to them in gratitude. On the second day, we will tell a story to a child, whether in our house or online, and count this telling as a sacrament. On the third day, we will eat and say to the earth how grateful we are for our bountiful meals, and we will save some of our food for the hungry. On the fourth day, we will pay attention to a plant in our home or garden, give that plant a name, and address it by that name. On the fifth day, we will celebrate the rain we receive as God's sacrament, God's pouring out of blessings on us, heaven and earth united in who we are: water. If there is no rain, our shower will be a sacrament and our washing of the dishes will be a sacrament of who we are. On the sixth day, we will count our neighbors as blessings and make sure they have what they need. On the seventh day, we will tend the earth and take care of the soil, the seeds, the plants, and so on. When we gather together in an online worship service, we will count the thousand sacraments we experienced during the week, tell each other how the bread and the wine were interspersed with daily living justly with the earth, each sacrament enriched by other sacraments, keeping our hearts glad all week long! These graces will be our sacrament.

Sacrament is that which is sacred. Now we will consider the whole earth sacred. Not just the bread and wine consecrated at the altar/table, not only the water prayed over baptism, but also the humus/earth that is in everything and the water that makes 90 percent of our bodies; everything will be sacred, a sacrament. We do not need to be blessed as sacred since we have always already been a sacrament—as have the plants, the rivers, the trees, and animals. In these ways, even if they are different from what we have known before, people are not only part of the sacrament, but *are* the sacrament.

Perhaps the biggest challenge here is to transform our pneumatology, the doctrine of the Holy Spirit, into something frighteningly more expansive, more real, more vivid, and more communal, trusting that God will do more than we could ever imagine or would even allow God to do. In this way our ecosystems become sacraments, as God moves around, in, with, under—but also dwells within—it all.

Lastly, let us not forget that even our technological resources are not a given. Such resources come from the earth arriving in our homes by way of phones and computers. We are devouring the earth with machines, phones, clouds, and virtual gatherings. We have no limits! We just feel entitled to have as much energy we want, as much of anything we desire, including technology. Yet, technology is also the earth's body, the earth's being! This will not be able to continue. We will pay for it. Will COVID-19 change our ways of living, being, believing, and consuming? Will this strange time cause us to change everything including our rituals? Will the death of George Floyd make us become open and unapologetically antiracists? Will COVID-19 help us gain awareness and engage in true reciprocity with the earth?

Conclusion

In addition to the laws of belief, prayer, and ethics, we must engage first and foremost the law of nature according to which we shape our liturgies. If we think, believe, and live together from the perspective of earth as sacrament, racism will also be destroyed because the *oikos* of God is for everyone. Our rituals must help us create solidarity with Black people, people of color, and the poor. Our rituals must change and help us learn a new reciprocity with the earth—one of protection, reparation, and healing. Then, the doing and the saying of our rituals will mirror the earth's movements and the healing of the nations.

We are a much larger assembly, one made of creatures, plants animals and all forms of life, a myriad of affections and relations. If we as Christians refuse to honor the earth in its fullness, we cannot celebrate the fullness of God in Christ. Liturgical theologies oriented around the ways of the earth, protecting the biome in its intense and immense diversities will result in liturgical politics that will orient us toward the earth with love, calling each plant by its name. Our God can only be found within the earth. Our spiritual work is to tend our hearts and our relations with the earth, as Gilberto Gil, a Brazilian artist, sings.

> *If the fields cultivated in this world*
> *They are too hard*
> *And the war-torn soils*
> *Do not produce peace*
> *Tie your plow to a star*
> *And then you will be*

The crazy farmer of the stars
The peasant loose in the skies
Since the further away from the earth
So much further from God[16]

Can our theologies be seeds in the ground and plows to tend the earth? Can our prayers be a mantle to protect trees from being cut and our anointing lead to the survival of forests? Can our singing protect the rivers and the mountains? Can we all fight for the plight of Black people and support their demands? Can we shake off the mantle of coloniality, of modernity, of progress, of extractivism, of capitalism, of racism, of patriarchalism that has been bestowed upon us, and join the fights on the streets, as well as the bees, the dolphins, the moss, the caterpillars, the birds, the trees, the rivers, the sea? All of us, a single bundle of humus!

The evidence will be in the performance of our faith in both our rituals and our lives, in our saying and in our doing. All of us, a single bundle of humus!

CHAPTER SEVEN[1]

Class, Interreligious Borders, and Ways of Living with Pachamama

Carine Shresta Bollam, 7 years old

This chapter was written in Kenya and so I begin by honoring the 42 peoples that compose the beauty of this country. Moreover, we must also celebrate not only the human beings who live there, but also all the animals and plants and mineral worlds that have lived here for ages. The first species of homo sapiens appeared in Africa, and this is the springboard of what constitutes our fundamental understanding of the Anthropos in all its metaphysics of human exceptionalism in relation to other forms of life. This notion of human exceptionalism has brought us to the possible end of our human world. According to Déborah Danowski and Eduardo Viveiros de Castro, we must begin to think in the space between a "world without us," and an "us without the world."[2] The intricacies between humans, economy and class, religion and the earth will guide our thinking here.

If Marx said, "Philosophers have only interpreted the world, what matters is to change it."[3] we might say "Religious thinkers have tried to keep their worlds intact, what matters is to change it." We feel and believe that our religious worlds and traditions have all it takes to tackle the world we live in. Almost as discreet entities, our religions feed off their own worlds and our work is to discover these worlds deeper and better so that we and the world can be fully lived, saved, or enlightened.

Perhaps in some sense, there is a class/caste system embedded in the structures of our religious beliefs that is organized around hierarchies, power, and control. In some cases, these systems are also organized around exploitation and expropriation, centered in the notion of the Anthropos, marking vividly a deep sense of human exceptionalism that not only considers few humans, but does not consider anything that is not human.

I can surely speak about that from a Christian perspective. Christian denominations are often organized around class structures. Many churches hold large amounts of money. In the US alone, Presbyterians have five billion dollars in the market. Methodists perhaps have 20 billion. Money keeps these denominations together, and within Christian denominations we find the same neoliberal system with a few churches accumulating loads of money, a number of churches squeezed in the middle, and a fast-growing number of churches trying to survive. In New York we have one single church that has five billion dollars in their assets. How is this really Christianity? People lack housing, health care, and food while a single church hoards these assets! This is a mark of what Christianity has become: a sustainer of class struggles. The Christian denominational structure is a cup full of class identities and struggle, but the church necessarily remains oblivious to those struggles, so it can continue its public mission of being the church of Jesus Christ.

For non-Christians who are not aware of Christian liberation theologies in the 20th century, there was a theological group called EATWOT, *Ecumenical Association of Third World Theologians*, who put together liberation theologians from Asia, Africa, North America, and Latin America. EATWOT was a place for theological battles. Each continent brought a distinct critique to the other. Africans challenged other theologians: where is the place of culture in your theologies? Black theology from North America demanded Latin Americans talk about race because there was no discussion of race in most or any of their works. Latin Americans got back to North Americans asking: where is the notion of class in your empty discourses of race? And Asians complained with everyone else that nobody had the slightest idea of what it meant to live in an interreligious world. From EATWOT we must move forward in different forms of relations. These discreet forms of theologies must now be placed alongside and mixed with each other. As my brother Joerg Rieger reminds us, class "needs to be considered as a relational term."[4] We must expand these relations from other places: from the end of the world as we know it; from the places where the poorest of the earth live; from the conditions in which the poorest earth itself is living now. I will talk from a position that aims to be nearer to the poor but struck by what Isabelle Stengers calls, "the intrusion of Gaia."[5] Before this, though, let us look at the economic sovereignty of capitalism.

Economics and the End of the World—
A Perspective from Latin America

Fredric Jameson said "Someone once said that it is easier to imagine the end of the world than to imagine the end of capitalism. We can now revise that and witness the attempt to imagine capitalism by way of imagining the end of the world."[6] How long until capitalism destroys us all, along with our religions?

We can divide historical times within the Western world and name some of their major aspects from the Middle Ages to our present time. These characterizations are filled with generalities and inconsistencies, but I hope to give a sense that throughout this time, the "civilizing" process of colonization was nothing more than a project of barbarism, plundering, stealing, and destruction. It helps us to understand the current spiritualities present in *Abya Yala*,[7] and mostly the southern part of it that was called Latin America. In broad categories, we might understand the Middle Ages in this way:

→ **Middle Ages**

    → **Feudalism/Land Production**

        → **Kings/Queens**

            → **Empire as Colonialism**

        → **Roman Catholicism**

    → **Extended Family/Community Networks**

→ **Rural Areas**

Feudalism transformed into other forms of dominating the land and people after the Treaty of Tordesillas happened in Latin America in 1506. Pope Julius II divided Latin America into two parts and gave them to Spain and Portugal. The colonization of Latin America resulted in the killing of millions of Indigenous people, and the theft of Latin America's rich resources that fed the wealth of Europe. The political idea of the two kings—God and the Pope/kings—was a mirror of the theological understanding of the transcendent/immanent presence of God, which organized people's tutelage by laws, the domination of the land, and the implementation of a cosmovision that was to be assimilated by the Indigenous and African peoples.

The battle between different forms of religion and cosmovisions were at the heart of the colonization process. Now, the broad categories look like this scheme, *on the next page.*

The Reformation would only come later to Latin America, even though John Calvin sent missionaries to the coast of Brazil during its earliest years. Those missionaries were killed by Indigenous people, but the plundering of Latin America continued, despite Indigenous resistance, as the industrial revolution created a more urgent need for natural resources. The lower castes of Europe were sent to Latin America to build the new world as well as Africans, who were enslaved. It is from this period to our current day that African Latin Americans have suffered and continue to be oppressed.

Christian spirituality, over against African and Indigenous spiritualities, became the ground of the civilization process and the measure of humanity. This process that claimed the power of a proper God who demanded a proper way of living with proper ritual actions, proper relations, proper bodies, proper thinking, and proper spiritualities. The break and battle between Roman Catholicism and Protestantism with their intense fights over proper Christian forms of spirituality lay dormant until our current time, when Christian Churches mix theologies and spiritualities that feed off one another even though Pentecostal, Neopentecostal, and Protestant Churches see Roman Catholics as enemies.

The second world war spread the presence of fascism even to Latin America and it has never left. Fascism could be called a byproduct of coloniality which was not new to Latin America. The period immediately after World War II marked the reconstruction of Europe and catapulted the United States into the position of a global empire. What is now known as the *Trente Glorieuses*, or the *glorious thirties*, was the period between 1945 to 1975 where countries in Europe grew economically under the Marshall Plan. Growth of economies, industrialization, increase of private possessions, expansion of the job market and the creation of a "welfare state" with labor rights, health systems, and retirement plans marked this

→ **Reformation/Renaissance/Enlightenment**

 → **Capitalism/Industrial Revolution**

  → **Nation/States and the transatlantic slave trade**

   → **Colonialism around the world: conquest and plundering; formation of race**

  → **Roman Catholics and Protestantism supporting colonization and persecuting and killing non-Christians**

 → **Nuclear Families**

→ **Urban/Suburban Areas**

period.

This era also saw the growth of the U.S. as a global militarized empire and the creation of global institutions such as the United Nations and the World Health Organization as mechanisms to counter movements against democracy or the possibility of another global war. It is during this time that the Declaration of Rights was created.

The underside of this picture is that this entire movement was a global colonized domination by the U.S. and Europe. It was Africa, Latin America, and Asia that provided the resources for Europe and the U.S. to grow. The creation of a social state for the wellbeing of most citizens with social security, retirement and workers' rights was nothing more than a state capitalism of maximum integration destined to benefit a certain part of the population, mostly the white, middle and upper classes. This form of the welfare state was also copied by many countries in Latin America.

While power and money continued the globalization process, the perfect model of economic management was created by other institutions: Brenton Woods/IMF/World Bank/Federal Banks that started to give money to the so-called third world countries to enhance their economies. Behind the borrowing of money was a strategic agenda to control political positions, fiscal legislations, educational programs, and industrial preferences, creating huge forms of dependency in Latin American countries.

These global organizations were responsible for disseminating an idealized world of modernity and its universal forms of humanity. It was a soft form of domination where richer countries, under the banner of human rights and democracy, controlled the agenda, presence, and knowledges of the rest of the world. These geo-economic and political movements had huge consequences for the spiritualities of Latin American people. The state-sanctioned forms of life and organization created rules and emotions, translated into forms of religion, to support these forms of politics. Worship services were an arm of the state with their spiritualities of steadfastness, order, and progress, assuring God's presence in the social realm. However, the economic gap produced by these social forms of state policies gave rise to the ongoing pauperization of Latin America's population. It is within these forms of oppression that popular social movements and liberation theology arrived, fighting against the domination of the United States and its political and missionary right wing through conservative and militarized governments in Latin America.

The end of the 20th century and the beginning of the 21st century have seen enormous changes in the entire landscape of Latin America. Socialists or leftist movements that happened throughout Latin America from the 1960's to the beginning of the 1990's began to fail. Governments

→ Post-World War II/Cold War

    → Brenton Woods/IMF/World Bank/Federal Banks

        → Nation States promoting the social common grounds with social securities, pension, worker's rights

            → United Nations, World Health Organization, The International Labor Organization, Organization of American States as legalized forms of accepted colonialism

        → Vatican II and the church openness, Liberation Theology and later the crush against communism, the beginning of new forms of Pentecostalism

    → Gay and Lesbian Rights becoming more accepted

→ Megacities, rural areas being dominated by agrobusiness

like Bolivia, with a strong connection to Indigenous people, and Brazil, with a president committed to the poor, both had public policies created to give voice to vulnerable communities. However, to do that, their central commitments were to the economic sector, and eventually their allegiance turned to right-wing politicians who swallowed these so-called leftist governments.

Conservatism and fascism are growing throughout Latin America, and the private economic sector supports conservative politicians and movements. The coups in Brazil and Bolivia, the recent domination of neoliberalism in Argentina and Chile, and the rise of conservative religious movements everywhere are all reshaping politics in Latin America. Christian Churches are also supporting these movements and are inserting their presence into ever higher political positions. By supporting conservative political parties and movements, they can receive the benefits of radio, television distribution, and forgiveness of federal debts. Christian spiritualities during this period are in a state of evulsion, marked by a desire for wealth, social ascension, and survival.

The mission of these spiritualities has been the recessive colonial notion of a political project of conquest and the "canceling" of other religions. Religions of African descent have been the targeted by Christian churches, whose love of God is regimented by a militarized war against the devil. The devil in these spiritualities has been named as gender theory, the LGBTQIA+ community, non-Christians, and everyone who is against right-wing "family values."

While Christian spiritualities cater to the desires of individuals, public spaces have been encroached upon by the private sector. Since the world is coming to an end with the coming of Christ, the biomes and forests and rivers, which are now the domain of agribusiness, do not matter. Jesus is coming, thanks be to God! Why bother with the Indigenous and Black people who continue to live through endless genocides?

Economy and Interreligious Dialogue

I wonder why interreligious dialogue ignores the ways in which economy marks our religious perceptions in the world. I wonder why our religious perceptions have not adhered to more substantial notions of the sacred. Is it because we only know how to talk about religious dogmas and textual hermeneutics? Is it because class does not belong in this dialogue? Is it because the very notion of our religious assembly does not need, or is even able, to engage with class as a fundamental issue in religious formation? Or is it that class is an ideological notion, and religion cannot deal with Marxist notions of religion as apparatus of the state?[8]

→End of the 20th Century and the First Decades of the 21st Century

    →The total ruling of the market without limits

        →The rise of leftist governments while International Corporations began to dominate the world as Nation States rules was only to support corporations and the neoliberal premises

            →Churches and conservative religious groups pressing to debunk United Nations, World Health Organization, The International Labor Organization

        →Explosion of New Pentecostalisms

      →Explosion of nuclear forms of families and decentralization of gender and sexualities

→Encroaching on every form of eco-system, destruction of rural and farmer workers, "agrobusiness is pop" and explosion of megacities.

As mentioned earlier, Joerg Rieger's notion that class is "a relational term," must be taken up and related to religious structure and strictures. The relationality of religion and its modes of production must be deeply related to the ways in which capitalism creates the means of production. Capitalism would not work without the unrelated-related religious connections. Religious silence, worldly detachment, and various forms of theocracy have offered support, organization, and very few limits to the ways that the market organizes itself around the world today. It is clear to see how Christianity has not only been an ally to capitalism, but it also made capitalism possible from its onset and has helped it continue its trajectory all the way through liberal and neoliberal economic formats. In what ways have other religions related their religious worldviews with the capitalist views of the world? How much of our religious rituals rubber stamp capitalist forms of living?

The manifested claws of capitalism, white supremacy, and state violence are everywhere, and their goals are clear: to attack Indigenous people for their lands and destroy their understanding of land as non-property and logic of non-desire; to attack women for their ability to sustain familial networks of sustenance that do not rely on massive modes of production; to attack LGBTQIA+ communities to maintain the supremacy of heterosexuality and conservative "family values"; to attack immigrants for their threat to civilized social accomplishments; to attack Black folks in order to maintain white supremacy undisputed; to attack the poor for their excess and negative surplus of existence.

Interreligious dialogue must not be afraid to get messy and name the ways we, as religious people, have participated and built capitalist systems of oppression and destruction. How much have our religions contributed to forms of capitalism that are destroying ourselves and the earth? How have religions supported the attack on queer folks, Indigenous peoples, Black folks, women, children, and the poor? How have our religions established local worshiping communities around class? How are the poor are allowed to ask for alms but are not permitted to be fully a part of these communities? The economic plundering of the world is also associated with the project of colonization and major religions are marked by it. If capitalism has destroyed local forms of the means of production and small business, the major religions such as Buddhism, Christianity and Islam have also diluted, destroyed, or absorbed most of the Indigenous religions around the world.[9] Thus we can say that the colonization process has created many forms of big corporations and big religions.

The Logic of Capitalism and The Logic of Religion

The logic of colonialism is the logic of coloniality, which involves emergent patterns in colonial locations/time that reproduce themselves beyond time and place. The logic of coloniality is the same logic of capitalism and the same logic of religion: stealing, plundering, controlling, imposing, and destroying. The amount of stolen land in the hands of religions can also be added to this scheme. In Christianity, accumulation by dispossession is the logic of spiritual catharsis and ritual practices. The notion of public in Christian public religion is set by way of its private properties and accumulation of wealth. Perhaps Marx can help us here.

Capitalism from its onset depended on forms of accumulation based on uprooting people from their own lands, the enclosure of the Commons, and the exploitation of free labor. We see it everywhere, in the loss of labor rights, the reinstatement of slave labor, the automatization of work, and the work of extractivism. Dispossession on steroids! At the hands of the neoliberal market, Nation-States now do the dirty work of legislation and police enforcement to continue the expropriation and dispossession of people and the earth and the transfer of capital from social welfare into private sectors. As Brazilian philosopher Marilena Chauí puts it, the very notion of the State today thinks of itself as private.[10] When Ronald Reagan said to the people of the United States that the nine most terrifying words in the English language are, "I'm from the government, and I'm here to help." and when Margaret Thatcher said, "There's no such thing as society. There are individual men and women and there are families." they were both instituting the realm of the neoliberal state, where the private state must relate to the private individual in a market that is private but protected by the state. This is the other side of the market coin.

The centralization of the market comes from the stealing/dispossession of small communities and their assets, all organized around class struggle. Examples:

(1) *Small farmers losing their land and assets to big multinational companies. Bayer and Monsanto modifying seeds and taking over lands from small farmers.*

(2) *Big fish industries destroying eco-systems of fish where small fishing communities live. The industry uses massive ships that outcompete small boats from small villagers, who also cannot compete with the price of the fish in the market.*

(3) *Workers losing their rights everywhere, working extra hours for the same amount of money. They are also losing their pensions and their welfare protection.*

(4) *Health systems turned for profit, incentivizing hospitals, and health insurance companies to fight against universal care.*

(5) *Education turned for profit, making research and teachers dependent on the private sector and their priorities.*

(6) *Taxing the poor and giving a break to rich people. Donald Trump's secretary pays more taxes than Trump himself.*

(7) *Neighborhood gentrification. Eviction and expulsion of local people from their own homes to distant places for the arrival of upper classes.*

(8) *Predatory credit lines for small business who depend on the flow of the market. and whose assets and profits will be liquidated so they can be easily bought by bigger companies.*

(9) *International organizations such the IMF and World Bank loaning money to countries to boost their economies and asking them in return to produce specific economic, educational, and state agendas within these countries, which makes it easier for large foreign companies to come in and take over local frail markets. As a Java Film Executive from Indonesia says:*

> *So, all these big, developed countries, they have their own protection measures to face Globalization. But a country like us (Indonesia), we are so naïve, so innocent, so young. We are a developing country. We don't have expertise in making this kind of regulation. Indonesia in the end becomes the target market. We have opened our market, people come in. Some investments come in because our labor is very cheap. But in the end of the day, what happens? They are selling their products here, mostly, and we don't have any protection.*[11]

(10) *Wars and rumors of wars. The United States has been at War 222 out of 239 years. To become the Empire, it had to invade, kill, and massacre countries, places, and people. The militarized might of*

the United States is one of the worst institutions that dispossesses and expropriates people.

(11) Land grabbing and evictions. There are many cases with people having their lands stolen, legally or illegally. In São Paulo, for example, the State sets fire to whole communities of poor people to take their locations and expropriate their lands. In United States, about 30-40 million people are running the risk of eviction due to COVID-19.[12]

(12) Extractivisms. The most current form of dispossession and expropriation has been the development of extractivist forms of expropriating wealth. China, France, Holland, the U.S., and Canada are expropriating rivers, mountains, seas, air, rocks, lands, eco-systems, everything! As Barack Obama said during his presidency: "we are drilling all over the place." These countries go to countries with already fragile economies and buy/steal all they want. The extractivism of our time is the new raw destruction led by neoliberalism. For capitalism, the earth is a commodity, a place to extract for development and profit.

In all these examples the capital class is gaining more than the labor class. In all these examples we see *dispossession*. In all these examples, there is the expropriation of something: health, education, communities, networks, modes of being, communal sustenance and the notion of a common good. In all these examples, we see class struggle by domination and expropriation of people's lives. In all these examples, we see utter, disastrous, unspeakable forms of violence, which are the core of capitalism's soul--ongoing, always impending, vicious raw violence.

According to David Harvey "accumulation based upon predation, fraud, and violence," requires "A general re-evaluation of the continuous role and persistence of the predatory practices of 'primitive' or 'original' accumulation within the long historical geography of capital accumulation..." and so, still according to Harvey, there is a need to "substitute these terms by the concept of accumulation by dispossession."[13]

And as Indonesian Intan Suwandi, quoting Marx, says, "'The hidden abode of production,' which, in the era of global commodity chains, is located in the Global South."[14] Tony Norfield in *The City*, says that imperialism as it exists today in "the present stage of capitalist development" has its primary basis in the inescapable reality that "a few major corporations from a small number of countries dominate the world market, world finance and the global structure of production."[15]

A Religious Turn

Our religious commitment should be with the poor. I am more interested in the dialogue between Dalits from the Muslim, Hindu, Buddhist, and Christian traditions than the discussion of divine love from religious experts. Unless we turn our ears to the ground and listen to the poor, religious dialogue will not be able to offer much help for our calamitous situations. How can we break free from the forms of caste and class from within our religions?

One example comes from Jewish liberation theologian Marc H. Ellis. In his book *Beyond Innocence and Redemption*, Ellis talks about a "Liturgy of Destruction," a term he gets from David Roskies.[16] The idea of a liturgy of destruction is for Jews to find ways to respond to the Holocaust but also to the many catastrophes experienced by Jews in their history. Ellis mentions the liturgical day of Yom Hashoah, which is a special day to recall the untold sufferings of the Jewish people.

Ellis, however, goes beyond the boundaries of Jewish liturgy to insist that today, Jews cannot do the Yom Hashoah if the liturgy does not take into consideration what Israel is doing to the Palestinians. For Ellis, the only way to understand the Holocaust is by way of remembering the Palestinians. He says,

> *for many, the liturgy of destruction rings hollow when it does not acknowledge those who have suffered and are suffering today because of that liturgy, the Palestinian people, and reveals a hollowness, almost a deceptive quality that forces a reevaluation of the liturgy itself. A new inclusiveness in the landscape of the dead and dying is called for if the voices of the Holocaust are to be rescued from an artificial construct that threatens memory much more than the Bitburg affair did.*[17]

In other words, the very liturgical celebration of Yom Hashoah, the special day to recall the untold sufferings of the Jewish people, must also recall the sufferings of the Palestinians. Some Synagogues are doing this. Rabbi Brant Rosen at Tzedek Chicago includes other people's sufferings in the Yom Hashoah prayers. Here is a "A Prayer for Yom Hashoah" by Rabbi Rosen:

*Oh, Spirit of mercy, whose presence dwells in the highest heights and the
    darkest depths:*

*Shelter the souls
    of all who were oppressed and murdered during the years of the
    Shoah.*

*May the memory of those who were singled out, persecuted, and destroyed
    be sanctified for goodness
    and for peace:*

*Jews, gays, lesbians
    and political dissidents;
    communists, socialists,
    labor leaders and Soviet prisoners of war; resistance fighters,
    Roma,
    Freemasons and Jehovah's Witnesses;
    the disabled of mind and body;
    the homeless, the unemployed
    and the unwanted...*

*May all who were once left vulnerable
    remain protected beneath the soft wings of your presence that they
    may rest in peace.*

*Spirit of Compassion,
    help us to mourn their loss in such a way
    that our fears and our hopes will become indistinguishable from
    the fears and the hopes of all who are oppressed.*

*Help us turn isolation into wholeness,
    division into fellowship
    and bitterness into healing waters of liberation for all humanity.*

Amen.[18]

For Ellis, a liturgy of destruction must be more inclusive and engaging to become entangled and welcome the challenge to involve the Palestinians. For him, the reference point for Jews must be beyond themselves. Thus, to revisit the Holocaust is also to visit the destruction of the Palestinians. When one looks at the Palestinian erasure, Ellis says a Jew can say, "I've seen it, I know what that means." The liturgical texture that gives life to the individual and to the collective only happens by way of somebody else. The liturgical boundary is fundamental here, but the reason Palestinians are fully within this liturgy is because, as Ellis says, "Palestinians are within ourselves." The liturgical rendering of the Jewish history can only happen if the history of the Palestinians is also remembered and transformed.

Perhaps Christianity can learn, with Marc Ellis, his notion of an unstable self and an unstable God that can only find meaning in relationship with another people. If we can do that with other people's lives and history, then we will realize that all of us must have the same conditions of living, and thus the liturgical work is not only to include another people in the prayer, but to include another people in the land and in other forms of life and ways of living.

The main quest here, however, is not for religions to include other people for the sake of religious dialogue, but rather, to undo our religious beliefs and our forms of living. If we take seriously those who are at the bottom of societies, we must be transformed and change everything until we find a way that every single being can have a life with dignity.

A Larger Community

Unfortunately, praying with other people until we realize that we all must have equal forms of living is not enough. We must expand the notion of class beyond human exceptionalism. Many of us have learned that humans are the apex of the earth, and we talk only about human relations, human production, and human inequality. It is time for us to expand the notion of community to include the mineral, vegetable, and animal worlds. If we do not believe these other worlds are in deep relationship and connection with us, we will destroy everything. Scientists are telling us that we are marching fast towards the burning of the earth and the demise of human living. We are already at a place of no return but not many people seem to be concerned. If religions are to show their care for the earth, we must engage in thinking, praying, and producing forms of life that are beyond the capitalistic system.

So far, we have lived out our religions as if the earth is merely the background of our lives. We pray, perform our religious rites, and sing our songs without much concern for the earth. All we care about is dogmas, religious identities and holding forth the traditions of ancestors. What we have forgotten is the one ancestor of us all that keeps us alive: the earth! None of our religious structures will matter if we do not actually have a world to live in.

Isabelle Stengers says that Pachamama has come out of the background and is intruding into our lives. She calls it "the intrusion of Gaia."[19] This intrusion shows us that Pachamama has taken the stage and is ruling our ways of living more clearly, and roughly, than we ever imagined. We are now at the mercy of Gaia, and we are building a future of disastrous impending catastrophes.

This intrusion is already happening in places where the people of that land are not the ones responsible for devastating the earth. Africa is already feeling it, islands everywhere are feeling it, Central American and Asian farmers are feeling it. We already have 240 million climate change migrants. Our situation is a disaster. This impending disaster is already here, unfolding in proportions that no one can imagine.

This shift is Gaia saying that our capitalistic ways of living and being are eating everything alive, and there is no way that life, as we know it, can continue. As we ponder this, we must contemplate how our religions have somewhat been silent about the ongoing relationship of appropriation, dispossession, and destruction of the earth. The Christianity of "conquer and dominate" was a powerful idea that created structures that continue to sustain the forms of domination and destruction of the earth until today.

Fredric Jameson, Déborah Danowski, and Eduardo Viveiros de Castro in their book *The Ends of the World*, tell us how modernity and colonization have made the end of the world arrive much sooner and now we must wrestle not with the imagination of a future to come, but rather a future that is already here. Modernist cosmologies are in stark opposition to Indigenous cosmologies. Christian cosmologies are organized over against animals and nature, while Indigenous cosmologies organize with animals and nature.

In Christianity, humans rise above the stages of animality and nature to claim humanity and culture by way of their elevated mind and ability to use power. While in Indigenous ways of thinking and believing, there is deep relationality between humans and the earth, for the modernist capitalistic Christian, this relationship is one of use, domination, and pleasure. In Indigenous ways of thinking and believing, humans are just a part of a larger chain of interconnected kinship, of many natures, which stands in stark opposition to the modernist capitalistic Christian way, claiming that we humans are at the top of the chain, above the natural world.

Modernity, through Christian influence, turned collective ways of being into individual modes of thinking-being (Descartes), flattened the complexity of entangled lives and made us into discreet forms of subjects, detached from the earth and pursued (individual) happiness. Holding on to a transcendent God, we were dislodged from the supernatural world by way of our sin, and our task became to find ways to get back to it. Original sin was more than a desire for knowledge, it was a desire to be a single being on one's own. That is our paradise lost: our sense of disconnection, our longing for belonging. With our paradise lost, we also lost our interconnected identity, our ability to perceive things collectively. We became completely confused, trying to discern identity from race, class from conceptualizations, religion from supremacy, God from the market, religiosity from being modern. Everything became a matter of mastery, conquering, and owning. I must conquer the earth, women, lesser human beings, animals and all the beasts.

According to Danowski and Viveiros de Castro, we will be a people without a world soon, which does not correlate with the notion of the earth, for the earth will continue. They say:

> To put it at its simplest, we could start from the opposition between a "world without us," that is, the world after the existence of the human species; and an "us without the world," a worldless or environmentless humankind, the subsistence of some form of humanity or subjectivity after the end of the world.[20]

We will all be bereft of a world in which to live; "the next generations (the generations after us) will have to survive in an impoverished, sordid environment; an ecological desert, a sociological hell."[21] And, I would add. a theological and religious catastrophe.

Pachamama's intrusion is changing everything. Gaia will continue to bring us to the brink of chaos, destabilizing all our beliefs and practices. The discreetness of our religions will not be enough. Speaking for myself: my Christianity will not give me enough to live on this earth without the world we know. The only way to be is, and will be, in relationship with other religions.

Conclusion

At the end of the world, we will be left not only with class conflict, but all forms of conflicts. Conflicts not only come out of the structures of class struggles, but also out of the ways the earth lives. Capitalism has centered our conflicts on humans, but we have huge conflicts with other beings too.

We are in constant struggle against the elephants, the bees, the meadows, the rivers, the mountains, the trees. It is time for our religions to think in a new key, fundamentally from the perspective of the earth and the poor. We can do that and one way to start is to reshape our religions. Religious people have also the responsibility to help end capitalism and all its tentacles of death.

As global capitalism, colonization, and Christianity have shaped Latin America, there are also practices from below that shape Christianity differently and can help us change the way Christians see the world. Don Pedro Casaldáliga, a prophetic liberation theology voice in Brazil, has committed to the poor in the center of Brazil. His ministry provided a space where the poor were able to fight agribusiness and the white supremacist Brazilian State. Within his ministry other religions were able to flourish. Within his ministry, the earth was not destroyed completely. Casaldáliga knew only too well the class struggle at the heart of the Brazilian colonizing project. Once he said: "In the womb of Mary God became man. In Joseph's carpentry, he became a class." This is a transformation of how we see Jesus, not only entangled in divine promises, not only in spiritual practices but rather in "promiscuous incarnations"[22] and class struggles. We must expand our religious understandings of the world through class struggles and earth destruction. Perhaps Christians can add to Casaldáliga's saying: "In the womb of Mary God became man. In Joseph's carpentry, he was made class..." but in the desert, he was made rocks, soil, solitude.

Perhaps we might be able add the cries of the earth in our liturgies of destructions as we include other people and religions to radically change and challenge who we are. Perhaps Indigenous people can teach us to understand rivers and trees and mountains and animals as subjects and holders of their own lives. Instead of seeing ourselves as capitalism taught us, as single selves and fully responsible for our individual economic success, we might learn with the African Ubuntu, as co-participators in life, responsible for each other, together in the same village around the same trees and rivers. Perhaps Buddhism can help us listen to ourselves differently and see that the bird singing right in front of me is not a separate creature but myself, and her singing is my own singing too. Perhaps Candomblé will expose me to a much larger view of life and movements of energies in a world of spirits that demands necessary balance. In all these encounters, I will become more adept at living on a common earth with many worlds.

In Brazil there is an African-Indigenous religion called *Jurema*. *Jurema* is an amazing flux, entanglement, and mutual transformation of Indigenous and African religions. A fruit of their need to survive, Indigenous and Black people in Brazil not only organized themselves in social forms of resisting but engaged in new forms of re-existing by creating other forms of religion. They are the greatest common denominator of the Brazilian minimum religion.[23] To survive. To resist, but even more than that, re-exist! In a new key for a new time and space.

Finally, can we get to the point where we can turn our world of class struggles into a life lived *with* the earth, belonging to the earth, and never owning the earth or any private space? Can we all be called religions of the earth?

If so, we might be able to change Marx's famous adage. Instead of "The proletarians have nothing to lose but their chains," perhaps the quest for religious people would be "The religious people, by moving into other religions, and deeply into the earth, have nothing to lose but their religious chains."

CHAPTER EIGHT[1]

Birds, People, Then Religion:

An Eco-Liberation Theological and Pedagogical Approach to Interreligious Rituals

Peter Isaac Lindsey Perella Carvalhaes, 9 years old

What does it mean for us to do interreligious theological dialogue and engagement after the election of Donald Trump, whose rhetoric has at best validated, and at worst increased, xenophobia, the colonial economic powers, and the global movement towards hatred of the poor? Our challenges get bigger and more complex and difficult by the day. The world is on fire from fights about religious and cultural identity. Our situation is so confusing that even the IMF and the World Bank are concerned with the unequal distribution of the wealth in the world! Fear and anger are the world's most present feelings right now, thereby adding to the humiliation of the majority of people on our planet who simply cannot make it. The Spirit of development in the neoliberal system is crushing entire populations, taking not only our money but poisoning our souls and breaking our spirits. The earth is excruciatingly exploited, making poor people of all colors, religions, and places inhabit the same impoverished, squalid, sordid, neglected spaces.

Moreover, working in institutions that are heirs of colonial powers, we must deal with the shattering of the white liberal myth of the U.S. as a land of democracy and rights and care for all. Education has become business and schools mirror for profit agencies; unless we can gain results with clear outcomes, education cannot support and be part of the system. In the classroom, as well as in society, there is hardly any possibility to engage in of any sort of political cultural conversation across the divides, much less attend to religious conversations about diversity. Moreover, the same system is telling us that all we have is our own property: identities in body politics. I fight for mine; you fight for yours; and we fight with each other. Meanwhile the financial powers laugh at our very educated, proficient, and highly complex understanding of political identities and religious exclusivisms.

If we are to think about these dynamics in our educational systems and our classrooms, I wonder how can we engage in interreligious conversations? Since our classrooms are also mirrors of our communities, how do we think and do with communities who live in the margins? Is there any correlation with classrooms and our world at large?

I write as a Christian liberation theologian. My sense of God comes from my upbringing in poverty and being a shoeshining boy at 8 years old in Brazil. In that sense, I write to try to reach the same children and their families growing up in poverty. My (very dangerous) common denominator is the economic exclusion of people across the globe, in whatever religion they might or might not belong. The hope is to find a sense of a "body" where we work with, from and to, to find ways to transform these situations. In these attempts, there are many dangers, among which is the possible flattening of the concept of poverty and its given normative claims. Nonetheless, this is an attempt to find a location, that is, economic poverty, within diverse social, contextual, cultural, and religious locations, one in which we can perform interreligious engagements.

Setting the Ground

When the radical Brazilian Catholic Archbishop Dom Helder Câmara, known in Brazil as the communist priest for being on the side of the poor, received the Niwano Peace Price in Kyoto, in 1970, he also participated in the World Conference of Religion and Peace. In that meeting, he said that religions were able to share this:

> *A conviction of the unity of the human family and equality of all human beings; A sense of sacred in every individual and its conscience; A sense of value in the human community; The comprehension that strength is not reason that human power is not self-sufficient and absolute; The belief that love, compassion, detachment and interior strength of truth have a spirit that is stronger than hatred, enmity and egotism; A sense of obligation to be on the side of the poor and the oppressed, against the rich and the oppressor; A profound hope that goodwill will triumph.[2]*

For him, the commitment with the poor--to enter into a pilgrimage with the poor--was the very notion that would create utopias on the horizon of our thinking and our practice. For him, to be with the poor was the fundamental ground, path, motion, and notion that sustained our forms of actions, beliefs, and utopias. It is from this place that I want to speak: from the margins. Coming from my theological education in liberation theologies in Latin America, I firmly believe that the Christian God is a God of liberation! Jesus, as God Emmanuel, God with us, chose to live with us in the form of a boy who from birth was a refugee, with parents forced to run away from his own "country." This Jesus lived his life amidst the poor and the outcast and at the end was killed by the Roman empire. For Jesus, the final judgment of our own lives will not be what we believed but what we did for those cast aside of our societies: "for I was hungry and you gave me food, I was thirsty and you gave me something to drink, I was a stranger and you welcomed me, I was naked and you gave me clothing, I was sick and you took care of me, I was in prison and you visited me" (Matthew 25:35-36).

In Jesus, God makes a clear choice to be on the side of the poor. A God who does not make choices is a God of the powerful. A God of all is a God of nobody. A God who loves all is like saying all lives matter. A God who makes choices, who chooses the poor, is like saying Black Lives Matter. Clearly this preferential option does not mean to discard others, but it does mean to be on the side of those who are on the underside of history, of whatever religion or no religion. It is from this place that I pursue interreligious theological dialogue and study interreligious engagement through rituals. This is necessarily neither an exclusive Christian place nor an attempt to find Karl Ranner's notion of "anonymous Christians"[3] in other religions. As we will see later, the concern and deep care for the poor is present in many religions. This broad religious care for the poor can entail interreligious engagements and commitments that can create many forms of religious liberation,[4] decolonial thinking, pedagogies of insurrection, healing ceremonies, theologies of liberation, and rituals of deliverance that deal with the wounded knees and souls of our people and that pays attention fundamentally to the suffering of the people. To do that we must not pledge our allegiance to any flag, any single form of knowledge, some unmovable syllabi format, *a priori* learning outcomes, or repeated pedagogies. Our allegiances must be with the poor and our collective liberation in whatever material-spiritual, local-global, contextual-universal, immanent-transcendent form.

What would this mean ritually? How can we think about interreligious rituals and engagement from the perspective of the poor? The reference to our work from the perspective of the poor means engaging the life of the poor by being with the poor, with other sources of academic thinking, like organic liturgist-theologians, something akin to the Gramscian notion of the organic intellectual. How can our encounter with rituals of justice in one another's religion help us seek clarity within our own primary traditions? Is this an impossible theological/ritual task? Our specific task as ritual doers and theorists, is to combat a form of anti-intellectualism that is a contemporary plague in our academy that divides praxis and theory, keeping both as separate entities, antagonistic to each other. The fact that very few scholars engage in ritual or any other practice that is deeply related to their thinking shows how a certain form of thinking has detached itself from forms of praxis which are considered counter-productive to theoretical work and even "fluffy stuff" when related to proper forms of knowledge. That dichotomy has found its place in cultural forms through secular rituals that are often totally foreign to the religious theories that ground, through absentia, these rituals. Forms of life, experiences of resistance, and communitarian practices not carefully reflected not only make us lose the universal sense of our life but also make us run the risk of losing points of connection and contextual grounding situations that speaks to specificities, localized potentialities and lived antagonisms. In any doing, we need some theory. In any theory, we need some doing. In this way, present, past, and future, the sensual and the ideal, the sense of awe and beauty, the classroom and the streets, our life and the lives of our communities can only be organized and lived if theory and practice go hand in hand. There, at that juncture, we find our theoretical-theological contradictions, our ritual paradoxes, and our lives cross in between these impossibilities.

Thus, the starting point must be the lives of the poor--the economically poor--their honor and dignity above all else. Religion must come after, as a way to help us expand and challenge our thinking and theory, to make us more aware of why we do theology and liturgy, to empower our practice, to remind us to relate to sources of life, to ground us on earth, to help organize ourselves, to help us deal with and keep our diversities, specificities, distinctions, and pluralities, all while embracing the oneness of a body that struggles and fights for common causes. In that way, our interreligious dialogue and engagement should pay attention to suffering as its ground zero of belief and action. In the words of James Cone,

> It is common experience among black people in America that Black theology elevates as the supreme test to truth. To put is simply, Black Theology knows no authority more binding than the experience of oppression itself. This alone must be the ultimate authority in religious matters.[5]

Linda E. Thomas works from this grounding and expands it with regard to rituals:

> For African American male and womanist theologians, neither scholastic tradition nor scripture could be claimed as the primary/dominant sources for discerning the nature of God or God's will for creation. Rather, the experience of oppression forced upon black persons and communities became the primary arbiter of theological authority...[6]

But this is not only a Christian form of thinking. The Four noble truths of Buddha are grounded in the elimination of *duḥkha*, or suffering. Buddha sees people suffering from illness, old age, and death, and the way they related to their suffering makes him realize that their minds are attempting to grasp permanence and stability in a world where life is impermanent and unstable. The mind grasping itself and making everything permanent is the source of suffering, *duḥkha*, the self-clinging aggregation of the mind to form sensation, perception, and karmic formation and consciousness.

As academic thinkers and teachers working theoretically with sources of suffering and liberation, we also must work with our students to provide forms of thinking and practicing liberation. We must create pedagogies that demand ethical imperatives before any form of religion is possible. Peter McLaren says that in the "field of critical pedagogy today, there is a disproportionate focus on the critique of identity formation at the expense of examining and finding alternatives to existing spheres of social determination that includes institutions, social relations of production, ideologies, subjective formation and cultural imaginary – all of which are harnessed to value production."[7]

Caring for the Poor Interreligiously

Jewish Liberation theologian Marc Ellis proposes this: "There shouldn't be any religious ritual until there is justice." His claim points to the ease with which religious people perform their rituals without fully considering the suffering of oppressed people, or rather, despite the suffering of the people. In his words: "On Passover, once my favorite holiday. My passion for Passover left years ago. How to celebrate my/our liberation when we are permanently oppressing another people? Can't be done. No way. My attempt last year? Passover for Palestine. Results?"[8]

What if we take Ellis' challenge seriously for a moment? What if we would not be allowed to do our rituals until oppressed people have the possibility to live their lives fully? How can we infuse interreligious rituals and engagements with justice so that we become concerned with oppressed people and how their suffering challenges us to see and organize ourselves in the world? More than a rhetorical plea, Ellis' question challenges us to see our thinking and teaching in light of our praxis, ways of living, ritual production, and pedagogical praxis. Following this challenge, I think we can indeed create interreligious ritual practices that come out of our commitment with the poor and the work of justice. Our religious traditions already contain the requirement to seek justice and care for the poor, and this is the common ground we are seeking.

The Jewish prophets criticize worship when detached from works of justice. The Prophet Hosea says: "For I desire mercy, not sacrifice, and acknowledgment of God rather than burnt offerings" (Hosea 6:6).

From the Qur'an,[9] when Muslins are practicing fasting, they hear this from Sura 5:

> Be maintainers,
> as witnesses for the sake of Allah,
> of justice,
> and ill feeling for a people should never lead you
> to be unfair.

Be fair; that is nearer to Godwariness,
and by wary of Allah.
Allah is indeed well aware of what you do. (Qur'an 5:8)

From Christianity, Jesus gives two main commandments deeply related to worship and daily life: "Teacher, which commandment in the law is the greatest?" He said to him, "'You shall love the Lord your God with all your heart, and with all your soul, and with all your mind.' This is the greatest and first commandment. And a second is like it: "You shall love your neighbor as yourself" (Matthew 22:36-40).

One of the most chanted *Metta Sutta* of the Buddhist tradition says,

May all beings be happy,
May they be joyous and live in safety,
All living beings, whether weak or strong,
In high or middle or low realms of existence
Small or great, visible or invisible, near or far,
Born or to be born,
May all beings be happy.[10]

As we continue these ancient traditions in our days, we can see Christian, Jewish, and Muslim liberation theologies claiming God's liberation for the poor. Socially engaged Buddhism is also deeply entrenched in social liberation. The Indian Buddhist thinker Ambedkar once said, "Religion is for men and not men for religion." It is the experience of oppression that should guide us in our theological thinking, our interreligious thinking, and our forms of ritual engagement. In that way, I can see how this interreligious task is possible! *The Muslim Reform Movement* defines themselves in their declaration in this way: "Ideas do not have rights. Human beings have rights."[11] *Jews with Conscience* is a group of Jews that works on behalf of the Palestinians for justice and liberation. Christian liberation theologians have emphasized that God has a preference for the poor. These forms of tradition engage the praise, the "doxa," the glory of God in more concrete and material ways.

Following Marc Ellis, we will keep his guidance hovering over our practices, haunting us like a prophetic ghost. Our rituals are marked by notions of power, control, authority, and wealth. There must be a shift from these places, breaking the top-down structures of our religions and attending to what people are actually doing. Ellis points to this place, to the people, to mark our places of privilege and detachment from the people.

We must be aware of rituals emerging within communities of marginalized people, so that what happens in our classrooms can reflect the community.

Interreligious Rituals—in Classroom and in Chapel

The field of interreligious ritual and dialogue seeks ways to think and take seriously the theologies and/or religious thinking of religions along with the performative/ritualized forms of their beliefs. Marianne Moyaert says that, in this field, there are two forms of ritual: *outer facing* and *inner facing* rituals. She writes, "Generally speaking, however, one may distinguish between two types: on the one hand, ritual sharing that is responsive and outer-facing and on the other hand ritual participation that is inner-facing and follows the pattern of extending or receiving hospitality."[12] In this process, we look at history and see the development of interreligious rituals, which can lead in our current time to ritualizing new forms of interreligious engagements, dialogues and needs.

This new ritualizing or ritualization can happen in many places: worship places, streets, street gatherings, and conferences. Here I want to show how it can happen in classrooms. Let us start with this question: how do we connect the theoretical forms of justice purported by our religions in pedagogical and ritual ways so students can create/recreate forms of resistance and justice for their own communities?

In what follows we see a blended outer and inner ritual done by my class on *Postcolonialism and Liturgy* at Union Theological Seminary in New York City. It was a blended ritual because it was done interreligiously but also using the inner sacred sources of our religions, namely Latinx and Black forms of Christianity, Islam, and Indigenous religions (Americas and Samoa). The ritual was about addressing an issue in society but also about offering and receiving hospitality. Being aware of the distinctions and similarities of religions and diverse classrooms, we decided to start from below, our common place, what Walter Mignolo calls our "colonial wound."[13] This was a barely possible but necessary task, to keep some understanding of the Christian eucharist while opening it up for a more expansive relationship. The host became that which offers and receives the blessings and the transformations. The eucharist became a venue within and around which our people could talk. We stayed grounded in the "colonial wound," the places of hurt in our communities. While there was a strong presence of Christian theology in a Christian chapel, that presence was also challenged and somewhat undone by the movements and singing of our community's voices.

My students included a queer Black man with AIDS, a woman with European and Philippine belongings, a Muslim woman from Syria, a Central American queer man, an Indigenous man from Samoa and a man from Latin America. All of them came with stories of violence, loss, despair, and sadness, with coloniality traversing their own people. They were the organic liturgist-theologians of their own people. They represented their people and created a ritual that they could themselves do in their own communities. We put this worship service together in James Chapel at Union Theological Seminary in New York City. It was communion day. This is how it went:

We were welcomed into the space with an accordion. In the center was the Eucharistic table. Around it other tables.

Somebody speaks: *Welcome! We are here to share the sufferings of our people. To give light to the shadows where they live. And to figure out how to love our God in connected and distinctive ways. One of the main themes of decolonial thought is the loss, the tragedy, the trauma of something that has happened in the land, on people, culture, languages, Spirit...the colonial wound, the fact that regions and people around the world have been classified as less humane, unreasonable, underdeveloped physically, economically, and mentally, all of that have plagued us and our people, keeping us from living a just and dignified life. Colonial wounds that have historically dismissed our people and taken away their strength and power to continue. Wounds that can be seen and heard in the feelings and songs of melancholia, of the African Banzo, the longing for that which was taken away from us. Due to that, many of our people live in distention, in emotional distress, stretched too thin and without rest... And yet, we all continue to go on singing: "I Don't Feel no Ways Tired." As we go, we think about our wounds, we tend our wounds, we feel our wounds, and re-discover forms of resistance, and stubborn ways to continue with our lives.*

So now we are invited into a journey to different places and peoples. In each stop we will hear about a wound and will receive food for the journey. We begin singing "God have mercy" from an indigenous community in Latin America and we will walk around singing the same song. We will finish here at this table, where the Eucharistic table will be deeply engaged, transformed, expanded, and offered in many forms and ways to all of us. Let us walk. Let us go explore!

We walked around, we ate something different offered from each student/people, we heard stories, and we sang. At the gathering tables, we heard about the brutal disasters of colonization over Indigenous people and their land and culture in Samoa. We heard about the economic exploitation and death of the people in Central America. We heard about disasters of social climate change in the Philippines. We heard about Black ancestors and old and new stories of slavery and liberation. We heard a cry of a woman holding her dead son in her arms after a bomb exploded in her house while singing Allah, Allah, Allah without stopping. Then we went back to the final gathering table.

Somebody says: *Welcome back to this table after being at other tables with other foods and stories. T. S. Eliot says: "We shall not cease from exploration, and the end of all our exploring will be to arrive where we started and know the place for the first time." Back to this table, we will know this place again and yet for the first time. We heard from Jesus that we are to eat and drink in his memory, a memory of a wounded body, killed by those who tried all they could to get him down. But they thought that cutting the tree would be enough. That everything would end. They forgot however that Jesus was a seed, a seed that was to be reborn in many other people. Along through history, we saw many other seeds being reborn in other people and today we saw some of those seeds in the places and people we just visited.*

Now these seeds will continue to spread, will continue to be taken into different stories, meanings, and possibilities. From these seeds, we will now receive a drink that will serve to sustain you for the rest of our journey… until we meet again. From each cup, a blessing, a very different blessing, with different beginnings and ends, with different sources and beliefs, but blessings that will help us sing alleluias in the midst of the wounds of ourselves and our people. We are now invited to come to whatever cup you feel so moved to receive a blessing and then leave singing alleluia. Our hope is that you go out singing an alleluia to and from your own people. Whatever alleluia you might know, with other words or meanings. Let the seeds of this worship and of this week, the seeds of each people we visited today, the seed of each blessing flourish in you and in your people. Come to drink! And go strengthened by the power of the seeds!

We left empowered by the stories of pain and sorrow of our people and our lands. That made me think that we are desperately in need of another vocabulary for our pedagogies and our rituals. Perhaps if we start instead with the wound of the earth, we might be able to find ourselves there, deeply interconnected. But for that we need a new idiom so we can engage well with it.

Concluding

In that ritual, communities were remembered by individual stories that showed a larger social, economic, cultural, and political context. More importantly, every colonial wound mentioned in those stories was related to the earth--stealing, economic exploitation, social climate, slavery, wars--everything fundamentally connected with the earth. The social, economic, and cultural aspects of our analysis are not enough. We need to ground ourselves elsewhere to begin this work. We need to literally touch the ground, feel the wind, and give space to the ways we can connect to the earth. Religious scholars need to go outside and learn from the Indigenous people. To start where we suffer, we must be attuned to the movements and sounds of nature. What are the birds, the rain, the trees, the rivers, the earth, and the animals telling us about life and ourselves? They all hold forms of humanity, and unless we are deeply connected, we cannot pay attention to our collective suffering.[14]

The Zapoteca poet Natalia Toledo recited her work "The Reality" in a conference once saying, "What it is to be Indigenous? Here is my list: To have an idiom to talk to the birds who sing in the air, an idiom to speak with the earth, to talk with life… To be Indigenous is to have a universe and not to renounce to it."[15]

In order to have an idiom to talk to the birds and the earth, we need new sources, new practices, new thinking, new paradigms, new teachers, new classrooms, and new pedagogies. The pedagogies we already have do not help us to sing with, or to pay attention to the birds or the earth. Our pedagogies teach us to tackle productivity, to race after learning outcomes with clear forms of evaluation in order to meet budgetary demands. Our pedagogies center the control of the means of production and the goals of our consumerist desires, even before we get into the classroom. We are trapped in a pedagogical model that searches the earth for profit, that measures the birds by the number of bullets, that approves the variety and richness of our human life from dogmatic thinking, privileges minds over bodies and feelings, straight thoughts over zigzagging contradictory emotions of communities, and European sources over Indigenous wisdom.

Now, at the beginning of every class, we pause in silence to listen to the birds. If we cannot listen to the birds, then our classes are sad and unproductive. When we listen to the birds, we feel alive! We can connect through that which is our common ground. We can hear each other's voices and suffering. We can hear the earth's wounds. Religion? Comes after to heal the wounds of the earth and each other. For the assurance of our being alive, the very possibility of our believing, the ritualizing of our lives and beliefs, is the birds singing.

Thus, for interreligious ritual practices to happen, we first start with the wound of the earth. And for that, we need to learn how to listen, and to talk to the birds!

CHAPTER NINE[1]

White Reasoning and Worship Methodology

Olivia Maia Victoriano Pacheco da Silva, 1 year old

This essay[2] began as a contribution to the process of renewal of the *Book of Common Worship* of the Presbyterian Church, (U.S.A.).[3] I had hoped that this reflection could help us in the Presbyterian Church to pay attention to the ways in which our liturgical methodology was marked not only by a distinctive theology, but also, by certain class, race, gender, and sexual commitments. I did not intend to be adversarial to my sisters and brothers, or to dismiss the beautiful work that was already in process. Instead, I hoped to bring a vision from the underground, to surface a perspective from the fringes of our society and church that could expand the racial colors of our common faith, bringing light from the Black, brown, yellow, and red people of our society, from those who are undocumented, from sexually excluded people, and disabled people, in order to expand the possibilities of our worship services.

This work was just a small movement in the now vast and growing field of worship and diversity. I attempted to investigate, rather briefly, how the mindset of what I call white reasoning has placed minorities into the fringes of the *leitourgia*, liturgy, the "work of the people." We, the racially, sexually, and otherwise minoritized and minority people and communities, are at the receiving end of this liturgical enterprise, turned into peripheral categories by "universal" white reasoning. We are expected to receive the wisdom of our white brothers and sisters, ritualizing our loves and faith according to the grounds of wisdom and tradition handed to us. One form of knowledge, universalized, has served to deter other forms of knowledge in name of "tradition."

My point was not, and is not, to dismiss the wisdom collected in the prayer book, since the gathering of wisdom needs people of all races, gender, and sexual orientations. The problem was the absence of other people and other forms of thinking that would constitute a more complex notion of the common, at least to the point of not working with an unmarked and given sense of "common." Thus, my hope was *to expand the notion of what was "common"* to open spaces for other wisdoms, practices, and thinking from people historically colonized and designated improper, whose liturgical practices and thinking are often considered "low liturgy," "popular," "contextual," or even "cultural" liturgies, as if the so-called universal liturgy were not also based on a particular cultural and contextual understanding of the body, of life, of race, sex, class, and worship itself.

Throughout this essay, I attempt to evoke and encourage different or expanded ways of thinking, acting, gesturing, performing–indeed, different ways of living. I write with a performative mind. My main wrestling ground is an all-encompassing white reasoning that purports to be neutral, universal, and pure but instead is fundamentally patriarchal, heterosexual, colonizing, and grounded in exclusion.

Leitourgia:
Revising the Methodology of the *Book of Common Worship*[4]

What is our understanding of the word *leitourgia* as we undertake the process of BCW revision, or for that matter, any prayer book revision in a mainline Protestant denomination, beyond the PC(USA)? When I ask this question, I am inquiring not only into the meaning of the Greek word, but also into the theological sense of the assembly it brings with it, the understanding of "the people" we have in mind when we undertake our worship book revision.

In other words, I am asking, "What is the role of the assembly, of the people, in this project? Who and where are the people we are working with as we revise and renew the *Book of Common Worship*?" These fundamental questions need to be addressed prior to the decisions about what prayers and practices we will choose and give to the people— the assembly—to shape their worship life. The meaning of *leitourgia* as "the work of the people" with which we are working (either implicitly or explicitly) will define both what "work" and "people "mean when we engage in this process of renewal. With that, we may ask some obvious questions: What is actually the work of the people? Can the people, not (only) the ordained people, create liturgy? Who can create access to the holy things and decide who has access to them? What can people do in worship? To what fundamental "holy things"[5] should we ascribe and according to whom? What rubrics should be assigned? What are the holy things—symbols, ritual sequences, forms of prayer—we are going to offer to our people? What proper action or behavior will we allow in our worship spaces? What sources are we using and authorizing? And before all this, what kind of liturgical theological choices are we making?

All these questions bear witness to the notion of "common." Who is the *common* in this book of prayer or whose *common-ality* are we talking about? I am not concerned in this discussion with the number of prayers of confession, the litanies we create, the clarity of the movements, whether Eucharistic prayers are to be short or long, whether the presider should raise their hands when leading, how many feet away from the table they should stand, or how we condense, combine, and/or collapse services. I know this will be there.

What is at stake for me is the common or the measurement by which we decide what being human is all about. What form of humanity is contemplated here under the generalized sense of common? What forms of thinking, of relations, of human experiences, of knowledges, practices, and wisdom we are talking about when we talk about a "common" book of prayer?

"Common prayer" often means a form of experiences and way of living that shapes the beliefs, hopes, and troubles of one group that prays and worships together. Books of common worship are a historical report of one group of people at the expense of others. If not, why do we not have prayers and songs and litanies and confessions that are fully antiracist and deeply committed to the eradication of the systemic racism that kills and imprisons Black people? Why do we not have relentless woes and curses against white supremacy at each liturgy? Why do we sustain a bland universal form of worship that does not name the violence against LGBTQIA+ people at every corner of our common history? Why do we never talk about colonization and the ongoing genocide of Indigenous people and the endless de-sacralization of their sacred lands? Caught in the dualism of the transcendence/immanence of God, these books are always above the earth, never praying with the earth, but holding up a sovereignty that rules over the Earth and over other animals or forms of life.

In that way, books of common prayer are religious documents of white supremacy and white civilization, soft colonial support for politics of exclusion, white jurisprudence, and the control of land and riches, a hidden manifesto on class struggles, and a clear orientation of the heart, the mind, and the body towards particular forms of social, political, economic, and religious control and dominance. It is hard not to add the books of common worship to the other civilizational documents mentioned by Walter Benjamin: "There is no document of civilization which is not at the same time a document of barbarism."[6]

The content and forms of our prayers have to do with power dynamics and how this form of power is dispersed within our forms of relationship to oneself and self with others. We must ask what understanding of self is proposed in our prayer, and in relation to what? Also, how is the earth part of this common sense of life? Over against what strictures (strict structures) will we work in order to make sense of our sense of God in the common life of the people? The *Book of Common Worship* will surely enhance and close off spaces for liturgical possibilities, imagination, and context, giving a full sense of humanity and what is common. Moreover, we must say that in comparison to the 1993 *Book of Common Worship*, we can name several changes: material in three languages, more emphasis on freedom (in both the rubricized prayers and the insistence in commentary sections that liturgy is contextual), and new sections on the care of creation and justice and reconciliation. In this way, the Presbyterian *BCW* is already much more open to creativity and is more contextual and more expansive than other denominational books of common worship.

My work is to try to figure out what kind of reasoning is underneath this process, the reasoning that will make us describe what it is to be human, humus, earth, relationships, God, and each other. Thus, our work is not only to keep asking how many prayers we need to add to the book but rather, to ask a more difficult question that comes before and that has to do with the methodology of our book of common worship, its theological commitments, the people we are serving, the worlds of injustice we are dismantling, and the worlds we are creating, all marked at the beginning and at the end of this project, sometimes clearly noted, sometimes hidden in a given, expected sense of *leitourgia*.

One of the main issues for me has to do with the place in which we are to start as well as our relationships and the forms of power dynamics that exist among us. These issues define our class belongings, our access to material and other goods, and our relation to race, social access, and power. Since we hope to locate ourselves in the best sources of our tradition, often our liturgies get swallowed into a clear un/conscious purpose to reflect unspoken locations, as if the liturgy and its starting location float somewhere universally in order to keep local people and its class commitments protected. Who are we "representing"? Who are we working with and for? To what purpose? We just assume that we are doing the work of God for "all" and that is enough. This reflects a strong sense of acquired power through tradition.

A pastor friend of mine is trying to bring poor youth into the churches she is working with, but time and again these young people have nothing to do with our liturgies or our ways of being in the world. Are they the very reason for our desires to create the forms of our worship? Are we working for those who lack institutional power to find their own way within our society? Must they conform to the institution and the divine liturgy? Are we working to make worship services that condemn and resist racism and homophobia in our society?

The PC(USA) denomination is mostly made up of small, struggling congregations in quite different conditions and circumstances. We have a huge economic gap between the "tall-steeple" rich churches and the struggling churches. Is this condition of being church what marks our liturgical efforts to make a "common worship book"? We cannot hide inside "universal" liturgies when we live in such an unequal and diverse national situation. This situation presents us all with a tremendous challenge overall, and in our liturgies.

Liturgical methodology must consider for whom and with whom we are doing this work. It must consider going from neutrality to clear choices and situated language and commitments, from the fiction of the purity of our faith and clear proper identity to the ongoing mixture of beliefs and multiple identities. The end result is often more attentive to "the tradition" than to the lives of the people. Can worship be the same in radically different locations? How can radically different churches pray the same prayer? How do we care deeply for poor, struggling churches and people under strenuous forms of oppression? How do we help create liturgical language to tackle racism, poverty, climate change, and economic inequality in our society? What does the grammar of our faith teach us to speak about?

Thus, finding better prayers—or just more choices of prayers—will not do if we refuse to tackle the national sins of our country. What we actually need is to find a new methodology, one that is contextual, one that comes out of living with people, so we can find the feelings, the hurts, the settings, the situations, the relationships, the power dynamics, the ideologies, meanings and challenges of our realities. A key point here is to realize that any liturgical methodology needs to know what kind of people we want to sit with as learn and to pray together.

If *leitourgia* is the work of the people with God, what kind of people are we talking about and whose God are we talking about? Who and where are they? What is the earth they are living on? Who owns that land?

The current prayer book methodology tries to respond to a metaphysical God, a white God who lives in and through purity, universality, a certain neutrality, and a-historicity. This "neutrality" can be seen, for example, in the Eucharistic prayers. We tell the history of salvation as narrated in the Bible and then we stop. We do not allow God's action to be named within either older (than biblical history) or contemporary radical events of liberation/salvation. Once we land in the current history of our time, our liturgies become political in the sense of being actual living in the *polis*, the city, the world, something we try to avoid at all costs. As if our traditional liturgies were not political! We are certainly not trying to make liturgy a political act in the sense of political parties. Liturgy is the way we love God, and our common prayers honor and give worth to God. However, we need to wrestle with a politics of the understanding of "common" in our tradition. This concerns what is at the heart of our reasoning.

A Detour: White Reasoning

There is indeed something called white reasoning. In the book *Critique of the Tupiniquim Reason*--which he also understands to mean "Brazilian reasoning"--the Brazilian writer Roberto Gomes says that Brazilian reasoning could only take place through fiction, a fiction that begins by negating and denouncing reasoning without color, reasoning supposedly grounded in neutrality and universality.[7] White reasoning invented the

Western canon from a mythic place of purity, a zero point of thought where everything is born a self-enclosed essence and everything that is strange to that essence is shoved aside, excluded, or simply ignored as non-existent. Our Indigenous peoples and their reasoning, which are considered mythical or fictional themselves, could never beat the historical Greeks, we reason.

In his *Critique of Black Reason*, Achille Mbembe, a thinker from Cameroon, also criticizes white reasoning.[8] White reasoning is inevitably related to a specific culture, the European culture descended from Greek-Hellenistic sources. White reasoning was created through the colonization process in the meeting of Europeans with Asian, African, and Indigenous peoples. These encounters troubled Europeans' awareness of their own identity. By encountering other people, they had to make a double movement to define themselves: they had to both distinguish and equalize themselves with the people they encountered, establishing a deep distinction from Indigenous and African peoples, and establishing some kind of sameness when encountering Asians, or the "Orientals." The way to do this was not only to use power and brutal force to win over and subjugate these peoples, but also and fundamentally, to create a sense of identity through a developing form of reasoning established by slavery, the trans-Atlantic slave trade, the plundering of lands, and the exchange of merchandise. Through this process, the Europeans' given sense of humanity had to be discussed, theorized, racialized, and composed through colonizing and modernity, the whitening of reason. In this process, conquering was marked by a sense of civilization, purity, and salvation.

All non-whites became the source of European identity: European colonizers and their compatriots and coreligionists negated the other so as to affirm themselves. By establishing the lack of humanity in everyone else, the colonizers fulfilled their own sense of humanity. In other words, during the colonization process from the fifteenth century on, there occurred a racializing of the ones who were to be conquered, the strange, the foreign. "Neutrality" became a code for God's will driven by ferocious forms of power and dominance, as if the rulers of the faith were saying, "All we want to do is God's will."

After severing people's lives from their land, displacing the earth from knowledge, connection, cosmology, living, and survival, one of the tactics of this white European reasoning was to avoid relationship to the earth, the soil, and where one lives. Abandoning local geography as the structuring of life, the subconscious avoidance of one's own cultural, social, and historical context was translated into universal truths. Thus, from the small towns of Germany, Belgium, England, Switzerland. and Scotland, the premise was that the (European) Christian way of thinking was a universal way of thinking about humanity. The local thinking of these places crushed the local knowledges of other places by enforcing a universality of thinking (cosmologies), feelings and behaviors (civilization), and religion (Christianity). With the advent of colonization and the uprooting of the conquered, a focus on space gave way to a focus on time; a variety of spiritualities and forms of worship had to give way to one form of liturgy and spiritual practice, and a particular tradition was turned into God's desire. Anything that did not resemble this way of reasoning—and the related spiritual practices and understandings of God—was not proper Godly reasoning and was thus in need of correction, illumination, order, and organization.

We can see three major aspects of this totalizing way of thinking: universality, neutrality, and purity. A socially and culturally unmarked white reasoning shaped the world and marked everything with a certain truth, with "universal" (though in fact particular) values. Its ethical demands are always shaped from within that reasoning. So too in the realm of theology. The continent of Africa could never be as wise or important as Greece, the purported cradle of humankind. Western and Eastern Asia--"the Orient"--could never be the location of the most significant historical accomplishments and human creativity. Indigenous peoples could never be seen as bearers of foundational cosmologies and civilizations. White reasoning is neither naïve nor innocent, for it enforces the thinking, the appearance, and the behaviors that define—from the perspective of its own logic—what human life is about. For the purposes of our discussion here, we can say that precision of reason, historical authenticity, and coherent logic are European characteristics and that any form of reasoning that does not assume these characteristics, or reflect them as mirrors to oneself, must be considered less human, uncivilized, barbarian, or at least poorer, or not academic enough, or "popular," an offense to the tradition.

This colonial dominance continues today even under rubrics of niceness and openness to other cultural forms of worship. The central, centripetal, non-negotiable forms of believing and worshiping must always be the ones coming from the tree of white reasoning. If we look at our customary liturgical resources, what do we know or teach about theological, philosophical, or liturgical reasoning from Africa, Latin America, Asia, or Indigenous peoples of any continent, in our seminary courses? Their forms of knowledge were destroyed in what is now called epistemicide[9] or epistemological genocide. If they exist in that setting, they are present as adjunct knowledge in relation to the more enlightened fundamentals of white reasoning.

But let us go back to the historical forms of white reasoning. During the Enlightenment of the eighteenth century, says Mbembe, white reasoning was marked by "white thinkers' indifference to slave trafficking." There was little writing or fighting against slavery, if any. This indifference was already shaping Black people's lives in relation to white Europeans'. Indifference, couched as neutrality, was a way of denying, diminishing, concealing, and killing Black people. This indifference was not neutral; instead, it created the contours of white reasoning, based on a racist core, dealing with anybody "other," in this way: the stranger was to be de-nigrated, turned Black.[10] Anyone who was not white was thrown into a Blackness that served to form and define its opposite, whiteness.

In other words, it was now necessary to respond to the force of race, and the answer was to turn all those who were not white into the categories of impure, lower races and groups: Black people, Jews, Muslims, Natives, women, children. Over against this Blackness, Mbembe talks about not only the presence of whiteness but the necessary *appearance* of whiteness. He writes,

> *The work of racism consists in relegating it to the background or covering it with a veil...Racism consists, most of all, in substituting what is with something else, with another reality. It has the power to distort the real and to fix affect, but it is also a form of psychic derangement, the mechanism through which the repressed suddenly surfaces...I have emphasized that racism is a site of reality and truth—the truth of appearances. But it is also a site of rupture, of effervescence and effusion. The truth of individuals who are assigned a race is at once elsewhere and within the appearances assigned to them. They exist behind appearance, underneath what is perceived.*[11]

This appearance, which shows up as neutrality and universality, indifference, and violence toward the Blackened races, dismantles particularities. Its mythic purity serves to render everything else impure. All these dimensions of white "reality"–neutrality, universality, purity— must be enforced. Threatened by the Blackness of others, white reasoning had to deploy a whole complex of power dynamics to sustain its validity. Exploitation, control, and even annihilation, of the newly Blackened world was necessary. We see a "reasonable" movement of brutal forces moving throughout five hundred years of colonization of the Americas up until today, imposing structures and strictures of behavior and thought upon Indigenous, Black, and brown people.

Coloniality is the reasoning of white supremacy at work, conjuring up a complex plethora of forced activities, a network of violence that aims at control and domination. As Mbembe says, "colonial violence is a network, "a node of encounter between multiple, diverse, re-iterated and cumulative forms of violence," experienced as much on the level of the spirit as in "muscles . . . and blood."[12]

Major forms of control and annihilation of these three groups of people have included old and new forms of theft and occupation of lands, slavery, socio-economic apartheid, mass incarceration, elimination of opportunities and resources, material and psychological barriers, economic constraints, and deportation. Most of the wealth of the Americas today, including here in the U.S., is in the hands of white people as a result of these centuries of theft and oppression. The private land in this country is stolen land, and now we all believe in a democracy that supports the rights of private land ownership. Despite color-blind rhetoric and the myth of shared public space, white dominant economic groups and private owners try to use media to shame Black people for "their" violence when they take to the streets, claiming that their intent is to riot and destroy "public common things."

White reasoning is not the privilege of white people only: colonized people of any color have participated in the same ways of thinking by adhering to orders, hopes of power, and acceptance by white masters. When properly "ideologized" and tamed, people of color are used to defend the white, hierarchical (and heteropatriarchal) establishment. The dominance of white reasoning has buried knowledge and weakened resistance by dark or Blackened people

Let me be clear that I do not write this chapter as a personal critique of my precious Christian brothers and sisters. There is truly nothing personal here. What I am trying to do is to show the systemic ways many Christian denominations, and not only Presbyterians, have used their books of common prayer as a particular book of experiences with God and turned these experiences into universal claims. People on the receiving end have used these books in different ways. Some have embraced these books; others have rejected them; many transformations have taken place.

I think, write, and perform from within as well as from outside of white reasoning. I understand my work as a counter-tradition, as resistance to and dismantling of a colonizing white reasoning that totalizes and neutralizes. I engage our worship and theology of worship as a Latinx, but a Latinx placed outside the dominant Latinx realm since I am a Brazilian-born American and Spanish is my third awfully broken language. In strange ways, I am also grateful for the faith I have received.

As we examine the methodology of the *Book of Common Worship* and work toward its renewal, I hope we will challenge white reasoning by building our foundation with other forms of reason—of wisdom, of beliefs, cosmologies, cultures, movements, performances, symbols, languages, and rituals. In other words, I hope that we will consider and engage different ways of being human. I am concerned that this has not been done.

Expanding the Commonality
of Liturgical-Theological Reasoning

Our reasoning must be expanded if we are to continue to be both Reformed and reformed. Without fear! We need a more concrete sense of the people we are serving and working with so that our God will make sense in our liturgies. Coming from liberation theology, I would say that the choice of our theologies should follow God's choice: the marginalized and the oppressed. There, with the poor, where it hurts, is the place where we should start figuring out our prayers, confessions, sacraments, preaching, and praise.

This feels like a dangerous move. What happens to our tradition and identities if we commit to the poor? To loosen our tradition might be a way to lose our sense of white belonging, and I imagine this is the source of our fear and resistance to transformation of our liturgies. What is the judge of our present liturgies? Jaci Maraschin, one of the most important liturgical theologians in Latin America, delves into these questions:

> *The liturgical moment is always a kind of center where the memory of the divine lives in the past, yet facing the challenges and the exigencies of what is to happen. If the gathering emerges from tradition, but does not close itself to this tradition, its very nature is to be open to what has not yet happened, and turns tradition into a model for the future with the clear presupposition of a critique. That is why the judgment of the present precedes the celebration of what happened in times of liberation, and it is animated by the hope of what might happen because of our commitment to this common decision...However, what kind of gatherings do we have now? Assemblies eaten away by the commitment to the powers of this world and captive to the social, political, and economic system, in which we live. That is why, in general, liturgical gatherings become tiresome, devoid of the vital element that would make them interpreters of reality, exulting in joy.*[13]

Thus, the judgment of the present is fundamental for our task here and it puts tradition in a place of vibrant force, one of possibility and empowerment. The choice of which people we want to serve has also to do with the methodology of this renewal.

We participants in the consultation about the *Book of Common Worship* renewal received a survey about the prayer book. The survey was essentially technical, since it is concerned with form, structure, and order. The survey was intended to be expansive in trying to encompass a variety of liturgical resources, but it failed to hint at something else, perhaps a more fundamental move: the survey did not take into account a contextual and embodied reflection. In other words, it did not reflect the pain and hurts, racism, and economic hardships of poor people since we as a church are a white middle-class people. The survey imagines a world without racism and with a lot of entitlement.

I wonder, what is our understanding of "our people"? The formality and shape of our survey responses limits and defines our work, a work somewhat detached from our bodies and any kind of real life. The survey comes before and after the body, never with it. What is expected in this survey is not a change in the ways we do the liturgical work of the people, as a possible way to become agents of our own histories with God, or how we live our prayers or check our confessions from harsh realities. The church of our survey is a church that has a clear sense of class—and a commitment to remaining of a particular class. The survey was a renewal of the (same) forms and (expansion of the same) contents of the book. If one looks at the previous *Book of Common Worship*, created twenty-five years ago (1993) and at the new one (2018), the only difference, it seems, is in more alternatives for prayers and greater ease of use. The main concern is with formality and not with the situation of our country and world.

Could we foster a movement of the church toward lower classes and the margins of society and be with them in praise and worship? If we fight for this to happen, then we might have a more just distribution of resources to our people, and we can understand better what "common prayer" might mean. If we can listen to the earth, we can start perceiving our deep belongings: common realities and symbols, materiality, and spirituality, money, and social conditions in the same breath as prayer.

For our prayer book to be fully accomplished in its commonality, it must be constituted of liturgies that would bring symbols and practices from beyond white churches and their theologies. A truly common worship book would have to have a diversity of expressions and forms. We need to have a variety of understandings of "decency and order" that go beyond a white reasoning imposing conformity, forms of understanding that would not only expand the understanding of time, of use of space, forms of worship and of cultural differences but would see racism as the utmost indecency, and social inequality as a fundamental worship disorder.

Back to *Leitourgia*

Let us go back to our sense of *leitourgia*. How do we understand the work of the people when we think about creating liturgies and liturgical spaces where the people of God can be reformed by God? If we are to do liturgy as the work of the people for the common good, we may need to pay attention to what Ruth Meyers wrote in *Missional Worship, Worshipful Mission:*

> *Leitourgia is formed not directly from laos, "people," but from leilos, which means "concerning the people or national community"—that is, "the public" of the "body politic."...When I use the term "liturgy," I have in mind both the structured ritual activity that involves texts and actions, using symbols, speech, song, and silence, AND the assembly's work for the common good, its public service as a gathered community and as the people of God in the world. Liturgy as work for the common good is thus a form of participation in the mission of God.*[14]

This definition, while still constrained by an unmarked sense of liturgical reasoning, an absence of pluralities and diversities of being with each other and in relation to the earth, is still a good understanding of *leitourgia* as it relates to the common good. Thus, I wonder if our group of liturgical experts has been working *on behalf of the people* and not *with* the people. If we understand liturgy as being with the poor, then, we must notice that we are mostly working in a safe environment telling people in dreadful situations what is common to our group and how to pray our way. But if our sense of liturgy is to serve mostly a middle-class community, then the understanding of "the people" might mean those currently counted in our formal statistics. There is something wrong with this scenario. "Our people" must include those whom we are called to join: the least of these, those outside the four walls of the church. Could we think about moving to the first theological choice: be with the ones abandoned by everyone? Then we could start a new way of revising the prayer book.

A group reforming the denomination's prayer book should begin by gathering its content, not by a new-old formal shaping of an already fixed source and understanding of liturgy, but rather, begin in reality, in specific places, in context, with issues that are killing our people and destroying the earth. From there we will shape our *lex orandi/vivendi/credendi,* or in other words, what is common, how to resist the forces of death and destruction, and how we can share a bit more in life as we say these prayers. Then a sense of universality could finally, miraculously, be achieved.

We need a new methodology for the creation of a book of common worship, a methodology that actually takes us to the places of pain, hurt, injustice, and death and that will help us pray and sing from these places.

If that is the task of the *Book of Common Worship* and other prayer books, we cannot avoid the very naming of places, situations, contexts from and with which we must work, and we must address this naming fully. If we look at reality, three major threads are shaping the United States which should shape our worship services as well: the patriarchal fascism that is taking over this country, the war against the poor, and the extractivism of the earth. Our worship book should not only offer prayers and instructions on what to pray, but also be a source of resistance for our communities to 1) gain consciousness about these issues; 2) gain new language to pray about these issues and respond to these realities, and 3) create forms of resistance and reciprocity. In this way, reformed worship services would be faithful to our tradition's core sense of constantly being reformed, but also assist in the undoing of the structures of evil that swallow our glorias and take away the breath of our praise to God

It is safe to say that our predominantly white church does not feel the need to think much about racism. We are "safe" and determined to keep our spaces safe. Most of our white middle class churches' members do not worry about their children arriving home safely or getting sick from working in unsafe conditions. Our church is one of the institutions that, when it does not consciously and vigorously denounce racism, contributes to social and racial injustices and divisions. How can the pain and despair of Black folks be in a book of prayer that wants to be "common" when these experiences are not common to most of this denomination?

Thus, if we speak the names of the devil in our worship to God, such as racism, patriarchalism, xenophobia, sexism, social exclusion, and depletion of the earth, in their local and broader contexts, we might gain a better sense of the hardships and the difficulties of the struggle for hope against these evil forces, both within and beyond ourselves.

Let me say that I am not advocating superpowers for liturgy, as if we could change the world from that one place. Our rituals of worship are just one aspect of our faith. Nonetheless, every part of our faith, and fundamentally our liturgy, where we learn so much of our Christian faith, should be a part of our bending with the arc of justice, a vision of our empowerment by the grace of God, through faith, hope, and love, to speak plainly and openly about God's reality in a way that names, and thus in some sense removes, the mystifying power of a racist agenda.

Subverting our Liturgies:
Naming Our Racism

Speaking to my class, *Worship and the Arts*, McCormick Professor David Daniels once said that we have to create "disruptive liturgies," liturgies that subvert white privilege by interjecting anti-racist forms of worshiping God." In the making of our liturgies, he said, "We should ask: does this liturgy mention the Black Jesus? From whose points of view is liturgy done? Is our white view privileged? Are the views of people of color privileged in the liturgy? Are races present? Does [the liturgy] deny despair?"[15]

The white reasoning of which I spoke earlier is also mirrored in what Daniels calls white-Anglo liturgy. He defines a white-Anglo liturgy as "shaped by white concerns such as white guilt, shame, culpability, alleged innocence, love without justice, peace on white terms, and/or bewilderment, a liturgy focused on ministering to white people. A liturgy tied to a progressive white frame of seeing as a frame of reference"[16]

If a book of common worship is always a reflection of its time, what are we saying if our worship resources do not bring ways to undo racism and confront an evil that is literally exterminating the Black people of this country? Does our liturgy make us complicit? And let us not forget the Native Americans who are almost exterminated. Our *Book of Common Worship* should struggle against five hundred years of colonization, which include its universal, white, unmarked worship services.

This means that the new *BCW* should help move us all towards places of hurt and exclusion and disaster. From these places—prisons, the wall between Mexico and the U.S., poor neighborhoods, failing school districts, neighborhoods controlled by drug dealers, modern slavery, racism, economic exclusion, and poverty—we will create prayers, choose songs, frame our worship services, decide about our Eucharistic food, and shape our liturgies, calling people to worship God. From places of violence and abandonment, we will confess at the baptismal font our complicity with the economic system, preaching against the hegemonic forces of the state against the poor. At the Eucharistic table, we will announce that no one goes hungry, that everyone is the *imago Dei*, and that freedom, equality, and social justice are possible. The table of communion will be a table filled with food and reciprocity, where we learn with each other and are forever changed. From dirty rivers, we will confess to the waters our lack of care for God's earth and commit to taking care of the rivers near our homes until they are alive again. This is what a liturgical methodology and a liturgical theology must consist of for our new worship book.

This methodology will foster and bring forth a mixture of several reasonings so that it can help undo the violence of a hidden white reasoning that is grounded in a certain cultural sense of order and decency. We need to add other forms of reasoning. David Daniels talks about African American liturgical reasoning giving us "a liturgy shaped by African American concerns such as racial equality, justice, empowerment, anger, reconciliation, disillusionment, and despair. A liturgy focused on ministering to Black and non-Black people. A liturgy tied to a progressive 'Black' way of seeing as a frame of reference."[17]

If we continue to add different frames of reference and a variety of cosmologies, we may start to dismantle white reasoning by infusing transformative liturgies that belong to other forms of reasoning. With this variety of non-white reasonings, with all their dangerous ways of being human, we can foster not only different liturgical theologies but different worldviews and possibilities for life, living into different senses and forms of thinking, trusting God and each other until we develop a true priesthood of all believers in worship.

The priesthood of all believers is a whole community accountable to each other as its members break systems of poverty and all become equal before God and one another. This community will not turn worship into its own image, as another consumerist good to buy, but rather, its members will be challenged in their desires and in their actions, and they will be able to search Christian history and find sources of empowerment, liberation, blessings, and solidarities.

I can only believe in a *Book of Common Worship* that is a garden with a variety of seeds for flowers and plants of all kinds and from various places. Perhaps we should visit congregations across the United States that are poor churches populated by undocumented people, talk to the Black Lives Matter Movement, visit Indigenous people, and learn from them, do chaplaincy in prisons, listen to the birds. Perhaps our children should tell us what is common. That would finally be the common place, the common good, the common life for us all.

Only in this way can we learn from various peoples across the nation what they say and do, what feelings they have, what emotions they cherish or wrestle with, what local symbols they use or how they use the Christian symbols to survive, what songs they are singing to sustain their own faith and in what conditions they are living God's grace in and through their bodies. In this movement, we would open to a sustained sense of how our bodies live out, are marked, punched, moved, filled, transformed and trans-versed by this faith. Then we would come with our expertise and prayers and songs to perhaps expand the sources of liberation and offer something that is not already there. I am calling us to do what the philosopher Antonio Gramsci calls the work of the "organic intellectual." We the organic liturgists, preachers, theologians, Bible experts, adding our expertise to the expertise of the people and the wisdom of *la vida cotidiana*, the quotidian life.

Then we can begin to distribute the sources of our faith to the poor—and not only our prayers but the monetary resources of our institutions. In this way, we will have a worship book that carries the possibility of a common life. What if we go be with the people who are hurting, to early pick-up lines for day jobs, and stand there with them? Or go with undocumented immigrants working on tomato plantations, or stay with homeless people on the streets to understand what it means to be homeless? Or listen to Black communities always under vicious attacks and learn how racism is deeply woven into the threads of our society? Or go and listen to Native Americans and see and hear the ongoing violence against their lands and lives? From these places we can sit down to hear and cry together and learn prayers and songs that we can bring back to our communities.

Professor Daniels gave to my class the trajectory we must follow, an exceedingly difficult one. What should our liturgies do? He answered, "expose, subvert, and transcend."[18] And I add:

Liturgies will expose our racism and injustices and hatred and class struggles.

Liturgies will subvert economic disparities and will restore our prayers for equal distribution of wealth, within the church and in the world.

Liturgies will transcend the limitations of our situations, fomenting and creating places, contexts, relations, and power dynamics that will show the real work of the people with God and the commonality of our lives. In this way, we will learn that liturgies, as well as theologies, should always be a second step, to be done after being with people.

An Example:

Let it Burn! (Pentecost 2020)[19]

One example of how to orient the liturgical calendar and our common resources is to read from a particular place, paying attention to the surroundings and the commitments our faith must make along the way. I wrote these words after the death of George Floyd and the burnings around the country. The idea is to show how the thinking of a liturgical time from the perspective of the margins, from perhaps another form of reasoning, can foster other forms of prayers, liturgical actions, preaching, and sacramental emphasis. I wish to show a way we might orient our faith from real situations. From a local place, we say a prayer to the world.

George Floyd, a forty-six-year-old Black man, was mercilessly killed by the police in Minneapolis. João Pedro, a fourteen-year-old Black boy, was playing with his cousins at his house in Rio de Janeiro when the police shot his house seventy times and killed him.

The streets and buildings of Minneapolis and other cities are burning. Like previous burnings in Baltimore, the burnings are signs of power, resistance, and a deep awareness of Black people and what it means to live in a country dominated by a white elite ever since the invasion of the Americas by the white culture that permeates every inch of this country. Only Black mothers and fathers know the fears of not having their children back home at the end of the day. This white culture is spread through every street of the U.S. and within the whole democratic system, including forms of legislation. It invades every single institution, from local political groups to local churches, gerrymandering, and voter regulations, from lack of workers' rights to wage disparity, from political party systems and legislative representatives to the Supreme Court and the White House. Everything is infused with forms of living, thinking, and organizing that comes from white values and their forms of living, perceiving, and feeling. This structure trickles down in every form of local power dynamic, school districts, poisoned waters, state austerity budgets, male domination, military might, jail and prison systems, school access, and police forms of domination.

All of the historical processes that built this country have served only to fuel a fire that was already running underneath the social threads of this country and that is and will always be ready to explode. There is no way that this country, ruled by predatory capitalism, will not have its buildings burned and its fortunes and ways of ruling put at risk. It is part of the game. White supremacy and fascism are foundational parts of capitalism and as long as we have capitalism as the system of organizing life together, there will be no way to dismantle racism, white supremacy, and fascism, or not to have buildings burned.

Since crisis is built into the capitalist system, crisis will always be necessary. The crisis of the neoliberal capitalist system tends to be economic, with the crashing of the market once in a while for more domination and stealing, but also by using natural disasters. Water spilling into New Orleans' Lower Ninth Ward gave way to the economic advantages of vultures sucking the blood of the poor. Along with a growing number of deaths caused by COVID-19, especially of the poor, we see that the world's richest billionaires have continued to enrich themselves.[20]

Our hopes have been crushed. We all feel the closing in of public spaces, the shortening of resources, the destruction of the earth. The increasing pauperization of the world will grow exponentially, and crisis will continue—we just do not know to what point or extent. The earth is giving us ample signs that we are killing ourselves and there will be nothing left for us if we do not change. The burning of Minneapolis is also telling us that if we do not change, something else will happen that will be worse than we imagine.

The death of George Floyd in Minneapolis set the Black community on fire in a country where people go on with their lives pretending that everything is all right and this is the greatest country in the world. George Floyd's death shows us that this country is a nightmare for many of its own people.

The fires on the streets are signs of life from Black people putting themselves into re-existence, the loud "language of the unheard," as Martin Luther King, Jr. put it. As I see it all, I join them with my heart and soul. I will never condemn them for doing what they are doing, for they are trying to survive in this country. I would rather condemn the politicians (be they Republicans or Democrats), the market, the banks, and financial corporations for what they do. They should be persecuted for what they have historically done to Black folks and Indigenous people and brown and yellow people with the stealing of the land, erecting of walls, and building of private jails and concentration camps. I will never condemn Black folks for their strength and bold courage for saying no, for saying "No more!" Theirs is the kingdom of God! They are my people! In fact, they are breathing the breath of God into us, the fire of the Holy Spirit. Pentecost! From the lives of Black people! A gift from God!

The whole Gospel for Pentecost Day is in a speech by Martin Luther King, Jr.:

I think America must see that riots do not develop out of thin air. Certain conditions continue to exist in our society which must be condemned as vigorously as we condemn riots. But in the final analysis, a riot is the language of the unheard. And what is it that America has failed to hear? It has failed to hear that the plight of the Negro poor has worsened over the last few years. It has failed to hear that the promises of freedom and justice have not been met. And it has failed to hear that large segments of white society are more concerned about tranquility and the status quo than about justice, equality, and humanity. And so, in a real sense our nation's summers of riots are caused by our nation's winters of delay. And as long as America postpones justice, we stand in the position of having these recurrences of violence and riots over and over again. Social justice and progress are the absolute guarantors of riot prevention.[21]

In Acts 2:2-3, we read, "And suddenly from heaven there came a sound like the rush of a violent wind, and it filled the entire house where they were sitting. Divided tongues, as of fire, appeared among them, and a tongue rested on each of them." Pentecost can be understood through three lenses in this year 2020:

Fire

". . . for indeed our God is a consuming fire." (Hebrews 12:29)

Fire! We need fire! Fire that will burn buildings, systems, oligarchies, "democratic" systems, pretensions of common life and fake mutual care. Fire that will burn religions, scholarships, spiritualities, forms of knowledge and financial exchange that contribute to the collective death of us all. Fire!

> *Our God is a consuming fire!*

> *Consuming fire* that puts down any human project made of injustice and the appearance of fairness.

> *Consuming fire* whose uncontrollable choreography will dance around our protections and pretenses, order, and decencies.

> *Consuming fire* consuming every private property so we can finally understand that nothing is private but belongs to all. Burning the privacy of excused treaties, secret changes in

political offices taking away resources from the poor time and again and giving them to the rich.

Consuming fire that burns private ownership of anything.

Consuming fire burning false spiritualities of Christians who think that holding worship on Sundays will be enough to hold onto the name of Jesus.

Consuming fire burning every liturgy or sermon that does not say the name of George Floyd with a loud voice, churning stomach, and trembling heart.

Consuming fire to any rationalization of the protests that does not take a clear side with Black people.

Consuming fire that compels our work around public gestures of change to local policies, police forces, and demands that legislators change, listening to the voices of those abandoned.

Consuming fire to the nuanced and blunt entitlement of white folks, be they liberal, very liberal, conservative, or of any other political ideology.

Consuming fire to any church who does not start an anti-racist workshop and teach its folks about the history of African Americans in the U.S., Black theologies, Womanist theologies and Black religions.

Consuming fire to any confession of sins that does not pause at the death of George Floyd.

Consuming fire to any blessing that is not preceded by "woes to" those who are keeping racism in place.

May the fires of Baltimore, Minneapolis, and other places spread across the world so that our faith can be enflamed by the presence of a burning Spirit who is unruly and will not accept anything less than a life fully committed to all of the abandoned, enslaved, oppressed, jailed, poor people in this country and elsewhere.

Fire everywhere! So, we can rebuild from ashes. Ashes not only from our Ash Wednesday evocation of ashes, but ashes that come from the fire of the Holy Spirit who burns works of injustice and white supremacy.

Ashes

The ashes of Minneapolis's burned buildings are clear signs that this time, our time, is over. Time cannot wait anymore. Nothing else is working. It did not matter that Black people used their music, art, knees, and protests, screaming "Black Lives Matter!" Nothing could change the minds, souls and structures of a country living off the oppression of Black people. Ashes! Time is up! Time is over!

Ashes will tell us that a new time has arrived, a time that is uncountable and uncontrollable and cannot be narrated any more, since time will be counted by the nobodies of the world. *They* are the agents of this new time. The nobodies of this country are saying to all, we are nobody for you, but in our communities, we are somebody, and it is this somebodiness that will destroy the pretense of nobodiness that you threw us into. We are more! Look at your streets: the ashes of your buildings are the signatures of the nobodies! We are the nobodies whose names you cannot speak in your clubs, houses, churches because silence is what you have chosen. Now take a look here and see our names, nobodies!

We are the fire that turned your world into ashes so we can perhaps start in a different time with new narratives, new legislations, a new life together, mutual respect, and new forms of distribution of wealth. Your safety is not as safe as you thought. All of us, not only Black people but also all of the Blackened people in this country, all who were made nobodies, we are back to terrorize your kindness and your niceness. We are coming and will be coming back again.

Remember the fears you have lived with your whole life but tried to deny time and again so it would not be embarrassing? The fears deep inside that used to flare up when we got close to you? You thought that controlling the fear would keep you safe, didn't you? I know you did not want to live this way. But you did not do much to change, right? So, the nobodies—they are the very measure of life you thought never existed. We came back with a vengeance. We came back as the nightmares you have decided not to pay attention to. We are the ashes of your world.

Ashes upon ashes, the debris of a world that did not work when organized just for a few, even though you thought it was for all. As we are taught, let the injustice be without making too much of a fuss, and things will find their way to oblivion and cultural structures of normalcy. Ah, you thought we were defeated, but you should never underestimate the power of those who have survived centuries and are still standing. We have seen wars of all kinds and we have survived. We are still standing. From Brazil, a country that also knows Black oppression, philosopher Vladimir Safatle writes:

> *It is true, we lost several times, but we were never defeated. For our defeats are, in fact, the high fire that forges the steel of our victories. Every true victory is the result of a profound loss. It reverberates with the animal desire to never lose again. Therefore, only those who fell and patiently out for a second chance will win. It will come sooner than we expect. That's what leads us to affirm that such losses are not defeats at all.*[22]

We will multiply, we will resurrect! Our ancestors will come back for us, and they are telling us that the time is over. Our memories, our songs, our ways of being will sustain us. We will use everything we can and want.

We have prayed over the ashes of our sons and daughters for too long. Now you will know what it means to face our strength. Not for revenge, for we have no business in revenge. But simply because of the law of circularity. We harvest what we plant. Roughness is the new harvest, and our love will not be easy. In hope, the Spirit of ashes will resurrect all of those who enter into this new time, a time of the Spirit, a time unknown, a time for deep changes, a time to lose individually, gain collectively, a time not merely to change our prayers, but to change the world.

Breath/Spirit

This change can only happen if the breath of the Spirit is breathing our lives together. This breath is fundamental to our living. The coincidence of COVID-19 and the extinguishing of George Floyd's breath is stunning. In the pandemic, we have been attacked in the most precious thing we have: our breath. We have put our knee on the necks of animals, destroying their own spaces. We have invaded their habitats and used them for our own sake. Now we are living with the result of the overuse, abuse, and dominion of the earth. Capitalist white society has put its knee on the necks of Black and Blackened people (Indigenous, brown, yellow, poor), stealing their resources, uprooting them from their lands, and then abusing them, displacing them through redlining, gerrymandering, throwing them into the corners of our cities and giving them the opportunity to come back to work for whites in the same cities.

In the U.S. and in Brazil, there has been a genocide of Black people and Indigenous people. The structures of racism are murdering Black people everywhere. The lack of care for the most vulnerable during the onslaught of COVID-19 is taking its toll within the Indigenous, Latinx, and Black communities. Everywhere, people literally cannot breathe.

Frantz Fanon has seen the difficulty of breathing in many cultures; he sees this not in one group but in an expansive "we" who cannot breathe. In *Black Skin, White Masks*, he writes, "When we revolt it's not for a particular culture. We revolt simply because, for a variety of reasons, we can no longer breathe."[23]

George Floyd couldn't breathe, Black people can't breathe, Indigenous people can't breathe, the brown people at the borders can't breathe, the earth can't breathe, a whole population of humans and species and plants and forests can't breathe either. If anything, this Pentecost reminds us of our collective breathing: breathing life together into new worlds and other ways of living. For we either breathe together or no one will breathe at all.

The breathing of the Spirit is the breathing of life. This Pentecost, we are challenged to see the fire in the world and give thanks for it. We are challenged to see the ashes of a world that did not work. And we are challenged to see the possibility of breathing new life-giving breaths together. May the memory of George Floyd and João Pedro bring about new worlds for us to breathe together.

CHAPTER TEN

Queering Christian Worship Services

Janet Walton and Cláudio Carvalhaes[1]

Cecilia Anne Perella Carvalhaes, 13 years old

True love is born from understanding.

The Buddha

Prologue

Our rituals are our collective work. Together we remember where we have been; together we listen anew to where we are going. Each one's story matters…each one's sorrows, each one's dreams. In our worship we have the responsibility and the opportunity to lean in, to hear from one another with a posture of humility—that is, an acknowledgment of what we do not know with a willingness to learn—to adjust, to try what we have not done before, to change. This posture of heart and mind undergirds our examination of what is emerging among us in our present time.

In particular, we desire to bring our attention to the glaring exclusion of the stories of LGBTQIA+ people in our worship services. LGBTQIA+ communities have invited us to think differently about our rituals, to "queer our worship services." This is a work of liberation, and thus of justice. It is a work of breaking down white supremacy. It is a call towards loving "them" as "us", a journey into learning, listening, and changing ourselves. It is an invitation to transgress the boundaries of "us" and "them" as we consider the queer and transgender nature of the *imago Dei* itself. We write at the threshold of liturgy, worship, and ritual where the boundaries between body and spirit fragment and blur. We write from how we have been changed ourselves through encountering the ways LGBTQIA+ communities have embraced ritual. We write to acknowledge that we do not control the boundaries of the sacred. As J Mase III and Lady Dane Figueroa Edidi say in *The Black Trans Prayer Book*:

> *Ritual is a grounding exercise, a reminder of the power of our imagination, and that we can receive from the well if only we journey towards it… Ritual is the recurring daily, weekly, or monthly ask from Spirit for you to show up to the stage, whether you feel like it or not. Whether we fail or not.*[2]

To speak of queering liturgies includes all our bodies, our hearts, our minds, and our souls. Our society normalizes certain kinds of bodies and sexes; we name what is outside a "normal" range as abject, troubled, sick, aberrant, un-natural. To move from an essentialist understanding of sex and sexualities we also must move away from an understanding of any one form of ritual as a fixed form of religious identity.

This posture of the heart and mind, to destabilize and queer our rituals, brings us closer to the pain and fear suffered by LGBTQIA+ people. Each day brings uncertainty as to who we might find in the next corner we walk, each encounter filled with the potential for sanctuary or violence. The work of a ritual is to be the gathering a place where all can rest, be renewed, and empowered. Our task is to create ritual that provides sanctuary particularly for those who live outside prescribed borders.

We learn with Judith Butler in Gender Trouble that gender is not something fixed or destined but is rather inscribed on us by cultural norms and religious fixations of forms of specific moral life. We perform our living, our sexualities, our bodies, our religion. We play on the moveable, the never-ending flux of life, the fullness of God always passing, moving. We must subvert our forms of belief so others can join the fold. One way to subvert is to reconstitute our worship services in ways that reshape our theological thinking, ecclesiastical understandings, and our common life through a love that infuses life into each other. As Marcella Althaus-Reid said:

> The point is that what cannot be made indecent in theology is not worth being called theology because it will mean that 'God', 'Jesus' and 'Mary' only may have a meaning in a determined heterosexual economic system.[3]

Thus, at worship we turn the exclusion of LGBTQIA+ people into gifts, trouble into blessings, abjection into fullness, abnormality into a joyous way of living. In worship we can enter and risk new prospects as Nathan Carlin says in his essay "Pastoral Theological Reading of Middlesex" (a story centered on the character of Cal, a man with an intersex condition):

> Can we risk loving, and being loved by, a God like this? Perhaps reading about the courage of others such as Cal will give us assurance to go out on the limbs of life that are sure to break, for in such breaking there is, as Dittes so beautifully put it, not only crisis and disaster (i.e., knowledge of our estrangement) but also "the prospect of new revelation and new creation and new relation" (i.e., knowledge of our essence).[4]

This article is our own way of loving through a new understanding, to learn and lean towards these ways of risking and creating new prospects that will hopefully foster new ways of thinking, doing, feeling and being together. It is just a beginning, but we have started.

Introduction

Not long ago, a friend of mine went through a time of challenges. One day his adult child came to him and his wife and said: "I am not a man; I am a woman. I need to go through a process of bodily changes and from now on my name is Jenna." Paul and his wife did not know what to say or to do…They were not prepared and had no internal resources to help them re-organize themselves around this news. That night, they nodded to Jenna and said, "We don't know how this is possible, we don't know what to do, but we love you and accept you the way you are." Over time, my friends had to do a lot of research and listen to transgender people until they started to figure out how not only to accept but to embrace the new identity of their daughter.

This event sums up how many of us might feel when we try to make our worship services inclusive for our LGBTQIA+ community members. One person within LGBTQIA+ communities explained that for queer people a primary consideration is the fluidity of their gender identity. Another person told me that, at least for some trans folk, there is a fixed notion of seeing themselves as a particular gender. How can we understand it? What can we do not only to know but to embrace and offer deep solidarity to queer folks? When we meet queer and trans people in our churches, we also might not know how solidarity is possible, and we might not know what to say or do. Even here we acknowledge that "queer" is not the same as LGBTQIA+, and that in our attempts at play with language we may fall short. But we must stretch our thinking and our feelings in order to embrace our friends (and ourselves) and answer the invitation to transgress and grow.

Janet and I believe that rituals carry a certain knowledge that can help us process and expand what we might think of what to be human is all about. This is what is at stake in our worship services: to celebrate an expansive way of being human. In this present time, we have been thrown into a flagrant dispute of what to be human is all about: What constitutes our lives? What makes us humans? What are the boundaries of our own selves? How, with whom, and to what do we relate ourselves? Our LGBTQIA+ communities invite us to consider these questions more fully.

History shows us that the measure of our humanity is bound to the ways we have received one another's understandings of life, how our world defines the very core of what it is to be human, and how we are each responsible for adopting and living out of these perspectives. In the early Christian churches, we see a variety of understandings of the world. We see in the gospels Jesus lifting up women and taking sides with the poor, but we also see in the epistles the subjugation of women, the condemnation of homosexuality, and the support of slavery. What are we to make of this?

Today we are still wrestling with issues around gender status, sexualities, immigration, nationalities, religions and so on. Do Muslims or immigrants or LGBTQIA+ people have the same rights as other human beings? Shall we consider the earth as a fundamental part of the humus of humanity, making us and the earth and animals all equals? Or shall we exhibit through entrenched power dynamic structures that we see the earth and animals as not worthy of our care, good only for our consumption? Will we acknowledge the humanity of Muslims, immigrants, or LGBTQIA+ people only to the extent they disappear or enable others' humanity?

Or, to state this in theological terms: Who bears the mark of God? What do we do with the idea of the *imago Dei*? As Christians, we are called to expand our ways of thinking and feeling about what it is to be human, to engage in their limits and borders. These borders are also present and in tension in our worship communities. When you go to a worship service is there a hierarchy of humanness? What are the borders between us humans, between us humans and the animals, the earth and the universe?

In a recent series of lectures entitled *The Origin of Others*, author Toni Morrison talked about the necessity to put ourselves, "in the middle of life, talking back to the world" to join the movements that, "put us at borders, the porous places, the vulnerable points.... where alarm hovers by an uneasy relationship with our own foreignness, our own rapidly disintegrating sense of belonging."[5]

Cláudio and I have been thinking about the challenge Morrison offers as it relates to our worship. We believe that we need to act as if we are all vulnerable, in a way, foreigners wrestling with boundaries. We have come up with questions: How do we model a way of living in our worship that "puts us in the middle of life?" Who do we mean by us? How do we acknowledge our fears? When we worship together, how do we claim responsibility for those whose humanness is marked by exclusion, cruelty, and shame? And finally, for now, what can we do together to continually re-discover where each of us is vulnerable?

We begin with our body — the personal and collective body. The body that is made of humus, deeply related to the earth. The incarnation of Jesus, the crux of the Christian faith, is the body where we live and die, where we suffer and rejoice, where we have orgasms, where we relate and where we face our limits. It is in the bodies of people that frames are constructed, and boundaries produced. As Ivone Gebara wrote:

> ... the body is the starting point for theology... My option is for the body, the human body, lived, center of all relations, bodies from which all the

problems begin and all the solutions converge into solutions. Bodies where we affirm the beauty... place of the signs of the realm of God, place of resurrection. To start from the body is to begin from the first reality that we know and know. It is to affirm and recognize the body in its wonder and at the same time, the impossibility of anything without it.[6]

Implied also for Gebara is the human body as it is deeply connected with the earth, Pachamama and all of its natural, social, racial, sexual and cultural correlations. With that cluster of relations in mind we ask: how do we engage the many relationalities and complexities of the body within the organization of our ritual structures? Our worship services are rituals that carry information framed around bodies and boundaries. These ritual frames and boundaries assemble a precise circumscription, a circulation and inscription of the bodies, around a certain understanding of what life is all about. The boundaries of bodies, ours and others, constitute the fundamental framework of worship. They are inextricably connected to many other issues such as: climate change, gun control, immigration and healthcare.

In the midst of these urgent issues, we have been asked to focus on the implications of gender identity in our worship — what we can draw from our memories about a deep cherishing of one another and, particularly, what we can imagine that prompts new responses to the challenges we face today. Can we imagine something different that interrupts what we have assumed to be acceptable and predictable? Can we engage new forms of what it means to be human? What is it that shakes our certainties as it makes space for something new? Philosopher Judith Butler has something to say about this: "To intervene in the name of transformation means precisely to disrupt what has become settled knowledge and knowable reality, and to use, as it were, one's unreality to make an otherwise impossible or illegible claim. The norms, themselves, rattled, become open to re-signification."[7] We understand Butler as saying that what we take for granted needs to get upended in order for the ways we see and accept each other to change.

Our plan is to address some of the ways in which our bodies are circumscribed, circulated and described within the forms that are already in place in our rituals. We begin with one example of the frames and boundaries of the body within a Eucharistic liturgy.

During a eucharistic liturgy in James Chapel at Union Seminary in New York City and just before we shared the bread and the cup, the presider said to us, "The gifts of God for the people of God are now ready, but we cannot receive them." Silence and confusion were palpable. What prompted the student presider to say this was an ethical concern, shared by others, that the administration was in a process of unfair negotiations with the people who cleaned our buildings. For him, and others, it was dishonest to act as if we were a community that prided itself on being advocates for justice while we were denying it to the very people whom we saw and depended on every day. A faculty member stepped up, put his arm around the student's shoulders and said: "These are the gifts of God for the people of God. It is not for you to determine who can and cannot have them." Then the faculty member turned to the assembly and invited those who wanted to, to come forward to share communion. Some did; some did not.

That liturgy took place "in the middle of life", that is, our day-to-day routines. A predictable action, eating and drinking as a body of Christ, required a decision whether to participate in communion or not. It was a ritual meal connected to real human issues. It embodied what justice requires of us. The experience did not end there. Discussions continued in every class and into the next day, when, as a whole seminary, we talked about what had happened. Communion in that Chapel was never the same again.

This experience is an example of crossing boundaries, of frames of knowledge being challenged and perceptions being transformed and expanded. We had come to worship expecting a predictable, routine regimen for eating and drinking. Instead, something disturbing happened; something that made us think more deeply about what we were doing. It was a moment that required each person to choose what participation in communion means now, in this very moment. And it was about power, public advocacy for the maintenance staff and a challenge to the authority of the administration.

In Ivone Gebara's words: "resistance in search of life with dignity, a spiritual experience from one's deepest being searching for freedom." It is this expansive form of knowledge of what human life is all about that we want to circumscribe in our rituals and worship services. Liturgical scholar Mary Collins puts it this way: "we must develop a way of looking beyond what has long been felt to be the truth of things."[8]

Boundaries as Frames,
Adiaphora, and What is Life

Frames

Worship services maintain and cross borders of all kinds: religious, racial, gender, sexual, cultural and class. Through living within and outside of these liturgical borders we define and frame the very question: what is life? This liturgical frame conveys values. It determines worth and sets up demands. As Jonathan Z. Smith wrote, rituals take place somewhere, orienting us and creating *"a mode of paying attention."*[9] By paying attention we recognize ways to think and act. Church and state often share the framework that defines what is acceptable. For example, one could leave the church to escape patriarchal power but still be subjected to its domination in an authoritarian state. Judith Butler wrestles with the notion of *framing* as it affects relationships: "The 'being' of life is itself constituted through selective means. It is through the mechanism of power that life is produced, shaped and recognized"[10]

In our time, amidst global movements and changes of all kinds, the familiar frames we were accustomed to still frame perceptions of our reality and our own rituals, definitions, and boundaries. Sticking to these perceptions is both an individual and social attempt to keep what we know unchanged and thus cast fear away. It is within these imaginary systems in which we are complicit that we need to work so that something new can arise without fear but instead as forms of blessings marked by the constant reframing and redefinition of our *oikos*, our common house. It is this new reframing that we are addressing today. How do our religious rituals reinforce or contest what limits the life of any human being? How do we not get trapped into the reification of issues of person and not-person within Christian rituals?

Frames shape our perceptions. They influence our decisions about what we receive or reject, who is in or who is out, welcomed or sent away. We can draw an example from the art world. In the art world frames differentiate the art from the spaces around it. According to some art theories, the borders and frames around religious art suggest that there is a clear boundary between the sacred and the non-sacred, what is exterior and interior to the Christian faith.[11]

Philosopher Jacques Derrida argues that frames are never neutral. Rather they are both the commentary and the very "essence" of the work of art itself. Derrida's theory is seen in the work of Lutheran theologian Gordon Lathrop. He explores how Adiaphoras are related to Christian worship rituals. For Lutherans, the Adiaphoras, the mediums of the worship ritual such as place, architecture, music, chalice, paten, clothing etc., are secondary to the centrality of bath, word, prayer, table, and the assembly. Nevertheless, both the primary and secondary sources of Christian rituals are fully intertwined. Sometimes, the Adiaphoras are perceived to be more fundamental to the essence of the worship of God because they are more visible and tangible. For example, a font of water can appear to be more important than the bath itself.

Today, we suggest that we think about how the frames of our worship services help us understand what is important for the life of every human being particularly those who are cast out because of gender. The

Lutheran liturgical frames of *Gathering, Word, Table/Bath and Sending* help us define what we can and must recognize as human. For a long time, these liturgical frames did not recognize women, or Black or Indigenous people and were far removed from the lives of the poor. The whole notion of gathering and sending excludes the daily struggle of the poor and the struggles of people in general. Today we still do not recognize the presence of refugees or queer people or people who are poor at least not in a way that they can fully participate in the life of the church without fear or shame.

Perhaps we have failed to live out the theological concept of the *imago Dei*, the belief that every single human being has honor and value, that each human being is drenched with the spirit and image of God. This notion demands that we treat those we have ignored, disrespected and feared with dignity. A practice of mutual respect affirms all sexual possibilities of the body, reinforces mutual relations, and creates a deeply ecological connection with nature.

Here is one powerful issue that we cannot ignore: How do we understand patriarchy as a frame? When I was a student at Union Theological Seminary, I took a course called "Women's Experiences: Resources for Worship." My advisors, Delores Williams and Janet Walton, taught it. Because I was the only man in a large class of women, I found out, for the first time in my life, what it felt like to be in the minority in this particular way. One class requirement for each of us was to create two rituals. In the first one I naively preached about how "manhood" was the most appropriate way to live in the world and serve God. Needless to say, it did not go over too well. In my second chance I was only allowed to do the final benediction. I asked five women to read it ahead of time so I would not get into trouble. During the de-briefing of the ritual an African American student said to the class the ritual was good, but she did not need my benediction. She added, there was nothing wrong with the benediction; we just did not need it. I was crushed. How come she did not honor my role in the ritual? It took me a while to realize that her critique was related to the way patriarchy has used rituals and hierarchical assumptions.

So, what did I learn from this class? As an outsider, I was filled with fear. I was knocked out of my comfort zone while preaching. I had the profound sense that women do not need men to lead worship for them. And to name just two or three lessons I learned, I also noticed that I can be patriarchal without even trying. Masculinity can be toxic. Men are brought up thinking we can dominate and define the worlds we want to live in and what it is to be human. To avoid being dominated I thought I needed institutions and women to always support me. This class began a shift in my own understanding of gender, both within myself and in the world.

The patriarchy created a God ready to fight, rule and control. To please God is to support the patriarchal and hierarchical structure of society and religion. These religious and political ideologies led to the formalization of laws regarding gender and sexuality thus placing at the margins, gay, lesbian, bisexual, asexual, queer, straight, transgender, transsexual, non-binary, gender fluid, gender queer people and viewing them as deformed, sinful, evil and a threat to the whole edifice of white patriarchal supremacy.

Unframed Women Crossing Boundaries

The challenges are dangerous, persistent and ever present. Listen to this selection of examples:

> 1) *March 2018, The New York Times acknowledged that since 1851 they had skipped over women, people of color, openly gay people, transgender and Native American people when choosing individuals to honor with an obituary.*

> 2) *An 11-year-old girl living in a gated community had been repeatedly raped over seven months by trusted employees of that community. These men did not look at her as a child, but merely an instrument to satisfy their lust. (New York Times A5, 7/19/18)*

> 3) *In Wikipedia, the fifth most visited website in the world, only 18% of its biographies are of women. 84-90% of Wikipedia's editors are men! (Get Wired, 08/03/18)*

And on a hopeful note, consider these encouraging stories:

> 4). *A public library in Albany, New York, sponsored the "Drag Queen Story Hour" to give children glamorous, positive and unabashedly queer role models.*

> 5) *In May 2018, there was a photography exhibit in James Chapel at Union Seminary. It was entitled "Silent Tears." The photographer Belinda Mason, and artists with disability Dieter Knierim, Margherita Coppolino, Denise Beckwith, created photos to draw attention to the stories of women with a disability who have been subjected to violence and women who have acquired their disability caused by violence.*

These large transparent and translucent images portraying the everyday lives of these women are not easy to look at, not only because of the topic, but also because of the artistic medium. The photos come into focus gradually and only with a lot of effort. We are looking through tears of women.

At first the images in this exhibit felt quite overwhelming, so large and so aimed at violence. However, a panel of women invited to speak at the opening of the exhibit, provided helpful perceptions. What marked their presentations was a sense of profound gratitude and hope. Here was a space where these women could tell their stories. Every time they did, it added another layer of healing. For the Union community, to worship surrounded by these images was sobering. We recognized our own naked truths, our experiences of domination and fragility, and we renewed our determination to struggle for dignity marked by the collective faith.

As a woman on the faculty at Union Theological Seminary in New York and as a woman who grew up as a Roman Catholic, I have had countless opportunities to reflect on gender issues during worship. Within two years of my tenure at Union in 1982, my colleagues and I found ourselves in the process of voting on a proposal about a commitment to use inclusive language in our classrooms and chapel services. That led to questions about the breadth of the symbols we used in worship, the texts we heard, and also about who could and who could not preside at our communion services.

Many women and men have contributed to the stories we will share with you later today, people who live in boxes on the streets as well as colleagues and students with whom we work daily. For now, I will focus on the work of two theologians who took risks speaking and publishing about what they learned from their own lives. In each case, what they had to say exacted a cost in terms of their reputations and, often, their careers.

My colleague, womanist theologian Delores Williams and I taught a course for many years at Union called "Women's Experiences as Resources for Worship," Every year the syllabus and classroom experiences were different. We were learning along with our students about how to imagine what we had <u>not</u> seen or heard or felt in our regular worship occurrences. We called upon women from a broad span of human experiences to share their stories with us. Together, we tried to unearth what we and others deeply desired. We practiced creating rituals about what we were coming to know, haltingly and bravely.

Williams and I urged our students not to think of worship as an experience that exists primarily "to reinforce doctrines and abstractions but rather as a space and time to express life as it is lived, to create liturgies from it that are alive, improvisational, experiential, embodied and that contest the world of dominance and subjugation and disrespect that is rampant in women's lives." To describe both the theology and liturgy we were imagining, Williams used the word, *organic*. For her, organic affirms the importance of the imagination in receiving and interpreting knowledge of the sacred as it is actually lived. This phrase "as it is actually lived" is pivotal. In every class we repeated these questions: What do women need? How do women define values? What do women expect from their relationships, with each other, with themselves, with what is sacred? What does a mother know? What does a sexually violated woman feel? How does a woman carry on who is silent in the face of discrimination?

Do not ask narrow, loaded questions, said Williams, that is, what is the meaning of Christology or eschatology? Rather ask theological questions about the heart of our living and dying, essential questions that challenge our liturgical norms. Hear the cries to a God who is mother to the motherless, sister to the sisterless. Listen to those moments where God helps women to survive and to hold on to their self-esteem even as they were raped by any white man who felt like doing it.

To that end, we explored broadening the scope of what we called, "sacred texts" in our worship services to include slave narratives, Indigenous stories, overlooked texts from the bible and everyday life. We imagined and used a broader range of symbols that expressed resistance and courage, such as, an overturned pot. It not only brought back memories of slave gatherings where a simple pot masked the sounds of singing and dancing, but it reinforced the belief that God supports us in resistance.

To place particular and diverse ways of living and dying at the center of our liturgies challenges singular, hierarchical sources of power. It identifies the patriarchal holds (or frames) on them. It disturbs expressions of all-knowing. And it requires each person to identify meanings that connect with our lives now. To start from where we live is messy work. Our tangled-up lives are fraught with pain, misunderstanding, and love. Layered expressions of faith from the margins are necessary and costly. It is important to say that these are mostly cis women's experiences of patriarchy and its possible answers.

As a scholar, Delores Williams was publicly criticized for her contributions to womanist theology most famously for her convictions and research about an alternative theory of atonement. We do not need folks hanging on crosses, she argued. Instead, we need them to more closely listen to the life of Jesus. What seems simple and even logical today was deemed irresponsible and wrong by many of her colleagues.

Theologian Elizabeth Johnson addressed another pivotal aspect of a re-imaging our faith that strikes at the heart of women's experiences, that is, the naming of God with both female and male images. In her words:

The fundamental capacity to be bearers of the image of God and Christ is a gift not restricted by sex. New religious experience of women's selves coupled with feminist theological analysis, has resurrected this insight at the same time that it vigorously gives the lie to any views that shortchange women's theological identity.[12]

I offer this example from my own experience:

In the early 1990s I was asked to help some faculty, alumnae and parents plan a Roman Catholic Eucharistic Liturgy to commemorate the 125th anniversary of a catholic girls' school. The mission of the school included developing active members of a faith-filled community as seekers of truth, moral decision makers and confident leaders. Given these commitments I began our planning by asking how their mission is reflected in the content of the liturgy. After several meetings, I invited them to think about how these girls relate to God. Since everyone on the planning committee was female and all the students, too, I asked them to pause for a moment and think about what it would be like for them to call upon God as mother and father. Some felt it was heretical. Others said it would be disruptive, all except one woman. I saw tears running down her face. She said, I am a mother of five children. I have never thought of myself as an image of God.

To use a variety of female images for God is a pursuit of truth and justice that requires revolutionary and moral change. Some say, "we don't know this God." It tears the fabric of comfort and certainty. Yes, and as it did for the woman mentioned above, the interruption stirred up awareness and connections. What felt foreign at first, felt right, true and affirming. It pushed out the boundaries of understanding as it opened new possibilities for moments of love and respect.

Queering/Quareing Worship Services

Up to this point in the article we have presented a discussion of queering the liturgy in the most general understanding of the term, that is, taking the worship structures off of their center, unbalancing the weights of method and value, expanding the terms of the conversation and calling attention to boundaries and stories often buried under the proper order and wording of Christian rites. But what would need to be queered, made strange in the structure of the worship, in order to welcome someone going through a process of transitioning in their bodies? What would have to give in order to honor such a moment fully? To honor this person as we honor God. Not just for the sake of the private life of someone but for the fullness of life lived in a community who cares and walks along with this person.

We start by listening. Here are some excerpts from a sermon given by Terry Cummings, a graduate of Union Seminary in which she described what the process of transitioning requires.

> *Imagine what it would be like if you had to hide the very essence of who you were from everyone. To not only have to keep your very soul under a lock and key, but to feel so ashamed of who you are deep down inside that you deny your own identity because of what you learn during your childhood about what it means to be normal. Imagine feeling scared of the unbearable humiliation you would suffer, at the very least, if you revealed who you really are to the world? And then imagine what it would be like to know that if you didn't live as your authentic self you might never know what it was like to be happy, or free.... I believe that making worship space welcoming of all, with a variety of gender/sexual orientation is about using words and rituals, bells and smells, in order to eliminate fear, fear of the queer folks, fear of the transperson. Worship services are to open up a much broader horizon so the congregation can go from fear to trust, from self-enclosed identities to a plethora of identities that includes the transperson and defies the binary world of worship.[13]*

To hear Terry's story required mutual trust. She counted on the congregation to listen to her account of the realities and demands of being transgender and to believe her. In turn, they expected honesty and respect from her, including the space and time to feel and work through their own vulnerabilities. It was an example of putting ourselves in the middle of life, to feel unease, even fear, to see beyond rejection and exclusion, to be "other", together. A sacred moment.

At the end of the video that chronicled her experience she was asked if she would do it again: *If I had to do it over, I would do it in a heartbeat. I live now in the state of grace.*[14]

But we cannot queer worship services without paying attention to the racial composite of our social life. Taking sexualities and gender without race or class is to perpetuate forms of living that are forever divided by forms of racialized language hidden in universal religious claims. As we find ways to queer our worship services, we must consider the ways Black queer folks live, process and perform their sexualities and gender lives. Embracing the word *quare* from E. Patrick Johnson, Jennifer S. Leath, tells us how queer/quare, or what she calls "Quareing," is fundamental to the religious work we must do. Leath says:

Given Johnson's definition, to "quare" justice, normatively speaking, is to awaken visions and expressions of justice that insert off-kilter blue notes, troubling epistemological and ontological certainties or arrogances with primary perspectival regard for the subjectivity of LGBTQ persons of color who love other people and appreciate Black culture or community. And it means to do this in a way that is holistically committed to the struggle against all oppression, in a way that reflects the connection between gender, sexuality, and race, and in a form that engages situations deeply instead of "throwing shade."[15]

In order not to throw shade we must again listen to LGBTQIA+ persons of color in order to learn and gain a new understanding so our ways of knowing, living, relating, believing can be transformed. In a ritual called *A Ceremony of Body Celebration*, in the Black Trans Prayer Book, Rev. Louis Mitchell writes, "Many of us walk through the world holding our breath, not only fearful of what the world might think of us, but equally full of loathing for our own bodies. Some of us celebrate the diverse configurations of us, but many of us dream of having different parts and pieces, sizes and shapes to affirm our identities."[16] To recognize transgender folks in our worship services is to hear their stories, their ways of living, relating, and believing. Their lives demand from all of us a new way of acting, performing and worshiping, one that expands the possibilities of life within a radical sense of love that comes from the assurance of transgender people as carriers of the *imago Dei*: to think what is to be human in a much bigger way. But to accomplish this change, our sense of human boundaries must be undone, replaced, expanded and dissolved.

We need a *queering/quareing* liturgical theology that radicalizes the fundamental notion of the Christian incarnation in worship. The incarnation of Jesus Christ as the site/locus of God's manifestation turns the body into the heart of Christian theologies and liturgical actions. If Jesus' body is fully human, it carries colors, race, sexuality and gender. If feminist and queer/ quareing theologies bring us an expanded form of humanity not contemplated before, transgender people bring a new foreground to our conversation and practices that allows us to think life and God in different ways and challenge our assumed frames as God's frames. Worship needs to begin this conversation and practice especially in regard to how boundaries shift, especially in conversation with racialized bodies, and the forms of loss, joy, anger and hopes queered/quared worship may embody. The full embrace of a trans person must transform our understanding of the forms of God's love and our own forms of love.

Fear and hatred, disguised as righteousness and used to justify the diminishing and the killing of women and queer folks in the name of God, must be confronted and removed from our worship. Transgender people know too well this hatred and are forced to protect themselves from deep violence against them. No wonder the Translatinx activist slogan is "Mi Existir es Resistir" (My Existence is Resistance). Within the Christian faith, to resist is to make precious bodies and lives not only recognizable as fully human but also loved and cared for. Worship is a privileged site where we learn a new grammar of love through prayers. By praying, we learn about a radical love that turns fear and anger into deep physical love. We are all called to re-frame the frames of our worship, the boundaries of our heart and physical spaces, in order to re-structure the very core of our understanding of what life is all about and expand the possibilities of different knowledges not yet known or explored by Christian churches. Patrick Chung, a queer theologian says that this process entails:

> *Radical love… a love so extreme that it dissolves our existing boundaries, whether they are boundaries that separate us from other people, that separate us from preconceived notions of sexuality and gender identity, or that separate us from God… the connections between Christian theology and queer theory are actually much closer than one would think. That is, radical love lies at the heart of both Christian theology and queer theory.*[17]

Radical love comes from a deep understanding. A deep understanding creates a radical love. That is the circularity between Christian rituals and queer theory and LGBTQIA+ people.

Rituals that Heal and Transform

Here are some suggestions we hear from our transgender colleagues as we prepare our worship services:

> Ask transgender people what they need and do not need. In the words of Jennifer Finney Boylan, we do not need more think pieces about the legitimacy of our lives. What we need and what we deserve is justice, and compassion and love. What we need is freedom from violence, and protection from homelessness and the right not to lose our jobs, or our children or our lives.[18]

Evaluate the liturgy from the perspective of the dignity of every person: diverse images of relationships, leaders that reflect a queer community, a variety of texts, traditional and new symbols that stretch the boundaries of what is safe and predictable.

Counteract the image that LGBTQIA+ bodies and practices are the negation of all that is good in the flesh and consequently, historically and theologically outside the image of God. We must create a strategy that calls for a fundamental shift in the organization of power that arises not from experts but rather from the community, not a hierarchical method, but a dialogical one, acknowledging the resilience and goodness of LGBTQIA+ bodies, individuals, and communities.

Include moments when there is an invitation to feel what is foreign, marginal, and gain an awareness that rituals are not to keep a world intact but rather, to help us move into another world that grows within and around us. For instance, a student from Union once taught us in worship how some queer people in Harlem, New York dance and how their dance is a way of embodying resistance and love.

Acknowledge the relationship of shame and queer identity that has been so cruelly imposed on queer folks.

Tony Morrison tells of an art experience at the Venice Biennial that can help us acknowledge our fear when engaging with others. At this art place, she entered a dark room facing a mirror:

In a few seconds a figure appeared, slowly taking shape and moving toward me. A woman. When she (rather, her image) was close to me, same height, she placed her palm on the glass and I was instructed to do the same. We stood there face to face, unspeaking, looking into the eyes of the other. Slowly the figure faded and shrank before disappearing altogether. Another woman appeared. We repeated the gesture of touching our palms together and looking into the eyes of the other. This went on for some time. Each woman differed in age, body shape, color, dress. I must say it was extraordinary—this intimacy with a stranger. Silent, knowing. Accepting each other—one to one.[19]

This experience can be used in our worship services to help us move and be moved. as we add in the complex issues of shame and internalized oppression.

The Black Trans Prayer Book brings beautiful rituals that gives us a sense of what it means to accompany and be with LGBTQIA+ friends, and the words remind us of the separation and pain we have caused through our exclusion, racism, and transphobia. From a ritual called *A Contemplation for Disabled/ill Trans Folks*, written by Wit Lopez:

> I am not broken
> I am not damaged
> I am not a burden
> I am not a curse[20]

To listen is to hear and remember why such a ritual is necessary and life-giving to those we have harmed.

Conclusion

The challenge for Christian communities is to turn a critical understanding of both constructed and essentialized forms of identity. We might start, perhaps, with the notion of identity in difference that José Esteban Muñoz procures, and then move into what Muñoz proposes as *disindentifications,* a term Muñoz learned with queers of color.[21] We must challenge ourselves to keep on reconsidering, shifting, and changing the very notion of community and what *us* means. We might start to have a sense from what Muñoz says from the work of Marga Gomez, claiming to be full drama queens:

> *In Gomez' comedy, we locate a disidentificatory desire, a desire for a queer life-world that is smoky, mysterious, and ultimately contestatory. More than that, we see a desire to escape the claustrophobic confines of community, a construct that often deploys rhetorics of normativity and normalization, for a life.*[22]

As we finish (for now), we believe that the presence of the Holy Spirit can be, within the Christian faith, the most transgressive person/wind/disruptive presence and concept we have. The Spirit is that which is untamable, crossing boundaries and reframing our understandings of sexes, genders and identities as the very work of God. The breathing of life within us is that which moves us and expands our knowing/doing/feeling/sexing assured frames, twisting our boundaried protections, helping us breathe life in more expansive ways, ritualizing a difficult love in constant solidarity with border communities. Ashon T. Crawley writes about the Holy Spirit from a Blackpentecostal perspective:

> *Blackpentecostal Breath argues that blackness is released into the world to disrupt the institutionalization and abstraction of thought that produces the categorical distinctions of disciplinary knowledge. To make a claim for belief— in and of Black Study— is to trouble and unsettle epistemological projects founded upon pure reason, pure rationality, in the service of thinking with and against how that which we call knowledge is produced and dispersed.*[23]

How can the Holy Spirit queer our minds to shift us lovingly into new understandings, new risks and new prospects? Can the Holy Spirit expand our horizons, ground us in ecological relations, and enlarge our ways of living multiple bodies and sexualities? We believe this is possible and that this is the beginning of our work.

CHAPTER ELEVEN

God's Petticoat and Capitalism—Full Fashion

Nancy Cardoso Pereira and Cláudio Carvalhaes[1]

Sarah Grinaboldi Ortiz, 3 years old

Marcella once said that to do theology is "to raise up God's dress."[2] We want to hold on to that suggestion, that precious and dangerous combination, as we search for dresses, skirts, clothes, fabrics, and the textures of rags. All of them: materiality of the divine. We will also conjugate the verb "to raise" . . . without knowing for sure if it's in the future – "we will raise" – or in the subjunctive – "if we raised." This is because we are learners of indecencies, and we live with grammatical rules and a very strict and repetitive theological lexicon. We want dresses, skirts, pants, miniskirts, underwear, and petticoats . . . the body. Life.

We choose a certain look. Without fearing the shortness of the narrative, we choose to talk about pants from what a woman said. A partial and temporary look: texts, like life, are always in movement. A little poetry here will not harm anyone, and if we use poetry and metaphors, we do it for didactic as well as theoretical purposes:

> *The figurative use of language can, naturally, be very important in theoretical works. Not only for didactic reasons, or as the author's stylish ornament, even though these two aspects are obvious. The important philosophical point here, however, is that the figurative expressions can reflect the very process of intuition.*[3]

Between history and literature there is the living materiality that restores dignity between thing and word. Thus, we will occupy ourselves with the fantastic and the concrete, with the unusual and the daily. To locate theology at the place of the fold, between the fantastic and the imaginary, does not authorize us to dissolve the material and the concrete that sustain our dreams, visions, oracles, and daily clothes. Theology, between history and myth, is the word reconfigured and located, filled with materialism: the dresses!

Ah! God's dresses: divine! So much going on under those divine dresses! However, we were told to turn our eyes away, to avoid looking at the dresses of God and the substances under the clothing of our narratives. "There is nothing to be seen," they told us.

> *We often think that we meet God where our body ends: and we make it suffer as we turn it into a machine, obeying orders, as an enemy to be silenced, and then we persecute the body to the point of making a eulogy to death into the path towards God, as if God preferred the smell of the sepulchers to the delights of paradise. And we became cruel, violent, allowing exploitation and war. For if God is to be met beyond the body, then anything can be done to the body.*[4]

Against the body, without the body, beyond the body: meta-physics. God is spirit and that's why God wears neither dresses nor pants ... but God's representatives do wear pants! Under clerical vests, ecclesiological underwear. Maybe! Clerical collar and theological collar: those little leashes on the neck, that subtle distinction that does not want to call attention to itself but divides the priest/reverend in two pieces ... demanding that I look at the theologian, the priest, the bishop, from the neck up. Nonetheless, theology is done down below: raise up the dresses? No, this is out of order! Here is the clerical fashionista explaining:

> *Wearing an ecclesiastical vestment, the priest will not fall into the vanity of lay clothes that will make him 'beautiful', 'charming', 'attractive'. The robe places the clergyman in his right place, at the same time that it removes human honors that he must sever even more radically. The ecclesiastical vestment, since it standardizes those who wear it, also impedes the flourishing of human vanities and its use serves as a therapeutic discipline against tendencies that are out of order.[5]*

But we insist on the dress, on clothes! So religious are the clothes! *Ikomojadê*: the ceremony of the children in Candomblé, a piece of cloth entwined by the hands of the mother, the grandmother, or Godmother. The child laid upon the ground over this special cloth with sacred words and the name that will follow her or him to the end of life: "This white cloth will accompany you forever," explains Egbomi Cici.[6]

The other woman and I meet in the bathroom. She smiles at me, sweating from the heat of a burning Friday morning. She is dressing up and so am I. In that little space we share our lives, and her long dress fills the space with laces and ruffles. In the corner, I am also dressing up in my original African celebration dress. Compared to the excesses of the other woman's dress, mine simply disappears. Her dress is from Umbanda, a reinvention of Africa in Brazil.

She wears many multicolored necklaces. I have my açaí beads in two long loops around my neck. We greet each other. She says: "I am Mother Ziza." I say: "I am Pastor Nancy: we are going to celebrate together." She smiles and asks if we are late. I say that I will ask and leave the locker room, still impressed by the beauty of the white laces and the handmade details in white and yellow on that older, more beautiful woman.

Outside, people are arriving for the celebration of *Black Consciousness Day*. The Roman Catholic priest greets me and asks if we should wear clerical vestments. He looks at *mae* Ziza and me and decides not to wear them. "I brought the robe, but I am not going to wear it. I don't like to look different in the middle of the people." While the drums gather people for the beginning of the celebration, I realize that all of the women, from Christian and Umbanda traditions, are dressed for the celebration … Dressed as what? As god? Is the yellow dress of that *mae de santo* part of the Bible?

A piece of cloth can symbolize the survival of the whole identity of a group and maintain the fundamentals of a culture. Mormon underwear, for example, is the same as other, regular clothes, but it needs to be all white, symbolizing purity, devotion, and cleanness.[7] The top part of their garment is similar to a shirt and covers the shoulders and a little of the arm. The lower part should cover the skin to the knees. The underwear should be worn directly on the skin. For the women, even bras should be placed over this special garment. According to the Mormons, their underwear is part of the Bible.

The Poetic Exercise of Raising Up Dresses and Pants

A Brazilian poet: Adélia Prado: a Brazilian poet.[8] We confess to reading her all the time. We read her as if her texts were very complicated lexicons always in need of translation and study.

> *Poetry, salvation, and life*
> *I wonder:*
> *What are those blue pants of Mr. Raul's*
> *They have to do with the moment*
> *When Pilate decides to inscribe*
> *Jesus Nazarenus REX JUDEORUM.*
> *I do not know what it is,*
> *But I know that there is a grain of salvation*
> *Hidden in the things of the world . . .*
> *The pants of Mr. Raul*
> *To me*
> *Are part of the Bible.*
>
> —Adélia Prado

Adélia Prado's poetry is confessional. Her religiosity does not lend itself to an ethic or system but is instead a trip through the divine that spills over the catechesis of the countryside of Brazil's Minas Gerais and into her prayers addressed from the everyday. Her poetry is neither feminist nor gendered, and it does not want to be. It does not need to be like that. The woman who speaks, moans, and makes comments from the side of her mouth, by folding parts of her body, is a country woman, repetitive and erotic, softly touching the skin of the ordinary with the paradoxes of her tongue. In Adélia Prado, mystery is not the totally other, but instead the totally ordinary, common, known, as transfigured by the sacred. Colloquial epiphany. Revelatory apparition. The Verb becoming the everyday. In her poetry, the Bible is always present in titles and epigraphs, as if it were impossible to say anything without the Scriptures. A theology made of vocatives.

Made up neither of messianic promises nor of rigorous programs, her Christianity is taken from the streets and enameled through the difficult art of poetry. In her poetry, one can see that she holds back any messianic move. In her poems, people's religion is presented in simple and dramatic gestures, without evaluation. She embraces the immediacy of the faith of the man and his pants.

She makes human frailty evident without massacring the body that experiences a continuous reality of exposure to the forces of death, non-coincidence to itself, and the unquenchable forces of its desires. Adélia Prado makes simple and common what systematic theologies have tried to construct for centuries: heavy, complex sounding Christologies. In her insistence on lightness and abyss, triviality and materiality, her poetry – going the wrong way, backwards – dismantles the exclusivity of Christological dogma and its superiority. She explodes theology from inside and invents other places for it, like, for instance, Mr. Raul's pants. Exegetical and dogmatic formulas of salvation are incapable of accomplishing this mixture of the sacred and profane, this rubbing between the less divine and the more humane.

> She (poetry) will save me. I don't speak to the four corners,
> because we have doctors, ex-communion
> and the scandal of the weak. I don't fear God.
> What other thing is poetry if not God's face slapped
> By the brutality of things?
>
> —Adélia Prado

She knows she offended against the Christological meta-narrative and that is why she fears the doctors, ex-communication and the scandal of the weak. About God, Adélia Prado will only speak the divine face slapped by the brutality of things: poetry.

This image of the face of God suffering a blow is strange. She inverts the formula that recognizes divinity in an outer reality, indifferent and incapable of being reached, and with her poetry she projects things in the theological arena with brutality. Revelation is reversed: it is the brutality of things that reveals God as poetry. There is no God outside of this daily reality, outside of things and their fabrication: the pants!

Without juxtaposing speeches, preventing the confrontation, and without the simulacra of the identity of the theologian: there! This scratch at the pubis, indecent and neither wanting nor needing to be: atavism.

> *Atavism*
> *Oh God, Don't humiliate me anymore*
> *With this scratch in the pubis.*
>
> —Adélia Prado

Mr. Raul has pants. She, the theologian, has a pubis. And does God have a dress?

Poetics feeds on materials, relationships, and concrete meanings … this materiality is what creates the objective and subjective conditions of subsequent readings and their interpretations of the autonomy and cohesion of the same texts. A fantastic materiality.

Searching for a definition – poor and temporary – for *fantastic materiality* we need to keep the objectivity of Per Johns who presents fantastic Latin American literature this way: "And by fantastic one wants to designate the state of the spirit who picks the unusual from the everyday, without losing either the everyday or the unusual."[9] Fantastic realism is, simultaneously, a technical narrative and an instrument of experimentation that places readers at the frontiers of the real and the insolid, revealing mechanisms that structure discourses of reality and their conflicts. Literature reveals the fable of the real, its fissures, and its very imperfect connections in order to generate a vital epistemological doubt: false or true? Possible or impossible?

To describe and explain is not enough. There is a sense of urgency – of *apo kalypto* – that is, of taking away, of uncovering that which covers, hides, conceals, veils. To unveil take the veil. To reveal. To raise up the dress.

The use of dresses and pants in texts can suggest a simple reference to things, as an externality of representation. Language, however, deals with *materialities*, thus, it is necessary to take dresses and pants not as external references only, but rather to ask for the objective and subjective conditions of these materials/things in the metabolism of production, reproduction, and consumerism.

To see dresses/pants as final and conclusive visions implies an unveiling act in the process of making and supporting an image as representational. From a materialist perspective, these questions about conditions need to be asked, and they can be answered only partially by the limits of this work.

The immediacy and naked severity of dresses/pants can be understood as a question of the concreteness of the clothes and their fabrication, of their usage and value and also, of their conditions of work. Mr. Raul's pants are blue. Is blue currently in fashion? Are blue pants fashioned?

The Miracle of Transubstantiation: Full-fashion Capitalism

When goods are exposed, during the time called the *Relative Form of Value*,[10] merchandise gains life in Marx's analysis: "Linen recognizes in the coat, even buttoned down, its own soul through value. However, the coat cannot represent value for the linen without assuming to its own eyes, the figure of a coat."[11] From a macroeconomic perspective, the fashion industry has an expressive function in the scenario of the globalized economy. Fashion connects a productive chain that articulates rural production into the idle world of luxury consumerism, passing through oil, chemistry, and textile industries; confections; craft workers, leather and shoes industries; the metallurgical industry; shopping centers; stores; publicity agencies; media and their professionals; and the industry of events, models, stylists.[12]

The attention of consumers turns to futile objects and the taste to consume—exemplars of a new formatting of capitalism in which subjects, when they consume, no longer have the preoccupation of searching for durable objects as they existed in the announced stability of *Fordism*.[13] This is because, in market logic, exchange relations assume money as the language of value without having to use the language of necessity.[14] An abstraction becomes concrete! Nobody sees it but everybody experiences the miracle of transubstantiation: "The exchange value attached to the body of the merchandise longs to be redeemed by the money format."[15]

Miracles happen when the person fulfills her/himself as a consumer. In the consumer act, merchandise and money kiss each other and profit, which promises to gather the whole of society one day into the total market. Or not: what matters are that profit and value reproduce themselves and fulfill themselves.

It is a complex and at the same time simple operation, very sensual and totally metaphysical. It has to do with realities, things, substances, objects, this and that which, when touched by the language of value, are transformed by subjectivities into needs. The material and concrete realities are stripped of their daily value and usage in order to put on the metaphysics of exchange value: "Anxious for the money, the merchandise is created in capitalist production to meet the image of the anxiety of the consumers. This image will be developed later by propaganda, already devoid of the merchandise."[16]

Things and bodies lose their immediate materiality to be mediated by the consumption of the merchandise. The body becomes the merchandise. Anxiety. Love. Image. Seduction. Words that don't seem appropriate for an economic discussion ... however they are words that perhaps best express the process of fabulating aesthetics for merchandise, especially in the fashion industry.

Merchandise-clothes desire to be consumed, need to be chosen, and in order to accomplish this, they make themselves into something lovable, desirable. Moreover, merchandise-clothes want to know the desires of consumers or invent them by offering an aesthetic stimulus. It is necessary to induce new forms of pleasure, always submitted to the maintenance of the capacity for reproduction of capital itself.

> *The principal strategy of capital is not to create new markets ... what is more important now is the rationalization of existing markets; to multiply the potential of their capacities of realization without necessarily implicating the growth of the number of consumers. That is the radicalization of a trend: birth and death of merchandise.*[17]

Presented as a stimulus to freedom and to difference, in fact, the fashion industry homogenizes by creating a multitude of anonymous people who follow religiously the directions of the specialists, the priests/priestesses. Within the frantic consumerism, the subject, without the capacity to elect and impose its own taste and will, makes an effort to copy, with whatever she/he can, the aesthetic knowledge that is on offer. Fashion moves by discarding things. The user/consumer becomes a non-subject: individuals do not dress themselves; they are dressed up. Through fashion, the market offers social mobility without establishing patterns and parameters, forcing mass-consumers to keep their agility by continuing to consume, which in turn warrants the reproduction of capital-fashion.

To Bourdieu, within the metamorphosis of taste, a trend is a mark that, without changing the natural sources of the materials used, alters the social relation of object-cloth.[18] The apparent frivolity and lucidity of the fashion world hides perverse relations of production, archaic forms of work payment, and manipulations of taste and consumerism. Even the geniality of stylists and their creative freedom are dependent on technological determinations established by the industry and the capital of the fashion world: "Industry establishes a chain of causations that start way before any creation when, for example, the chemical industry agrees about the set of colors that will dictate subsequent fashion collections. It starts with the yarn; goes through automobile production and many other products to end up, later on, in sanitary objects and construction material."[19]

Fashion and Religion

In the introduction to the *Artist Clothing Catalogue 2004/2005*, Otto Von Busch presents similarities between religion and fashion, especially the ways in which fashion influences dreams and conceptions of reality: "The fashion system is a metaphysical system closely guarded by sects and hermeneutic schools."[20] This system has its mystical professionals and interpreters – *cardinals and priests*. What brings fashion and religion together, however, are not their structured and hermetic hierarchies but instead, their liturgies, i.e., the rituals that reproduce belief in the ideal of a beauty that is within the reach only the initiated.

> *Fashion is alchemy.*
> *Ritual and magic.*
> *Faith and religion.*
> *Sacrifice and devotion.*

The fashion world is idealized *in extremes* and by the mediation and correction of lenses, make up and computers, human imperfections disappear into the transfiguration of the *most beautiful specimen*. Not a single hair is out of place, no wrinkles, no fat, no smell. It is the body in its maximum exposure ... only, at this point, there is no body present anymore: "This holy moment is totally unique, but later reproduced into millions of copies, and made for us believers to be used as an ideal for living."[21]

The fashion religion demands of its faithful observation, contemplation, surrender, and sacrifice in exchange for oils and potions that promise eternal life. This relation is perceived in the marks of capitalism that are turned *into the most refined magical system*, a system of meanings that deals with *freshness, sexiness, and beauty*.[22] Away from this world, everything is messy, disordered, and chaos reigns. *Everything is doomed to be ugly, dull, and grey.*

For von Busch, the fashion system is the spirit of capitalism connecting the fetishes of merchandise with religious fetishes unequivocally: "Fashion cannot have any meaning, because then it would already be out of fashion."[23] It is a closed and self-sufficient system that deals with oppressed sights, dreams, and desires projected beyond the objectivity of dress and its fabrication, yet the system keeps consumer exigencies busy and alive, renewed by its rituals and objects. In that sense, fashion exists but cannot make itself seen. Yarn, gestures, mouths, and the ritual paraphernalia are visuals that blind its implications, blurring if not eliminating private and public notions of body, market, and capital. As in religion, the fashion world has its rules. Among them are: "Don't make images and don't have other gods," that is, interdiction of models and voluntary servitude. At fashion shows, however, images multiplied thousands of times hold success, nauseating any value making while models bring their bodies to inhuman size in order to serve (the kingdom of) capital. Capital possessing bodies.

The authors present the catalogue believing that a middle terrain between fashion and art creates the possibility of fissuring the monoculture of the religion-fashion system: "Fashion is closing in from the side of art which gives it freedom by being outside the production of the system and can therefore reveal this landscape under a fresh aspect."[24] It is not an enlightenment project *to end the alchemy or magic of fashion,* but the mixture of two mystical worlds *merging into one.* The hybridity of art and the fashion world creates a space for discussion about the complex phenomenon. This is a tight space that can, however, open the possibility of critiquing the fashion system within itself.

Theology of the Petticoat: of the Avoidance of the Body

If I ask the economist: do I obey the economic laws if I get money from the sale of my body to pleasure someone else? (The industry workers in France call the prostitution of their wives and daughters the nth hour of work, which is literally right); don't I act economically when I sell my friend to the Moroccan people? (The direct sale of men in the market that recruits people has a place in all civilized countries); the economist answers me: you don't act against my laws but look at what Madam Morality and Madam Religion say; my moral and religious economy has nothing to censor you. Then, who should I believe, the political economy or the moral? The moral in political economy is profit, work, savings, and sobriety, and political economy promises to satisfy all of my needs.

Karl Marx[25]

Marx introduces two madams: Madam Morality and Madam Religion. These two Madams are completely obsolete and unnecessary as regards the economic law: the moral in political economy is the profit that undermines these two madams by its logic through an efficient metabolism of alienation. Well said! Within this full fashion capitalism, it is religion that adapts to the economic laws of consumerism and the reproduction of the more-value system that legitimates the Fall-Winter collection.

It is the theological petticoats, yarn, and clothes that prevent the visualization of god, its flesh, the very core of what it is made of, its sexualized belonging to the world of bodies. Theology offers itself as prudish clothing around God's hips ... pure discursive decency incapable of fissuring the monolatrous, monotheistic monoculture. Systematic performances, lucrative performances. Spectacles that do not let us see, either by authentication of virtue or market.

Thus, theology is a discursive textile that does not let us 'see' the inner parts of God, in a game of hide and seek that ends up hampering any consideration of what God is and of how God manifests itself in theophanic experiences. The exegetes and researchers turn their faces away, avoiding the text as if they are performing the experience of fear and trembling. In particular this avoidance is located in the treatment of the body of God that the experience/text entails. The body of God is avoided as a way to hide the body of the man who is writing, rendering the experience asexualized, as if he could avoid his body while thinking.

Virtuous theologies wear extremely decent, heavy, and redundant petticoats. These theologies are the same ones that read and reread the same author over and over, or perhaps another author who can be included in the same new authorial simulacrum ... anything that impedes the nakedness of reality, of sexualized bodies and their human, erotic miseries and economies! In the fashion world of theology, the body is idealized *in extremis* and by the mediation of letters and words, make-up and computers, where the imperfections of the human being disappear in the transfiguration of the *most beautiful specimen.* Not a single hair is out of place; there are no wrinkles, no smell, and no sex. It is the body in its maximum exposure when there is no body there.

On the other end of the religious phenomenon, religion offers itself to the market world of entertainment with the launching of ardent, frivolous products that are everywhere in t-shirts, I-pods, and shows that reproduce themselves in singers and its aesthetics of spiritual fervor ... moans and praise to King Jesus! The wheel of consumerism turns, and capitalism doesn't even pay the tithe.

Conclusion: Mr. Raul's Pants are *Queer!* So is God's Petticoat

What is the blue of Mr. Raul's pants? Hidden under the things of the world, are Mr. Raul's pants the grain of salvation? Without trying to repeat what the poem has already said and without trying to exhaust its possibilities, we come close to its brutality. We connect the scope of the language of poetry to the things of the world and so learn.

The blue and the pants belong to Mr. Raul. He does not disappear either before the power of fashionable inscription already there or before the power that wants to script something, represented in the poem by Pilate.

Mr. Raul's blue pants are part of the Bible and can be a grain of salvation because he is wearing them. Mr. Raul's pants are unique even while being the same as many others. In Adélia Prado's poetry, the pants transgress the larger narrative and escape from their schemes of domination. Mr. Raul's pants are iconoclastic, not by complementing the individual, but by their ambiguity and resistance: "I don't know what it is, but it is part of the Bible."

Mr. Raul's pants are not *avant-garde*, nor do they submit themselves to the logic of being easily discarded. They are blue pants filled with interruption, strangeness, and suspension. And if we say that the blue pants of Mr. Raul crash the bourgeois order, I want to say that they do so by opposing the repetitive gesture of the ever 'new' in the fashion world. Mr. Raul's pants are a grain of salvation because they denounce, from a collective singularity, the religious character of fashion as inscription. The poetry/scripture of Adélia Prado functions, using Barthes's terms, as a "negativity, as the social limit of the possible."[26] Mr. Raul's pants contest, break, steal, pulverize, and ironize the model of power manifested by the inscription and the script of theology, making theology unrecognizable:

> The only possible answer is neither confronting nor destroying, but rather, stealing: to fragment old texts of culture, science, literature and disseminate their traces according to unrecognizable formulas. (The scriptures) exceed the laws of society, an ideology, a philosophy that gives or concedes to itself in beautiful gestures of historical intelligence.[27]

Mr. Raul's pants are an irony: "irony is nothing more than a question asked to language by language."[28] Mr. Raul's pants are queer because they are strange, indecent, ironic, because they disrupt the serious aspects of both inscription and the one inscribing. Adélia Prado asks herself: "I wonder if the pants have to do with the moment of decision." And she answers: "I don't know what it is." The ambiguity is kept:

> Ambiguity is understood as, first, a form of resistance to a system, any given system, that establishes rules and patterns of behavior ... Second, besides thinking ambiguity as a form of resistance, ambiguity is a space (or spaces – plural) for production of meanings that extrapolate imposed limits by hegemonic systems, founding another logic and opening the possibilities for other forms of knowledge and theoretical reflection.[29]

In the same way as Mr. Raul's pants, God's petticoat is ambiguous because it is touched by the ambivalence of human skin, its possibilities, desires, strengths, and frailties. The ideological aspects of theological inscriptions, with their sexual/economic values, forms of exchange, and market usage, try to define the very fabric of God's petticoat. However, God's petticoat resists every theological attempt to turn meaning into commodity, to control its truth by assigning it value. By negating theological dogmas, contradicting the rules of capitalism, and resisting any attempt for singularity of thought/global market grasp, God's petticoat lurks around the possibilities of other worlds, without the hegemony of the new.

To sum up, Mr. Raul's pants, as well as God's petticoat are queer because they are equivocal, plural, hybrid, simultaneous, fluid, relational, polyphonic, syncretic, mobile, transgressive … all of the terms and concepts that are associated with the notion of ambiguity that allow one to glimpse possibilities for the construction 'of ambiguity' as an epistemological category.[30]

CHAPTER TWELVE[1]

Ecclesiologies as Foreign Ecclesiologies:
Worshiping with the Homeless

Mabel Bastos Chiavegatti, 2 years old

Every people felt threatened by a people without a country

Jean Genet

Introduction—Welcome Church[2]

A group of people gathers together at Logan Square or Suburban Station in Philadelphia, PA, every Sunday afternoon. They call themselves a church without walls because they do not have a building. The members are people from different Christian churches and homeless people. The liturgy is mostly from the Lutheran Church, but it changes and adapts and adds what is needed. One day they were not having Eucharist, but a homeless person said, "what about our eucharist today?" the pastor said, "we didn't bring the elements." She then opened her bag, took a loaf of mushy bread and said: "I got it." And eucharist was celebrated and shared.

On Ash Wednesday this church celebrated death and life in the midst of a bitter cold winter at Logan Square in Philadelphia.[3] We heard stories of extreme poverty, abandonment, frostbitten feet, and dignity not heard elsewhere. On Good Friday, we walked through the main points of the Suburban subway station where homeless people stay to hide from the cold. This church started outside of the restrooms of this station, and on this day the stations of the cross were the many places within this station, places to rest, dollar stores, abandoned places where they could hide, warm places, a women's store, a place to eat and so on. In each station, a song, a prayer, A Bible text, a story of pain and hurt and perhaps some redemption. Somebody gave them $ 10 gift cards from McDonalds to get some food. From there they returned to the streets to hunt for the next meal.

Once I asked Pastor Violet C. Little to describe how the relationship between worship, homeless people, food and social justice form her ministry and this is what she said:

> "… there is a witness to a different way of being and relating in our very midst. The sacrament of the Eucharist is the in-breaking of God's economy of abundance in the midst of human economies of scarcity. It is the creation of free-flowing relationships of power in which the roles of server and served are blurred and reversible. This establishes a community of partnership and cooperation wherein each experiences, elaborates, and shares her or his humanity as a free gift of God's grace. When we gather at the communion table, we form a circle; for the One towards whom we move stands in our midst answering the needs of each with the same gift of love and mercy given without stint to all… Homeless? Perhaps, though we need to be aware of how many reject that title because they have learned

that they do have a home among God's people and within God's Kingdom. And above all, none of us are any longer nameless and invisible. That is a source of strength we all need when we next have to lay aside our dignity and stand in line like supplicants to receive food, or clothing, or the simple respect that is due to all of God's children... We ask the volunteers who bring snacks for Coffee Hour to serve the food they bring, to circulate and share what they have brought. That is why we ask all who are present to share in that process. Yes, I have seen someone grab a whole case of crackers and run off. But that is what happens to people when they have spent too much time standing in lines. They lose their awareness of community and of themselves as members of a community. This is the terrible cost visited upon those living in the extremes of poverty; and this is what I believe God is calling us to address by attempting to instantiate, each time we gather, a taste of that Beloved Community that awaits us all. "[4]

Every week somebody is missing, disappearing, dying. Pastor Little holds together the vivid tension of life and death pulsing in every breath of this community. While Welcome Church is a local church supported by the Lutheran (ELCA) and Presbyterian (PCUSA) churches, they challenge their denominational ecclesiological boundaries and expand the markers of the church. What kind of ecclesiology is this?

This essay wants to comment on the life of the Welcome Church with homeless people and propose a new form of ecclesiology, one that migrates from buildings to where the poor, the displaced, the disfranchised and the homeless people live. This article proposes a conversion to lower classes of people and create liturgies that literally sit on the disasters of the world. At the end, the hope is that using the fourfold use of one of the liturgical orders: Gathering, Word, Meal and Sending, can be a source for the migration and beginning of a new development of this foreign ecclesiology.

A New Ecclesial Base Community?

In some new ways, the Welcome Church is a legitimate heir of the Latin American Ecclesial Base Communities CEB. Fundamentally there is a deep shift in the theological/ecclesiological thinking/practices of both communities. Both events start where the poor live, the liturgies and the idea of the community is done by and on behalf of the poor; both invert the hierarchical structure of the church; they are bound to a context and work from their locality; they start with the difficult socio-economic conditions of the poor; they make a clear social and class choice to work with the poor based on God's preferential option of the poor; they re-allocate spiritual and economic resources to where the poor live; they read the Bible and build a movement from these frail locations.

In Latin America, the disastrous socio-economic condition, coupled with military interventions, caught the attention, energy and commitments of priests and theologians who were social agents of change using the theological, ecclesiological and religious symbols of the church. How were they to think about faith from the marginal places where the poor were mercilessly thrown? The reading of the Bible by the poor was one of these powerful new practices, a new reformation of the Catholic Church. This commitment entailed the beginning of a new form of church that challenged the religious, social and political powers that be--not only the Roman Catholic Church, but the CIA as well and together they worked hard to dismantle the CEB.

However, it was a time of change and dreams and utopias. The church organized a place in between the political party and the social struggle, fostering people's agency in the larger social political scenario. As Michael Löwy says, "(...) a significant sector of the Church (both lay and clergy) in Latin America, changed position in the area of social struggles, going with their material and spiritual resources to the side of the poor and to the struggle for a new society."[5] The church not only paired the reading of Bible with social reality, but made a choice to be on the side of the poor, strengthen grassroots social movements such as local labor union, and empower them with the strength and weight of the institution of the Roman Catholic church.

In this process, liberation was more than a theological, doctrinal concept; it was an experience with Christ the liberator in the community, as faith and work were juxtaposed with the holy things, namely baptism, eucharist, preaching, praying, reading the Bible and so on. The social and individual body of the poor lived in the everydayness of life became the crucial (crux/cross) point of articulation of liberation theology. The historical materiality lived through theory-practice, faith/experience was lived/thought together, one fixing and expanding the other. As Frei Betto says: "there is no theology without experience, without liberating practice (...)."[6]

At Welcome Church, the social analysis is not as deep as it was developed with the CEB's but there is no way to serve and worship with the homeless without thinking about the inequities, social exclusions and disasters of the larger society. It is one thing to worship in the midst of a well-fed group and another totally different experience to worship with the outcast of society, discarded people who have nowhere to go. At Logan Square some of the prayers are the same as are said in worship services that use worship books, but they are also very different from the ones pronounced in the church due to the concerns and urgency of homeless people. Preaching is a different beast! The sacraments are the lifeline of people. Literally!

CEB's and the Welcome Church are clear departures from the established churches, theologies and practices in secluded places marked by class preferences and belongings. CEBs and WC make a choice to live and work and be with the poor. They chose to serve the disfranchised people of God on the streets instead of feeding the already well-fed middle and higher class. In that seemingly small way, they redistribute the wealth of society.

To be with the poor is to start to understand the social economic conditions of their disastrous situations and when put in relation to the gospel of Jesus Christ, it reflects back on our own Sunday practices and commitments. In these excluded settings, with precious people turned into the disposable garbage of our society, we are confronted with the *imago Dei!* Ecclesiologies, salvation, evangelization, liberation, social movements have everything to do with critical seeing/thinking/judging/naming the evils of our social structures and with grassroots, activist political/social/sexual/gender movements of transformation.

In this piece, Frei Betto is talking about the CEBs in Brazil but could be describing the Welcome Church in Philadelphia:

> *(...) Small groups are organized around urban or rural parishes by lay people, priests, or bishops, and usually meet people from working classes, who belong to the same Church and live in the same region (periphery, squatter areas, slums, or on the margins of the big cities). They all have the same problems of survival, shelter, fighting for better living conditions, and have the same longings and hopes for liberation.[7]*

These two churches help us think and experience church in ways many of us never did. The Welcome Church challenges power structures inside the church and in the public domain, subverting the generally accepted laws that allow only certain people to be the holders of the divine and social resources, pointing to injustice, segregation and social exclusion. The Welcome Church turns the eyes of God to the homeless and places them as the privileged loci of God's epiphanies. Immanuel, if Immanuel, God indeed with us, must be primarily in the midst of the poor! In a dialectical movement, the *imago Dei* re-presented in this community is disconnected from exclusive powers that control the sacred and yet, it is deeply connected with the God they belong, represent or point to. The Welcome Church is a temporary, foreign, frail and dispossessed movement without hierarchical sustenance. Since it is made possible by the offerings of these churches, it can disappear at any time these churches do not want to support it anymore. But perhaps not anymore. The church has created such a crowd of supporters that it will continue no matter what happens to their funds because the movements of the Spirit cannot be tamed or controlled.

At the heart of this church, the work of the people stands out as a true practice. The hierarchy lived in these communities is based on a common sharing of activities; everybody can lead the worship and preach and sing and decide what the worship should do and be. A showing of a doing, these communities are great interpretations of the "priesthood of all believers" (1 Peter 2:5).[8]

Leonardo Boff describes the Base Communities in Latin America as a response to the hierarchical structures of the Roman Catholic Church:

> *Theologically they signify a new ecclesiological experience, a renaissance of the very church, and hence an action of the Spirit on the horizon of the matters urgent of our time. Seen in this way, the basic church communities deserve to be contemplated, welcomed, and respected as salvific events.*[9]

The salvific events might be altogether unrecognizable by official ecclesiological parameters, but they are found, appropriated, elaborated and represented by this community in ways that the people who participate need it to be. The Welcome Church places, perhaps inadvertently or unwillingly, the class struggles right in front of our eyes and under our noses so we cannot avoid it when worshiping God. More than that, they steal the holy things from those who own them and divide them up accordingly, preferentially to the poor, doing what we mentioned before: redistributive justice.

Thus, liturgies (work of the people), churches and society are reflected in this worship, in this gathering and we see, perhaps, that there is something wrong in our safe, insulated ecclesiologies and our ways of living and worshiping. The Welcome Church makes it clear by where they worship and people with whom they worship, that something is going wrong not only with our societies but also with our safe, protected and detached ecclesiologies.

The poor disrupt the sacred since they "steal" the perceived/known sacred sense of the worship space, the use and meaning of the holy things and locations and place it all in the hands of the homeless. Jamal, Ana, John, Tirone, Ann and many others have no building, and churches would not allow them to sleep in their sanctuaries. The very gesture of worshiping on the street, for many months in the bitter cold of Philadelphia, clearly shows the class differences between homeless Christians and Christians who have warm sanctuaries and do not want the poor in their buildings with them.

Thus, our homeless people, or the absence of them in our worship services painfully attest to the dissymmetry of our theologies of class: we discard the homeless in favor of the middle- and upper-class church people as evidenced by Christian ecclesiologies, which we sustain through our theological confessions, homiletical statements, missiological programs and liturgical practices.

The marks of the church foment ecclesiologies that internalize this larger system of oppression in society that keeps the poor and the homeless away from the symbolic and material production of wealth and the holy. That means that the "faithful ones occupy objectively distinct social places according to the situation of their class. This situation makes them perceive reality as corresponding to its social condition, and make them interpret and live the evangelical message according to its class function..."[10]

Urban Design: Ecclesiological Walls and Theological Spikes

Church buildings, fundamental parts of our ecclesiologies, contribute to the social urban design. Ecclesiologies build walls and theologies build spikes so we can protect our sense and experience of God. Churches are markers of urban design, and our theologies are stories of many sorts and kinds that foster and confirm our ecclesiologies. In this world of disasters, we have so many competing buildings and stories.[11]

Recently, there have been new stories of urban design around the world that are developing ways to keep the poor/homeless away from site/sight. Here is the news from London, England: "... any Londoner will know that the number of so-called bum-proof benches has risen sharply. Wave-shaped benches with central armrests made from slippery or buttock-numbing materials such as stainless steel are designed to prevent the homeless from kipping in public. Sloping seats at bus stops barely provide a perch, let alone a place to actually sit."[12]

From São Paulo, Brazil, the journalist Sakamoto tells of strategies in urban design intended to get rid of the homeless: "Bridges and tunnels closed with gates and concrete, streets with some inclination, pieces of glass on concrete, or metal. Showers on front stores to disperse enough water to wet the homeless, chemical products placed on streets, walls, shortening the size of sidewalks."[13] There are spikes placed all around the world now, making it impossible for the homeless to sleep in places they could find a little more comfortable or warmer.[14]

These ways of treating urban design are influenced by our church walls and lack of work with the homeless. The lack of the presence of homeless people in our churches evidences the spikes in our class ecclesiologies. Welcome Church shows us that we too have theological spikes and strategies to make the gospel easy to take, comforting to live, and away from the poor. Mainline Protestant churches have moved up the letter and have made clear commitments to a middle and higher class. That commitment makes it difficult for us to engage with lower class people. However, a call to conversion is at stake for us all! We must move our ecclesiologies/theologies to the places the poor live. For any theology that does not articulate the pain and the hurt of the poor is a theology covered with spikes that prevents people from changing, moving, and transforming social situations of oppression. For instance, the budgets of Christian denominations, seminaries and institutions poured into the financial market feed this scheme of injustice that produces the end product of spikes on the streets.

Our ecclesiologies should be thought/done with denominational budgets on our minds. What kind of ecclesiology must come out of the $9.2 billion assets of the Presbyterian Church (USA)? Budgets are stories of people that depict the ways we worship, understand, and do mission. Along with budgets, salary differences between employees of these churches also show the spikes in our faith, marking an inequality never mentioned in our ecclesiologies. Unless we can see the central armrests in our ecclesiological benches, the spikes in our detached theologies, and the walls of our buildings that do not serve the poor, the oppression against the homeless will continue. Unthought-of. Unaltered. As if they are not the results of our political inaction and contribution to the urban design of our societies.

When we worship with the homeless, we hear stories and parables and tales that can transform reality and sustain people and narratives of liberation that create the possibility of ongoing changes. When describing the stories that sustain the Vietnamese people, Trinh T. Minh-ha says,

With the creative works of the disfranchised and of political prisoners around the world in mind, one can say that just as poetry cannot be reduced to being a mere art for the rich and idle, storytelling is not a luxury or a harmless pastime. It is, indeed, in the tale that one is said to encounter the genius of a people. Tales are collective. The tales not only condense certain characteristics of the everyday person and the people's customs, they often also deal with complex social relations... As with stories among oppressed and disfranchised groups around the world, the Vietnamese tale allows its tellers to allude to issues of poverty, social injustice and class conflict. Tales often read like profound strategies of survival. In them, divergence and inequality, if not conflict, are often set within the framework of a patriarchal economy. The human condition and its dilemmas are featured in the fate of an individual who is likely to be poor, unfortunate, rejected or plainly stupid, but whose honesty and goodness usually lead to a rewarding ending.[15]

Ecclesiologies should be collective stories of justice, social and individual liberation, stories of people meeting God and each other and turning the world into the *imago Dei*. For we have lost the *imago Dei* by our sinful ways of living, relating and organizing our social economic life together with God. What is the true hope of the gospel manifested in our ecclesiologies that can offer liberation to our brothers and sisters on the street? What tales and parables are we creating with our ecclesiologies? Our ecclesiologies are thin ropes of hope that sustain us before falling into homelessness, as well as ropes that take us back out of homelessness. Relating ecclesiologies as tales of hope we can associate with Trinh T. Minh-ha says:

> *Hope is, however, always kept alive in the tale… through the forces that exceed the lifetime of an individual, that people who knew the lore of survival seek to solve difficult situations and social inequity. As Native American storytellers remind us, stories are what we have to fight off illness and death, they make medicines and are a healing art. Bringing the impossible within reach and making us realize with poignancy that material reality is only one dimension of reality, tales address our longing of a more equitable world built on our struggle as well as on our dreams, our aspirations and actions for peace.*[16]

Any ecclesiological story/tale that disrupts the urban design of rural and urban settings must create a space for refugees and prisoners, displaced and homeless people. Every ecclesiology, as well as any theology, comes from the choices we make, fundamentally marked by an understanding of social political structures where we live. Ecclesiologies must influence our theologies as our understanding of the "assembly" articulates the shift towards the poor and build a beloved community, a house, an *oikos* in our midst. Such articulations must provide the conditions of the possibilities for the crucial shift in the living of our faith(s) and the undoing of the spikes already embedded in our insulated, wall guarded, monitored self-protected theologies/ecclesiologies and its consequent high-class suburban commitments, faith-in-budgets mission and hidden and disastrous financial investments.

Our ecclesiologies thus must help us to dislocate ourselves towards the areas of no-people's land and enable just, fair and equal ways of living together. Then, as a second act, our worship services will be able to provide a space where everybody is foreign, non-documented, a refugee camp turned into home, a displaced place transformed into this place of love.

How do our ecclesiologies and theologies respond to that? Perhaps our understanding of the worship might help us.

Moving With Our Worship

Worship is what we, together, decide it will be! The is always in flux. Don Saliers tells us that in worship, Christians are always caught up between the is and the should be.[17] The is entails a correlation between the conditions in which the world is living at this present time and how it should be lived from the perspective of justice rehearsed in liturgy for the sake of the poor. In other words, worship hangs between what we hope for and that which takes away our hope; between the discourses of hatred and exclusion and the counter discourses of love and inclusion that we rehearse/enact in our worship services. Janet R. Walton talks about the work of worship. She says,

> *"Living in a fluid, interdependent world, where so many people are constantly dealing with war, starvation and violence, requires responsible citizenship. Worship plays an important role in developing just living by embodying the legacy of a living, day after day, week after week, and year after year. Worship enacts faith and just living in process, in sight, but not yet, fully, in hand."*[18]

It is said that the world is in constant change, and it begs for some kind of constancy. If that is true, then our constancy is to stay at it, being fluid with it, moving with it, fighting its processes of extermination, struggling against the forces of evil that erase the poor and criminalize actions of resistance. Ecclesiologies, like our liturgies, are moving vessels, moving along with God's love and those who resist the forces of death, without excuse to give in, to give up! In the midst of war, starvation or every kind of violence, our worship services should stand as a sign of peace and resistance, building opportunities for people and the earth to utter, joyfully, "glory to God, peace and joy to the world." In the midst of violence and bombs, we stand up shielded by the gospel with the work of pacifists and lovers of justice. We kneel and stand, offering prayers and songs and acts of change. Carrying a kernel of revolution, we share treasures old and new, helping each other to dream, to organize and to deal with the brutality of symbolic and concrete realities of our lives and our societies. "Embodying the legacy of living," a fair, honest, dignified living for all is our ecclesiological/ liturgical task. It is the mission of God in our midst, rescuing the dignity of the *imago Dei* in the bodies of our brothers and sisters diminished by the powers that be; in Jesus' name!

We need ecclesiologies focused less on buildings and more on using resources to impact people's living conditions! Within these communities of the suffering, we bring a word of faith and life that mixed with their own words will create smoke signs of strength so those in need will see they are not alone, and they can endure the fight! Together, in the midst of the debris of our societies, we, the church of Jesus Christ will blow the smoke of our rituals of resistance, love, desire for change and support of our brothers and sisters in this and other societies. In Jesus' name we cry out loud: "Glory be to God, hang on! The death of Jesus and many of us will be turned into a resurrection event! As the death of Jesus became a resurrection event, so too promises of love, rescue, miracles, changes, transformation and healing are on our way brothers and sisters!! Hang in there! Let us sing alleluia and offer God sacrifices of praise!" How do we embody, ecclesiologically, "the legacy of living well?"

Quoting Urban Holmes, Aidan Kavanagh says that "liturgy leads regularly to the edge of chaos, and from this regular flirt with doom comes a theology different from any other."[19] Yes! Only when we see the disasters of the world, the destruction of the earth and possibilities of our own annihilation can we create theologies that can make a difference in our world. Otherwise, theologies are no more than the scratching of empty ideas and belly buttons. At the edge of chaos, before God, Kavanaugh says that liturgy always calls us to convert, to change our lives. When we are before God everything is transformed, everything we are can be changed. At the edge of chaos, we are always about to lose everything.

Where is the "edge of chaos" in our worship services, our ways of being church? We have turned this chaos, meaning this moment/space where everything can fall apart, into a comfortable sanctuary where God is our butler. Nonetheless, the liturgical space is as it should be, fundamentally, a place for conversion. Far from being committed to the gods of our world (money and privacy, the status quo, the preservation of social class, liturgical order theology or ecclesiology), our most important commitment is to Jesus who lives with the least of these. In that sense, it does not matter much which liturgy we use or what ecclesiology we decide, as long as it issues a call for us to convert to God in Jesus Christ in the service of the poor. Change is indigenous to liturgy, and liturgy's "nature" is a call to radical changes. What, then, are the liturgical/theological/ecclesiological consequences of a church that is brought to the edge of chaos, time and time again?

Liturgical Ecclesiologies

It is with and for the sake of the poor, the destitute, and the lame, that we must begin to practice and to think about our provisional liturgical ecclesiologies. With any liturgical order, theological treatise, or ecclesiological creed, if we are not fully and totally committed with Jesus to care for the poor, we must rethink our very understanding of what being a Christian is all about. In Jesus' name, the poor, the oppressed, the excluded are the privileged locations of our allegiances.

In these worship spaces, no documents are required! No proper theological trajectory demanded, since it is the Holy Spirit who will be drawing the lines of our direction/orientation to encounter God. Our worship spaces, thus our ecclesiologies, are the places for those who do not have anywhere else to go, in the world. For Jesus did not have a space to recline his head either (Matthew 8:20).

My God has many names, tattooed upon the diverse lives of the poor, in the mind of the afflicted, in the empty belly of the hungry, in the shame of the outcast, in the territories of those whose lives and homes were taken by the powerful, in the cries of those who live under utter injustice! Those who hunger are the ones who should interpret faith and give me a better sense of my own theology. They are the ones to tell me who God is, and what my ecclesiology is all about. They are the ones who will help me enact my faith, embody God's grace, teach me to pray, help me choose a song to glorify God, and help me organize my/our common life. Thus, my theology/liturgy/ecclesiology depends on the non-documented immigrants around the world, the millions of children suffering from malnutrition, illiterate people, the Palestinians in their stolen land, the battered women across the globe, the orphans and the children on the street, the communities of transgender people torn apart by hatred and vicious violence, the Syrian refugees! They will give the limits and the possibilities of my faith.

Our worship spaces are too safe. We should sell our churches and move ourselves into zones of conflict to bring peace! Churches without walls! We should worship at the walls/borders of U.S. and Mexico, Israel and Palestine, with heavy military presence between us. We should learn how to say our alleluias and glorias at Catatumbo, one of the most dangerous places in the northeast of Colômbia, where guerrillas and the government battle everyday! We should learn how to say our prayers in the midst of narco-traffic where there is no infrastructure and violence is rampant. These foreign spaces must be our places of worship! We would quickly learn that half of our prayers are good for nothing except to embellish our aesthetics, our sense of safety and protect ourselves from God. At these places, as Zizek says: "What cannot be said must be shown."[20] We are people who do our faith, called by God to live out this love which sets people free! We must become used to living like undocumented immigrants: no place is mine; we are always in a foreign space.

In the gospel of John, true worship is done neither in Gerazin nor Jerusalem but somewhere else.[21] There is a third space where we all meet, which is a frail, provisional tabernacle made of things that move, that we carry along the way. It is in this third space, neither yours nor mine that the worship of God can become a space for immigrants. It is only when we learn that we are all immigrants walking through confiscated land, pilgrims in private places, displaced people on soil constantly stolen by governments and agribusiness, that we will be able to see the face of God in the face of those who are the wretched of the earth. Then, we learn that along with people, we need to resist, occupy, produce, that is, to resist those who want to take the land from the poor, occupy territories that want to serve private interests and produce food for all to eat. Our worship is always a concrete place, a place of resistance and change!

As Jesus said, we do not belong to the world, but we are sent to the world with a mission. In this endless movement around the globe, we gather in "rest areas," places that belong to none and to all, to worship God. In these provisional spaces, we learn what we need to see, we shift our ideas, we gear up to go in new directions, we renew our struggle for the poor, we make sure every traveler is doing well, we honor each other along the way, we heal each other's wounds, we wash each other's feet, we feed each other's mouths, and we move along, until we meet again. When we meet, we are continuously undoing the sense that worship spaces belong to denominations. When we worship God, we learn that we are each other's keepers. In God´s *oikos*, God's house, we live together in all our differences and receive those who come to us.

Ecclesiological Liturgies

Every time we meet to worship God we have to ask again and again, "What now?" What should we do now in our liturgies, in light of daily tragedies? What is this call to worship demanding from us now when we are together with non-documented people and women who have been raped? What does the remembrance of baptism have to do with this situation and what does this situation have to do with the remembrance of baptism? What should we sing, now that we are sealed off in this refugee camp? For what should we ask forgiveness? What is this gospel saying to us? How are we to be converted? What dialogue is spurred from this sermon, as we look in the eye of this storm and the debris of its devastation? Where does the feeding and eating of the Eucharistic service takes us? What kind of acts of love is this place/people/ecclesiology are asking? What testimony and witness should we offer? Who is here that needs to be lifted up? Protected? Cared for?

Christian worship (space, actions, gestures, utterances, songs, movements, things, words, etc.) can interrupt and change our chaotic world. The worship space as a foreign space is a way of creating "inventive engagements,"[22] with the world; imagining understandings and practices of worship that can foster a material space for those who are displaced, engaging in a certain power that will provide conditions for the least of these to live a just life.

When we answer these questions, we will speak with one another, on behalf of each other, learning with one another, for the defense of each other and all those who are poor, fighting each other's battles for the sake of dignity, justice and the *imago Dei* in each other![23] Unless we see all of us as displaced (foreigners, idiots, fools, lost, immigrants) and in constant need of shelter and safety, we will continue to think that we are "God's employees," i.e., owners of worship spaces, theologies and ecclesiologies.

Conclusion

Having been changed by the Spirit to God's preferential option for the poor, and having committed ourselves to the disfranchised and displaced, now we can migrate, move and make the *oikos* of God where the poor live in order to start to see how our ways of being a church can happen. As a consequence, we will all feel like living our faith in a foreign space where nothing is completely comfortable or safe, but nothing is completely unknown as well.

As a second act, our ecclesiologies we will form our assemblies from the crumbs and debris of society and from what we all bring. Within this ecclesiological sense of migration, the fourfold liturgical structures can be of help: gathering, word, meal, and sending, can frame and offer a response to the social disasters of our time as we juxtapose our holy things with the disastrous places of the world. The church cannot be a mirror to itself and work only inward with its own symbols and sources. We have become an insulated community that does not know how to open itself to the world. We attract only those of our own culture, and we expect that folks will come to us and agree with our ways. But the Christian faith is a troubling faith that entails negotiations of beliefs, liturgical practices, social sources and capital.

Let us consider the movement of the fourfold of this one liturgical order in our new ecclesiological, missional, and theological understanding of faith:

Gathering – We go to where the homeless are, bringing our material and spiritual resources. We will spread a tent for all to be under, clothes for all to be warm, coffee and bread. There, we remember the Psalmist and say together: "I was glad when they said to me, 'Let us go to the house of God!' Our feet are standing within your gates, O United States!"[24] We call each other to worship God saying: "God owns the earth and all there is! Everybody has the right of shelter and if one person doesn't have a roof no one does. "Ho, everyone who thirsts, come to the waters; and you that have no money, come, buy and eat! Come, buy wine and milk without money and without price."[25] There we ask God forgiveness for not caring for the earth and one another. We remind ourselves that our world is sinful, that we are disconnected from one another and the earth. And we sing what people bring from their own backgrounds.

Word – The very precious word of Gods is what challenges us to live together trusting God's mercy to live faithfully bounded in this sinful-diabolic-disconnected world. We read the Bible together in the midst of cultural class differences, intellectual challenges, emotional gaps and linguistic accents. Because of so much difference, we must read the word of God very slowly, listening very carefully to one another. In the word of God Christ is in our midst, challenging us to serve each other and God's earth.

Meal – The Eucharistic meal consists of what people bring with them. Everything will be connected with the life and death and resurrection of Jesus Christ. People suffered from violence and died on the streets yesterday and we sing our kyries and sad songs to remember those who were crucified in this world like Jesus. We share the stories of violence and horror and death that are all around us. Then, the revolutionary memory of Jesus' life and death will fill us with stories of hope from amidst the community. We will eat and drink a full meal. At the table, whatever table/altar, we cry out loud: Under the name of Jesus Christ NO one goes hungry in this city!

Sending – When we are ready to go, after burning with this passion, we will check on each other and make sure that everybody will have enough to go through the week: shelter, food, health care, school. And we will only leave after all are insured in the wrapping up of this full and caring ecclesiology."

Jaci C. Maraschin, an Anglican liturgical theologian from Brazil said that "Any liturgical reform should also be related to the mission and should be based on a new theology, mission related to joy and freedom. Liturgy and mission are sisters dancing together towards the beauty of God's kingdom."[26]

CHAPTER THIRTEEN[1]

Praying from the Ends of the World

Elizabeth Kathryn Perella Carvalhaes, 15 years old

Faced with pain that rips apart, we cry out in one voice,
* Intercede with us,
O solidarity Lord.

Faced with death that wounds,
And marks with pain,
* Give us the strength of an embrace
And the peace that your love gives us.

Faced with injustice that kills
And cries out for conversion,
* Move us to transform the world
And let all death become a song.

In the face of desolation and crying,
Faced with impotence and frustration,
* Come to our side,
Sustain us with your life, Lord.

You are the God of the poor, the One who sows hope,
* You are the God of solidarity, the One who gives love.

You are God with us, the Eternal, the Great I am.
* God of the embrace, God of song, God who caresses,
God who strengthens, God who surrenders, God of action.

O Lord of Solidarity: Your kingdom come to the mourner,
Lean your ear to the cry,
* Your sons and daughters are coming
To show your great love.[2]

From Places of Violence:
The Dissonance Between Belief/Prayer and Action

In a township in Johannesburg, a group of people from several African countries and I were walking around to learn about the situation of the people there. We came to a church where people were worshiping. The gate had a lock, and we could not enter. We said, "We are Christians from various places, can we go inside?" "No," came the response, "no stranger can come in." A conversation ensued during which the members of that little church said, "This is a very dangerous neighborhood, so we come here to church to feel safe. But it is also very dangerous to be here in the church because people come and steal from us." In the same place, there were feelings of freedom and a state of being locked in and fearful. There people prayed.

At a gathering of women in the Philippines, the women were crying. They had lost their sons to the war on drugs President Duterte declared. None of the seven women knew why their children had been killed; most of them had been killed "by mistake." We held a worship service and as they told the stories of their dis-grace, we could hear their wailing. They could barely talk. We were there to pray.

In Jamaica, behind a mountain of garbage, one of the dumpster places of the city, lives a group of people abandoned and forgotten by everyone. They are remnants of a community into which the police came, raped the women, threw children out of a third-floor window of a building, and killed all of the men. How could we pray?

Breonna Taylor, George Floyd, and Ahmaud Arbery in the U.S., and João Pedro Matos Pinto in Brazil, are Black people killed by the police. The world is burning. A colonial disaster of global proportions has taken over the whole planet. Violence and death are alive, vivid, palpable, and visible in proportions much greater than we can count in words. Psalm 139 can be said in this new way for our days:

> *Where do I go to escape the presence of violence?*
> *If I go to Manila, violence mounts everywhere,*
> *killing Indigenous people.*
> *If I go to Johannesburg, violence engulfs*
> *the spirit of the South Africans in the townships.*
> *If I go to Minneapolis, Louisville, or Rio de Janeiro, blood on the streets*
> *overwhelms over our eyes.*
> *If I go to Jamaica, the violence of discarded people*
> *is beyond our reach.*

*If I go to Europe, the violence of turning away refugees
exposes their sheer desperation.*

How can we pray in those places? How can we pray in situations where it seems there is nothing to be said and yet everything to be processed, learned, and explained? To go where violence abounds is to ask the question "Should there be a God?" To pray in those places is to face the absurdity of life and also discover the resilience that only those living in these situations can muster. To go there is to discover ourselves being reviled and killed. How can we let our own people be treated this way? How can we do this to ourselves? Why do we keep destroying people and the earth mercilessly without care of any kind? How should we even pray? And if we pray, to whom do we pray when we pray to God?

How can we reconcile our beliefs with the life of the world? Marc Ellis has said that "systematic theology is a reduction of cognitive dissonance." We try to turn down the volume of absurdity and dissonance, but can we even do that? Systematic theology committed to knowledge without bodies, blood, or (lack of) breath cannot do much to reduce the cognitive dissonance. Can the written prayers of the church even respond to the pain of the world? In one of my classrooms, a well-known visiting lecturer said to our students, "Recite the prayers of the prayer books for twenty years, and only after that can you write your own prayer." While this is a way to uphold the tradition of the church and a proper understanding of proper prayer, I wonder if the prayers in our prayer books can still hold the pain of the people and the flooding of violence everywhere.

We are all feeling, in one way or another, that we are moving toward an impending collective death. The vast majority of people around the Earth are poor. Social and economic inequality is growing. Oxfam reports that "the world's 2,153 billionaires have more wealth than the 4.6 billion people who make up 60 percent of the planet's population."[3] We live in an alarming earth catastrophe that does not always make headlines; some call our era the anthropocene (the era when the human being—in Greek, *anthropos*—determines and dominates what happens on the planet) but also capitalocene, plantationocene, or chthulucene.[4] Humans, who have placed ourselves above any other form of life, are extracting more from the earth than its limits permit, and the earth is losing it balance. Global warming, the melting of polar ice caps, uneven seasons, droughts, overpopulation, forests devastations, the warming of the oceans, the extinction of many species are everywhere. Geopolitical configurations are marked by an expanding movement of migrants and refugees due to climate change and civil wars. Democracies are collapsing, nation-states are dissolving into dictatorships, public spaces are contested or shrinking, and fear is the political emotion of our time. Many forms of destruction and violence are becoming normalized, and the consequences of an unrestrained neoliberal economy are thrusting us toward a place of no return.

In these calamitous times, what prayers are we called to pray? The condition of our world begs for prayers and forms of prayer different from the ones we have prayed thus far. As we witness the pain of the poor, the collapsing of the world we know, the natural disasters around the globe, there seems to be no prayer that can respond to it all. Where should our prayers come from? What prayer may Christians offer to God and the world?

If we are to pray today from real historical and social locations, from places of deep pain, and from places that are almost entirely foreign to us, we Christians must learn a new grammar for our faith. We must learn new prayers and new ways to pray.[5] We will have to look at tradition differently and use our current prayer books with fresh eyes. Our prayer will have to delve into other prayers, the ones made in the midst of disasters, to engage with the earth more fully, in order to respond to the excruciating poverty and the demise of our planet. We also need to be more open to other religions in order to become a different kind of church. I wonder if the grammar of the prayers we currently have and use is enough to sustain us, or the world.

If God's voice in the world can be expressed in our prayer, we are called to be radically converted in our ways of praying. We are called to go deeper within ourselves, to relate more deeply with nature, and to be radically converted toward forms of action that heal, recuperate, reconfigure, restore, and restitute our communities, the earth, and our social and natural systems. May it be anathema, we pray—any form of government that sustains war, that oppresses people, animal, mountains, oceans, and the whole earth! Instead of placing us apart from the world, prayer can reconcile us back into a deep sense of communities. And blessed be those who understand that we live *en conjunto*, together, all with the same rights and responsibilities.

Only a prayer that has its ear attached to the earth and hears the cries of the oppressed, a prayer that has its eyes upon those who suffer, and hands stretched in solidarity, can help us pray better and help us realize our distance from God and a world in flaming pain. If prayer is about loving God, then prayer is also about building a house for the abandoned, becoming a wall of protection for the vulnerable, and giving our life away for those who are on the brink of disappearance. When we lose our entitlements, our class protections, our fear of others, and realize our deep connection with the poor, the stars, the animals, and the whole earth, prayer becomes breathing God's breath in the world. Prayers are a continuation of Jesus' life and thus prayer must express a radical commitment with the poor. The building of a common happiness, and place of safety for those vulnerable is an absolute imperative in our world today.

Many Christians have created a faith that avoids the poor. Some of our denominations have become gated communities protecting a privileged class. However, in different parts of the world, there is a Christian renewal thriving amidst the poor, at the bottom of economic systems, on the fringes of Empire. This neo-Pentecostal Christian renewal is taking place through worship, ritual, and prayer. It is exploding everywhere,[6] offering a new grammar of faith that gives strength, mission, and purpose to those abandoned by the state and exposed to social threats, chaos, and loss. These churches are embracing the poor, speaking from places where abandoned people live, and from there a new grammar of faith has been developed, often giving people tools to survive in the midst of violence, social and personal trauma, illness, anxiety and depression, deep economic hardship, and close acquaintance with death. In the midst of these conditions, people worship to ask God for protection, to ask for healing, and to imagine promises of a better financial life and happiness. Their churches offer something real, local, named, visceral, that resonates within these realities, most of which we, in our context, cannot imagine how to engage.

Many of us would surely criticize this form of Christianity and say that it is not good theology, not the best way to help people worship God, not the appropriate way to help people find their sense of self-worth. Meanwhile, on this side of the world, the First-World-traditional-bourgeois-white-middle-class theologies that sustain many of our dying churches serve to appease social upheaval and maintain a psychologically neutralizing boundary, a rationalization for self-protection in faith, and an impediment to getting closer to those who are racialized and those living in the lower classes under the sign of poverty and violence. While many of the neo-Pentecostal churches exploit people, they also offer sanctuary and hope to those who are impoverished and suffering miserably by creating new songs and prayers—new ways to pray, sing, and listen to the word of God. Theirs is a grammar of faith whose prayers find fertile ground in the hearts of those who are unwanted around the world but wanted by God.

Praying with the Wretched of the Earth:
Learning a New Grammar of Faith

Blessed and supported by the Council for World Mission,[7] a group of some one hundred people from various Christian traditions, theologies and types of churches, of different races, ethnicities, sexualities, and walks of life in fifty or so countries, gathered together during 2018 and 2019 in four different countries on four continents. The group of participants in the project (named "Re-Imagining Worship as Acts of Defiance and Alternatives in the Context of Empire") was made up of pastors, theologians, students, artists, and activists. Our purpose was to learn how to pray with local communities and to create liturgical resources for Christian communities around the world. This project was rooted in God's demand for us to live a life of compassion, listening to those who are suffering and learning how to pray with them. We hoped that together, in the desire of God and the strength of our faith, we would respond to the challenges of our world today. We reached and stretched toward an alternative to both the traditional prayer books of Christian liturgies and neo-Pentecostal cultic prayers. Always, the main question for us, as for me in these pages, was "How are we to pray with the unwanted of the world? How can our prayers not only address the disasters of the world but also offer, in God's love, hope and actions of transformation?

During the four gatherings, we lived and engaged with people who are poor and disenfranchised and wrote prayers and stories of people who live the Christian faith in abandoned places. The encounters were short but intense. Eventually we produced a rich and rich and varied collection of liturgical resources—prayers, songs rites of healing, baptismal and eucharistic prayers, meditations, and art—from varied communities contending with violence, migrants and refugees, drugs, land grabbing, war on the poor, attacks on women, militarization, and climate change. But first, we listened. And we prayed.

After living with communities of people on four continents, we realized that we had actually been learning how to pray. When we prayed, we were not only praying with those affected by violence and poverty, we were also praying for ourselves. By praying with those living in inhumane conditions, we were challenged to change. Wrestling with many contradictions, with heavy and full hearts, bringing together our own struggles and the ones from the communities we visited, we created prayers for our own churches, not for the poor, with the hopes that we might learn how to pray for ourselves and move into deep change, for the sake of the most poor. In a circular movement, we were also, through our own prayers, praying with those at the ends of the world.

Our project brought together a mix of voices, those of the travelers--the visitors--who participated in this project and those of the people who accepted and welcomed us to be with them for a while. We continued to wrestle with the tension between witness and solidarity on the one hand and "poverty tourism" on the other. In our prayers, we came to profess and confess both. Our work was only a gesture toward a necessarily long and deeper stay with those who suffer at the ends of the world, until we are finally in and of the same place, together. From the ends of the world, we came out praying, singing, creating art, crying out loud for the mercy and power of God. The experiences reflected in the resources we created aim to give churches and Christians a new methodology and a new vocabulary to pray, so that we might reorient ourselves in the world. Figuratively and concretely, we became part of a wave of liturgies coming from the bottom up.

Manila, Philippines

In Manila we experienced what the world will become in the future. After many years of colonialism, the Philippines is a fertile ground for fascism. The country is controlled by a few rich people and neoliberalism is the preferred weapon of the state. A fascist government led by Rodrigo Duterte is in place, using martial law and extrajudicial killings as necropolitics, expelling Indigenous people from their own lands, and selling the country's natural resources to agribusiness. The government is in the hands of China's economy and U.S. militarization and does not know how to address poverty. The fifteen richest Filipinos have 57 billion dollars— more money than the remaining 79.6 million people together. Hundreds of thousands of jobs have been lost in the agricultural sector due to the spread of agribusiness. There are no workers' rights, and most jobs offer low wages.

On this leg of the journey, a diverse religious group of two dozen people from more than fifteen Asian countries gathered to begin this work. At first none of us had any idea of what would happen or what kind of result we would have. We trusted each other and stayed together from beginning to end. We laughed and cried and shared life together. This bonding provided a model for the gatherings to come on other continents.

In Manila we visited four communities: 1) Indigenous peoples' communities in the Province of Rizal, victims of militarization, forced evacuations, demolitions, and extrajudicial killings. They are continuously harassed by land grabbers, mining companies, and the government military forces; 2) Workers' organizations in the province of Bulacan and Southern Tagalog areas. The workers are victims of unfair labor practices and two workers' organizations located in different communities are currently on hunger strikes; 3) Urban poor communities, victims of demolition because of development aggressions; 4) Peasant communities in the Batangas and Kalinga Areas, victims of land conversions, militarization, demolitions, and extrajudicial killings.

On the first day, after engaging in a powerful worship and being welcomed by our hosts, we heard a presentation about the socio-economic and political situation of the Philippines and an introduction to the communities we would be visiting. After this, a member of the National Council of Churches of the Philippines spoke to us about safety. We were advised to be alert about how we talked, both with people with whom we gathered intentionally and with people we met on the street, and not to use social media. We were also told that if the police were to put us in jail, a group of lawyers would try to help, but that even with its planning and anticipating, the Council of Churches was not able to promise that nothing bad would happen to us.

When we returned each night from our visits to poor communities, we were emotionally exhausted. We had seen so much pain and death that we were deeply disturbed. We met mothers who had lost their sons to police brutality and to the war on drugs and mothers who wailed in pain during our worship services. We wept with Indigenous children whose schools have been bombed by the government and paramilitary movements because they were considered havens for revolutionaries. We cried with workers who earned so little that they did not have enough money to take back home and thus needed to sleep on the streets.

It was after these visits and during the two subsequent days of writing liturgical resources that we finally felt life coming back to us. Writing prayers was a life-giving time when we found ways to address people's pains and to connect God to real-life situations and to liturgy. It was during this process of writing that we found the life of our faith and the faith of our life.

As part of the project, we were tasked to write prayers to engage our own rage and anger. One of the prayers written by a group of participants was filled with curse words. In any other place or time, this prayer would have been considered blasphemous and outrageous, but within this group, as theologically diverse as we were, there was a deeper understanding at stake. These prayers were about the life of the disenfranchised under the brutality of the Empire. They were about the pain of our brothers and sisters in such a way that cursing was a "theological" way of expressing that for which we had no words. We all prayed those words together.

In the midst of all this, a source of immense joy was learning from local Christians in all the communities we visited. The church is well and alive in the Philippines!

Johannesburg, South Africa

In Johannesburg, we experienced the remarkable development of South Africa in the midst of its still deeply entangled history of racism and colonialism. The brutal history of apartheid has racist historical consequences that continue to plague the country. The South African theologian Vuyani S. Vellem expresses it as follows: "Racism in our times is thus an ethos, an imperial spirit, innate to the socio-political, ecclesial organization and institutions of management and learning in our society."[8] Trapped in these "fraudulent, race-blind, normative invisibility and elusiveness of race, doubt," the presence of racism has the power to "castrate the goals and agency of Black Africans against this problem."[9]

Still sunk in a deep wound opened by white settlers, South Africa is still wrestling to find ways out of this complex situation. Here we questioned whether and how we could help when the situation was so difficult and seemed to require years of knowledge. In spite of these challenges, we tried to learn both from our insurmountable limitations and our struggle to write something about experiences and events that seemed indescribable. Holding on to these dilemmas, we gathered, thirty African scholars and I, not only to talk about South Africa but to make a composition of African spaces and situations and to pray from that web of issues, histories, pain, violence, and struggles.

We visited four communities:

(1) Marikana, where there is exploitation of workers that closely resembles slavery, as capitalist corporations profit at the expense of human dignity by taking away the community's resources;

(2) Soweto, a township of the City of Johannesburg Metropolitan Municipality in Gauteng, South Africa, bordering the city's mining belt in the South. Its name is an English syllabic abbreviation for South Western Townships (So-We-To). Formerly a separate municipality, it is now incorporated into the city of Johannesburg. Soweto has become synonymous with the South African struggle, as we think of protest and the 1976 Soweto uprising. Soweto is also the home of many liberationist leaders. In Soweto, Moroka has become Johannesburg's worst slum area, where residents have erected their shanties on plots measuring six by six meters with only communal bucket-system toilets and very few running water taps;

(3) Alexandra, another township in the Gauteng province of South Africa, commonly known as "Gomorrah" among local residents. It is one of the poorest urban areas in the country and at one point made the news during xenophobic attacks by residents on foreigners living in their midst;

(4) CBD, another community in Soweto, where we were able to experience the life of economic and political refugees. Johannesburg gave us the opportunity to interact with the brutal effects of wars, economic looting, and political instability. It also helped us to engage the realities of displaced communities which are mostly undocumented local residents and refugees.

Being in these townships as foreigners was a source of anxiety and fear for us. The shacks where people live, their difficult living conditions, and the violence within the villages showed us how Empire destroys entire communities by moving, shifting, and dumping people into places that they do not know and where they have to fight for their lives by being set against each other.

As our group came back from our visits to the communities, the conversations about liturgy became very difficult. We discussed the notion of praying for "those who are lost," since this form of prayer implies that "we" are not lost and have accomplished something that places us above "them." Questioning the very task of liturgy and its workings was paramount to this process. This group left nothing unchallenged or uncriticized, and in so doing, showed an extraordinary commitment to name uncomfortable feelings and to wrestle with thorny situations.

Kingston, Jamaica

The third leg of this global project took place in Kingston, Jamaica. In keeping with the model of the workshops held in Manila and Johannesburg, this workshop had a variety of participants from American countries, an ecumenical group of scholars, pastors, students, and church leaders who came with the desire to create something new in the realm of liturgy. We examined evidence and causes of such realities as violence, urban displacement, land grabbing, neoliberal policies, corruption, climate change, poverty, hunger, and violence. We divided into four smaller groups for our visits to local communities.

We visited Tivoli Gardens, where seventy-three people were shot in a massacre by the state in 2010. Local residents claim that the government figure of seventy-three dead was low, and that at least one hundred and possibly two hundred people were killed. With our leader and guide, social activist Lloyd D'Aguilar, we heard the searing testimonies of people who survived the shootings and visited neighborhoods abandoned by the government with no concern, care, or help. Our group also experienced the ways in which religion can transform the lives of the people. It was powerful to walk the street markets of Kingston and hear people speak of Mr. D'Aguilar as "our good Samaritan."

We also visited August Town, Trench Town (the home of Bob Marley), and displaced street workers in both of those districts. All these communities struggle with poverty and neglect. Our people walked on the streets and in marketplaces with pastors and local leaders and listened to their stories and to those of community residents. We also heard the heart-wrenching testimonies of workers who were going to be displaced from the market where they had lived for the last fifty-five years because the place was sold to the owner of a nearby shopping mall. We were able to have a worship service organized by Jamaica Theological Seminary with the vendors about to be evicted.

We spent time, too, at the Bobo Shanti Rastafari community in Bull Bay, a thriving community of Rastafarians in the woods. Members of our group were able to participate in worship services and to learn about the community's life and beliefs and its proposal for a new society. Finally, our visits took us to two rural communities in Low River and Manchester. These small rural farming communities received our group with joy and taught our people how to care for the earth as they do. We also heard about their struggles to survive against extractivism and big corporations.

After our visits, participants spent two intense days of writing resources. Their experiences with poverty provoked differing reactions; some participants experienced more difficulties than others in fully giving themselves to the poor. Thus, we were reminded that our presence in Jamaica and in our group was not to defend a personal position nor to share a paper or intellectualize the situation, but to be a witness to the people, to become a sounding board for their cries, and to learn how to pray with the poor, as church. The mix of participants— local participants and people from South, Central, and North America—helped us to understand the plight of the Jamaican people, and it shaped our efforts to create a new grammar for the Christian faith through prayers, songs, and liturgies of liberation. In Jamaica, we were able to engage with the local situation more fully with regard to the content of our faith and through our liturgical resources. Bob Marley's "Redemption Song" echoed throughout the days.

Every gathering on each of the continents produced something new in the context of unique challenges. At this particular gathering in Jamaica, we experienced liturgy unfolding into many new possibilities. Liturgy has the power to offer inner and outer transformation, and doing liturgy together was a way of connecting with people, our own selves, and our faith in a new way. At the same time, this liturgical work was also a way of seeing our immeasurable distance from those who are suffering, our inability to say things properly, our powerlessness before such suffering, and the insufficiency of trying to do what we were hoping to do.

Scicli, Italy

The fourth and last meeting of this global project took place in Scicli, Italy. This small town in southern Sicily on the shores of the Mediterranean Sea receives and welcomes refugees and immigrants from the African continent, Syria, Iraq, and other parts of the world. We were hosted by the Mediterranean Hope Refugee and Migrant Programme, a migration project recently conceived by the Federation of Protestant Churches in Italy in association with other Protestant churches in Europe. Federation members helped us to understand the situation of migrants and refugees and we heard testimonies from people who had dealt with violence across the globe. This gave us a window into a reality we do not pay much attention to and helped us to gain a new language for our prayers. All the participants in our ecumenical group were troubled by the ways in which European countries mistreat migrants and carried in their hearts a desire to create something new to respond to these situations in ways that help to shape our Christian spirituality and mission. We intended for our worship services to reflect the voices of the poorest people in Europe by offering solidarity, resistance, and defiance to the forces of death of Empire in this particular context.

The first day of our visit, we gathered to learn about the overarching effect of European laws on immigration and the powerful resistance work of the Christian churches in Scicli. We learned from Ciccio Sciotto, a pastor of the Italian Waldensian church, about the ways in which the European continent is closing borders. We were also offered theological perspectives to better understand migration. Pastor Sciotto spoke of migration starting when Adam and Eve were expelled from the garden of Eden and then explained human movements as part of the world's history. He described how Italians were shipped to other countries and how Italy exported violent groups such as the Italian mafia. The problem, he said, is not migration but how we talk about it, condemning migrants and refugees without addressing the sources and reasons for the intense movements of people on our planet and in our regions. We then heard stories from refugees and immigrants about their difficulties, including that of two young boys who came in small boats from Libya to Italy and struggled to survive near-death experiences several times during their journeys. We shared a meal with refugees at Mediterranean Hope;

this became, for us, the event that most closely mirrored what the realm of God can be. We were all deeply moved by it.

One of our unforgettable moments was having dinner with refugees from many countries at the Casa delle Culture, a sanctuary receiving people in conditions of particular fragility and vulnerability from around the world.[9] We were able to break bread together and gesture kindness to each other. Since we could not speak each other's languages, we smiled and served each other in the best way we could. We heard some of the guests' stories and at the end, we played and laughed out loud with all of these precious children.

As we had in Manila, Johannesburg, and Kingston, after our two days of visits we engaged in two days of writing liturgical resources. It was difficult to figure out how to pray with those affected by policies of death and destruction. We wept and prayed together using theater, art, singing, and writing in collective ways. The result was beautiful, powerful, and challenging.

A new movement is required for this time: not to abandon the prayers of the church, but also to pray new prayers in new ways—for others and ourselves, in a constant movement of God's grace into an expansive mindfulness, transformation, and recreation of ourselves and the world. This will mean learning how to pray differently, to be faithful to Jesus in these devastating times by praying with and for the unwanted— those who are the "undercommons,"[10] including not only humans, but also the whole earth and other animals, because their conditions of living are also the conditions of existence for all of us.

Our prayers must help us navigate new changes and challenges. Through our collective prayers, with those we are called to listen to, serve, and fight for, God calls us to live our faith in much deeper ways, understand the world we are living in broader ways, and make a radical commitment with the poor in the name of God. Praying with one another teaches us that we are never done. Through prayers, we can imagine a radical moral imagination of new worlds! By the grace of God, we can birth these new worlds through *ora et labora*—our prayers and our work in solidarity.

> *A lost voice. Squatting in my little street corner this very dark night. It is cold and the darkness is scary. Who can hold me – the hand of God. Is there a God out there? God if you are there – if you can hear me, hold me through the night. I really want to sleep but my belly is rumbling. Please don't let them find me here, stop them from taking and hurting me. God – if you are there – hear my voice!*

Prayers and Empire

The extensive context of the four-continent project was and is (the) Empire: institutions, networks, individuals, mindsets, that control power, money and authority embedded in nation-states, tradition, rationalities, reasoning, science, references, epistemologies and knowledge production, illustrations, academic work, dualities, fake news, values, policy, patriotism, social construction, culture, history, forms of identity, race, gender, patriarchy, heterosexuality, wars, forms of religion, religious care, prayers, songs, worship. We call ourselves out as we name this. We are all entangled in Empire and what we can do to find awareness, conscientization, and contribute to fracturing the porous walls of dominance and injustice.

The variety of knowledges in these prayers complicates any easy targeting of colonizer from the North and colonized from the South. Our group of about one hundred people show how colonized and colonizer are not only in external, fixed locations but inside of us all. Modernity has won the world and made it impossible to live without the present work of colonization and coloniality. Our hearts have become racist, imperialist, and colonizers just as much as we are colonized. A closer look at these prayers reveals a vast array of power dynamics with voices filled with colonized and decolonized struggles. This aspect of the group, coupled with the fact that we were not only praying with the poor but sometimes thought that we were praying on behalf of the poor, makes it impossible to idealize these prayers as a completely decolonized project. No! This is not a full decolonized project but a decolonial work in progress. It is a work made of expectations and guilt, embarrassment and attempts, limitations and desires, awkwardness and confusion, frustration, and joys. Even the use of colonial metaphors, expressed by us who are colonized, evidences the insidious nature of oppression: the language available to us for liberation in many cases is itself colonized. Nonetheless, this project also showed how people are trying to figure out the coloniality of our times and to respond to these forces of Empire in many ways. We start here praying with all the complexities, hopes, absurdities, im/possibilities, and beliefs that a new world structure is possible.

We who participated in the project have various forms of entanglement with Empire, but with the prayers that emerged from that entanglement, we seek to change how we think about ourselves and the world. We imagine that we can be transformed and offer resistance as we do the work of decolonization. This work of decolonization has to do not only with articles of faith or abstract beliefs systems but fundamentally with our relationality with the land. It must respond to the ways in which our spirits and our land were stolen. As Frantz Fanon wrote: "Imperialism which today is fighting against a true liberation of mankind leaves in its wake here and there tinctures of decay which we must search out and mercilessly expel from our land and our spirits."[11] Prayers must help us transform our thinking, feeling, and ways of living which includes the land, the law of the land, who owns the land, what is the history of the land and all its inhabitants, namely the trees, the rivers, the birds, etc. To pray with the wretched of the earth is to pray without a sounding board from the land we use to belong since we were made into immigrants, nomads. To pray with the wretched of the earth is to pray with all the people disenfranchised and made poor. To pray with the wretched of the earth is to pray with all of the more than human beings of that patch of earth. To pray with the wretched of the earth is to pray with all of the spirits of that place. To pray with the wretched of the earth is to pray with all of the dead ones of that place and all their presences and absences. To pray with the wretched of the earth is to attend to the madness of our lives stolen, destroyed, made barren. To pray with the wretched of the earth is to work on the cognitive dissonance between the Christian faith and its practices (place/time), as the Christian Empire and the Christianity that works as resistance to the same Empire. How does placing colonized people at the center of Christian prayers affect the praying of Christian colonizers? Considering the complexity of the colonized and the colonizer in this work is paramount. All of the people participating in this work had large or small ties to this complex relationship. Races and ethnicities mixed, sexualities and genders blurred, high and low classes combined, theologies and liturgical practices were placed in dispute and tension.

The power of prayer offers resistance to the Empire: to orient our hearts, embolden our souls, strengthen our spirits. No Empire can resist the work of the Spirit who keeps things alive, show us ways out of no ways, breaks down barriers and walls, and makes us sing a song of victory and freedom at last!

Lex Orandi, Credendi, Vivendi, and Naturae

How do we connect our faith, the *polis* and the *oikos* (community and economy) of God? We have received from the tradition of the church the expansive notion of the *leges* (plural of *lex*, law in Latin) of the church: *lex orandi*, *lex credendi*, and *lex agendi* or *lex vivendi*.

How does the law of prayer challenge Empire?

How does the law of our beliefs defy the self-enclosed sense of self that is not correlated to the earth and its suffering?

How does the law of *vivendi*, the way of life, our ethical mode, based on a just way of living, help transform the logic and practice of our prayer-beliefs within a sordid economic system?

Often the relationship of the *leges* happens within a theological inner circle that protects the boundaries of faith by analyzing liturgy with liturgy. In spite of all of the dialogue liturgy has with other areas of knowledge, the praying and believing of liturgy seem to be encircled within a tradition that looks mostly inward upon itself. We juxtapose liturgical things with liturgical things: gathering with word, water bath with eucharist, word with sending, and so on.[12] We need to expand these notions of the *leges* and put prayer at greater risk through a perhaps frightening series of "external" juxtapositions: placing prayer alongside wars, praise alongside all forms of violence, confession alongside poverty and patriarchy, word alongside ecological destruction, sending forth alongside refugees and migrants. This is what I am proposing: the relation of the internal *leges* with the "outside" of the church's worship, including nature, and all the world that is not human.

If we think about these juxtapositions, we can easily realize how much the church has kept its worship sacred by avoiding "worldly" issues. The naming of these issues is tangential and irrelevant to sacred ritual. The multi-continental project—and my proposal in these pages—connects the inside of the church with the outside by organizing our center not from tradition, but from the voices of the poor, from the places of pain and violence. It is women losing their children to state violence that make us define our prayer. It is the extreme poverty of people without humane living conditions that shapes our faith. It is refugees drifting in the midst of the sea without help who define our worship. It is global warming and drought that make us confess and ask for God's mercy. It is violence against women that makes us pray prayers of anger. It is the utterly desperate condition of a vast majority of people that is the *lex* of our prayer, faith, and life.

There is a need for another *lex*, a liturgical law for our time. This law has been more recognized in the past than in our modern-day traditions. It is the *lex naturae*, the law of nature. Given the climate disaster that is coming to us all with all its effects and already taking place all over the globe, *lex naturae* becomes a pre-condition to the laws of prayer, belief, and way of life for our common survival. *Lex naturae* must be our guiding principle in praying by providing an orientating ground from which we can learn how to pray, to believe and to act. Thus, to pray becomes an orientation toward Gaia, the Earth, in this time of Anthropocene. *Lex naturae* helps us to pay attention to the cries of the earth, the burning of God's *oikos*, the desolation of peoples' lands across the globe and the extinction of many species. We are called to *ora et labora* with the earth and with those who live everywhere on the Earth.

Praying Locally:
Challenging Christianity's Universal Dominion

The goal of our group of liturgists was to learn and work from the self-determination of people, their resources of daily life, their art, dreams and struggles, their vulnerabilities and forms of resistance, paradoxical structures, and idiosyncratic languages. By attending to these forms of life, our prayers mark the historical, patriarchal, political, economic, sexual, cultural, and class loci of enunciation of our utterances in order to show the dynamics of power at stake in each place. These locations, sites of enunciation of the poor, became fundamental to our understanding of the Christian faith, theologies, liturgies, reading of the Bible, sacraments, and prayers.

This work/ing of prayers from the ground shifts and creates both a new vocabulary and new forms of prayers for the Christian faith by "simply" praying with the poor. These prayers do not seek to change the poor, but fundamentally ourselves, the ones praying to God. When we pray with other people, our field of recognition shifts and change. Being with people who are not within the horizon of our ways of knowing and living places us in a new territory where we must reframe, transform, and restore our own ways of knowing, of making sense of the world and of ourselves, since we are now "affected" by the presence of somebody else, with whom we are now praying. To come to the knowledge of somebody else's praying, believing, and living, must change my own ways of praying, believing, and living.[13]

Prayer that shows the dis-ease within the Empire in Christian liturgical resources disrupts assumed liturgical ways of thinking, believing, and being that shape people that are marked by an expansive whitening/witnessing of European liturgical local histories made universal. Instead of prayers demanding to be prayed, prayers come from a belief in the sovereignty of local people praying to God and each other their own struggles with their own voices and full bodies. These prayers beg us to darken our liturgical resources.[14]

To pray with is to bear witness, to walk together, to be a companion, from the Latin com-pane, "with bread", sustaining, filling the path with enthusiasm, with God, offering a shield. To pray is to take side with the ones with whom we are bearing witness, protecting, giving ourselves, transforming our sense of self, changing our consciousness, telling the story from the perspective of the ones with whom we are praying.

One of the challenges of this process of praying with the wretched of the earth is to figure out our own condition, our own complicity with power, our distance from those suffering, the relation between "our" inclusion and "their" exclusion. This methodology sheds a light into our common history, and we are challenged to read it differently, asking who owns what and how, who has been a part of this "common" history, who has been erased, to whom do we pay attention and honor, to whom do we not, and in all of it, why?

When we pray from the underside of Empire, the entire dynamics of prayer, its content, forms, mechanics, social places, tonalities of voices, breathing intervals, body strength, heart condition, and rationality changes, since everything starts elsewhere, namely, where it hurts. There, from these places of pain, our voices quiver, we are always at the edge of our strength, we can't speak, we mostly scream when we can. I remember that when I was growing up in Brazil, my voice always quivered.

When Christianity is on the side of Empire, it controls the sources of domination and as such, it prescribes the proper prayers, while not allowing prayers in forms of rupture, dissonance, screams, curses, woes, "disrespect," demands, breaks, and radical transformations. Instead, it keeps our emotions under a certain understanding of humanity, mostly defined by forms of doctrinal control, allowing people to pray in some ways, and at the same time denying prayers as social reaction against oppression and consequent radical social responses.

Amidst theological quibbles and fables and edited histories chosen by official liturgical theologies, liturgical resources have been composed to actually prevent such radical prayers from ever touching the horrors done by humankind—especially when such horrors go beyond the suffering of white middle-upper class folks. Liturgical history is often the repetition and confirmation of official history through dogmas and documents, confined to very well-crafted liturgical texts, restricted to the inner conflicts of doctrinal interpretation, recollecting doctrines and forms of belief that only serve to confirm the official history, which is always a "universal" history of Christianity created by local peoples living in Europe, wholly accepted and necessarily regurgitated everywhere else. Our common ground is not somebody else's history but the common struggle of those from below.

If we are to pray with the Jesus who was killed by the violent state of his time, we must create liturgical resources in the shadows of colonization, modernity, and slavery. Only by reading the history of liturgy with those who are damned, whom Frantz Fanon called the wretched of the earth, can we start to be faithful to Jesus. Thus, the only way to pray a Christian prayer today is to pray with those who are exploited, crushed, killed and oppressed, on the sides of our societies; to pray against liturgical thinking that is still wrapped up in white supremacy, colonial capitalist power, and the slavery mentality of those who have invaded and plundered lands everywhere, destroyed local people's history, and massacred their offspring. And are still doing it.

Thus, to pray with the poor is to take a step beyond our comfort zone moving to a different location to begin our theological thinking. To be on the ground with those suffering without any security of their own is to gain awareness of our own groundlessness, of our distance from those with whom Jesus lived and taught us to pray. Praying with the poor shifts the center of prayer. Oaths are shifted, commitments are challenged, emotions are evoked and expanded, beliefs are questioned, compassion is issued, and theological positions are placed at stake.

A New Grammar of Faith

Prayer is the grammar of faith and doctrine is the grammar of colonization—at least for the most part. The history of Christian prayer, associated with powers of destruction, has created a grammar of faith that has been also a form of wounding. The colonizers made us repeat their words, words that made sense to and in their own worlds and their own pain. Surely, they reasoned, the prayers of the church can be said by people anywhere and that can be the healing of entire communities.

We need a new grammar of faith, a grammar that is born from the streets, from the abandoned corners of the earth, from the wisdom of the people buried under the powers of dominance, exploitation, and extermination. We need a new grammar of faith that can help us sense the dissonance between the promise of the presence of God and the dissonance of the felt absence of God in the miserable situations of so many.

In each place we went, we witnessed pain and hurt. We experienced the cognitive dissonance between the language of our faith and the conditions of violence present in each location. Thus, these workshops were about the possibility for all of us to be transformed by the Holy Spirit as we were present to a certain incarnation of Jesus, one whom we, as a church, mostly avoid. This event was a life-changing experience, a denunciation of our detached liturgical resources, and a call into a life of deeper connections and fullness sparked by prayers resounding with the pain and joy of the unwanted.

We witnessed how Empire can make us feel terribly frail, and at the same time we experienced how prayers permit us to discover a God who is much more vivid than our imagination. We discovered how prayer is a way to find ourselves in the midst of others, a way to breathe in the wonder of God and to create conditions of resistance. Prayer helps us to "organize" forms of consciousness that give us a sense of agency grounded in the power and love of God. Although it may seem that prayers are almost nothing with which to fight Empire, they can crack its walls with their sound and persistence. As we read in Ezekiel 22:30, we must "stand in the breach" between the Empire and the unwanted, the powerful and the least of these, the center and the periphery, listening to the local stories of the margins, learning their wisdom and knowledge, providing spaces for sustenance and expansion. Prayer carries an immense possibility of breaking the structures of evil and violence. Within and outside.

In one way or another, praying in situations of suffering changed us. Most of the workshop participants' testimonies pointed to that transformation. Many of them never thought that the church could be so important and could mean so much to so many people. At the same time, it is impossible to capture the experiences of the people who participated. Through this project, many of us experienced how it is possible for Christians to be challenged, to decolonize ourselves and reclaim patterns of words and actions in liturgies that can open fissures within the walls of Empire. We realized that by creating liturgies from the places where vulnerable people live, we ourselves gain a more radical voice, one closer to where Jesus lived.

Christians must build expansive practices of compassion and solidarity with those who are deemed to die. We must realize our deep connections with all from the lower classes, all the poor, of any religion or color, and expand this solidarity with animals, rivers, ocean, birds, and the whole earth. Prayer reminds us that through God, we understand that to become human is far more than the indoctrination of any human dominion. Instead, we learn that we are always collective, in our communities and with other species and the earth. Through our prayers and liturgies, God transforms the world through us. Only through that confluence of mutualities and belonging does our prayer become God's breath in the world. In that way, prayer becomes a continuation of Jesus' prophetic life, expressing a radical commitment with the poor. A new grammar of faith.

What is the grammar of our prayers when we write them with an empty stomach, a bleeding wound, a terminal illness, without any provision of health care or medical intervention? What is the grammar of our prayers when there is no redemption anywhere? When our prayers and liturgies are disconnected from the forces of death, we cannot reach the forces of life. When we pray under the power of Empire without vividly naming the powers of death, we are offering a soft support to the powers of destruction and domination. Soft, but support: enabling conditions for the hard power of destruction to continue.

When we pray our liturgies within situations of terror, we need a grammar that names and responds that situation, a grammar of awareness, of rebuke, of resistance, of transformation, of life pulsing in the midst of death. We do not have such a liturgical grammar for our prayers and for that we need to engage our worship to God and our worship services from a different perspective, not that of the rich or the comfortable, but of the poor and those being attacked mercilessly. The Hagars and the cast-out concubines of our time also need prayers, anamnesis, and liturgical care. We need liturgies that can rage against all forms of destruction and prophesy against local injustices by helping to dismantle violent forms of power that kills: patriarchy, racism, sexism, economic injustice, and earth extractivism.

In sum, how can we create a grammar of faith that pauses and reckons deeply with violence, and at the same time, carries the urgency of those who are about to die?

Christian women and feminist scholars have developed an entirely new way of doing liturgy. Some of the liturgies respond to violence against women based on their own experiences with evil structures. Others speak from and to other concrete situations and life transitions.[15] These practitioners and scholars "do liturgy" not for the sake of some male liturgical traditions, but for the sake of the healing and well-being of women. In the same way, Pentecostal churches are responding in prayer to the disasters of our world. Other Christian communities have developed the work of liturgy from the context of local experiences of suffering, vulnerability, and strength that can offer resistance the political-economic forces of Empire.[16]

When Christians are not seen as a danger to any of the powers that be, the church has lost its core meaning and purpose and prayers and liturgies are only a perfunctory act of self-conservation. "Prayer is meaningless," wrote Rabbi Abraham Joshua Heschel, "unless it is subversive, unless it seeks to overthrow and to ruin the pyramids of callousness, hatred, opportunism, and falsehoods."[17]

Prayer as a Circular Movement

Prayer does something. It is a potent ritual action. Prayer effects a deep circular movement within us, moving between our inside and outside without separation. When we pray to God, our prayer first changes us and then, while the movements of our hearts go toward God, our prayer has ripple effects into the world, affecting the course of our individual and communal life. Prayer effects changes in our personal and political thinking, feeling, actions and ways of being. In the United States, when there are disasters or mass gun shootings that kill many people, including children, or even now in the midst of COVID-19, politicians typically say they are sending "thoughts and prayers" to the victims. But most of the time, this is empty rhetoric, since nothing else happens, nothing really changes. The public quickly learns from the rote repetition of this expression that prayers do not really matter.

In these cases, however, we can see an obvious circularity: prayers and thoughts not accompanied by socio-political and economic actions and changes are not really genuine prayers. When we think of our prayers, we have to remember Jesus saying: "You will know them by their fruits" (Matthew 7:16). When we pray, the fruits of gratitude, solidarity, justice, and compassion are seeds that, once planted in us, make the soil of our hearts and communities rich and grow into new gardens of collective harvest and bounty. When we pray together no one should go hungry or go abandoned. When we pray, genuinely, for families who have lost their children to gun violence, to jail, or to poverty, a whole network of life and solidarity must come to fruition and be turned into laws against guns, against social disparity, against systems of death and exclusion. If prayer has a live and full circularity within one's body and spirit, the whole community will breathe this prayer and be connected in love and true solidarity. Prayer can be the starting point for change.

Praying is about bringing people into re-existence. We are called to pray into re-existence those hidden and forgotten in the shadow of oblivion, into abject and obscure places where life is considered a thing to be disposed of. To pray people into re-existence is to bring them closer to our hearts and our neighborhoods, rewriting laws and offering a new way of organizing and living our social life. For those abandoned at the ends of the world, we pray God to bring them into full existence against the necropolitics of Empire that only tortures and exterminates the poor. We are called to pray like the women in the movie "Pray the Devil Back to Hell", who, amidst civil war, prayed the devil away from their lives by facing warlords so that children could get out of the hands of armies and return to a peaceful life.[18]

Our times demand courage. We must do more than hope. Waiting is often a form of apathy or complacency. As the Spirituals says, "We are the ones we've been waiting for."[19] God is calling us all to offer solidarity, and the way to do it is by giving our hearts to it. As we get closer to those who are suffering in our communities, we may feel lost and unsure what to do. We may experience a mixture of gratitude, exhaustion, longing, impotence, pain, discomfort, excitement, and confusion. At the same time, we may learn as we go that prayer has the power to keep us going! Our hearts may be open to courage in ways that we will only know as we pray, work, sit, meditate, listen, and act.

There are actions done with people around the world that can help spark our imagination. For instance, we can take a line of actions from Babasaheb Ambedkar, who wrote the Constitution of India, a social reformer and liberationist. Fighting with and for his own people, the Dalits, he proposed: educate, agitate, and organize. From Catholic Social Teaching, a methodology to change social reality using this pedagogical pattern: see, judge and act. From the large social movement around the world called the Landless Movement, a pattern of actions with the most impoverished people: occupy, resist, produce.

Korean American theologian Anne Joh bluntly says of solidarity:

> *You don't just pull solidarity out of your ass. Solidarity/solidarities is an act now or for hopeful futures. It's un/learning ways of cultivating relations with others, it's learning to hear, embrace, to speak and to even fight differently. Solidarity is a labor of love, repentance and choosing to risk oneself in being with another whose life and living, whose histories and politics may not even resonate or be in direct opposition from what may be familiar to oneself. Solidarity is being with another in acts of dissensus that most likely will be the target of systemic and social wrath. Stand up. Speak/shout up, act up!*[20]

Whatever path we take, praying with those who are at the ends of the world will be hard. It takes an immense amount of courage and a conversion of the heart. As Professor Mayra Picos Lee reminded me during our journey, when I was feeling lost and frail,

> *Courage comes from the Latin cor, which means heart. Courage means "with heart," or to pour one's heart into action. As such, your courage reflects your heart's strength, which needs those moments of confusion and chaos to pump harder and to become stronger. This is the gift of growing one's heart in adversity, the story your project tells in so many ways from so many places and through so many people, including you!*

Dear readers, take heart, and draw closer to those who are suffering—with full ears, compassion, courage, solidarity and hearts open to be completely transformed.

CHAPTER FOURTEEN

African-Indigenous Jurema:

The Greatest Common Divisor
of The Brazilian Minimum Religion

Nancy Cardoso and Cláudio Carvalhaes[1]

Davi Chiavegatti Scaff, 7 years old

To Afonso Maria Ligório Soares
who taught us to do theology as pilgrims,
from tent to tent,
in transitory ways, but animated,
since our pilgrim bodies are always
the home of the Spirit.

Over the course of the last few decades, questions surrounding what encompasses a minimally Brazilian religion (MBR)[2] have been discussed and debated in conjunction with the consolidation of the religious studies field. One of the most significant attempts to address the issue was articulated by André Droogers, who gathered contributions made during the '70s and the '80s in the Revista Religião e Sociedade (1987). Brazil is a country that has had to overcome its own self-understanding as a Catholic Christian country and to acknowledge its religious polyphony over and above any attempt by the Church to establish cultural consensus. This process of acknowledgment remains an important task today, as this process is still incomplete, and the religious field has only become increasingly complex.

Carlos Brandão identifies "a great symbolic matrix of common use, onto which each group edits and adds its own repertoire of beliefs", and Pedro Ribeiro de Oliveira considers that "...there should be more than one set of religious elements available to different religions," suggesting that a possible MBR would stem primarily from popular Catholicism. Rubem Cesar Fernandes prefers to talk about a "common substrata capable of reaching an agreement among the many traditions" or "elements of general knowledge" that are shared by several religions with certain variations on the "relationship among each of the parties" (God, nature, human beings, deceased souls and both positive and negative deities). He particularly debates the role and function of the "clergy" as a "translator" in relation to the religious mass seen as "polyglot", yet unable to translate its contents on its own. Droogers, however, believes that the MBR is not dependent on intermediaries (translator priests), nor does it need recognition from so-called institutionalized religions.[3]

Based upon this debate, Droogers proposes the following concept for MBR:

> *It is a religiosity that is publicly manifested in secular contexts, that is conveyed by mass media, but also by ordinary language. It is part of Brazilian culture. It exists on a national level and can even serve nationalistic purposes.[4]*

Since its inception, this debate has developed in many ways and has continued to inquire about Brazilian culture and what might be unique to it in terms of its relevance to the religious question. This process of actualization has taken two discernible paths: a descriptive research method based on science and methodologies used in anthropology, sociology, history, etc., and research centered upon particular subjects' (women, Black people, gay people, etc.) modes of belief. While the first path has solidified the intuitions present among the "patriarchs" of religious studies, the second has acknowledged the divergence in dealing with religious power and its representations (class, gender, ethnic, etc.).

Two important examples of this second research trajectory deserve to be mentioned here: Brazilian feminist and Black theologies.

Ivone Gebara highlights the experience of poor, Black, native women in Latin America: prostitutes, women who were abandoned by their husbands, etc., and gives priority to women making choices for themselves as the first step toward determining the role and function religion serves for them. In this sense, a real "minimum" does not exist, but we should still ask what the "minimum" for women is. Gebara relativizes all efforts at a so-called women's "popular reading of the Bible" and identifies a potentially more meaningful set of realities and power relations.[5]

Similarly, Afonso Maria Ligorio deconstructs the debate on syncretism and religious enculturation, asserting that most efforts to establish a viable "minimum" end up reinforcing the "maximum" religion and its capacity of annexation. To Ligorio, displacing the issue of enculturation as a means of correcting a decayed and flawed syncretism fails to deal with the power issues present in the religious sphere.

Was it African and Indigenous people who corrupted Portuguese Catholicism, or it was the latter who violated the ancient traditions of the former?[6]

This question highlights an ambiguous relationship but loses its paradox to the extent to which the maximum religion occupies public space and defines the acceptable modes of belief through its visibility and ability to occupy mediums. This occupation confuses and/or erases the existing complex relations of power from view in the public space, and as a result, almost always lends support to hegemonic pretensions of power and knowledge--the very same ones that are laid down by the maximum religion.

Within this logic, creating a supposed single minimum not only loses sight of the existing and resilient elementary/minimum forms, it also loses sight of the disputes, conflicts and modes of belief that are involved in broader class struggles--modes that create a place of their own, grant access to public space and give a name to things and places that are both invisible and visible.

The descriptive and analytic efforts that identify an MBR through the use of public spaces end up strengthening the voices that intend to be "maximized" or "maximizing", particularly in theology. Three steps can be identified in this process of controlling the "minimum" religiosity:

(1) *Subordination of "minimum" expressions to the 'maximized' religions, so that the latter may appear to tolerate localized practices not likely to gain influence;*

(2) *Usurpation and co-optation of certain ritual elements, languages and objects that break with functional autonomies; as well as the theological displacement of experiences that are not easily tolerated or might gain influence;*

(3) *Prohibition of and the fight against religious practices/beliefs with the potential to gain influence and maintain their functional autonomy.*

The relationships between formal and informal religious systems are not limited to the (occasionally ineffective) attempts by certain institutionalized systems to subordinate, co-opt or abominate, but are marked by an ambivalence between accommodation and resistance on the part of certain popular religiosities, an ambivalence that creates this apparent minimum consensus or an equivocal/uncertain symbolic residue that will be accommodated as an MBR.

In this sense, the pursuit of common, shared or displaced elements from diverse religious registries cannot be "minimized" by using descriptive and analytic logic. These elements do not fit within a pocket-sized ecumenism that, intending to maintain a public space for religion (theology), also constrains diverse and divergent expressions. Religion, like culture, is full of conflict, disputes and violent power relations that legitimize subordination. Any expectation of an elegant appeasement of these rough edges is merely a restatement of the "maximum" modes of the Christian religion and its desire to maintain power in the public space. Public space does not appease the forms of colonization, slavery and domination that persist among us. Only a particular way of thinking that proclaims itself as universal, normative and superior (because it has been appeased!) can expect to look at such conflicts and identify the "minimum" of the others who are not as smart as they are.

If we must talk about "minimum" things, let us ignore the sanitized residues controlled by the patriarchal, white and colonized voice of science and technology.

> *Two elements help us understand a position that radically rejects a syncretic process in the Christian system. The first one is the self-understanding of Christianity as a religion that holds the only and true revelation from God. At the core of such pretension would be a concept of static (ahistorical) revelation that, based since its inception on facts of faith, would immunize this tradition against the several levels of syncretism that constitute any and every religious group along its historical development. Such a stance inevitably leads to an artificial conflict (ideological, ahistorical and idealistic): the kerygma revealed (by God himself) to the Christian community versus other religions that were subordinated to the laws of sociology.[7]*

This discomfort is particularly important in helping Latin American feminist liberation theology to resist co-optation and falling into an easy "I-want-to-be public" theology. The ever-present challenge of dramatic social inequality and structural racism do not allow for any form of reduction.

Following the suggestion of a "minimum religion", we might also ask what a maximum Brazilian religion would be look like--perhaps a fact that comes before any interpretation, with a pretension to plenitude, purity, and authenticity, and to being tasked with organizing the world as democratic and universally representative. In contrast, the minimum religion would be viewed (because it would be interpreted as such) as partial, unofficial, deconstructive, dangerous, destabilizing and unrepresentative except for in a few sectors of society.

Jurema's Multi-sensory Polyphonies

The women of the Agro Ecologic Web of the People of Bahia[8] gather to play ancient songs and produce dances and rhythms that continue to enchant the southern part of Bahia. "Enchanting" here involves being taken over by memory, by ancestors who were not defeated by death, invasion or oblivion. All of southern Bahia is inhabited by enchanted men and women, orixás and caboclas. There on the coast of Brazil, in between the forest and the seas, the first native communities met with invaders 515 years ago. The excessive conquering of the land, tearing down the forest and enslaving the people served to de-evangelize the local people forever, making their gods and goddesses more beautiful and necessary. Bahia's history demonstrates the radical resilience of people and of their modes of belief as they fight for their land and territory.

The women first gathered two months before the event and anticipated their fourth full organizational gathering in December of 2015. It was an opportunity for 60 women to live together and talk to each other. The Agro-ecologic Web of the People of Bahia believe in

> *the need to articulate our struggles against racism, religious violence and other colonizing and euro-centric practices that came with the ships of discovery and are still repeated, day after day, as if there weren't another way, as if we were beyond repair... it is time to cultivate a land where alliances are forged and we UNITE ourselves in wisdom and joy to defend our cultures, cosmo-visions and territories.*[9]

What brought the women together for this meeting were questions of practices and debates on agro-ecology in a difficult and contentious political scene, as well as within a context of increased artificial planting of eucalyptus, pasturage set aside for cattle, and the growth of touristic enterprises. The Cabruca designates the forestation and way of life of traditional peoples of southern Bahia. The Cabruca includes both the preservation of large old trees as well as new ways of planting, interspersing cocoa among the fruits and trees of what remains of the Atlantic Forest. It is both from and in the Cabruca that the people of the forest draw their sustenance, maintain their pleasures and flavors, and delight in life.[10]

The articulation of traditional peoples' struggles for land and territory in the region joined together with the materiality of both the Atlantic Forest and of the Jurema and their rituals. In between conversations on agro-ecology, we met under the shade of Jurema and African-Indigenous pluralities.

Alternating between Black and Indigenous beats, smoke bathed the women and invited them to the circle. Inside the circle we wove a web through the necessary, urgent and extremely beautiful articulation of people fighting for their land. Jurema created for us and in us the opportunity and means of doing so. Each one danced in her own learned rhythm, but we let go, and an overwhelming sense of joy took over the space.[11] In between conversations, I asked the other women: what is Jurema? how does it work? The answers came mixed with stories and examples that spoke of individual and social bodies and territories: Jurema opens the body, opens paths, gives joy to festivities and rituals; Jurema closes the body and protects it from diseases and hazards; it prepares and strengthens the body for work, and sustains it in struggle and hardship.

323

The Meeting of a Rural Social Pastorate:
A Theology of Good Living and Jurema

At the 2015 national meeting of the Rural Pastoral Commission,[12] the experience of *sumakkawsay* (good living) was discussed. More than a concept or a phrase, *sumakkawsay* is an experience of the ancestry of native Andean communities that is reflected in projects advocating for life, and even in the constitutions of Bolivia and Ecuador. The question that was posed was whether the traditional peoples in Brazil also understood "good living" as an ancestry that projects itself as the uniting element in their struggles. Someone commented, "Sumakkawsay— would that be the same as our understanding of an earth without evil?" Then, someone from the Northeast of Brazil said, "We have Jurema!"

Each one then shared what he or she knew about Jurema and what it meant to the traditional peoples in the Brazilian Northeast. Long-standing questions and intuitions were awakened: remedy, ritual element, medicinal plaster, beverage, multiple uses of plants that make up the imagination and daily life of many groups in the country and in the cities. It is both Indigenous and bears African roots. It is a relationship with nature, with place, with ancestors.

> *Jurema is a typical religious expression of northeastern Brazil. It is both a rural and urban religion, but scholars have only recently become interested in the urban Jurema that involves the confluence of other religious expressions such as umbanda, Catholicism, candomblé and voodoo from Maranhão. Its name, of Tupi origin, is linked to some species of trees found in the dry region of the northeast: Mimosa hostilis (recently reclassified as Mimosa tenuiflora), Mimosa verrucosa and Vitexagnus-castus, respectively known as black, gentle, and white juremas. The black jurema is used to make the beverage that gives the name to this religious world. It probably originated in pajelança and toré, religious systems that are at the base of indigenous sacred understanding.*[13]

Jurema as a Smoking Hybridization

At this gathering of women, the paradigm of cultural and religious pluralism was essential to create unity among peasant, Indigenous and quilombola women, as well as among students and representatives of environmental organizations.

The economic models in place in southern Bahia have always favored large cacao, cattle, and more recently, artificial eucalyptus farms, creating an environment where people and other living beings have been exploited and exterminated for the last 500 years.

The arrival of men and women from various parts of Africa reinforced in the territory the despair of not belonging. With no knowledge of language or place, these sequestered and enslaved people, through songs, prayers and memory, maintained a sense of origin that was incredibly resilient. Demonized and silenced by their owners' faith, they quickly had to become familiar with the land, and they used names that they brought with them to designate rivers, rocks and trees. De-evangelized by the love of the Word and the litanies imposed on them in an attempt to mirror European beliefs (in which they were unable to see their own reflections), Black people opened their ears of resistance and learned how to listen for the singing of *torés* and how to recognize who they were without losing themselves or disappearing. In the eyes of the Indigenous people, they saw windows of reconciliation with this place.

Nobody knows the exact moment when Jurema's smoke left the toré to beautifully envelop the powerful rhythm of African religion reinvented in Brazil. It may be that in the ancient quilombos the common fate of natives and Africans created a spark of conviviality between the circles of the two and, at some point, Jurema's actions and infinite manifestations in the forest began to be shared by _torés_ and *catimbós*. And thus, Brazil was created... even if only in its potential one day simply to be.

Political practices and daily struggles also accompany an articulation of the culture and religions of the local people. In one of the first Portuguese colonization attempts, native peoples of Southern Bahia were quickly evicted and suffered a lengthy process of annihilation, assimilation and alienation from the land. There were also Black slaves, who were an important piece of many economic cycles, working on the land but remaining alienated from it. The landless were farm workers imprisoned by the coronels, whose stories reach far beyond the tales found in Jorge Amado's novels[14] and continue to permeate power dynamics in the region.

For years, each group resisted and fought these powers in its own way. However, with various successes in regaining the land and fighting repression, these movements began to grow closer and work together. At this particular gathering of women, we celebrated this trend of approximation and mutual recognition. Beyond objective goals of organization and creating a deeper political understanding, means of resistance and struggle reflect the wisdom and embrace of the mystical that spring forth and integrate profound discoveries and intuitions that serve us on our path to theology and spirituality. This is an uneven path, marked by many forms of violence, including the violence of strategic invisibilities that left deep scars still open in Brazilian religious history.

> *At this point, we wish to point out that most likely the reasons for the invisibility reside in magic/religion dichotomy as value judgments. The persecution of terreiros, especially during the years of the Estado Novo (New State), occurred under police control as they considered terreiros under the term Charlatanism. In 1933, the Mental Health Service was created in Pernambuco, led by Ulysses Pernambucano and other intellectuals such as Gilberto Freyre, Gonçalves Fernandes, and René Ribeiro. Quite simply, the SHM was an attempt to raise Candomblé to the category of religion, considering it a component of the formation of Brazil, thus removing terreiros from police jurisdiction. However, that shift didn't happen to Jurema, which continued to be recognized as charlatanry and primarily accused of using false medicine for healing work. This attitude towards Jurema made Jurema's religious altars to be hidden within terreiros.*[15]

This unfortunately did not happen to Jurema and its healing rituals, which continued to be understood as magic and not a formal religion, and which are constantly accused of charlatanism and the practice of false medicine. The fear of constant attacks caused Jurema to place its altars within terreiros, a movement apropos of ecumenism or religious pluralism. A deep solidarity based in shared strategies of survival connected Jurema with the terreiros, one sustaining the other, each protecting, honoring, guarding and expanding the other. At the core of Jurema is an influx of religious energies, all joined to protect and empower the lives of its people.

The Role of Mística/Mystique

Jurema is like an old conversation between Black and Indigenous people that lingers in Brazilian history. It is a liturgical gathering in response to oppression. The *mística* is created by and comes in the wake of the struggle, thus becoming and continuously transforming itself into the plural identity of Indigenous and Black peoples. The *mística*, the spirituality of the people and their possible theological progress, comes from the continuous fight for life and survival.

> *In brief, instead of providing a representation "of its own", Jurema multiplies the representations. It is not a single plant but encompasses the (polysemy of the) whole forest. Its feet are cities. It resembles a woman, cabocla, a beautiful indigenous dark-skinned woman... Powerful, heir of*

an oral culture, she roots herself in words: "its" natives sometimes manifest themselves as spiritual beings similar to romantic literary constructions or to images from civic celebrations (Santos, 1995); sometimes, when they effectively resemble people and indigenous communities, at least in part, they receive such an identity from concepts taken from literary anthropology.[15]

The memory of violence that lacerated (lacerates) the flesh of native and Black people in Brazil creates trenches, prayers, movements, visitations and healing. A shared solidarity and *mística* capable of recreating known and unknown worlds, categories of thinking and sacred movements ignored by the oppressor, was maintained and continuously revived in the forest and in the encounters needed to live, however big or small. The spiritual promiscuity between Indigenous people and spirits, Black people and enchanted ones, as well as their oral nature, reflects its maximized *mística*, exhausted by the immediacy of the full life that is necessary to strengthen a celebrating people. With that, it confuses, deafens and makes a mess of the metaphysically barbed Christian canon.

Mística does not happen within forced doctrine or confessions of faith but emerges out of a materiality of the dances and smoke that traverse unauthorized spaces and mystify people united against the violence of the law. Mystified, they live and survive; they rearrange their spaces and symbols. The *mística* softens identities, skin colors, histories, legacies, traditions and whatever else is needed. The enchanted ones and the spirits mobilize themselves to ensure the survival of the people. What once was distinct is now common; what was once separated now lives in and through relationship; what asserted itself as autonomous now participates in the dance of intersectionalities, in a continuous re-discovery that recreates worlds of life and ancient wisdoms.

When the people say, "We have Jurema," they are saying, "We have a measuring rod and compass, and we do not need your precision." In the fight for the lands that were taken, for the lives cut short, for the rights that were stripped away, decolonized bodies live their life-and-death struggle, trying to return to what was once theirs: their home.[16]

Possessed by Enchantment

In contrast to the obsessive controls of Christianity, the Indigenous and African-based religions are directed by the orixás and the enchanted. Control is lost, and all is subjected to the directions and charms of the enchanted ones and the orixás. This possession defines what was and what will come to be, transfiguring identities and states of mind. It is a power that takes over, directing and organizing everything. The possession of these wonders goes beyond the formal analysis of a descriptive and defining theology that comes before living. Instead, they are concerned with the composition of energies and synergies, with the compensation of good for evil, the preservation of the good, and caution in the face of evil, without the particular polarities found in Christianity. The meeting space is always sacred, and it is in the trance, in the body, that the communication between distinct realities takes place.

Jurema and Space

Jurema's *mística* is not timeless but keeps track of time through the space and the ground that provide life and harvest. Jurema is both a tree and a beverage with religious and medicinal properties to care for the people who gather; it is an entity, a place of worship and ritual, a metaphysical Indigenous woman, a long line of enchanted people and caboclas, men and women from the desert and the water's edge, an object, a forest, a tree trunk. Many orixás landed here with the Africans, escorting their sons and daughters, and partnered with the local entities, because African religions leave a space open for gathering and adding various religious expressions. In the wake of those developments, Jurema expanded the African pantheon, and the orixás expanded themselves by living together with Jurema and the enchanted ones.

In this deep solidarity and highly particular confluence, the space of *mística* establishes itself in the communion of Indigenous people, Black people, and caboclos.[17] Jurema is found in settlements. With the alienation of Indigenous and Black peoples from the land, their livelihood moved from the forest to the spaces of Umbanda. It lives in the interchange with the Umbanda rituals. But the notion of settlement links itself with the settlement of excluded people in lands that were stolen from the natives. Black people were settled in this land, and now they need to assert their rights to it. Uprooted, Jurema's roots in the settlement create a notion of belonging, even though a deadly melancholy remains its most primal song. Cosmogonies became intertwined and transformed. Settled in this land-life, Jurema reconfigures the dimensions of public space, determines anew to what and to whom it belongs. This reconfiguration happens in the mixed reordering of Indigenous and Black cosmologies. African-Indigenous entities live off their deep relationship with nature. Thus, the struggle of the women from the Ecologic Web of the People of Bahia is this symbiosis between spirits and nature, tribes and quilombos.

Jurema as One Who Redefines Class

The welcome of Jurema within the diversity of oppressed people recreates class structures. The expansion of the concept of and access to the sacred is plural and is detached from monetary value. Quite to the contrary, it breaks and balances out diversities, thus redefining class systems. Everyone sits at the Jurema table, and its table extends itself throughout the entire forest.

Parallels and Disconnects with Christianity

In the complex Brazilian religiosity, Jurema is a minimum-maximum religion, a non-religion that unsettles Western thinking. The very notion of religion is put to the test, since the concept of religion is a Christian invention that symbolizes the *religare* of the creation removed by sin from the God that created it. Jurema does not fit into this or any other notion of religion, but is rather a set of understandings, practices and wisdom that arises from the ground and ingrains itself in the daily lives of peoples in all its forms, colors and challenges. Jurema does not claim, nor does it desire a status, be it minimum or maximum.

On the contrary, it is the remaking of life, the sacred without dichotomy, immersed in life and things. It does not organize or accomplish anything by holding a view of the secular as being opposed to or different from the sacred. For Indigenous and African peoples, everything is sacred, a dwelling of the spirits. Thus, the body, also sacred, gives itself to life lived with enchantment, the life of the body in all its fullness, without denial or guilt. The body is elevated when it is in a trance and meets the spirits, in contrast to Christianity, which denies the ability of the body to act as a sacred proxy. Spirituality/*Mística* happens through the materiality of dances, the rhythm of instruments and congas, and smoke. All covered in a haze, perhaps like the mysterious God *absconditus* of negative Christian theology.

As a set of understandings and practices, the label of minimum-maximum does not fit Jurema, because it is at the same time both minimum and maximum, escaping pseudo-Christian definitions.

Jurema's Crossbred Liturgy

Jurema is a shared table of conviviality, relationships and interchanges of power, a place of celebration, the enchanted world manifesting its charms and creating a hybrid, mestizo, "Brazilian" spirituality that is both disliked and feared by the minimum and maximum religions that breed through authentications completely foreign to Jurema's movement. Jurema is marked by its singularity and multiplicity: a place of multiple representations, it welcomes, expands and reconfigures the needs of the oppressed--people shared by distinct gods who became common to all, for their well-being and survival. Jurema, a tree-root-trunk that through daily experiences lived with the people, becomes the potential of oppressed peoples', natives' and blacks', survival.[18]

Jurema's crossbreeding comes from its originality and capacity for mutation and mutual involvement. In this sense, it is cannibalistic and symbiotic, becoming, from its originality, something else, beyond itself and because of itself. The very plurality of Jurema and its multiple forms are made not only of spirits but also of things and places, a materiality of the enchanted and charmers.[19] Thus, it confounds and defies the trinity that intends to unify Christianity. Jurema is much more than three persons. Its representations more closely resemble the multiple sacramental understanding that comes from Orthodox Christian theology than the Western Catholic-Protestant understanding of sacraments built on anywhere between two and seven sacraments.

Reality and representation are mixed in several spiritual, mental, bodily or even natural realities that are sometimes not embodied. Jurema can be drunk, the bark from its roots or trunk made into a beverage like the God that offers itself in the bread and wine. But Jurema may be mind-altering, while in the Eucharist there is still total control of God through the forms of the ritual and possibilities of meaning.

Contributions of a Brazilian Black Liberation Theology

Understanding Black theology in Brazil requires a broader perspective, since liberation is found not only in Blackness, but also in the composite colors of theology. No theology that feeds on itself can be upheld in the face of the white colonizer's power. The crushing of identities in the theological quehacer (the doing of theology) seems to be one more way to provide an ideology of conquest rather than an autonomous or self-determining mode of thinking. We propose a Black theology based on its deepest shades, in the idea of a Latin American Pan-Africanism and its stories in relation to Indigenous hues. This co-relation, based on a profound religious pluralism, seems to us deeper, more congenial and capable of offering not only anti-colonial resistance but also new ways to live and reproduce life.

Diego Irarrázaval gives us four points to consider in the dialogue of Christianity with African religions:

(1) celebrate and think in accordance with African ways about a recreation of the world;

(2) identify ourselves and our continent as Afro-American;

(3) celebrate the mystery of an African form where the body has a fundamental place in both revelation and the sacred;

(3) engage with syncretism and with the particular wisdoms and sources we bring.[20]

What is missing here is what Gebara reminds us of: the well-being that is the life of the earth and of the entire ecosystem.[21] The very life of the native and African nations is fully embodied in the movement of biodiversity. Similarly, we need to celebrate and think about Indigenous forms of recreating the world. We must identify ourselves as the Indigenous and consider our continent as being originally owned by the native peoples who were here first. We must understand the body, community and environment as sacred places, and engage with syncretism.

Thus, the reconstitution of a Latin American Black theology would rescue a pluralistic, cultural, religious, and class paradigm that aims to liberate native and excluded people and sees life on the planet as a fundamentally plural place full of meaning.

No theology in Latin America can or should exclusively uphold Christianity. To base a Black theology solely on Christian grounds would constitute the disempowerment of Latin American Black plurality. Consequently, a Black theology is only possible if it is deeply intertwined with all religions of African, Indigenous and Christian hues. For this reason, the inter-religious movement is essential, and Jurema can be a concrete space where this sharing happens.

In brief, we propose that any liberation theology in Latin America:

(1) needs to be done with the earth, on the land one lives, with the seeds, rivers, trees, animals rocks and spirits;

(2) needs to be constructed out of the relationship with Indigenous peoples; needs to intersect race, gender and class;

(3) has to be mestizo and hybrid, and include women, gay people, and oppressed people, because all Black theology is composed of mixtures and intersections where oppressed people gather to discuss plans of resistance and transformation;

(4) should always be a theology of settlement and class struggle: a theology of invasion, of reclamation of ownership, and of conquering by force, using all the resources of mystical symbols and the spirituality of oppressed peoples;

(5) should be done over time to refine its actions, belongings, subjects, subjects and forms of life, ongoing struggle and resistance.

There will no longer be a search for minimum-maximum religions.

CONCLUSION

Avery Leigh Frantz, 8 years old

Faith + Class= Style

I write this conclusion from my house, a private property who once belonged to the Lenape, Susquehannock, Shawnee, and Iroquois nations. So strange how we made all this to be normal. Yes, through a huge civilizing process, we made the laws, we made the lawyers to write the laws and contracts, we invented paper, and we invented the right to own somebody else's lands. We just confiscate their land, we made it ours--so much so that we feel entitled to "own" land, even when so many people do not have housing.

No, we do not own the land--the land always owns us. I live in this land without knowing anything of it: its stories, its enchanted people, its rivers, its more than human people, its cosmological relations. There is so much for me to truly inhabit the land and to fully land where I live. And yet, each chapter I wrote without much acknowledgement of where I was. My concepts float above the earth. And yet, I am searching for my sacred song. I hope the earth will give it to me at some point.

I am reminded of my mother's words every time I call her in Brazil: "Mom how are you doing?" And she would always say: "I am going... with faith and class." I asked my mother what she meant by that, and she said, "faith is to know that our Lord Jesus Christ is always with me, and class is not to lose your joy for life." I don't remember her exact words, but it was something to do with this: class is to know how to be in life but also above life. Perhaps my mother's faith and class can be called her *style*, something akin to what Cornel West and Edward Said have developed in their own thinking.

Cornel West talks about Black folks' style as a way of living in the *funk*, responding to disaster, despair, and anxiety with smiles, joy, singing, playing, dancing, poetry, and so on. In his words, Black style is about "ordinary people exercising a certain kind of free agency always under severe constraints, but a sense of style, or a sense of smile, or a sense of laughter"[1] In a strangely similar way, Edward Said says of style, calling it lateness, "artistic lateness, not as harmony and resolution but as intransigence, difficulty, and unresolved contradiction?"[2]

That is it! My mom's faith and class are a way of smiling without resolution of her problems, engaging intransigence, difficulty, and unresolved contradiction with joy. It is about a dancing Sisyphus who made the boulder a friend to walk with instead of pushing against himself. In my first book I said that to create borderless borders in liturgies was an endless Sisyphean process, but I never paid attention to the boulder. This is what we tend to do: talk about the processes, the condemnation, the work that entails this course, but the rock is never to be considered.

Style with a dancing Sisyphus is about telling the rock: we have got to do this, so let us do it together until we don't need to do it anymore. And while the rock and Sisyphus go up and down, they plot a way to move away from the curse. For any destiny can be traced and changed. No curse from the gods has an eternal grip on us. We learned with Glicéria Tupinambá in the introduction that if the land dies, the enchanted beings die, and we die too. So, the point of Sisyphus' dancing curse is to become the rock, and by becoming the rock, end the curse. That might be a tale for our times. Not to pay attention to the earth, but to become the earth. Not to pay attention to the trees and the forests but to become the forests.

A Sensuous Grammar of The Body

I do this by discerning the sensuous ways of my body and the diverse forms different parts of my body, head, heart, naval, feet, hands connect without compartmentalization. With that I am trying to spell capitalism and modernity from my body and my thinking by relating to the earth in some way or another. By reading and being with people attached to the land, I'm trying to get to that point where Mary Oliver said, "All important ideas must include the trees, the mountains, and the rivers."[3]

Indigenous leader Sonia Bone Guajajara, the leader of the Association of Indigenous People of Brazil, told us that we need to reforest our minds: "Reforesting minds is necessary for a future we want for ourselves and for the future generations."[4] But how do I reforest my mind? If we think with people attached to the earth, Indigenous people from everywhere, then we must realize that knowledge is not a production of truth collected from books only…it is not about academia, statements of cohesive thoughts, or conceptual stratagems only…but also stories and rituals related to the earth and the sky and all its inhabitants.

When I think about rituals as someone whose grandparents were uprooted from the land, I feel lost--no connection whatsoever. In order to change my own form of thinking, I have to engage my body in relation with the earth in other forms of knowing. I think about rituals as a form of tapping into other forms of knowledge production. But to think about rituals, I must think not from a transcendence/immanent framework, but rather an animist pantheological perspectival way of relating with more than humans. First, I must see myself as an environment relating with other environments--me, as a person, relating to other beings as persons: the tree people, the river people, the bird people, the vegetable people, the fish people and so on. When I do that, I don't search for truth but for relationality and reciprocity which places me in the realm of protocols and diplomacy.

As I engage with the patch of land I live in, I want to deeply relate and create kinship. I search even for other forms of ancestry that didn't influence my upbringing, as I now belong here in this land, and these are the ancestors who live in this land. I need to listen to them as my elders.

I honor the Lenape people who first lived here and were decimated from their land. I go to the Codonoguinet river and honor the river as my elder. I try to listen. Then I go to Wonder, the tree with whom I have established a respectful relation. I honor Wonder in his/her 5 trunks. I breathe as I try to hear her breathing. Every time I do this I feel, think, and learn something different. As I touch Wonder my body enters into a different form of thinking.

My body's sensory cells are devoted to touch--all 600 million receptors in my skin, the receptors in my muscles, tendons, and joints. I need to sense/feel with different bodies, air, skies, rocks, trees, water. I need a different time, with a pace that is slower than I can even imagine.

I need a strange, new grammar of a sensuous language, one that teaches me to relate with the natural world. Perhaps if I turn the educational pattern known as "to see to judge and to act" into the repeated ritual of "to see, to listen, perhaps to touch, and very occasionally to talk," then I can learn more about the place where I am, the land that is receiving me, the people who live here, and how I am not only a part of them through many processes of symbiosis, but I *am* them too. I hesitate, but start by asking my companions:

> *My dear elder Codonoguinet creek: why do I feel you so estranged from you? How have I forgotten all the rivers of my life and never paid much attention to them? What happened to me that makes it so hard to talk to you and relate to you as my elder? How can I reciprocate your care for me?*

> *My dear Wonder: why have I never paid attention to you and all the trees as tree people? What happened to my people that we have lost any sense of relation and reciprocity with you and all the animated natural world? How can I reciprocate your care for me?*

By asking these questions I circumambulate my own self in relation to humans and our ways of being that extract everything: coloniality and the uprooting of people and all forms of life from the land.

I learn that my language must acquire flesh--a flesh made of feelings and sensibilities that can be tuned with more than humans. A language that is not mine and yet, it lives within me. It feels like a foreign language, one that makes me breathe and yet, it is not habituated into my lexicon. My words so confusing and fearful, my ways of living too distant, my culture opposed to other living presences, and this land, next to my house, is nothing less than a foreign country.

To learn this language, I need all my senses and a sixth one I haven't yet discovered. As an Indigenous shaman told me once: you need the sacred song now. Yes, I do! I need a song that sings and listens to other forms of sacra-mentality and a language that dislodges the configuration of my culture-nature world. I need a language without words to attend to a thousand hierophanies, cataphatic native languages, to compose ten thousand cosmological pantheologies. I need a language that provides space for a river to be my most important reference, the tree system my conceptual way of thinking, and the seeds as my revolutionary manifested resistance.

If we start to see, and feel and touch differently, we can perform other forms of relation and create space for different worlds to live together. If we start to see and feel and touch differently, we might be able to engage knowledges that pertain to entirely different ways of living long ago set aside and uprooted by extractivism.

To finish, I wonder how can we think forms of decoloniality from the presences of trees and forests? How can we think of the production of knowledge in the presence of rivers? How can we think about patriarchy in the ways we slaughter animals? How can we think about capitalism through the ways we relate with the oceans? How can we think about racism by the ways we relate to fracking? How can we think about poverty and exclusion by the ways we relate to seeds and monoculture plantations and poisoning? All of these relations are based on dominance and mastery, and we need something else. we need something like what poet Tomas Tranströmer says:

> Tired of all who come with words, words but no language I went to the snow-covered island. The wild does not have words. The unwritten pages spread themselves out in all directions! I come across the marks of roe-deer's hooves in the snow. Language, but no words.[5]

Rituals are forms of knowing across all the many languages that offer ways to think/feel/relate with the natural world to create pluriverses and multiple worlds so that we can live together. I finish with a blessing.

A Blessing to you all

Inspired by "Thesis for an Atomic Era"
by Günther Anders[6]

A life better lived is a life where blessings, that is, forms of wishes, hopes, desires and modes of life circulate around people as care, challenge, and sustenance. You have blessed me during this learning, so I now bless you with these blessings.

I bless you with all that is sacred, the sacred that flows in energies, mutations, symbiosis, and transformations.

I bless you with the God of life that keeps changing and moving, dying, and living, recreating itself in thousand flows, and unexpected possibilities.

At the end of our time on earth, I bless with an anti-apocalyptic blessing, against all apocalypses created by "men," and the blessing that refuses to assume the end of times. Thus, I bless you with the end of times that is always unending.

I bless you with a faith that can be easily called stubbornness, which is the positionality of standing with those whose lives are constantly taken away, opening yourselves up to be affected by them, pledging your allegiance with them, and not giving up on the possibilities of transformations and healing.

I bless you with the recurring awareness that we are earth, humus! In other words, I bless you with what Saint Augustine said of the sacraments: "Receive what you are."

I bless you with the immanent grace of bodies of all kinds, human and more than human people to keep us ready to disarm bombs in the middle of minefields where bombs are ticking and already exploding.

I bless you with a certain form of sustenance that you can stay standing in the presence of enemies while dismantling the atomic bombs they are igniting.

I bless you with the awareness of standing on your ground, and land, as atomic bombs of racism, extractivism, colonization of the earth and of the moon extinguish what took millennia to come to life.

I bless you with the loss of the transcendent as a new way of finding immanent forms of life, freedom, and the fascination of living amidst so many beings/agents all around us.

I bless you with the expansion of your horizons as you start to see God more in the immanent life than in a transcendent one, more in the symbiosis of life than in stagnated creeds.

I bless you with the abdication of the hope to live better after this life and so that you may live fully in this life. Even if you can't.

I bless you with the sense that we are all too close to each other and that proximity can either be something to fear or it can help us make kin of all the species and agents of life near us. May this closeness help us see that our interaction with vast forms of life is a witness to the fact that we are never alone and that we can always produce life and death.

I bless you with the healing leaves of trees and the force of every root.

As we live in this society of surpluses and endless developments, I bless you with the ability to move beyond those desires so we can substitute these forms of creation with other ways of being in this world.

I bless you with the death of our age and time! May your mourning be devastating, yet also glorious, as we mourn that which once constituted us, moving through the cracks opened to think/imagine/act new worlds of life and modes of being.

I bless you with determination as you lose the signs of this time, the ones created and circulated by capitalism and its metaphysics of the now. May we lose our grip on that which kills us.

And since the future has already happened and we are creating it every day, I bless you with horizons of destitution: the destitution of the machinery that rips the earth apart, the end of massive fishing, excessive meat for meals, accumulation of anything, the end of all jails and police around the world, and the destitution now of all of those who rule the financial market and the politic arena from any political party. And I bless you with horizons of newness: a world of small farming, sufficient energy for all, basic salary for all, fewer hours of work for all, health systems for every single human and non-human being, and a democracy from below, starting with those who were always destitute from any democratic life: the poor, the trees, the rivers, the soil, the animals. May they tell us what we need to do to live collectively.

I bless you with a "Productive Frustration." [7] Our efforts to fulfill the imperative "Expand your capacity to be afraid and make it commensurate with the immensity of the effects of your actions" maybe frustrated or unsuccessful. But even this failure should not intimidate us; the repeated frustration does not refute the need to reiterate the effort. May every new failure bear fruit and alert us to initiate other actions whose effects transcend our ability to be afraid.

Since we are incapable of measuring the disasters and catastrophes that are continuing to come and will continue to come, I bless you with the ability to see ourselves not as special beings, or kings and queens of nature, or anything else except nothing more than a speck of life filled with luminosity just like an ameba, the singing of a bird, the yawning of a bear or the ruffling of fins of fishes within the water.

I bless you with the thought that we are "incapable to imagine what we are in fact producing" and that alienation will continue to take us to places of extinction and death.

More, I bless you with a new binarism: our ability to "produce in opposition to our power to imagine... since not only is imagination no longer up to production, but feeling is no longer up to responsibility. Moreover, we live in a world where the stimulus is too large to produce any reaction or activate any brake mechanism." So, I bless you with forms of imagination and sacred abilities to produce a brake in consumption, a limit to accumulation, and a strong halt to processes of development.

I bless you with strength as you live with debts that the system of oppression and colonization imposed on you and now, they say it is all your fault!

I bless you not with hope but courage.

I bless you as you muster the courage to know that we are the only ones taking care of ourselves, nobody else: not politicians, not democratic systems, not companies, not priests, not religions, not authorities.

I bless you with communities that will relearn how to sustain a whole village and care for those who are sick and provide for the unemployed and for those who are unable.

I bless you with the awareness of all those who died for we must fight for them! Every day, remember those who died and go into the fight for them!

I bless you not with the insistence of resistance which can be a mode of weakness, but the courage to know limits, to say we are lost, and to encounter the strength within ourselves and within those who have seen the world end so many times before. May we know that nothing can destitute us because we have already destituted ourselves even of ourselves. Now we are free from grasping any hope or waiting for anyone. We will now have the courage to cultivate what is worth living for, honoring, and fighting for.

I bless you with perceptions of reality that come from communities on the bottom--those forgotten, named as thugs, garbage, escoria do mundo. I bless you with new senses of perception to make allegiances with those communities who are outside of the system, beyond official theologies and political hopes. May we implode the very forms of power that constitutes them and our system. I bless you with the ability to move away from forms of under the control of coloniality and massive forms of ideologization of necro-powers that only work against the vast majority of the people.

I bless you with the capacity to fear fully and not to hide under the incapacity to fear. I bless you with the fear that is part of the struggle against forces of death. I also bless you with a "1) a fearless fear, since it excludes fearing those who might deride us as cowards, 2) a stirring fear, since it should drive us into the streets instead of under cover, 3) a loving fear, not fear of the danger ahead but for the generations to come."[8]

I bless with you the urge to say this mantra: "I don't need this; I don't need that either."

I bless you with the demand to continue the mantra: "Who am I responsible for today? And tomorrow? And after?" And also, to be responsible for those who died: rivers, people, trees, birds...

I bless you with the ability to live in truth and to know the difference between truth and lie. For we are living under a "Deceptive Form of Current Lie: The examples of camouflage teach us something about the contemporary type of lying. For today, lying no longer needs to be affirmed by affirmation; ideologies are no longer needed. The type of victorious lie today is one that prevents us from even suspecting that it could be a lie; and this victory became possible because, today, to lie it is not necessary to hide behind affirmations. Until now, in honest hypocrisy, the lies pretended to be true, they are now camouflaged with a completely different costume."

I bless you with a life away from a sense of Truth, but if truth is necessary, I bless you with the truth that every lie is a form of giving up responsibility.

I bless you with the sanity to live in a world where the repression of forms of evil and perversion have now been freed from the gates of our un/conscious and are now flooding the world with the ugly parts of ourselves and taking the shape of politics, means of relation, moral and religious feelings, and forms of law.

I bless you with a shift to our questions. If the basic moral question of previous times was "How should we live", we must now ask "Will we live?"

I bless you with the blessing of the lawyer from the movie Dark Waters: The most important thing I learned in my life came from a small farmer without much education: that nobody will take care of us: not politicians, governors, churches... We will take care of ourselves. May your most important sacramental allegiances be with those who have been crushed by this colonial system. I bless you with the sacredness of small farmers, of collectives of women, of peasants and landless people, of people in jail, homeless, enslaved, abused, destroyed. Or what Brazilian singer Emicida said of Black people, which can be also said of Indigenous people, colonized and wronged people: "And everything, everything, everything, everything we have is us."[9]

I bless you with the courage to let go of this isolated human centered world, Let the anthropocentric world die! And I bless you with the exciting joy of finding anew thousands of worlds of so many beings and agents living in full reciprocity and mutual care: plants, animals, rocks, sky, cells, flowers, birds, rivers, fishes, things and on and on and on.

I bless you with a faith without belief and full of relationship. But if belief is needed, I bless you with the belief only in the impossible for the possible is not worth fighting for. And for that, I bless you with the strength to work that will give body to the impossible.

As we finish this book, I pledge my allegiance to you. I will be here for you with you. Together we will go, together we will take care of each other. I will be responsible for your well-being, and you will be responsible for mine.

Knowing that all the blessings I send you is mostly the things I need to be blessed by, may these blessings be what Jewish thinker Marc Ellis calls a "dystopic solidarity" with you.

Finally, as you go, I bless you with a God (that) is all the stuff that makes the world.[10]

NOTES

Foreword

1. Translator's adaptation.

Introduction

1. This phrase was projected on the buildings of the Brazilian Federal Congress by the Brazil's Indigenous People Articulation on the Indigenous Day April 19, 2021. https://ifnotusthenwho.me/who/articulacao-dos-povos-indigenas-do-brasil-apib/

2. Milton Schwantes, "A Teologia E O Direito Dos Pobres--Entrevista com Milton Schwantes," *Associação Rumos* (blog), March 30, 2012, http://www.padrescasados.org/archives/3313/a-teologia-e-o-direito-dos-pobres-entrevista-com-milton-schwantes/?fbclid=IwAR0sH3rvqIdnkMgtE7bhpC-XaV69FtPE_0o_NqVAYHyN1ebr_R3zWO7Evnw.

3. Ailton Krenak, *Ideias para adiar o fim do mundo* (São Paulo: Companhia das Letras, 2019).

4. Glicéria Jesus da Silva, Daniela Fernandes Alarcon, and Vitor Flynn Paciornik, *Os Donos Da Terra* (São Paulo: Editora Elefante, 2020).

5. Julie Dorrico, "Nascidos e criados da terra, Ao longo de sete narrativas, HQ mostra o processo das retomadas de terras e o cotidiano dos Tupinambá na Bahia," *Quatro Cinco Um,* February 1, 2021, https://www.quatrocincoum.com.br/br/resenhas/quadrinhos/nascidos-e-criados-da-terra.

6. Davi Kopenawa and Bruce Albert, *The Falling Sky: Words of a Yanomami Shaman,* trans. Nicholas Elliott and Alison Dundy (Cambridge: Belknap Press: An Imprint of Harvard University Press, 2013).

7. Davi Kopenawa, *A Última Floresta,* directed by Luiz Bolognesi (2021; São Paulo: Gullane), documentary.

8. I have to thank all of my students for giving me wonderful feedback for this chapter.

Chapter 1

1. "Eco-Liturgical Liberation Theology" had different iterations as Liturgical Liberation Theology in two previous publications: "Teologia Litúrgica da Libertação," in *Estudos Teológicos, Dossiê: Decolonialidade E Práticas Religiosas* 58, no. 2 (2018): 338-355, Programa de Pós-Graduação em Teologia, Escola Superior de Teologia, São Leopoldo, Brazil. / "Liturgische Befreiungstheologie," in *Called to Worship - Freed to Respond,* ed. Dorothea Haspelmath-Finatti (München: Gütersloher Verlagshaus, 2019), 90-110. Beiträge aus der international en Liturgischen Theologie zum Zusammenhang von Gottesdienst und Ethik, Gütersloher Verlagshaus, Gütersloh 2019. Both publishers kindly granted their permission.

2. Ivone Gebara, *Teologia ecofeminista: ensaio para repensar o conhecimento e a religião* (São Paulo: Olho D'Agua, 1997), 124. "Graças a Deus, choveu no sertão. Graças a Deus, o milho brotou. Graças a Deus, o gado não morreu. Graças a Deus, estou curada. Deus, como chuva, milho, gado vivendo, cura... Deus, como esmola, ajuda, pão. Deus, como pedindo em mim, pedinte nos outros (as). Deus, como comida. Deus, como carência, sem omnipotência nem ciência... Deus, como trabalho, casa, companheiro... quebra minha solidão, grita comigo, suspira comigo, busca comigo."

3. Ignacio Ellacuría, "Liturgia y liberación," in *Escritos teológicos IV* (El Salvador: UCA Editores, 2002), 31.

4. Dietrich Bonhoeffer, *Letters and Papers from Prison,* ed. Eberhard Bethge (London: Folio Society, 2000), 16.

5. Edward Said, *Representations of the Intellectual* (New York: Vintage, 2012), 35, 113.

6. Don E. Saliers, "Afterword: Liturgy and Ethics Revisited," in *Liturgy and the moral self: humanity at full stretch before God: essays in honor of Don E. Saliers,* eds. E. Byron Anderson and Bruce T. Morrill (Collegeville, Minnesota: The Liturgical Press, 1998), 214.

7. José Comblin, *Introdução geral ao Comentário Biblico: Leitura da Bíblia na perspectiva dos pobres* (Petrópolis: Vozes, Imprensa Metodista e Editora Sinodal, 1985), 15.

8. Jonathan Z. Smith, *To Take Place: Toward Theory in Ritual* (Chicago: University of Chicago Press, 1992), 103.

9. Michel de Certeau, *The Practice of Everyday Life* (Berkeley: University of California Press, 2011), 117.

10. Bryan D. Spinks, "Imagining the Past: Historical Methodologies and Liturgical Study," in *Liturgy's Imagined Past/s: Methodologies and Materials in the Writing of Liturgical History Today*, ed. Teresa Berger and Bryan D. Spinks (Collegeville, MN: Liturgical Press, 2016), 6-7.

11. Graham Harvey, *Animism: Respecting the Living World*, 2nd ed. (London: C Hurst & Co, 2017), 32.

12. Nathan D. Mitchell, *Meeting Mystery: Liturgy, Worship, Sacraments* (Maryknoll, NY: Orbis Books, 2006), xiv, 14.

13. Ronald L. Grimes, *Reading, Writing, and Ritualizing: Ritual in Fictive, Liturgical and Public Places* (Washington DC: The Pastoral Press, 1993), 52.

14. Martin D. Jean, "Foreword," in *Liturgy's Imagined Past/s: Methodologies and Materials in the Writing of Liturgical History Today*, ed. Teresa Berger and Bryan D. Spinks (Collegeville, MN: Liturgical Press, 2016), x.

15. In all the syllabi on liturgical theology courses I checked, the bibliography used was basically made of the same white male liturgical theologians, with the exception of Teresa Berger and few others. We surely need a new bibliography for the field that includes, along with the traditional ones, the work of Jaci C. Maraschin, Julio de Santa Ana, Leonardo Boff, Scott Haldeman, Kristine Suna-Koro, Tissa Balasuriya, Jay Emerson Johnson, Dorothy Beatrice Claudette McDougall, Tércio Bretanha Junker, Siobhán Garrigan, Marianne Moyaert, Gerald Liu, and others.

16. Willie James Jennings, After Whiteness: An Education in Belonging (Grand Rapids: Eerdmans, 2020), 10.

17. Gustavo Gutierrez, *A Theology of Liberation: History, Politics, and Salvation* (New York: Orbis Books: 1973), 167.

18. Gutierrez, *A Theology of Liberation*, 171.

19. Eduardo Viveiros de Castro, interview with Eliane Brum, "Diálogos sobre o fim do mundo," *El País*, 10/29/2014, https://brasil.elpais.com/brasil/2014/09/29/opinion/1412000283_365191.amp.html?fbclid=IwAR2UzGFHENEID4ooQsV8VU5ZvOUXgpMdZJITBdG6wF9GjYtGe5cnG13X5mg.

20. Vladimir Safatle, "Another Kratos for the Demos," https://www.academia.edu/36864867/Another_Kratos_for_the_demos, (accessed July 3, 2021).

21. Safatle, "Another Kratos for the Demos."

22. Isabelle Stengers, "Autonomy and the Intrusion of Gaia," *South Atlantic Quarterly* 116, no. 2 (2017): 398, https://doi.org/10.1215/00382876-3829467.

23. Marisol de la Cadena and Mario Blaser, eds., *A World of Many Worlds* (Durham, NC: Duke University Press, 2018).

24. Cf. John 10:10.

25. Edward Said, *Orientalism* (New York: Vintage Books, 1978), 25.

26. Boaventura de Sousa Santos, *Epistemologies of the South: Justice Against Epistemicide* (London: Routledge, 2014).

27. Enrique Dussel, "Anti-Cartesian Meditations: On the Origen of the Philosophical Anti-Discourse of Modernity," *Journal for Cultural and Religious Theory* (January 13, 2014): 11-53, https://jcrt.org/archives/13.1/dussel.pdf.

28. Ramón Grosfoguel, "The Structure of Knowledge in Westernized Universities: Epistemic Racism/Sexism and the Four Genocides/Epistemicides of the Long 16th Century," *Human Architecture: Journal of the Sociology of Self-Knowledge* 11, no. 1 (Fall, 2013): 73.

29. Gloria Anzaldúa, *Borderlands / La Frontera: The New Mestiza* (San Francisco: Aunt Lute Books, 1987).

30. Desmond Tutu, *No Future Without Forgiveness* (New York: The Crown Publishing Group, 1999), 31, Kindle.

31. I am still wrestling with this incredible concept. I read several interpretations of it and here is one that helps: McKenzie Wark, *Eduardo Viveiros de Castro: In and Against the Human,* https://www.versobooks.com/blogs/3265-eduardo-viveiros-de-castro-in-and-against-the-human.

32. de Castro, *Cannibal Metaphysics,* 63.

33. For more information see Nancy Cardoso and Cláudio Carvalhaes, "African-Indigenous Jurema: The Greatest Common Divisor of The Brazilian Minimum Religion," *CrossCurrents* 67, no. 1 (March 2017): 86. Also reprinted with permission in chapter 14 of this book.

34. Cardoso and Carvalhaes, "African-Indigenous Jurema."

35. Michelle Gonçalves Rodrigues and Roberta Nivar Carneiro Campos, "Caminhos da visibilidade: a ascensão do culto a jurema no campo religioso de

Recife," *Afro-Ásia* 47 (2013): 271, http://dx.doi.org/10.1590/S0002-05912013000100008.

36. Every time I use the term "patch of land" I am referring to the ways Anna Tsing, Andrew S. Mathews and Nils Bubandt use it. "Patchy Anthropocene" is a conceptual tool for noticing landscape structure, with special attention to what we call "modular simplifications" and "feral proliferations." Anna Lowenhaupt Tsing, Andrew S. Matthews and Nils Bubandt, "Patchy Anthropocene: Landscape Structure, Multispecies History, and the Retooling of Anthropology: An Introduction to Supplement 20," *Current Anthropology* 60, no. 20 (August 2019), https://www.journals.uchicago.edu/doi/full/10.1086/703391.

37. Eduardo Viveiros de Castro used this phrase in one of his lectures.

38. Pedro Casaldáliga, "Pobreza Evangélica" in *Antología Personal* (Madrid: Editorial Trotta, S.A, 2006), 35.

39. Aimé Césaire, *Discourse on Colonialism*, trans. Joan Pinkham (New York and London: Monthly Review Press, 1972), 3.

40. Alfredo Bosi, *Dialética da Colonização* (São Paulo: Companhia das Letras, 1992), 16.

41. Marc Ellis, *Facebook posts*, April 2016, https://www.facebook.com/marc.ellis.1291.

42. Ellis' claim points to the ease with which religious people perform their rituals without fully considering the suffering of oppressed people--or rather, despite the suffering of the people. In his words: "On Passover, once my favorite holiday. My passion for Passover left years ago. How to celebrate my/our liberation when we are permanently oppressing another people? Can't be done. No way. My attempt last year? Passover for Palestine."

43. Cláudio Carvalhaes, Introduction to *Da Leveza e da Beleza — Liturgia na pós-modernidade*, by Jaci Maraschin (São Paulo: ASTE, 2010).

44. Júlio de Santa Ana, *Pão, Vinho e Amizade: Meditações* (São Paulo, CEDI, 1986).

45. From these sources and many others, I have attempted to develop, in the North of the globe, a liturgical liberation theology. See Cláudio Carvalhaes, *Sacraments and Globalization: Redrawing the Borders of Eucharistic Hospitality* (Oregon: Wipf & Stock, Pickwick Publications, 2013) and *What Does Worship Have to Do with It? Interpreting Life Liturgically* (Oregon: Cascade Books, 2018).

46. Nathan D. Mitchell, *Meeting Mystery: Liturgy, Worship, Sacraments* (New York: Orbis, 2006), 37, 150, 185.

47. Jonathan Z. Smith, "Religion, Religions, Religious," in *Critical Terms for Religious Studies*, ed. Mark C. Taylor (Chicago: The University of Chicago Press, 1998), 269-284. This notion expands from Jonathan Z. Smith's notion of religion as that which binds people.

48. Ellacuría, "Liturgia y liberación," 31.

49. Catherine Bell, *Ritual Theory, Ritual Practice* (Oxford: Oxford University Press, 2009), 3.

50. Aidan Kavanagh, *On Liturgical Theology* (Collegeville: A Pueblo Book, 1992), 73-74.

51. Richard Schechner, *Performance Studies: An Introduction* (New York: Routledge, 2013), 28.

52. Bernd Wannesnwetsch, *Political Worship*, trans. Margaret Kohl (New York: Oxford University Press Inc., 2004), 5.

53. Júlio Cézar Adam, "Liturgia como prática dos pés. A Romaria da Terra do Paraná: reapropriação de ritos litúrgicos na busca e libertação dos espaços de vida," *Sinodal Ciências Humanas e Sociais* (2011).

54. Mitchell, *Meeting Mystery*, 2006, xiii.

55. Sunder John Boopalan, *Memory, Grief and Agency: A political Theological Account of Wrongs and Rites* (Switzerland: Palgrave Macmillan, 2017).

56. Dave Fagerberg, "Liturgy, Social Justice and the Mystical Body of Christ," in *Liturgy and Empire: Faith in Exile and Political Theology*, ed. Scott W. Hahn and David Scott (Steubenville, OH: Emmaus Road Publishing, 2009), 207. It is said that Aidan Kavanagh said this line in several of his classes.

57. Otto Maduro, *Maps for a Fiesta: A Latina/o Perspective on Knowledge and the Global Crisis* (New York: Fordham University Press, 2015).

58. Larry L. Rasmussen, *Earth-honoring Faith: Religious Ethics in a New Key* (Oxford: Oxford Press, 2015).

59. Natalia Lafourcade and Leonel García, "Hasta la Raíz," with the International Committee of the Red Cross (ICRC) and Playing for Change, 2020, https://www.youtube.com/watch?v=cUaKBGnn2DQ.

60. Cláudio Carvalhaes, "Theopoetics in Revolution: The Life of Ernesto Cardenal," *The Bias Magazine: The Voice of the Christian Left*, (March 12, 2020),

https://christiansocialism.com/ernesto-cardenal-liberation-theology-revolution-poetry/?fbclid=IwAR1_SuFNYIs7IkExhkvtunOSJ3UKdGwLmOynbwFhxsRCu_JZea9gbHBdmQU

61. Walter Benjamin, "Theses on the Philosophy of History," in *Illuminations: Essays and Reflections*, ed. Hannah Arendt (New York: Harcourt, 1988), 255.

62. Ailton Krenak, *Ideias*.

63. Cláudio Carvalhaes, Introduction to *With Many Voices: Liturgies in Contexts*, ed. Viji Varghese Eapen (India: DARE, 2020). This section evolved from this introduction.

64. Pamela Copper-White, "Union Ideas: Becoming Conscious of the Unconscious," (May 2, 2016), https://www.youtube.com/watch?v=4rmTmyvSW5c&t=17s.

65. Pamela Cooper-White, "The Ritual Reason Why: Explorations of the Unconscious through Enactment and Ritual in Pastoral Psychology," *Journal of Supervision and Training in Ministry* 19 (1998-99): 69.

66. Jacques Lacan, *Écrits A Selection*, trans. Alan Sheridan (London: Routledge, 1989), 126.

67. James Cone, *The Cross and The Lynching Tree* (New York: Orbis Books, 2011).

68. Leonardo Boff, *Cry of the Earth, Cry of the Poor* (New York: Orbis Books, 1997), 156, Kindle.

69. Leonardo Boff, *Princípio-Terra: A Volta À Terra Como Pátria Comum* (São Paulo: Editora Ática, 1995), 33.

70. Ivone Gebara, *Longing for Running Water: Ecofeminism and Liberation* (Minneapolis: Fortress Press, 1999), 2312-2313, Kindle.

71. Ivone Gebara, *Longing for Running Water*, 2430-2433.

72. Leonardo Boff, "O Cristo Cósmico: Uma Espiritualidade Do Universo," blog (September 23, 2016), https://leonardoboff.org/2016/09/23/o-cristo-cosmicouma-espiritualidade-do-universo/.

73. Clodovis Boff, *Theology and Praxis: Epistemological Foundations* (New York: Orbis, 1987).

74. Antonio Donato Nobre, "Um Novo Olhar Sobre a Vida na Terra," (December 8, 2020), https://www.youtube.com/watch?v=QtQ86Yfiks0&t=217s

75. Nobre, "Um Novo Olhar."

76. Jacques Derrida, *Rogue: Two Essays of Reason* (Stanford: Stanford University Press, 2005), 152.

77. Tissa Balasuriya, *The Eucharist and Human Liberation* (Eugene, OR: Wipf & Stock, 1977), 36-37.

78. C. J. Kaunda, "'Rituals of resistance, weapons of the weak': Toward an African Pentecostal transformative Holy Communion Missiology," *Theologia Viatorum* 40, no. 2 (2016): 94.

79. Kaunda, "Rituals of resistance."

80. Virgilio P. Elizondo and Timothy M. Matovina, *Mestizo Worship: A Pastoral Approach to Liturgical Ministry* (Collegeville: Liturgical Press, 1998), 6.

81. Elizondo and Matovina, *Mestizo Worship*, 6-7.

82. Melva Wilson Costen, *African American Christian Worship*, 2nd ed. (Nashville: Abingdon Press, 2007), 22 56.

83. Costen, *African American Christian Worship*, 1-6.

84. Thich Nhat Hanh, *The Art of Living: Peace and Freedom in the Here and Now* (HarperCollins, 2017), 76, Kindle.

85. Marcella Althaus-Reid, *Indecent Theology: Theological Perversions in Sex, Gender and Politics* (New York: Routledge, 2001).

86. By "Late Style Prophetic," I mean the prophetic tradition come alive in its deconstruction and in its committed waywardness, visible wailing and solitude--as a form of dystopic solidarity." See my book *Praying with Every Heart.* for expansion on this theme.

87. Mark C, Ellis, written in his journals on Facebook.

88. Delores S. Williams, *Sisters in the Wilderness: The Challenge of Womanist God-Talk* (New York: Orbis, 2013).

89. Richard E. Wentz, Introduction to *The Solace of Fierce Landscapes: Exploring Desert and Mountain Spirituality* by Belden C. Lane (New York: Oxford University Press, 1998), i, Kindle.

90. Bruno Latour, *Reassembling the Social: An introduction to Actor-Network-Theory* (Oxford: Oxford University Press, 2005).

91. Karl Marx, *A Contribution to The Critique of the Political Economy*, 91-93, Kindle.

92. Louis Althusser, *Essays on Self-Criticism* (New York: Verso Books, 1978), 37.

93. James H. Cone, *A Black Theology of Liberation* (New York: Orbis Books, 2010), 6.

94. Balasuriya, *The Eucharist*, 160-1.

95. Althaus-Reid, *Indecent Theology*.

96. Cláudio Carvalhaes, "Oppressed Bodies Don't Have Sex: The Blind Spots of Bodily and Sexual Discourses in the Construction of Subjectivity in Latin American Theology," in *Indecent Theologians: Marcella Althaus-Reid and the Next Generation of Postcolonial Activists*, ed. Nicolás Panotto (Alameda, CA: Borderless Press, 2016).

97. Jane Bennett, *Vibrant Matter: A Political Ecology of Things* (Durham, NC: Duke University Press, 2010).

98. Sherman Alexie, Vine Deloria Jr., Winona LaDuke, Davi Kopenawa, Eduardo Viveiros de Castro, Bruno Latour, Timothy Morton, Dorothy Roberts, Naomi Klein, Larry Rasmussen, George E. Tinker, and so many others.

99. Cláudio Carvalhaes, "Lex Naturae – A New Way into a Liturgical Political Theology," in *T&T Clark Companion to Political Theology*, ed. Rubem Rosário-Rodriguez (New York: Bloomsbury T&T Clark, 2018). See a full development of the notion of *Lex Naturae* I made in this article.

100. Pierre Bourdieu, *In Other Words* (Stanford: Stanford University Press, 1990), 12-13. *Habitus*: "the conditions associated with a particular class of conditions of existence that produce habitus, system of durable, transposable dispositions, structured predisposed to function as structuring structures, that is, principles which generate and organize practices and representations that can be objectively adapted to their outcomes without presupposing a conscious aiming at ends or an express mastery of the operations necessary in order to attain them... Learned and acquired through practice, habitus is embodied history, internalized as a second nature."

101. Craig Dykstra, *Growing in the life of Faith* (Louisville: Westminster John Knox Press, 2005), 37.

102. Jan Patocka, *Heretical Essays in the Philosophy of History* (Chicago: Open Court; 1999), 131.

103. Wangari Muta Maathai, *Unbowed, A Memoir* (New York: Anchor Books, 2008).

104. Krenak, *Ideias*, 33-34.

105. Gordon W. Lathrop, *Holy Ground: A Liturgical Cosmology* (Minneapolis: Fortress Press, 2009), 2332-2333, Kindle. "Does the Christian liturgy really do all this? Does Christian assembly in Word and Sacrament gather its participants into a worldview marked by reorientation and the hole in the heavens? Does liturgical life enable an open but critical dialogue with the other cosmologies by which we live? Does it propose a set of radically reoriented maps for our ethics? No, not necessarily."

106. Mayra Rivera Rivera, *Poetics of the Flesh* (Durham: Duke University Press Books, 2015), 90.

107. Ike and Cláudio, "Lettuce and Tomato," August 10, 2020, https://www.youtube.com/watch?v=c1WY5iZPXCE.

108. Mitchell, *Meeting Mystery*, 1984, xv. As Nathan D. Mitchell says: "At the end of the day, then, a liturgical theology begins not with historical reconstruction or even with our 'experience of worship's symbols, rites and texts,' but with the sober recognition that *we don't know what we are doing.*"

109. Luiz Fernando Lobo and Tulio Mourão, directors, "Louvação à Mariama" and "Marcha Final de Banzo e Esperança" from the show "Missa dos Quilombos," set up by the Companhia Ensaio Aberto for the musical by Milton Nascimento, Pedro Casaldáliga and Pedro Tierra. The video is a fragment of the DVD directed by Luiz Fernando Lobo and Rudi Lagemann. https://www.youtube.com/watch?v=BU6oz6DRBZw.

110. Email conversation between Nancy Cardoso and the author, October 30, 2020.

Chapter Two

1. "Lex Naturae – A New Way into a Liturgical Political Theology," was first published in *T&T Clark Handbook to Political Theology*, ed. Rubem Rosário-Rodriguez (New York: Bloomsbury T&T Clark, 2019), 449-466. By kind permission of T&T Clark/Bloomsbury.

2. Francesco Gagliano, "Pedro Casaldáliga, 90 años: bispo, poeta e defensor intransigente da dignidade humana," *Revista Ihu On-Line* (January 31, 2018), http://www.ihu.unisinos.br/78-noticias/575711-pedro-casaldaliga-90-anos-bispo-poeta-e-defensor-intransigente-da-dignidade-humana

3. Eduardo Viveiros de Castro, "A revolução faz o bom tempo," April 18, 2015, https://www.youtube.com/watch?v=CjbU1jO6rmE.

4. Nancy Cardoso Pereira, "V Congresso Latino-Americano De Gênero E Religião," Faculdades EST, August 23-26, 2017, http://eventos.est.edu.br/index.php/genero/Genero.

5. Leslie Head, *Hope and Grief in the Anthropocene: re-conceptualising human-nature relations* (New York: Routledge, 2016).

6. Bruno Latour, *Facing Gaia: Eight Lectures on the New Climatic Regime* (Cambridge: Polity Press, 2017), 4, Kindle.

7. Donna Haraway, *Staying with the Trouble: Making Kin in the Chthulucene* (Durham: Duke University Press, 2016), 2.

8. Larry L. Rasmussen, *Earth-honoring Faith*, 5.

9. Larry L. Rasmussen, "Bonhoeffer and the Anthropocene," *Ned Geref Teologiese Tydskrif* 55, no. 1 (2014), https://doi.org/10.5952/55-Supp%201-677.

10. Martin Luther King, Jr., "Letter from Birmingham Jail," in *A Testament of Hope: The Essential Writings of Martin Luther King Jr.*, ed. James M. Washington (San Francisco: Harper and Row, 1996), 190.

11. Robin Kimmerer, *Braiding Sweetgrass* (Canada: Milkweed Editions, 2015), 21.

12. Pedro Casaldáliga and Vitor Westhelle, "Creation Motifs in the Search for a Vital Space: A Latin American Perspective," in *Lift Every Voice: Constructing Christian Theologies from the Underside*, ed. Susan Brooks Thistlewaite and Mary Potter Engel (New York: Orbis, 1998), 148.

13. Latour, *Facing Gaia*, 11.

14. Amitav Ghosh, "The Great Derangement: Climate Change and the Unthinkable," Union Theological Seminary, New York, March 28, 2018, https://www.youtube.com/watch?v=9eFT_eb_jRk&t=4390s.

15. A few examples of environmental artists: Subhankar Banerjee, David Buckland, and Basia Irland.

16. Marty Haugen, "Gather Us In" (Chicago: GIA Publications, Inc., 1982), hymn.

17. Octavius Minucious Feliz, "8.4;9.1-2," in *The Change of Conversion and the Origin of Christendom* by Alan Kreider (Oregon: Wipf & Stock, 2006), 11.

18. Brigitte Kahl, *Galatians Re-Imagined: Reading with the Eyes of the Vanquished* (Minneapolis: Fortress Press, 2010). Further reading on the work of Paul.

19. Wendell Berry, "How to Be a Poet," in *Given: New Poems* (Berkeley: Counterpoint Press, 2005), 18.

20. Vitor Westhelle, *Eschatology and Space: The Lost Dimension in Theology Past and Present* (New York: Palgrave Macmillan, 2012), 2.

21. Yi-Fu Tuan, *Space and Place: The Perspective of Experience* (Minneapolis: Univ. Of Minnesota Press: 2001), 3.

22. Edward Relph in "Place and Placelessness, Edward Relph" by David Seamon and Jacob Sowers, *Key Texts in Human Geography: A Reader Guide*, 2nd ed., ed. Phil Hubbard, Rob Kitchin and Gill Valentine (London: SAGE Publications Ltd, 2008), 44-45.

23. David Harvey, "Space as A Key Word," Paper for Marx and Philosophy Conference, May 29, 2004, Institute of Education, London, http://frontdeskapparatus.com/files/harvey2004.pdf.

24. Winona LaDuke, "Our Home on Earth," excerpted and updated from "Voices from White Earth: Gaa-waabaabiganikaag," the Thirteenth Annual E.F. Schumacher Lecture, given at Yale University, October 1993. The lecture is sponsored by the New Economics Institute. This essay appears in OTC's book *All That We Share: A Field Guide to the Commons.* http://www.onthecommons.org/magazine/our-home-earth#sthash.HEifPfDt.kV1CNvWd.dpbs

25. Westhelle, *Eschatology and Space*, 13.

26. Glaucia Vasconcelos Wilkey, *Worship and Culture: Foreign Country or Homeland?* (Grand Rapids: Wm. B. Eerdmans Publishing Co., 2015). Anscar Chupungco was a Filipino Benedictine monk who led the way in studying these intersections. The Protestant response was the *Nairobi Statement on Worship and Culture, The Eucharistic Liturgy of Lima* and others. Recently, there has been an engaged conversation around all these issues, honoring Chupungco and expanding the Nairobi Lutheran declaration.

27. Dietrich Bonhoeffer, "Outline for a Book," *Letters and Papers from Prison, Dietrich Bonhoeffer: His Significance for North Americans* by Larry L. Rasmussen (Minneapolis: Fortress Press, 1990), 186.

28. Eduardo Viveiros de Castro, "A revolução faz o bom tempo," April 18, 2015, https://www.youtube.com/watch?v=CjbU1jO6rmE.0

Chapter Three

1. Kimmerer, *Braiding Sweetgrass*, 29.

2. The whole poem can be found here: https://www.claudiocarvalhaes.com/blog/honeyeaters-losing-songs-prayer/

3. Jeremy Siefert, Director, *The Church Forests of Ethiopia*, uploaded February 11, 2020, https://vimeo.com/390833915.

4. Siefert, *The Church Forests of Ethiopia*.

5. Kopenawa, *The Falling Sky*, xvii.

6. Westhelle has done a great work reminding us of our forgetfulness. Vitor Westhelle, *Eschatology and Space: The Lost Dimension in Theology Past and Present* (New York: Palgrave Macmillan, 2012). Also, John Inge, rightly praised by McGrath, has a very good work on space. John Inge, *A Christian Theology of Place* (Burlington: Ashgate, 2003).

7. Alister McGrath, *Re-Imagining nature: The Promise of a Christian Natural Theology* (Malden: Wiley Blackwell, 2017), 64.

8. McGrath, *Re-Imagining nature*, 23.

9. Eduardo Viveiros de Castro, *The Relative Native: Essays on Indigenous Conceptual Worlds* (Chicago: Haul Books, 2015), 215.

10. Ivone Gebara, Leonardo Boff and others have done great work on Eco-liberation theologies. Biblicists like Milton Schwantes, Carlos Mesters, Nancy Cardoso, Odja Barros and many others, move us even deeper by focusing on a patch of land and working with the people and their land.

11. I am grateful for Moses Bollam for calling my attention to these nuances and these notions.

12. Berry, *Given*, 18.

13. Richard Schechner, *Essays on Performance Theory, 1970-1976* (New York: Drama Publishers, 1976), 114.

14. Leonardo Boff, *Cry of the Earth.*

15. Bell, *Ritual Theory,* chapter 9.

16. Bell, *Ritual Theory,* 220.

17. Adrienne Maree Brown, *Emergent Strategy: Shaping Change, Changing Worlds* (Chico, CA: AK Press, 2017), 42, Kindle. "Mycelium is the part of the fungus that grows underground in thread-like formations. It connects roots to one another and breaks down plant material to create healthier ecosystems. Mycelium is the largest organism on earth. Interconnectedness. Remediation. Detoxification."

18. Gilles Deleuze, *Logique du Sens* (Paris: Minuit, 1969), 355. English translation (2003), 306, as quoted in Eduardo Viveiros de Castro, *The Relative Native: Essays on Indigenous Conceptual Worlds* (Chicago: Haul books, 2015), 10.

19. Grimes, *Reading, Writing, and Ritualizing,* 24, 22.

20. Manuel Vasquez, *More than Belief: A Materialist Theory of Religion* (Oxford: Oxford University Press, 2010), 12.

21. Mary-Jane Rubenstein, *Pantheologies: Gods, Worlds, Monsters* (New York: Columbia University Press, 2018), 5187-5193, Kindle.

22. Ronald L. Grimes, "Performance is Currency in the Deep World's Gift Economy," in *The Handbook of Contemporary Animism,* ed. Graham Harvey (London: Routledge, 2015), 510.

23. Lisa Friedman, "Biden Administration Defends Huge Alaska Oil Drilling Project," *Los Angeles Times,* May 26, 2021, https://www.nytimes.com/2021/05/26/climate/biden-alaska-drilling.html?fbclid=IwAR0iavbEuSZM6PYKCx0fYKNkAg1KaL4Xpm29fQR YkpG5gYnSy9xjMetYxFA "The administration says the country must pivot away from fossil fuels but backed a project set to produce more than 100,000 barrels of oil each day for 30 years."

24. Barack Obama, "President Obama Speaks on Expanding Oil and Gas Pipelines," March 22, 2012, https://www.youtube.com/watch?v=YxkODM6lzUk.

25. Lynn Margulis, *Symbiotic Earth,* dir. John Feldman, Hummingbird Films, 2019, Documentary.

26. Ronald Reagan "I'm from the Government and I'm here to help." (August 12, 1986), "President Ronald Reagan Quote "I'm from the Government and I'm here to help." (Uploaded December 31, 2020), https://www.youtube.com/watch?v=nCedOQJoZEA.

27. Marcia Bjornerud, *Timefulness* (Princeton: Princeton University Press, 2018), 7, 17, Kindle.

28. Donna Haraway, *Simians, Cyborgs, and Women: The Reinvention of Nature* (New York: Routledge, 1990).

29. Bruno Latour, *Critical Zones: The Science and Politics of Landing on Earth*, ed. Bruno Latour and Peter Weibel (Cambridge and London: ZKM and MIT Press, 2020), 13.

30. Donna J. Haraway, *Staying with the Trouble*.

31. Rubenstein, *Pantheologies*, 5237-5272.

32. Rubenstein, *Pantheologies*, 5295.

33. Smith, *To Take Place*, 103.

34. Kimmerer, *Braiding Sweetgrass*, 31.

35. Barbara Kingsolver, *Animal, Vegetable, Miracle: A Year of Food Life* (New York: Harper, 2007). A good example of these small and big changes can be seen in an experience Barbara Kingsolver did with her family for a year.

36. Latour, *Critical Zones*, 15.

37. Haraway, *Staying with the Trouble*, chapter 5.

38. Kimmerer, *Braiding Sweetgrass*, 376-377.

39. Kimmerer, *Braiding Sweetgrass*, 380-382.

40. Kimmerer, *Braiding Sweetgrass*, 328.

41. Grimes, "Performance is Currency."

42. Haraway, *Staying with the Trouble*, 2, 5, 10.

43. Winona LaDuke, *How to Be a Water Protector: The Rise of the Wiindigoo Slayers* (Nova Scotia: Fernwood Publishing, 2020).

44. Tyson Yunkaporta, *Sand Talk: How Indigenous Thinking Can Save the World* (Sydney: HarperOne, 2020), 245-246, 269-272, Kindle.

45. Yunkaporta, *Sand Talk:* 245-246, 269-272.

46. Rasmussen, *Earth-honoring Faith.*

47. de Castro, *The Relative Native,* 213.

48. Haraway, *Staying with the Trouble,* 12.

49. Haraway, *Staying with the Trouble,* 13.

50. Ronald L. Grimes, "Ritual theory and the environment," in *Nature Performed: Environment, Culture and Performance* ed. Wallace Heim, Bronislaw Szerszynski, and Claire Waterton (Oxford; Malden, MA: Blackwell Pub./Sociological Review, 2003), 44.

51. Haraway, *Staying with the Trouble,* 13.

52. Haraway, *Staying with the Trouble,* 12.

53. Brown, *Emergent Strategy,* 3.

54. Brown, *Emergent Strategy,* 13.

55. This notion comes from a Brazilian song called "Bola de Meia, Bola de Gude," from Milton Nascimento.

56. Grimes, "Performance is Currency," 508.

57. Déborah Danowski and Eduardo Viveiros de Castro, *The Ends of the World* (Maldem: Polity Press. 2017), 2112–2116, Kindle.

58. Grimes, "Performance is Currency," 510.

59. Cláudio Carvalhaes, "Why I Created a Chapel Service Where People Confess to Plants," *Sojourners,* blog, September 26, 2109, https://sojo.net/articles/why-i-created-chapel-service-where-people-confess-plants

Chapter Four

1. "Worship, Liturgy and Public Witness" was first published in *Companion on Public Theology,* ed. Katie Day and Sebastian Kim (Boston, MA: Brill, 2017), 466–486. By kind permission of Brill.

2. J.M.R. Tillard, *Flesh of the Church, Flesh of Christ: At the Source of the Ecclesiology of Communion* (Collegeville, MN: Pueblo Books, 2001), 28.

3. Cláudio Carvalhaes, "Eucharist and Hospitality and the Early Christian Meals." in *Eucharist and Globalization: Redrawing the Borders of Eucharistic Hospitality* (Eugene, OR: Pickwick Publications, 2013).

4. Michel Foucault, *The history of sexuality Volume 1: An Introduction* (New York: Vintage Books, 1978), 56-58. "Western societies have established the confession as one of the main rituals we rely on for the production of truth…(a) continuous incitement to discourse and to truth… that helped to give the confession a central role in the order of civil and religious powers."

5. Christopher Elwood, *The Body Broken: The Calvinist Doctrine of the Eucharist and the Symbolization of Power in Sixteenth–Century France* (New York: Oxford University Press, 1999). See this book for a wonderful take on the resignification of the Body of Christ during Reformation.

6. Carvalhaes, *Eucharist and Globalization*, 2033, Kindle.

7. The first question and answer of the Westminster Catechism is this: "What is the chief and highest end of man? Answer: Man's chief and highest end is to glorify God, and fully to enjoy him forever [sic]".

8. David Tracy, *The Analogical Imagination: Christian Theology and the Culture of Pluralism* (New York: Crossroad Publishing Company, 1981), 5.

9. Alonso Gonçalves, "Teologia Pública: entre a construção e a possibilidade prática de um discurso," *Ciberteologia, Revista de Teologia e Cultura* 8, no. 38 (August 1, 2015): 63-76, https://www.otroscruces.org/essential_grid/teologia-y-espacio-publico-segunda-edicion/.

10. Nicolás Panotto, *Teologia Y Espaço Público*, (Ciudad Autónoma de Buenos Aires: GEMRIP Ediciones, 2015). https://www.academia.edu/10964644/Teolog%C3%ADa_y_espacio_p%C3%BAblico_Libro_?

11. Nancy Cardoso Pereira, personal conversation through e-mails with the author.

12. Cláudio Carvalhaes, "In Spirit and in Truth: The Liturgical Space as Territory," in *Common Worship in Theological Education*, ed. Siobhan Garrigan and Todd E. Johnson (Eugene, OR: Wipf & Stock Publishers, 2009).

13. Jaci Maraschin, "Libertação da Liturgia," in *A Beleza da Santidade Ensaios de Liturgia* (São Paulo: ASTE, 1996), 133, 138.

14. Luke 12:51-53, *Holy Bible* (NRSV). "I have a baptism with which to be baptized, and what stress I am under until it is completed! Do you think that I have come to bring peace to the earth? No, I tell you, but rather division! From now on, five in one household will be divided, three against two and two against three; they will be divided: father against son and son against father, mother against daughter, and daughter against mother, mother-in-law against her daughter-in-law and daughter-in-law against mother-in-law.'"

15. Soren Kierkegaard, *Works of Love*, (New York: Harper & Row, 1962), 114.

16. Edward W. Soja, *Thirdspace* (Malden: Blackwell, 1996), 57, 61.

17. Henri Lefebvre, *The Production of Space* (Malden: Wiley-Blackwell, 1992).

18. Homi K. Bhabha, *The Location of Culture* (New York: Routledge, 2004).

19. Gloria E. Anzaldúa, "(Un)natural Bridges, (Un)safe Spaces," Preface *to this bridge we call home*, ed. Gloria E. Anzaldúa and AnaLouise Keating (New York: Routledge, 2002), 1.

20. *The Epistle of Mathetes to Diognetus*, Chapter 5 https://www.scriptural-truth.com/PDF_Apocrypha/The%20Epistle%20of%20Mathetes%20to%20Diognetus.pdf.

21. Mitchell, *Meeting Mystery*.

22. Flávio Irala and Elsa Tamez, "Venham, celebremos a Ceia do Senhor - Convite ao compromisso," June 26, 1983, IECLB, visited the site on August 26, 2015, http://www.luteranos.com.br/conteudo/venham-celebremos-a-ceia-do-senhor-convite-ao-compromisso

Chapter Five

1. "From Multiculturalisms to Multinaturalisms: Liturgical Theological Shifts" was first published as "Theological Shifts: From Multiculturalisms to Multinaturalisms," in *Vulnerability and Resilience: Body and Liberating Theologies*, ed. Jione Havea (Lanham, MD: Lexington & Fortress Academic Press, 2020), 159-172. By kind permission of Lexington & Fortress Academic Press. All rights reserved.

2. Michel Foucault, *Power/Knowledge. Select Interviews and Other Writings, 1972-1977*, ed. Colin Gordon (New York: Pantheon Books, 1988), 81.

3. Danowski and de Castro, *The Ends of the World*, 28.

4. Westhelle, *Eschatology and Space*, xiv-xv.

5. H. Richard Niebuhr, *Christ and Culture* (New York: Harper & Row, 1975).

6. Sandra Maria Van Opstal, *The Next Worship: Glorifying God in a Diverse World* (Westmont: IVP books, Intervarsity Press, 2016); Eunjoo Mary Kim, *Christian Preaching and Worship in Multicultural Contexts: A Practical Theological Approach* (Collegeville: Liturgical Press, 2017); Brian K. Blount and Leonora Tubbs Tisdale, *Making Room at the Table: An Invitation to Multicultural Worship* (Louisville: Westminster John Knox Press, 2000).

7. *Nairobi Statement of Worship and Culture*, The Lutheran World Federation. https://worship.calvin.edu/resources/resource-library/nairobi-statement-on-worship-and-culture-full-text

8. Eduardo Viveiros de Castro, "Cosmological Deixis and Amerindian Perspectivism," *The Journal of the Royal Anthropological Institute* 4, no. 3 (1998): 473, http://www.jstor.org/stable/3034157, accessed: June 11, 2017.

9. de Castro, "Cosmological Deixis," 470.

10. Eduardo Viveiros de Castro, "Perspectivismo e multinaturalismo na América indígena," *O que nos faz pensar* 18 (September 2000): 239, http://oquenosfazpensar.fil.puc-rio.br/import/pdf_articles/OQNFP_18_13_eduardo_viveiros_de_castro.pdf, accessed November 6, 2017.

11. Eduardo Viveiros de Castro, "Perspectival Anthropology and the Method of Controlled Equivocation," *Tipití: Journal of the Society for the Anthropology of Lowland South America* 2, no.1 (June 1, 2004): 6, http://digitalcommons.trinity.edu/cgi/viewcontent.cgi?article=1010&context=tipiti accessed November 6, 2017.

12. Nancy Cardoso Pereira, "Da agropornografia à agroecologia: uma aproximação queer contra as elites vegetais," in *História, saúde e direitos: sabores e saberes do IV Congresso Latino-Americano de Gênero e Religião*, ed. André Musskopf and Márcia Blasi (São Leopoldo, RS: CEBI, 2016), 35-41.

13. https://www.merriam-webster.com/dictionary/cult.

14. Jaci Maraschin, *"The Transient Body: Sensibility and Spirituality,"* paper presented at the event "Liturgy and Body," Union Theological Seminary, New York, October 20, 2003.

15. Leonardo Boff, *Essential Care: An Ethics of Human Nature*, trans. and notes by Alexandre Guilherme (Waco: Baylor University Press, 2008), 138-39.

16. Rasmussen, *Earth-honoring Faith.*

Chapter Six

1. "The Christian as Humus: Virtual/Real Earthly Rituals of Ourselves," was first published in *Liturgy* 35, no. 4 (2020): 25-33. By kind permission of The Liturgical Conference. All rights reserved.

2. James Baldwin, *I Am Not Your Negro* (New York: Vintage International, 2017), 47, Kindle.

3. Louis-Marie Chauvet, *Symbol and Sacrament: Sacramental Reinterpretation of Christian Existence*, trans. Madeleine M. Beaumont and Patrick Madigan, SJ (Collegeville, MN: Liturgical Press, 2018), 328.

4. Balasuriya, *The Eucharist and Human Liberation*, 2.

5. See Don E. Saliers, "Liturgy and Ethics: Some New Beginnings" and "Afterword: Liturgy and Ethics Revisited," in *Liturgy and the Moral Self: Humanity at Full Stretch Before God*, ed. E. Byron Anderson and Bruce T. Morrill (Minnesota: Pueblo Books, 1998), 15-37 and 209-224, respectively; for including nature in this movement of *lexes*, see Cláudio Carvalhaes, "Lex Naturae: A New Way into a Liturgical Political Theology," in *T&T Clark Handbook to Political Theology*, ed. Rubem Rosário-Rodriguez (London: T&T Clark, Bloomsbury Publishing, 2019).

6. Leonardo Boff, *Sacraments of Life: Life of the Sacraments* (Washington, DC: Pastoral Press, 1987).

7. Walter Benjamin, *Understanding Brecht*, trans. Anna Bostock (New York: Verso Books, 2003), 1.

8. Cláudio Carvalhaes, "Liturgical Liberation Theology," Liturgical Conference Hildesheim, Germany, August 27-29, 2018.

9. Jason Byassee, "Maybe the body of Christ has always been both virtual and physical," blog, *Faith and Leadership*, March 2, 2011, https://faithandleadership.com/jason-byassee-virtual-theological-education. See also Deanna A. Thompson, "Christ is Really Present Virtually: A Proposal for Virtual Communion," blog, Lutheran Center for Faith, Values, and Community, March 26, 2020, https://wp.stolaf.edu/lutherancenter/2020/03/christ-is-really-

present-virtually-a-proposal-for-virtual-
communion/?fbclid=IwAR2UMm0coKFJgJvI_cg8bFKBUKNeoJRMsX5Dvfgll
RhyMrda2bxFobe7iYg.

10. Linda Gibler, *From the Beginning to Baptism: Scientific and Sacred Stories of Water, Oil and Fire* (Collegeville: Liturgical Press, 2010), 24.

11. Extractivism is the economy looking at the earth as profit, without any sense of life and dignity. Extractivism extracts fossil fuels, metals, minerals, from the sol, creates dams, turns forests into pastures, depletes the oceans from its inhabitants, removes mountain top, and so on. The processes of extractivism take away what some call "natural resources" from the Earth in order to make all sot of things and make money out of it destroying vast preserved lands of Indigenous people and wildlife. This form of relation with the earth sees the earth only as resources for our desires and not as a living organism that needs to be respected and lived with in reciprocity and mutual care.

12. James Lovelock, *The Revenge of Gaia* (New York: Penguin Books, 2007), 20. "We have to think of Gaia as the whole system of animate and inanimate parts. The burgeoning growth of living things enabled by sunlight empowers Gaia, but this wild chaotic power is bridled by constraints which shape the goal-seeking entity that regulates itself on life's behalf."

13. Latour, *Facing Gaia.*

14. Isabelle Stengers, *In Catastrophic Times: Resisting the Coming Barbarism* (London: Open Humanities Press, 2015), Chap. 4.

15. Sallie McFague, *The Body of God: An Ecological Theology* (Minneapolis: Fortress Press, 1993).

16. Gilberto Gil, "Amarra O Teu Arado A Uma Estrela," *O eterno Deus Mu dança* (Rio de Janeiro: Warner Music Brasil, 1989), CD.

Chapter Seven

1. "Class, Interreligious Borders and Ways of Living with Pachamama," was first published in *Faith(s) Seeking Justice: Dialogue and Liberation*, ed. Peniel Jesudason Rufus Rajkumar (Geneva: WCC, 2021), 220-239. All rights reserved.

2. Danowski and de Castro, *The Ends of the World.*

3. Karl Marx and Friedrich Engels, "Teses sobre Feuerbach," *A Ideologia Alemã* (São Paulo: Martins Fontes, 2001), 103. "Die Philosophen haben die Welt nur verschinden interpretiert: es kömmt drauf an, sie zu *verändern.*"

4. Joerg Rieger, *Religion, Theology, and Class: Fresh Engagements after Long Silence* (London: Palgrave Macmillan, 2013), 3.

5. Stengers, "Autonomy and the Intrusion of Gaia," 381.

6. Fredric Jameson, "Future City," *New Left Review* 21 (May/June 2003): 76.

7. *Abya Yala* is a name some Indigenous people from the Americas call the earth.

8. Althusser, *On the Reproduction of Capitalism.*

9. Alan Strathern, *Unearthly Powers: Interreligious Dialogue and the Whole World* (Cambridge: Cambridge University Press, 2019).

10. Marilena Chauí, "Crise do neoliberalismo tem como resposta o autoritarismo," Brasil de Fato, October 16, 2109, video, https://www.youtube.com/watch?v=ZYZqqwQjGws.

11. Intan Suwandi, *Value Chains, The New Imperialism* (New York: Monthly Review Press, 2019), 13.

12. "30-40 Million People in America Could Be Evicted from Their Homes by the End of 2020," National Low Income Housing Coalition, Aug 7, 2020, https://nlihc.org/news/30-40-million-people-america-could-be-evicted-their-homes-end-2020.

13. David Harvey in Raju Das, "David Harvey's Theory of Accumulation by Dispossession: A Marxist Critique," *World Review of Political Economy* 8, no. 4 (Winter 2017): 591-592.

14. Suwandi, *Value Chains*, 17.

15. Tony Norfield, *The City: London and the Global Power of Finance* (New York: Verso, 2016), 5.

16. Marc H. Ellis, *Beyond Innocence & Redemption: Confronting the Holocaust and Israeli Power: Creating a Moral Future for the Jewish People* (Oregon: Wipf & Stock, 2016), 95.

17. Ellis, *Beyond Innocence*, 102.

18. Brant Rosen, "A Prayer for Yom Hashoah," posted April 8, 2013, https://ynefesh.com/2013/04/08/a-prayer-for-yom-hashoah/.

19. Stengers, "Autonomy and the Intrusion of Gaia," 381.

20. Danowski and de Castro, *The Ends of the World*, 718.

21. Danowski and de Castro, *The Ends of the World*, 682.

22. Laurel Schneider, "Promiscuous Incarnation," in *The Embrace of Eros: Bodies, Desires, and Sexuality in Christianity*, ed. by Margaret Kamitsuka (Minneapolis: Fortress, 2010).

23. Nancy Cardoso and Cláudio Carvalhaes, "Jurema african-indigenous - the greatest common divisor of the Brazilian minimum religion," *CrossCurrents Journal* 67, no. 1, (March 2017).

Chapter Eight

1. "Birds, People, Then Religion—An Eco-Liberation Theological and Pedagogical Approach to Interreligious Rituals," was first published in the *Journal of Interreligious Studies* 21 (September 2017): 3-12. It is found here: https://irstudies.org/index.php/jirs/article/view/271)

2. Dom Helder Câmara, *Utopias Peregrinas* (Pernambuco: Editora UFPE, 2014), 107.

3. Karl Rahner, *Theological Investigations Vol. 14*, trans. David Bourke (London: Darton, Longman & Todd, 1976), 283.

4. Miguel A. De La Torre, editor, *The Hope of Liberation in World Religions* (Waco: Baylor University Press, 2008).

5. James H. Cone, *Black Theology & Black Power* (New York: Orbis Books, 1997), 120.

6. Linda E. Thomas, "The Social Sciences and Rituals of Resilience in African and African American Communities," in *The Cambridge Companion to Black Theology*, ed. Dwight N. Hopkins and Edward P. Antonio (Cambridge: Cambridge University Press, 2012), 46.

7. Peter McLaren, *Pedagogy of Insurrection, From Insurrection to Revolution* (New York: Peter Lang, 2015), 13.

8. Marc Ellis, Facebook posts, April 2016, https://www.facebook.com/marc.ellis.1291

9. Ali Quli Qara'l, *The Qu'ran, with a Phrase by Phrase Translation* (London: Islamic College for Advanced Studies; 2004).

10. Venerable Dr. Balangoda Ananda Maitreya, Mahanayaka Thera Abhidhaja Maharatthaguru, Aggamaha Pandita DLitt D Litt, and Jayasili, "The Discourse on Loving Kindness (Mettâ Sutta, Sutta Pitaka)," in *Introducing Buddhism*, trans. H.J. Russell-Williams and The Buddhist Group of Kendai (Theravnâda) (London: The Buddhist Society, 2003), 26.

11. *Our Declaration*, Muslim Reform Movement: A Global Coalition of Muslim Reformers, December 4, 2015, https://muslimreformmovement.org/first-page-posts/personal-marketer/

12. Marianne Moyaert, "Introduction: Exploring the Phenomenon of Interreligious Ritual Participation," in *Ritual Participation and Interreligious Dialogue: Boundaries, Transgressions and Innovations*, ed. Marianne Moyaert and Joris Geldhof (New York: Bloomsbury Publishing, 2015), 1, Kindle.

13. Walter D. Mignolo, "Epistemic Disobedience, Independent Thought and De-Colonial Freedom," *Theory, Culture & Society* 26, no. 7-8 (2009): 3, https://journals.sagepub.com/doi/pdf/10.1177/0263276409349275. Italics mine: "The de-colonial path has one thing in common: *the colonial wound*, the fact that regions and people around the world have been classified as underdeveloped economically and mentally."

14. de Castro, *The Relative Native*.

15. Natalia Toledo, Nación Zapoteca, México, "La Realidad," at XII International Poetry Festival of Medellín in 2002, https://www.youtube.com/watch?v=PcKlFJQ-q6g.

Chapter Nine

1. "White Reasoning and Worship Methodology," was first published as "What Is Common About Our Common Worship? A Methodological Critique of White Reasoning in the Process of Renewal of the Book of Common Worship, Presbyterian Church U.S.A." in Cláudio Carvalhaes, *Praying with Every Heart: Orienting Our Lives to the Wholeness of the World* (Oregon: Wipf & Stock, 2021). Used by permission of Wipf & Stock Publishers, www.wipfandstock.com All rights reserved.

2. The structure of this essay is somewhat strange. It hopes to show the reasoning that often undergirds and orders the ways of thinking and ordering liturgy and worship in Christian churches. Books of common worship are markers of this form of liturgical reasoning, often an unmarked white form of reasoning. But what is this white liturgical reasoning? To answer that, I will show the process of renewal of the *Book of Common Worship* of the Presbyterian

Church, (U.S.A.), the denomination of which I am a member and in which I am an ordained minister—as much as it might not look like it, this work is a work of love. I was invited to be a part of this process. As I describe the movement of renewal of this prayer book, I show some of its very problematic core issues, which is what constitutes white liturgical reasoning. Once I get to that point, I make a detour to show how a white reasoning was historically created and how it functions. Once this detour is made, I go back to the renewal process of the book of common prayer and wrestle with the very notion of the "common" in this book. As I finish it, working with an expanded sense of *leitourgia*/liturgy, I end with an example of how to think the season of Pentecost not from a white universal liturgical reasoning but from a historical situation. The death of George Floyd defines the season and where we should align ourselves as Christians.

3. Presbyterian Church (U.S.A.), *Book of Common Worship*, (Louisville: Westminster John Knox, 2018).

4. In September of 2015, a group of mostly white people, mostly men, leaders, and liturgy experts in the PCUSA and liturgical experts from other denominations, gathered at McCormick Theological Seminary in Chicago to continue the process of the renewal of the *Book of Common Worship*. This was not a decision-making group but a consultant gathering asking a variety of people to offer their wisdom to the people of the church who were leading the renewal. I had hoped to speak this at the meeting, but time constraints did not allow me to do so. I continue to believe that if we fail to attend to this concern, we will have failed our call and our people.

5. Lathrop, *Holy Things*.

6. Benjamin, "Theses on the Philosophy of History."

7. Roberto Gomes, *A Crítica da Razão Tupiniquim* (CRIAR, 2001).

8. Achille Mbembe, *Critique of Black Reason*, trans. Laurent Dubois (Durham: Duke University Press, 2017).

9. de Sousa Santos, *Epistemologies of the South*.

10. Denigrate: "If you "denigrate" someone, you attempt to blacken their reputation, with "blacken" here in its commonly accepted pejorative meaning. It makes sense, therefore, that "denigrate" can be traced back to the Latin verb *denigrare*, meaning "to blacken." When "denigrate" was first used in English in the sixteenth century, it was meant to cast aspersions on someone's character or reputation. Eventually, it developed a second sense of "to make black" ("factory smoke denigrated the sky"), but this sense is somewhat rare in modern usage. Nowadays, of course, "denigrate" can also refer to belittling the worth or

importance of someone or something." https://www.merriam-webster.com/dictionary/denigrate.

11. Mbembe, *Critique of Black Reason*, 842, 850.

12. Mbembe, *Critique of Black Reason*, 2266.

13. Maraschin, *A Beleza da Santidade*, 133–38. Emphasis mine. My translation.

14. Ruth A. Meyers, *Missional Worship, Worshipful Mission: Gathering as God's People, Going Out in God's Name* (Grand Rapids: Eerdmans, 2014), 672–73, Kindle.

15. David Daniels, class lecture at McCormick Theological Seminary in Chicago for "Worship and the Arts"

16. Daniels, "Worship and the Arts."

17. Daniels, "Worship and the Arts."

18. Daniels, "Worship and the Arts."

19. I write this in the living memory of George Floyd and João Pedro and all the Black people across the world who are killed daily by white supremacy, simply for being Black. *¡PRESENTE!*

20. Jonathan Ponciano, "The World's 25 Richest Billionaires Have Gained Nearly $255 Billion In Just Two Months," Forbes, May 23, 2020, https://www.forbes.com/sites/jonathanponciano/2020/05/22/billionaires-zuckerberg-bezos/.

21. Martin Luther King, Jr., "The Other America," in *The Radical King*, ed. Cornel West (Boston: Beacon Press, 2016), 235-244.

22. Vladimir Safatle, *Quando As Ruas Queimam: Manifesto Pela Emergência* (São Paulo: N-1 edições, 2016), 12. My translation.

23. Frantz Fanon, *Black Skin, White Masks* (New York: Grove Press, 1967), 305, Kindle.

Chapter Ten

1. Lecture at the University of Oslo, Norway – September 2018. We are very grateful to Katherine Wolk for reading this chapter, challenging us and helping us to learn and use a more appropriate language.

2. J Mase III and Lady Dane Figueroa Edidi, editors, *The Black Trans Prayer Book* (Lulu.com, 2020), 19, Kindle. https://theblacktransprayerbook.org/.

3. Althaus-Reid, *Indecent Theology*, 69.

4. Nathan Carlin, "Pastoral Theological Reading of Middlesex," in *Intersex, Theology, and the Bible: Troubling Bodies in Church, Text, and Society*, ed. Susannah Cornwall (New York: Palgrave, 2015), 113.

5. Toni Morrison, *The Origin of Others* (Cambridge: Harvard University Press, 2017), 94.

6. Ivone Gebara, *La Sed de Sentido: Búsquedas ecofeministas en prosa poética* (Uruguay: Doble Clic, 2002), 63.

7. Judith Butler, *Undoing Gender* (New York: Routledge, 2004), 27-28.

8. Ivone Gebara, "Spirituality of Resistance: a Latin American Perspective". Unpublished presentation, 2008.

9. Smith, *To Take Place*, 103.

10. Judith Butler, *Frames of War: When Is Life Grievable?* (New York: Verso Books, 2009), 1.

11. "Although enclosing borders were used in the art of Ancient Egyptians, it was in Europe that picture frames became a widely accepted norm in painting. It is also interesting to note that before the advent of the movable picture frame, paintings were built into altarpieces with unmovable frames that referenced the exteriors of churches. This indicates that in its inception, the picture frame was seen as part of religious architecture, and its function was to establish a visual relationship between a painting and its surroundings." Erdem Taşdelen, *The Logic of Parerga*, Studio Babak Golkar, http://babakgolkar.ca/the-logic-of-parerga/.

12. Elizabeth A. Johnson, *She Who Is: The Mystery of God in Feminist Theological Discourse* (New York: Crossroad, 1992), p 75. Elizabeth Johnson was the object of a multi-year investigation by the bishops of the United States for the errors of her feminist theology.

13. Terry Cummings, from a conversation between Terry Cummings and Janet Walton.

14. Terry Cummings with Janet Walton.

15. Jennifer S. Leath, "Is Queer the New Black?" *Harvard Divinity Bulletin* (Summer/Autumn 2015), https://bulletin.hds.harvard.edu/in-queer-the-new-black/.

16. Please read the whole ritual here: Edidi and Mase, *The Black Trans Prayer Book*, 40-42. https://theblacktransprayerbook.org/.

17. Patrick S. Cheng, *Radical Love: An Introduction to Queer Theology* (New York: Seabury Books, 2011), 114, Kindle.

18. Jennifer Finney Boylan, "Britain's Appalling Transgender 'Debate,'" *The New York Times,* May 9, 2018, https://www.nytimes.com/2018/05/09/opinion/britain-transgender-debate-caitlyn-jenner.html.

19. Morrison, *The Origin of Others*, 74.

20. Edidi and Mase, *The Black Trans Prayer Book*, 43. https://theblacktransprayerbook.org/
Also, Justin Edward Tanis writes about trans-gendered theology and has liturgical resources: *Trans-Gendered: Theology, Ministry, and Communities of Faith* (Ohio: Pilgrim Press, 2003).

21. José Esteban Muñoz, *Disidentifications: Queers of Color and the Performance of Politics* (Minneapolis: Univ. of Minnesota Press, 1998).

22. Muñoz, *Disidentifications*, 34.

23. Ashon T. Crawley, *Blackpentecostal Breath: The Aesthetics of Possibility* (New York, Fordham University Press, 2017), 3, Kindle.

Chapter Eleven

1. "God's Petticoat and Capitalism-full Fashion" was first published in *Dancing Theology in Fetish Boots: Essays in Honor of Marcella Althaus-Reid*, ed. Lisa Isherwood and Mark D. Jordan (London: SCM Press, 2010). © The Editors and Contributors 2010. Published by SCM Press. Used by permission. rights@hymnsam.co.uk.

2. Eliane Brum, "Teologia Indecente: An Interview with Marcella Althaus-Reid," *Revista Época* (n.d.), http://revistaepoca.globo.com/Epoca/0,6993,EPT805466-1666,00.html (accessed January 9, 2010).

3. I. Mészáros, *Filosofia, ideologia, e ciência social - Ensaio de Negação e Afirmação* (São Paulo: Editora Ensaio, 1993), 238; cited in Justino Souza, Jr., "Mercadoria,

fetichismo e discurso figurado n' O Capital," 8, available at: https://www.unicamp.br/cemarx/ANAIS%20IV%20COLOQUIO/comunica% E7%F5es/GT1/gt1m2c3.pdf.

4. Rubem Alves, Introduction to *Creio na ressurreição do corpo* (Rio de Janeiro: CEDI, 1984).

5. "Vestimentas Clericais Tradicionais Durante os Serviços Religiosos," *Comunhão Anglicana: Diocese do Recife* (September 17, 2009), http://www.dar.org.br/loc-2008/97-vestimentas-clericais-tradicionais-durante-os-serv/499-vestimentas-clericais-tradicionais-durante-os-servicos-religiosos.html, (accessed January 9, 2010).

6. Adriana Jacob, "Alta costura afro-baiana," *Soterpolitanos* (September 16, 2008), http://soteropolitanosculturaafro.wordpress.com/2008/09/16/identidade-ancestral/, (accessed January 9, 2010). *Ikomojadê* is the candomblé ceremony that introduces a child to the divinities sixteen days after birth. The cloth used in the ritual is washed, incensed and perfumed so that it can be kept throughout the life of the child. *Egbomi* is the person who has already gone through the rite of initiation in Candomblé. *Egbomi Cici* is one of the oldest mothers of the Terreiro Ilê Axé Opô Aganju, at Lauro de Freitas in the state of Bahia, Brazil.

7. Agnaldo Garcia and Mariana Grassi Maciel, "A influência da religião na busca do futuro cônjuge: um estudo preliminar em comunidades evangélicas," *Psicol. teor. prat.* 10, no. 1 (June 2008): 95-112.

8. All texts from Adélia Prado are taken from *Bagagem* (Rio de Janeiro: Imago, 1976).

9. Per Johns, "Realismo fantástico e floração ecológica," *Agulha: Revista de Cultura* 51 (May 2006), http://www.jornaldepoesia.jor.br/ag51johns.htm.

10. Karl Marx, *O Capital: para a crítica da economia política* (Rio de Janeiro: Bertrand Brasil, 1989), p. 59.

11. Justino Souza, Jr., "Mercadoria, fetichismo e discurso figurado n' O Capital," *Anais: Centro de Estudos Marxistas* (n.d.), https://www.unicamp.br/cemarx/ANAIS%20IV%20COLOQUIO/comunica%e 7%f5es/GT1/gt1m2c3.pdf.

12. Carlos Alberto Dória, "Moda: o inútil e a sua servidão," *Trópico* (n.d.), http:\\pphp.uol.com.br/_tropico/html/textos/2038,_1.shl, (accessed January 9, 2010).

13. Aldo Ambrózio and Paulo Alexandre Vasconcelos, "Baudrillard: especulações acerca da relação entre corpo e moda e outros teóricos que convergem para o

tema," *International Scientific Journal* 1, no. 3 (2008), http://www.interscienceplace.org/isp/index.php/isp/article/view/24.

14. Souza, "Mercadoria, fetichismo e discurso figurado".

15. W. F. Haug, *Crítica da Estética da Mercadoria* (São Paulo: UNESP, 1996), 30.

16. Haug, *Crítica da Estética da Mercadoria*, 35.

17. Francisco José Soares Teixeira, "O Capital e suas formas de produção de mercadorias: rumo ao fim da economia política," *Crítica Marxista* 10 (2000): 83.

18. Pierre Bourdieu, *A distinção* (São Paulo: Difel, n.d.), 82.

19. Bourdieu, *A distinção*.

20. Otto von Busch, foreword to *Artist Clothing Catalogue* (2004/2005), http://selfpassage.info/research/Fashion%20is%20alchemy%20ForeWord.pdf.

21. von Busch, *Artist Clothing Catalogue*.

22. von Busch, *Artist Clothing Catalogue*.

23. von Busch, *Artist Clothing Catalogue*.

24. von Busch, *Artist Clothing Catalogue*.

25. Karl Marx, "Manuscritos econômico-filosóficos (Terceiro manuscrito)," in *Manuscritos econômico-filosóficos e outros textos escolhidos* (São Paulo: Abril Cultural, 1978), 3-48.

26. Julia Kristeva, *Sentido e Contra-senso da revolta – poderes e limites da psicoanálise I* (Rio de Janeiro: Rocco, 2000), 334.

27. Kristeva, *Sentido e Contra-senso da revolta*, 336.

28. Kristeva, *Sentido e Contra-senso da revolta*, 338.

29. André Musskopf, *Via(da)gens Teológicas: Itinerários para uma Teologia Queer no Brazil* [Dissertation] (São Leopoldo: EST 2008), 221.

30. Musskopf, *Via(da)gens Teológicas: Itinerários*, 247.

Chapter Twelve

1. "Worshiping with Homeless: Foreign Ecclesiologies." was first published in *Church in an Age of Global Migration: A Moving Body*, ed. Susanna Snyder, Joshua Ralston, and Agnes M. Brazal (New York: Palgrave Macmillan, 2016), 131-146. All rights reserved.

2. http://www.thewelcomechurch.org.

3. Ash Wednesday in Logan Park with The Welcome Church, led by the Rev. Violet C. Little, February 13, 2013, https://www.youtube.com/watch?v=6t63AatspA4&index=60&list=UUTOc5P mgWWmdH_naVcNJx0Q

4. Rev. Violet C. Little, in an email sent to my class "Intro to Worship" at Lutheran Theological Seminary in Philadelphia. March 20, 2014

5. Michael Löwy, *A Guerra dos Deuses: Religião e Política na América Latina* (Petrópolis: Vozes/clacso/LPP, 2000), 12.

6. Frei Betto, *O que é Comunidade Eclesial de Base* (São Paulo: Brasiliense, 1981), 38.

7. Betto, *O que é Comunidade Eclesial de Base,* 7.

8. I made this video with Tirone, a member of Welcome Church: https://www.youtube.com/watch?v=48yV7ww2l6c&index=59&list=UUTOc5 PmgWWmdH_naVcNJx0Q

9. Leonardo Boff. *Ecclesiogenesis: The Base Communities Reinvent the Church* (New York: Orbis Books, 2012), 9.

10. Leonardo Boff, *Church, Charisma and Power: Liberation Theology and the Institutional Church* (New York: Crossroad Publishing Company, 1986), 189.

11. The following Story relates deeply what we are talking about in this article: John Burnett, "Statue of a Homeless Jesus Startles a Wealthy Community," *NPR*, April 13, 2014, http://www.npr.org/2014/04/13/302019921/statue-of-a-homeless-jesus-startles-a-wealthy-community

12. Maryam Omidi, "Anti-homeless spikes are just the latest in 'defensive urban architecture'" *The Guardian*, Thursday June 12, 2014, https://www.theguardian.com/cities/2014/jun/12/anti-homeless-spikes-latest-defensive-urban-architecture.

13. Leonardo Sakamoto, "Londres enxota sem-teto com pinos na calçada. São Paulo é mais professional," *Blog do Sakamoto, UOL*, October 6, 2014, http://blogdosakamoto.blogosfera.uol.com.br/2014/06/10/londres-enxota-sem-teto-com-pinos-na-calcada-sao-paulo-e-mais-profissional/

14. Colin Daileda, "Store Abandons 'Anti-Homeless' Spikes After Citizens Protest," *Mashable*, June 12, 2014, http://mashable.com/2014/06/12/anti-homeless-spikes-london/.

15. Trinh T. Minh-ha, *Elsewhere, Within Here: Immigration, Refugeeism and the Boundary Event* (New York: Routledge, 2011), 16-17, Kindle.

16. Minh-ha, *Elsewhere, Within Here*, 17.

17. Don Saliers, Speech given at Societas Liturgica in Wizburg, August 2013 (not published).

18. Janet Walton, "God," unpublished essay.

19. Kavanagh, *On Liturgical Theology*, 73.

20. Slavoj Zizek, *Less Than Nothing: Hegel and The Shadow of Dialectical Materialism* (Brooklyn: Verso Publications, 2013), 23.

21. John 4:1-42. Also, for a development of this theme please see my article: "'In Spirit and in Truth' The Liturgical Space as Territory," in *Common Worship in Theological Education*, ed. Siobhán Garrigan, (Oregon: Wipf & Stock, 2010), 118-132.

22. Derrida, Jacques, quoted by Elisabeth Weber, in "Introduction: Pleading Irreconcilable Differences," in Living Together: Jacques Derrida's Communities of Violence and Peace, Elisabeth Weber (Editor), (New York: Fordham University Press; 2012), 4.

23. To see the ways in which this can be achieved, please see Gayatri Chakravorty Spivak, "Can the Subaltern Speak," in *Marxism and the Interpretation of Culture*, ed. Cary Nelson and Lawrence Grossberg (Champaign: University of Illinois Press, 1988), 271-316.

24. Psalm 122 (my trans).

25. Isaiah 55:1.

26. Maraschin, *Da Leveza e da Beleza*, 21.

Chapter Thirteen

1. "Praying for The Ends of the World" was originally printed in a shorter version in Cláudio Carvalhaes, *Liturgies from Below: Prayers from People at the Ends of the World* (Nashville: Abingdon Press, 2020), 7-11. Used by permission by Abingdon Press.

2. The prayers in this chapter are part of the book *Liturgies from Below* (see n. 1 above), and many of the prayers from the project are available at the website of the Re-Imagining Worship Project, http://reimaginingworship.com.

3. "World's Billionaires Have More Wealth than 4.6 Billion People," *Oxfam*, January 19, 2020, https://www.oxfamamerica.org/press/worlds-billionaires-have-more-wealth-than-46-billion-people/.

4. Donna Haraway, "Anthropocene, Capitalocene, Plantationocene, Chthulucene: Making Kin," *Environmental Humanities* 6 (2015): 159-165.

5. Paul Holmer, *The Grammar of Faith* (New York: Harper & Row, 1978), 24. Holmer writes that prayer consists of structural languages that shape people's ways of being. The grammar of faith, for him, is marked by language *of* faith and not language *about* faith. Theology is done by the one praying and is not a comment or reflection on proper theology done elsewhere. Theology is a personal event. "Theology, he writes, "must always move toward a present-tense first person mood." With Holmer, I believe that every individual prays from their people's lives experiences. Prayers are the ritual and contents of theology. In other words, theology happens in the moment when one is praying, with one's personal and collective presence, with the conditions, situations and limitations of one's life. When we pray in places of hurt and violence, our theologies pulse with sweat and blood and a new grammar of faith ensues.

6. Jung Mo Sung, *Desire, Market and Religion: Reclaiming Liberation Theology* (London: SCM Press, 2007); "Pentecostals: Christianity Reborn," *The Economist*, December 23, 2006, https://www.economist.com/special-report/2006/12/19/christianity-reborn.

7. The Council for World Mission is a worldwide partnership of Christian churches, many of them with roots in Reformed tradition, focused on global resource-sharing for local mission. https://www.cwmission.org.

8. Vuyani S. Vellem, "Cracking the Skull of Racism in South Africa Post-1994," in *Who Is an African: Race, Identity, and Destiny in Post-apartheid South Africa*, ed. Roderick R. Hewitt and Chammah J. Kaunda (Lanham, MD: Lexington Books, 2018), 23.

9. Casa delle Culture is part of the Mediterranean Hope Refugee and Migrant Program of the Federation of Evangelical Churches in Italy (FCEI). https://www.mediterraneanhope.com/casa-delle-culture-scicli.

10. Stefano Harney and Fred Moten, *The Undercommons: Fugitive Planning & Black Study* (New York: Minor Compositions, 2013), 26-30, Kindle. Open access to this book is available at https://www.minorcompositions.info/wp-content/uploads/2013/04/undercommons-web.pdf.

11. Frantz Fanon, *The Wretched of the Earth* (New York: Grove Weidenfeld, 1991), 249.

12. On liturgical juxtaposition, see the work of Gordon Lathrop in *Holy Things*; *Holy People*; and *Holy Ground*.

13. When we read prayers of people far from us, we are always challenged. For those here in the U.S., especially white people, see DuBois, *Prayers for Dark People*; Mbiti, *Prayers of African Religion*; and Tutu, *African Prayer Book*.

14. See chapter 6, "Praying with Black People for Darker Faith."

15. The sources are vast and diverse, including *Walton, Feminist Liturgy*: Proctor and Walton, *Women at Worship*: Procter-Smith, *Praying with Our Eyes Open*; Procter-Smith, "Liturgical Responses to Sexual and Domestic Violence," and Berger, *Women's Ways of Worship*.

16. Among other works, see. Stewart, *Watered Garden*; Galbreath, *Leading into the World*; Lathrop, *Holy Ground*: Copeland, "Eucharist and Some Black Bodies;" West, "Liturgy: Church Worship and White Supremacy;" Haldeman, *Toward Liturgies that Reconcile*; Johnson, *Divine Communion*; and Bretanha Junker, *Prophetic Liturgy*.

17. Abraham Joshua Heschel, "On Prayer" in *Moral Grandeur and Spiritual Audacity: Essays*, ed. Susannah Heschel (New York Farrar, Straus and Giroux, 1996), 263.

18. *Pray The Devil Back to Hell*, directed by Gini Reticker (2008; New York: Fork Films).

19. Sweet Honey in the Rock, "We Are the Ones," Rykodisc, track 1 on *Twenty-Five*, 1998, CD.

20. Wonhee Anne Joh, Facebook post, July 19, 2019, 8:50 am. Joh is the author of *Heart of the Cross* and editor of other works such as Kim and Joh, *Feminist Praxis against U.S. Militarism*.

Chapter Fourteen

1. "African-Indigenous Jurema: The Greatest Common Divisor of The Brazilian Minimum Religion" was first published in *Black Theology in Brazil, CrossCurrents Journal,* CROS 67, no. 1 (March 2017): 86-104. Used with permission by the "Association for Religion and Intellectual Life."

2. "Brazilian minimum religion" can be somewhat related to the phrase "least common denominator" in English.

3. André Droogers, "A Religiosidade Mínima Brasileira," *Religião e Sociedade* 14, no. 2 (1987): 62-86.

4. Droogers, "A Religiosidade Mínima Brasileira," 65.

5. Ivone Gebara, "Que Escrituras são autoridade sagrada? Ambigüidades da Bíblia na vida das mulheres na América Latina," *Concilium: Revista Internacional de Teologia* 276 (1998/3): 10-25.

6. Afonso Maria Ligorio Soares, "Impasses da teologia Católica diante do sincretismo religioso afro-brasileiro," *Religião & Cultura Cenas da religião no Brasil* 1, no. 1 (2002): 66-76.

7. Soares, "Impasses."

8. The Agro Ecologic Web of the Peoples was created from the dialogues initiated at the I Bahia Conference of Agro-Ecology at the Terra Vista settlement in 2012. It is in charge of creating the annual agenda to support the development, empowerment and emancipation of communities and their connections. Quilombolas, native people, masters of oral tradition, peasants, students, scholars, educators, children, urban, and countryside youth participate in and build the Web. In: http://jornadadeagroecologiadabahia.blogspot.com.br/p/blog-page_11.html

9. VIII Afro-Ecumenical Meeting of the Caxuté Community. In: http://jornadadeagroecologiadabahia.blogspot.com.br/. Accessed December 20, 2015.

10. Cabruca is a traditional agroforestry system in the region, which understands cultures within the shade of the Atlantic Forest's native trees. Cabruca incorporates and enjoys the arboreal remnants of the great original forest, which is preserved. This creates much confusion in the process of classification or any attempt to differentiate Cabruca from the Rain Forest, because the cacao crops ended up inheriting spectral characteristics of the Rain Forest. In this logic, the forest needs to remain standing and be preserved, because other plants such as

cocoa, coffee, etc. depend on the shade of old trees to create an intricate system of permanence and newness. Cabruca, Planeta Orgânico, in: http://planetaorganico.com.br/site/index.php/cabruca/

11. Articulação Pastorais do Campo, 2015, http://www.cptnacional.org.br/index.php/publicacoes/noticias/acoes-dos-movimentos/2482-articulacao-das-pastorais-do-campo-realiza-encontro-sobre-desafios-pastorais-no-campo

12. Articulação Pastorais do Campo.

13. Rodrigues and Campos, "Caminhos da visibilidade."

14. Alexandra Prado Coelho. "O culto de índios e negros que chegou a Portugal," *Publico* (August 10, 2014), http://www.publico.pt/sociedade/noticia/o-culto-de-indios-e-negros-que-chegou-a-portugal-1665703 (accessed November 20, 2015).

15. José Francisco Miguel Henriques Bairrao, "Raízes da Jurema," *Psicol* 14, no. 1 (2003): 157-184, http://dx.doi.org/10.1590/S0103-65642003000100009, accessed on December 31, 2015.

16. Arnaldo Antunes, "Volte Para o Lar," *Álbum Um Som* (BMG Brasil Ltda, 1998): "Here in this house / Nobody wants your good manners / When there is food / We eat with our hands / And when the police, the disease, the distance / Or some quarrel do us part / We feel it never stops / To fill with pain our heart / But we don't cry for nothing/ Here in this tribe / Nobody wants your catechization / We may speak your language / But we can't understand your sermon / We laugh out loud, we drink and we curse / But we don't smile for nothing / Here in this boat / Nobody wants your direction / We have no prospects / But the wind guides us through / The life that drifts / Is what takes us too / But we don't follow for nothing / Go back to your home / Go back there."

17. "Jurema is a religious celebration (practiced differently by natives or caboclos) where the Jurema beverage is shared. Sometimes recognized as a specific religion in the complex scenario of Brazilian spirituality, the Jurema cult is diffused among religious practices where the beverage can have a more or less central role: pajelança, toré, catimbó, Umbanda, Candomblé de caboclo, etc. (Anthony, 2001)." M. Anthony in Bairrao, "Raízes da Jurema,"

18. "Sacred Jurema is what remains from the religious tradition of the natives that inhabited the shores of Paraíba, North Rio Grande and Pernambuco, and their pajés, experts in the mysteries of the hereafter, plants, and animals. When fleeing from the sugar cane plantations, enslaved Africans could find shelter with the indigenous tribes, where they exchanged religious knowledge with the natives. That is why, to this day, the greatest Jurema masters always have mixed native and black blood. Africans brought their knowledge about the egun worship of the dead and the divinities of nature, the orixás, voodoos and inkices. The natives

contributed with their methods of invocation of spirits from ancient pajés and work with the enchanted ones from the forests and rivers. That is why the Jurema is formed by two major lines: the Jurema masters and the enchanted ones." Jurema Medicina Sagradas, In Aldeia de Shiva, accessed on June 1, 2016. http://www.aldeiadeshiva.org/medicinas/jurema.html

19. For more information about the Jurema rituals, see Rodrigues and Campos, "Caminhos da visibilidade."

20. Diego Irarrázaval, "Salvação Indígena and Afro-Americana," in *Teologia Pluralista Libertadora Intercontinental,* José M. Vigil, Luiza E. Tomita, and Marcelo Barros (Orgs.), ASETT, EATWOT (São Paulo: Paulinas, 2008), 69.

21. Ivone Gebara, "Pluralismo Religioso, Uma Perspectiva Feminista" in *Teologia Pluralista Libertadora Intercontinental,* José M. Vigil, Luiza E. Tomita, and Marcelo Barros (Orgs.), ASETT, EATWOT (São Paulo: Paulinas, 2008), 298.

Conclusion

1, Cornel West, in Eduardo Mendieta, "'What it means to be human!': A Conversation with Cornel West," *Critical Philosophy of Race* 5, no. 2, (Special Issue: Race After Obama and Non-Racialism, Color Blindness, And Post-Racialism, 2017): 137-170. https://www.jstor.org/stable/10.5325/critphilrace.5.2.0137#metadata_info_ta b_contents

2. Edward W. Said, *On Late Style: Music and Literature Against the Grain* (New York: Knopf Doubleday, 2007), 7, Kindle.

3. Mary Oliver, "Leaves and Blossoms Along the Way," *Felicity* (New York: Penguin Press, 2015), 17, Kindle.

4. Sonia Bone Guajajara, *Facebook,* June 5, at 9:57 pm.

5. Tomas Tranströmer, in David Abram, *The Spell of the Sensuous* (New York: Knopf Doubleday, 2017), 143, Kindle.

6. Günther Anders was a Jewish thinker, Stern being his original last name, first marriage to Hannah Arendt, fleeing Germany in 1933 to France and the US, then after the war, living in Vienna. See his thesis here: Günther Anders, "Theses for the Atomic Age," *The Massachusetts Review* 3, no. 3 (Spring, 1962): 493-505.

7. Anders, "Theses for the Atomic Age," 498.

8. Anders, "Theses for the Atomic Age."

9. Emicida, "Principia," Album *AmarElo* (São Paulo: Laboratório Fantasma, 2019).

10. Rubenstein, *Pantheologies*.

PERMISSIONS

Chapter one, "Eco-Liturgical Liberation Theology," was originally published as different iterations in two previous publications, and presented here with their kind permission: (1) "Teologia Litúrgica da Libertação," in *Estudos Teológicos: Programa de Pós-Graduação em Teologia* 58.2 (2018, special issue, *Decolonialidade E Práticas Religiosas*); and (2) "Liturgische Befreiungstheologie," in *Called to Worship - Freed to Respond: Beiträge aus der internationalen Liturgischen Theologie zum Zusammenhang von Gottesdienst und Ethik,* ed. Dorothea Haspelmath-Finatti (Gütersloh, Germany: Gütersloher Verlagshaus, 2019).

"Lex Naturae – A New Way into a Liturgical Political Theology," chapter two, was first published in *T&T Clark Handbook to Political Theology,* ed. Rubem Rosário-Rodriguez (New York: Bloomsbury T&T Clark, 2019), 449-466. Published here by kind permission of T&T Clark/Bloomsbury.

"Worship, Liturgy, and Public Witness," chapter four, was first published in *Companion on Public Theology,* ed. Katie Day and Sebastian Kim, (Boston: Brill, 2017): 466–486. By kind permission of Brill.

Chapter five was first published as "A Theological Shift: From Multiculturalisms to Multinaturalisms," in *Vulnerability and Resistance: Body and Liberating Theologies,* ed. Jione Havea (Lexington & Fortress Academic, 2020): 159-172. By kind permission of Lexington & Fortress Academic Press. All rights reserved.

Chapter six was first published in *Liturgy* 35.4 (2020). By kind permission of The Liturgical Conference. All rights reserved.

"Class, Interreligious Borders and Ways of Living with Pachamama," chapter eight, was first published in *Faith(s) Seeking Justice: Dialogue and Liberation,* ed. Peniel Jesudason Rufus Rajkumar (Geneva: WCC, 2021): 220-239. All rights reserved.

"Birds, People, Then Religion—An Eco-Liberation Theological and Pedagogical Approach to Interreligious Rituals," chapter nine, was first published in the *Journal of Interreligious Studies,* 21 (2017). It is found here: https://irstudies.org/index.php/ jirs/article/view/271.

BIBLIOGRAPHY

Adam, Júlio Cézar. "Liturgia como prática dos pés. A Romaria da Terra do Paraná: reapropriação de ritos litúrgicos na busca e libertação dos espaços de vida." *Sinodal Ciências Humanas e Sociais* (2011).

Abram, David. *The Spell of the Sensuous.* New York: Knopf Doubleday, 2017. Kindle.

Althaus-Reid, Marcella. *Indecent Theology: Theological Perversions in Sex, Gender and Politics.* New York: Routledge, 2001.

Althusser, Louis. *Essays on Self-Criticism.* New York: Verso, 1978.

—. *On the Reproduction of Capitalism: Ideology and Ideological State Apparatuses.* New York: Verso, 2014.

Alves, Rubem. *Creio na ressurreição do corpo.* Rio de Janeiro: CEDI, 1984.

Ambrózio, Aldo, and Paulo Alexandre Vasconcelos. "Baudrillard: especulações acerca da relação entre corpo e moda e outros teóricos que convergem para o tema." *International Scientific Journal* 1.3 (2008). *interscienceplace.org/isp/index.php/isp/article/view/24.*

Anders, Günther. "Theses for the Atomic Age." *The Massachusetts Review* 3.3 (1962): 493-505.

Antunes, Arnaldo. "Volte Para o Lar." Álbum Um Som, BMG Brasil Ltda, 1998.

Anzaldúa, Gloria. *Borderlands / La Frontera: The New Mestiza.* San Francisco: Aunt Lute, 1987.

—. "(Un)natural Bridges, (Un)safe Spaces." Preface *to this bridge we call home,* 1-5. Ed. G. Anzaldúa and A. Keating. New York: Routledge, 2002.

Bairrao, José Francisco Miguel Henriques. "Raízes da Jurema." *Psicol* 14.1 (2003): 157-184. *dx.doi.org/10.1590/ S0103-65642003000100009,* acc. 31. Dec. 2015.

Balasuriya, Tissa. *The Eucharist and Human Liberation.* Eugene, OR: Wipf & Stock, 1977.

Baldwin, James Baldwin. *I Am Not Your Negro.* New York: Vintage, 2017. Kindle.

Bell, Catherine. *Ritual Theory, Ritual Practice.* Oxford: Oxford UP, 2009.

Benjamin, Walter. "Theses on the Philosophy of History." In *Illuminations: Essays and Reflections,* 253-264. Ed. H. Arendt. New York: Harcourt, 1988.

—. *Understanding Brecht.* Trans. A. Bostock. New York: Verso, 2003.

Bennett, Jane. *Vibrant Matter: A Political Ecology of Things.* Durham, NC: Duke UP, 2010.

Berry, Wendell. "How to Be a Poet." In *Given: New Poems,* 18. Berkeley: Counterpoint Press, 2005.

Betto, Frei. *O que é Comunidade Eclesial de Base.* São Paulo: Brasiliense, 1981.

Bhabha, Homi K. *The Location of Culture.* New York: Routledge, 2004.

Bjornerud, Marcia. *Timefulness.* Princeton: Princeton UP, 2018. Kindle.

Boff, Clodovis. *Theology and Praxis: Epistemological Foundations.* New York: Orbis, 1987.

Boff, Leonardo. *Church, Charisma and Power: Liberation Theology and the Institutional Church.* New York: Crossroad, 1986.

—. "O Cristo Cósmico: Uma Espiritualidade Do Universo." Blog (September 23, 2016). *leonardoboff.org/2016/ 09/23/o-cristo-cosmicouma-espiritualidade-do-universo/.*

—. *Cry of the Earth, Cry of the Poor.* New York: Orbis Books, 1997), Kindle.

—. *Ecclesiogenesis: The Base Communities Reinvent the Church.* New York: Orbis, 2012.

—. *Essential Care: An Ethics of Human Nature.* Trans. and ann. A. Guilherme. Waco: Baylor UP, 2008.

—. *Princípio-Terra: A Volta À Terra Como Pátria Comum.* São Paulo: Editora Ática, 1995.

—. *Sacraments of Life: Life of the Sacraments.* Washington, DC: Pastoral Press, 1987.

Bonhoeffer, Dietrich. *Letters and Papers from Prison.* Ed. E. Bethge. London: Folio Society, 2000.

Boopalan, Sunder John. *Memory, Grief and Agency: A political Theological Account of Wrongs and Rites.* Switzerland: Palgrave Macmillan, 2017.

Bosi, Alfredo. *Dialética da Colonização.* São Paulo: Companhia das Letras, 1992.

Bourdieu, Pierre. *A distinção.* São Paulo: Difel, n.d.

—. *In Other Words.* Stanford: Stanford UP, 1990.

Boylan, Jennifer Finney "Britain's Appalling Transgender 'Debate.'" *The New York Times* (9. May 2018). *nytimes.com/2018/05/09/opinion/britain-transgender-debate-caitlyn-jenner.html.*

Brown, Adrienne Maree. *Emergent Strategy: Shaping Change, Changing Worlds.* Chico, CA: AK Press, 2017. Kindle.

Brum, Eliane. "Teologia Indecente: An Interview with Marcella Althaus-Reid." *Revista Época* (n.d.). *revistaepoca.globo.com/Epoca/0,6993,EPT805466-1666,00.html,* acc. 9. Jan 2010.

Butler, Judith. *Frames of War: When Is Life Grievable?* New York: Verso, 2009.

—. *Undoing Gender.* New York: Routledge, 2004.

Byassee, Jason. "Maybe the body of Christ has always been both virtual and physical." *Faith and Leadership,* March 2, 2011. *faithandleadership.com/jason-byassee-virtual-theological-education*

Câmara, Dom Helder. *Utopias Peregrinas.* Pernambuco: Editora UFPE, 2014.

Cardoso, Nancy. "Da agropornografia à agroecologia: uma aproximação queer contra as elites vegetais." *História, saúde e direitos: sabores e saberes do IV Congresso Latino-Americano de Gênero e Religião.* Eds. A. Musskopf and M. Blasi. São Leopoldo, RS: CEBI, 2016. 35-41.

—. "V Congresso Latino-Americano De Gênero E Religião." Faculdades EST (23-26. Aug. 2017). *eventos.est.edu.br/index.php/genero/Genero.*

Cardoso, Nancy, and Cláudio Carvalhaes. "Jurema african-indigenous - the greatest common divisor of the Brazilian minimum religion." *CrossCurrents Journal* 67.1, (2017): 86-104.

Carlin, Nathan. "Pastoral Theological Reading of Middlesex." *Intersex, Theology, and the Bible: Troubling Bodies in Church, Text, and Society*. Ed. S. Cornwall. New York: Palgrave, 2015.

Carvalhaes, Cláudio. *Eucharist and Globalization: Redrawing the Borders of Eucharistic Hospitality*. Eugene, OR: Pickwick, 2013.

—. "In Spirit and in Truth: The Liturgical Space as Territory." *Common Worship in Theological Education*. Ed. S. Garrigan and T. Johnson. Eugene, OR: Wipf & Stock, 2009.

—. "Introduction." In J. Maraschin, *Da Leveza e da Beleza — Liturgia na pós-modernidade*. São Paulo: ASTE, 2010.

—. "Introduction." *With Many Voices: Liturgies in Contexts*. Ed. V. Varghese Eapen. India: DARE, 2020.

—. "Oppressed Bodies Don't Have Sex: The Blind Spots of Bodily and Sexual Discourses in the Construction of Subjectivity in Latin American Theology." *Indecent Theologians: Marcella Althaus-Reid and the Next Generation of Postcolonial Activists*. Ec. N. Panotto. Alameda, CA: Borderless, 2016.

—. "Theopoetics in Revolution: The Life of Ernesto Cardenal." *The Bias Magazine: The Voice of the Christian Left* (12. Mar. 2020). *christiansocialism.com/ernesto-cardenal-liberation-theology-revolution-poetry/?fbclid= IwAR1_SuFNYIs7IkExhkvtunOSJ3UKdGwLmOynbwFhxsRCu_JZea9gb HBdmQU*

—. "Why I Created a Chapel Service Where People Confess to Plants." *Sojourners* blog (26. Sept. 2109). *sojo.net/articles/ why-i-created-chapel-service-where-people-confess-plants*.

Casaldáliga, Pedro. "Pobreza Evangélica." *Antología Personal*. Madrid: Editorial Trotta, S.A, 2006, 35.

Casaldáliga, Pedro, and Vitor Westhelle. "Creation Motifs in the Search for a Vital Space: A Latin American Perspective." *Lift Every Voice: Constructing Christian Theologies from the Underside*. Eds. S. Thistlewaite and M. Engel. New York: Orbis, 1998. 146-158.

Caxuté Community. VIII Afro-Ecumenical Meeting. *jornadadeagroecologiadabahia.blogspot.com.br*, accessed 20. Dec. 2015.

Césaire, Aimé. *Discourse on Colonialism*. Trans. J. Pinkham. New York and London: Monthly Review, 1972.

Chauí, Marilena. "Crise do neoliberalismo tem como resposta o autoritarismo." Brasil de Fato, October 16, 2109. *www.youtube.com/watch?v=ZYZqqwQjGws*.

Chauvet, Louis-Marie. *Symbol and Sacrament: Sacramental Reinterpretation of Christian Existence*. Trans. M. Beaumont and P. Madigan. Collegeville, MN: Liturgical, 2018.

Cheng, Patrick S. *Radical Love: An Introduction to Queer Theology*. New York: Seabury, 2011. Kindle.

Coelho, Alexandra Prado. "O culto de índios e negros que chegou a Portugal." *Publico* (10. Aug. 2014). *publico.pt/sociedade/noticia/o-culto-de-indios-e-negros-que-chegou-a-portugal-1665703*, acc. 20. Nov. 2015.

Comblin, José. *Introdução geral ao Comentário Bíblico: Leitura da Bíblia na perspectiva dos pobres.* Petrópolis: Vozes, Imprensa Metodista e Editora Sinodal, 1985.

Comunhão Anglicana: Diocese do Recife "Vestimentas Clericais Tradicionais Durante os Serviços Religiosos" (17. Sep. 2009). *dar.org.br/loc-2008/97-vestimentas-clericais-tradicionais-durante-os-serv/499-vestimentas-clericais-tradicionais-durante-os-servicos-religiosos.html.*

Cone, James. *Black Theology & Black Power.* New York: Orbis, 1997.

—. *A Black Theology of Liberation.* New York: Orbis, 2010.

—. *The Cross and The Lynching Tree.* New York: Orbis, 2011.

Cooper-White, Pamela. "The Ritual Reason Why: Explorations of the Unconscious through Enactment and Ritual in Pastoral Psychology." *Journal of Supervision and Training in Ministry* 19 (1998-99): 68-75.

—. "Union Ideas: Becoming Conscious of the Unconscious" (2. May 2016). *youtube.com/watch?v=4rm TmyvSW5c&t=17s.*

Costen, Melva. *African American Christian Worship.* 2nd ed. Nashville: Abingdon, 2007.

Crawley, Ashon T. *Blackpentecostal Breath: The Aesthetics of Possibility.* New York, Fordham UP, 2017. Kindle.

Daileda, Colin. "Store Abandons 'Anti-Homeless' Spikes After Citizens Protest." *Mashable* (12. June 2014). *mashable.com/2014/06/12/anti-homeless-spikes-london/.*

Danowski, Déborah, and Eduardo Viveiros de Castro. *The Ends of the World.* Maldem: Polity. 2017. Kindle.

Das, Raju. "David Harvey's Theory of Accumulation by Dispossession: A Marxist Critique." *World Review of Political Economy* 8.4 (2017): 590-616.

da Silva, Glicéria Jesus, Daniela Fernandes Alarcon, and Vitor Flynn Paciornik. *Os Donos Da Terra.* São Paulo: Editora Elefante, 2020.

de Castro, Eduardo Viveiros. *Cannibal Metaphysics: For a Post-structural Anthropology.* Trans. P. Skafish. Minneapolis: Univocal, 2014.

—. "Cosmological Deixis and Amerindian Perspectivism." *The Journal of the Royal Anthropological Institute* 4.3 (1998): 469-488. *jstor.org/stable/3034157,* acc. 11. June 2017.

—. Interview with Eliane Brum. In "Diálogos sobre o fim do mundo." *El País* (29. Oct. 2014). *brasil.elpais.com/brasil/2014/09/29/opinion/1412000283_365191.amp.html?fbclid=IwAR2UzGFHENEID4ooQsV8VU5ZvOUXgpMdZJITBdG6wF9GjYtGe5cnG13X5mg.*

—. "Perspectival Anthropology and the Method of Controlled Equivocation." *Tipití: Journal of the Society for the Anthropology of Lowland South America* 2.1 (1 June 2004): 3-22. *digitalcommons.trinity.edu/cgi/viewcontent.cgi?article=1010&context=tipiti,* acc. 6. Nov. 2017.

—. "Perspectivismo e multinaturalismo na América indígena." *O que nos faz pensar* 18 (2000): 225-254. *oquenosfaz pensar. fil.puc-rio.br/import/pdf_articles/OQNFP_18_13 _eduardo_viveiros_de_castro.pdf*, acc. 6. Nov. 2017.

—. *The Relative Native: Essays on Indigenous Conceptual Worlds.* Chicago: Haul, 2015.

—. "A revolução faz o bom tempo." 18. Apr. 2015. *https://www.youtube.com/watch?v=CjbU1jO6rmE.*

de Certeau, Michel. *The Practice of Everyday Life.* Berkeley: U California P, 2011.

de la Cadena, Marisol, and Mario Blaser, eds. *A World of Many Worlds.* Durham, NC: Duke UP, 2018.

De La Torre, Miguel, ed. *The Hope of Liberation in World Religions.* Waco: Baylor UP, 2008.

Deleuze, Gilles. *Logique du Sens.* Paris: Minuit, 1969.

Derrida, Jacques. *Rogue: Two Essays of Reason.* Stanford: Stanford UP, 2005.

de Santa Ana, Júlio. *Pão, Vinho e Amizade: Meditações.* São Paulo, CEDI, 1986.

Dória, Carlos Alberto. "Moda: o inútil e a sua servidão." *Trópico* (n.d.). *pphp.uol.com.br/ tropico/html/textos/2038, 1.shl*, acc. 9. Jan. 2010.

Dorrico, Julie. "Nascidos e criados da terra, Ao longo de sete narrativas, HQ mostra o processo das retomadas de terras e o cotidiano dos Tupinambá na Bahia." *Quatro Cinco Um* (1. Feb. 2021). *www.quatrocincoum.com.br/br/ resenhas/quadrinhos/nascidos-e-criados-da-terra.*

Droogers, André. "A Religiosidade Mínima Brasileira." *Religião e Sociedade* 14.2 (1987): 62-86.

Dussel, Enrique. "Anti-Cartesian Meditations: On the Origen of the Philosophical Anti-Discourse of Modernity." *Journal for Cultural and Religious Theory* (13. Jan. 2014): 11-53. *jcrt.org/archives/13.1/dussel.pdf.*

Dykstra, Craig. *Growing in the life of Faith.* Louisville: Westminster John Knox, 2005.

Elizondo, Virgilio, and Timothy Matovina. *Mestizo Worship: A Pastoral Approach to Liturgical Ministry.* Collegeville: Liturgical, 1998.

Ellacuría, Ignacio. "Liturgia y liberación." *Escritos teológicos IV,* 17-45. El Salvador: UCA Editores, 2002.

Ellis, Marc. *Beyond Innocence & Redemption: Confronting the Holocaust and Israeli Power: Creating a Moral Future for the Jewish People.* Oregon: Wipf & Stock, 2016.

Elwood, Christopher. *The Body Broken: The Calvinist Doctrine of the Eucharist and the Symbolization of Power in Sixteenth–Century France.* New York: Oxford UP, 1999.

Emicida. "Principia." Album *AmarElo.* São Paulo: Laboratório Fantasma, 2019.

Fagerberg, Dave. "Liturgy, Social Justice and the Mystical Body of Christ." *Liturgy and Empire: Faith in Exile and Political Theology.* Ed. S. Hahn and D. Scott. Steubenville, OH: Emmaus Road, 2009. 193-210.

Fanon, Frantz. *Black Skin, White Masks.* New York: Grove, 1967. Kindle.

—. *The Wretched of the Earth.* New York: Grove Weidenfeld, 1991.

Feliz, Octavius Minucious. "8.4;9.1-2." In A. Kreider, *The Change of Conversion and the Origin of Christendom*. Oregon: Wipf & Stock, 2006. 11.

Foucault, Michel. *The History of Sexuality Volume 1: An Introduction*. New York: Vintage, 1978.

—. *Power/Knowledge. Select Interviews and Other Writings, 1972-1977*. Ed. C. Gordon. New York: Pantheon, 1988.

Friedman, Lisa. "Biden Administration Defends Huge Alaska Oil Drilling Project." *Los Angeles Times* (26. May 2021). *nytimes.com/2021/05/26/climate/biden-alaska-drilling.html?fbclid= IwAR0iavbEuSZM6PYKCxOfYKNkAg1KaL4Xpm29fQRYkpG5 gYnSy9xjMetYxFA*

Gagliano, Francesco. "Pedro Casaldáliga, 90 años: bispo, poeta e defensor intransigente da dignidade humana." *Revista Ihu On-Line* (31 Jan. 2018). *www.ihu.unisinos.br/ 78-noticias/575711-pedro-casaldaliga-90-anos-bispo-poeta-e-defensor-intransigente-da-dignidade-humana*

Garcia, Agnaldo, and Mariana Grassi Maciel. "A influência da religião na busca do futuro cônjuge: um estudo preliminar em comunidades evangélicas." *Psicol. teor. prat.* 10.1 (2008): 95-112.

Gebara, Ivone. *La Sed de Sentido: Búsquedas ecofeministas en prosa poética*. Uruguay: Doble Clic, 2002.

—. *Longing for Running Water: Ecofeminism and Liberation*. Minneapolis: Fortress, 1999. Kindle.

—. "Que Escrituras são autoridade sagrada? Ambigüidades da Bíblia na vida das mulheres na América Latina." *Concilium: Revista Internacional de Teologia* 276 (1998/3): 10-25.

—. *Teologia ecofeminista: ensaio para repensar o conhecimento e a religião*. São Paulo: Olho D'Agua, 1997.

Ghosh, Amitav. "The Great Derangement: Climate Change and the Unthinkable." Union Theological Seminary, New York (28. Mar. 2018). *www.youtube.com/watch? v=9eFT_eb_jRk&t=4390s.*

Gibler, Linda. *From the Beginning to Baptism: Scientific and Sacred Stories of Water, Oil and Fire*. Collegeville: Liturgical, 2010.

Gil, Gilberto. "Amarra O Teu Arado A Uma Estrela." *O eterno Deus Mu dança*. CD. Rio de Janeiro: Warner Music Brasil, 1989.

Gomes, Roberto. *A Crítica da Razão Tupiniquim*. CRIAR, 2001.

Gonçalves, Alonso. "Teologia Pública: entre a construção e a possibilidade prática de um discurso." *Ciberteologia, Revista de Teologia e Cultura* 8.38 (1Aug. 2015): 63-76. *www.otroscruces.org/essential_grid/teologia-y-espacio-publico-segunda-edicion/.*

Grimes, Ronald L. "Performance is Currency in the Deep World's Gift Economy." *The Handbook of Contemporary Animism*. Ed. G. Harvey. London: Routledge, 2015.

—. *Reading, Writing, and Ritualizing: Ritual in Fictive, Liturgical and Public Places*. Washington, DC: Pastoral, 1993.

—. "Ritual theory and the environment." In *Nature Performed: Environment, Culture and Performance*. Eds. W. Heim, B. Szerszynski, and C. Waterton. Malden, MA: Blackwell/ Sociological Review, 2003.

Grosfoguel, Ramón. "The Structure of Knowledge in Westernized Universities: Epistemic Racism/Sexism and the Four Genocides/Epistemicides of the Long 16th Century." *Human Architecture: Journal of the Sociology of Self–Knowledge* 11.1 (2013): 73-90.

Gutierrez, Gustavo. *A Theology of Liberation: History, Politics, and Salvation*. New York: Orbis: 1973.

Hanh, Thich Nhat. *The Art of Living: Peace and Freedom in the Here and Now*. HarperCollins, 2017. Kindle.

Haraway, Donna. "Anthropocene, Capitalocene, Plantationocene, Chthulucene: Making Kin." *Environmental Humanities* 6 (2015): 159-165.

—. *Simians, Cyborgs, and Women: The Reinvention of Nature*. New York: Routledge, 1990.

—. *Staying with the Trouble: Making Kin in the Chthulucene*. Durham: Duke UP, 2016.

Harney, Stefano, and Fred Moten. *The Undercommons: Fugitive Planning & Black Study*. New York: Minor Compositions, 2013. Kindle. *www.minorcompositions.info /wp-content/uploads/2013/04/undercommons-web.pdf.*

Harvey, David. "Space as A Key Word." Marx and Philosophy Conference (29 May 2004). Inst. of Education, London. *frontdeskapparatus.com/files/harvey2004.pdf.*

Harvey, Graham. *Animism: Respecting the Living World*, 2nd ed. London: C Hurst & Co, 2017).

Haug, W. F. *Crítica da Estética da Mercadoria*. São Paulo: UNESP, 1996.

Haugen, Marty. "Gather Us In." Chicago: GIA, Inc., 1982.

Head, Leslie. *Hope and Grief in the Anthropocene: Re-conceptualizing Human-Nature Relations*. New York: Routledge, 2016.

Heschel, Abraham. "On Prayer" *Moral Grandeur and Spiritual Audacity: Essays*. Ed. S. Heschel. New York: Farrar, Straus and Giroux, 1996. 257-267.

Holmer, Paul. *The Grammar of Faith*. New York: Harper, 1978.

Ike and Cláudio. "Lettuce and Tomato" (10. Aug 2020). *www.youtube.com/watch?v=c1WY5iZPXCE.*

Irala, Flávio, and Elsa Tamez. "Venham, celebremos a Ceia do Senhor - Convite ao compromisso." IECLB (26. June 1983). *luteranos.com.br/conteudo/venham-celebremos-a-ceia-do-senhor-convite-ao-compromisso,* acc. 26. Aug. 2015.

Jacob, Adriana. "Alta costura afro-baiana." *Soterpolitanos* (September 16, 2008). *soteropolitanosculturaafro.wordpress.com/2008/09/16/identidade-ancestral/,* acc. 9. Jan. 2010.

Jameson, Fredric. "Future City." *New Left Review* 21 (2003): 65-79.

Jean, Martin D. "Foreword." *Liturgy's Imagined Past/s: Methodologies and Materials in the Writing of Liturgical History Today*. Eds. T. Berger and B. Spinks. Collegeville, MN: Liturgical, 2016. ix-x.

Jennings, Willie. *After Whiteness: An Education in Belonging.* Grand Rapids: Eerdmans, 2020.

Johns, Per. "Realismo fantástico e floração ecológica." *Agulha: Revista de Cultura* 51 (2006). *www.jornaldepoesia.jor.br/ag51johns.htm.*

Johnson, Elizabeth A. *She Who Is: The Mystery of God in Feminist Theological Discourse.* New York: Crossroad, 1992.

Kahl, Brigitte. *Galatians Re-Imagined: Reading with the Eyes of the Vanquished.* Minneapolis: Fortress, 2010.

Kaunda, C. J. "'Rituals of resistance, weapons of the weak': Toward an African Pentecostal transformative Holy Communion Missiology." *Theologia Viatorum* 40.2 (2016): 84-101.

Kavanagh, Aidan. *On Liturgical Theology.* Collegeville: Pueblo, 1992.

Kierkegaard, Soren. *Works of Love.* New York: Harper, 1962.

Kimmerer, Robin. *Braiding Sweetgrass.* Canada: Milkweed, 2015.

King, Martin Luther Jr. "Letter from Birmingham Jail." *A Testament of Hope: The Essential Writings of Martin Luther King Jr.* Ed. J. Washington. San Francisco: Harper & Row, 1996. 289-302.

—. "The Other America." *The Radical King.* Ed. C. West. Boston: Beacon, 2016. 235-244.

Kingsolver, Barbara. *Animal, Vegetable, Miracle: A Year of Food Life.* New York: Harper, 2007.

Kopenawa, Davi. *A Última Floresta.* Dir. L. Bolognesi. São Paulo: Gullane, 2021.

Kopenawa, Davi, and Bruce Albert. *The Falling Sky: Words of a Yanomami Shaman.* Trans. N. Elliott and A. Dundy. Cambridge: Belknap/Harvard UP, 2013.

Krenak, Ailton. *Ideias para adiar o fim do mundo.* São Paulo: Companhia das Letras, 2019.

Kristeva, Julia. *Sentido e Contra-senso da revolta – poderes e limites da psicoanálise I.* Rio de Janeiro: Rocco, 2000.

Lacan, Jacques. *Écrits A Selection.* Trans. A. Sheridan. London: Routledge, 1989.

LaDuke, Winona. *How to Be a Water Protector: The Rise of the Wiindigoo Slayers.* Nova Scotia: Fernwood, 2020.

—. "Our Home on Earth." Excerpted and updated from "Voices from White Earth: Gaa-waabaabiganikaag." Thirteenth Annual E.F. Schumacher Lecture, Yale U (Oct. 1993). In On the Commons, *All That We Share: A Field Guide to the Commons. www.onthecommons.org/magazine/our-home-earth#sthash.HEifPfDt.kV1CNvWd.dpbs*

Lafourcade, Natalia, and Leonel García. "Hasta la Raíz." International Comm. Red Cross (ICRC) and Playing for Change, 2020. *youtube.com/watch?v=cUaKBGnn2DQ.*

Lathrop, Gordon. *Holy Ground: A Liturgical Cosmology.* Minneapolis: Fortress, 2009. Kindle.

—. *Holy Things, A Liturgical Theology.* Minneapolis: Fortress, 1998.

Latour, Bruno. *Critical Zones: The Science and Politics of Landing on Earth.* Ed. B. Latour and P. Weibel. Cambridge and London: ZKM/MIT P, 2020.

—. *Facing Gaia: Eight Lectures on the New Climatic Regime.* Cambridge: Polity, 2017. Kindle.

—. *Reassembling the Social: An introduction to Actor-Network-Theory.* Oxford: Oxford UP, 2005.

Leath, Jennifer S. "Is Queer the New Black?" *Harvard Divinity Bulletin* (2015). *bulletin.hds.harvard.edu/in-queer-the-new-black/.*

Lefebvre, Henri. *The Production of Space.* Malden: Wiley, 1992.

Little, Violet. "Ash Wednesday in Logan Park with The Welcome Church" (13. Feb. 2013) *youtube.com/watch ?v=6t63AatspA4&index=60&list=UUTOc5PmgWWmdH_naVcNJx0Q*

Lobo, Luiz Fernando, and Tulio Mourão, dirs. "Louvação à Mariama" and "Marcha Final de Banzo e Esperança" from the show "Missa dos Quilombos." Set up by the Companhia Ensaio Aberto for the musical by Milton Nascimento, Pedro Casaldáliga and Pedro Tierra. The video is a fragment of the DVD dir. by L. Fernando Lobo and R. Lagemann. *youtube.com/watch?v= BU6oz6DRBZw.*

Lovelock, James. *The Revenge of Gaia.* New York: Penguin, 2007.

Löwy, Michael. *A Guerra dos Deuses: Religião e Política na América Latina.* Petrópolis: Vozes/clacso/LPP, 2000.

Maathai, Wangari Muta. *Unbowed, A Memoir.* New York: Anchor Books, 2008.

Maduro, Otto. *Maps for a Fiesta: A Latina/o Perspective on Knowledge and the Global Crisis.* New York: Fordham UP, 2015.

Maitreya, Balangoda Ananda, et al. "The Discourse on Loving Kindness (Mettâ Sutta, Sutta Pitaka)." *Introducing Buddhism.* Trans. H. Russell-Williams and The Buddhist Group of Kendai (Theravnâda). London: Buddhist Society, 2003. Inside back cover.

Maraschin, Jaci. "Libertação da Liturgia." *A Beleza da Santidade Ensaios de Liturgia,* São Paulo: ASTE, 1996. 133-138.

—. *"The Transient Body: Sensibility and Spirituality."* Presented 20. Oct. 2003, Union Theol. Sem., New York.

Margulis, Lynn. *Symbiotic Earth.* Dir. J. Feldman. Hummingbird, 2019.

Marx, Karl. *O Capital: para a crítica da economia política.* Rio de Janeiro: Bertrand Brasil, 1989.

—. *A Contribution to The Critique of the Political Economy.* Kindle.

—. "Manuscritos econômico-filosóficos (Terceiro manuscrito)." In *Manuscritos econômico-filosóficos e outros textos escolhidos,* 3-48. São Paulo: Abril Cultural, 1978.

Marx, Karl, and Friedrich Engels. *A Ideologia Alemã.* São Paulo: Martins Fontes, 2001.

Mase, J. and Lady Dane Figueroa Edidi, eds. *The Black Trans Prayer Book.* Lulu, 2020. Kindle. *theblacktransprayerbook.org/.*

Mbembe, Achille. *Critique of Black Reason.* Trans. L. Dubois. Durham: Duke UP, 2017.

McFague, Sallie. *The Body of God: An Ecological Theology.* Minneapolis: Fortress, 1993.

McGrath, Alister. *Re-Imagining nature: The Promise of a Christian Natural Theology.* Malden: Wiley, 2017.

McLaren, Peter. *Pedagogy of Insurrection, From Insurrection to Revolution.* New York: Peter Lang, 2015.

Mendieta, Eduardo. "'What it means to be human!': A Conversation with Cornel West." *Critical Philosophy of Race* 5.2 (2017): 137-170. *www.jstor.org/stable/10.5325 /critphilrace.5.2.0137#metadata_info_tab_contents*

Meyers, Ruth A. *Missional Worship, Worshipful Mission: Gathering as God's People, Going Out in God's Name.* Grand Rapids: Eerdmans, 2014. Kindle.

Mignolo, Walter D. "Epistemic Disobedience, Independent Thought and De-Colonial Freedom." *Theory, Culture & Society* 26.7-8 (2009): 1-23. *journals.sagepub.com/doi/ pdf/10.1177/0263276409349275.*

Min-ha, Trinh T. *Elsewhere, Within Here: Immigration, Refugeeism and the Boundary Event.* New York: Routledge, 2011. Kindle.

Mitchell, Nathan D. *Meeting Mystery: Liturgy, Worship, Sacraments.* Maryknoll, NY: Orbis Books, 2006.

Morrison, Toni. *The Origin of Others.* Cambridge: Harvard UP, 2017.

Moyaert, Marianne, and Joris Geldhof, editors. *Ritual Participation and Interreligious Dialogue: Boundaries, Transgressions and Innovations.* New York: Bloomsbury, 2015. Kindle.

Muñoz, José Esteban. *Disidentifications: Queers of Color and the Performance of Politics.* Minneapolis: U Minnesota P, 1998.

Muslim Reform Movement: A Global Coalition of Muslim Reformers. *Our Declaration* (4. Dec. 2015), *muslimreformmovement.org/first-page-posts/personal-marketer/*

Musskopf, André. *Via(da)gens Teológicas: Itinerários para uma Teologia Queer no Brazil.* Diss. São Leopoldo: EST 2008.

Nairobi Statement of Worship and Culture. Lutheran World Federation. *https://worship.calvin.edu/resources/resource-library/nairobi-statement-on-worship-and-culture-full-text*

National Low Income Housing Coalition, "30-40 Million People in America Could Be Evicted from Their Homes by the End of 2020" (7. Aug 2020). *nlihc.org/news/30-40-million-people-america-could-be-evicted-their-homes-end-2020.*

Niebuhr, H. Richard. *Christ and Culture.* New York: Harper & Row, 1975.

Nobre, Antonio Donato. "Um Novo Olhar Sobre a Vida na Terra." December 8, 2020, *https://www.youtube.com/watch?v=QtQ86Yfiks0&t=217s*

Norfield, Tony. *The City: London and the Global Power of Finance.* New York: Verso, 2016.

Obama, Barack. "President Obama Speaks on Expanding Oil and Gas Pipelines" (22. Mar. 2012). *www.youtube.com/watch?v=YxkODM6lzUk.*

Oliver, Mary. "Leaves and Blossoms Along the Way." *Felicity.* New York: Penguin, 2015. Kindle.

Omidi, Maryam. "Anti-homeless spikes are just the latest in 'defensive urban architecture.'" *The Guardian* (12. June 2014).

www.theguardian.com/cities/2014/jun/12/anti-homeless-spikes-latest-defensive-urban-architecture

Oxfam. "World's Billionaires Have More Wealth than 4.6 Billion People" (19. Jan. 2020). *oxfamamerica.org/press/ worlds-billionaires-have-more-wealth-than-46-billion-people/*

Panotto, Nicolás. *Teologia Y Espaço Público*. Ciudad Autónoma de Buenos Aires: GEMRIP Ediciones, 2015. *www.academia.edu/10964644/Teolog%C3%ADa_y_espacio_p%C3%BAblico_Libro_?*

Patocka, Jan. *Heretical Essays in the Philosophy of History*. Chicago: Open Court; 1999.

Ponciano, Jonathan. "The World's 25 Richest Billionaires Have Gained Nearly $255 Billion In Just Two Months." *Forbes* (23. May 2020). *forbes.com/sites/jonathanponciano/ 2020/05/22/billionaires-zuckerberg-bezos/.*

Prado, Adélia. *Bagagem*. Rio de Janeiro: Imago, 1976.

Presbyterian Church (U.S.A.). *Book of Common Worship*. Louisville: Westminster John Knox, 2018.

Rahner, Karl. *Theological Investigations*. Vol. 14. Trans. D. Bourke. London: Darton, Longman & Todd, 1976.

Rasmussen, Larry. "Bonhoeffer and the Anthropocene." *Ned Geref Teologiese Tydskrif* 55.1 (2014). *doi.org/10.5952/55-Supp%201-677.*

—. *Earth-honoring Faith: Religious Ethics in a New Key*. Oxford: Oxford UP, 2015.

Reagan, Ronald. "I'm from the Government and I'm here to help" (12. Aug. 1986). *youtube.com/watch?v= nCedOQJoZEA*, acc. 31. Dec. 2020.

Relph, Edward. In D. Seamon and J. Sowers, "Place and Placelessness, Edward Relph." *Key Texts in Human Geography: A Reader Guide*. 2nd ed. Eds. P. Hubbard, R. Kitchin and G. Valentine. London: SAGE, 2008. 44-45.

Reticker, Gini, dir. *Pray The Devil Back to Hell*. New York: Fork, 2008

Rieger, Joerg. *Religion, Theology, and Class: Fresh Engagements after Long Silence*. London: Palgrave Macmillan, 2013.

Rivera, Mayra. *Poetics of the Flesh*. Durham: Duke UP, 2015.

Rodrigues, Michelle Gonçalves, and Roberta Bivar Carneiro Campos. "Caminhos da visibilidade: a ascensão do culto a jurema no campo religioso de Recife." *Afro-Ásia*, 47 (2013): 269-291. *http://dx.doi.org/10.1590/S0002-05912013000100008.*

Rosen, Brant. "A Prayer for Yom Hashoah" (8. April 2013). *ynefesh.com/2013/04/08/a-prayer-for-yom-hashoah/*

Rubenstein, Mary-Jane. *Pantheologies: Gods, Worlds, Monsters*. New York: Columbia UP, 2018. Kindle.

Safatle, Vladimir. "Another Kratos for the Demos." *academia.edu/36864867/Another_Kratos_for_the_demos*, acc. 3. July 2021.

—. *Quando As Ruas Queimam: Manifesto Pela Emergência*. São Paulo: N-1 edições, 2016.

Said, Edward W. *On Late Style: Music and Literature Against the Grain.* New York: Knopf Doubleday, 2007. Kindle.

—. *Orientalism.* New York: Vintage, 1978.

—. *Representations of the Intellectual.* New York: Vintage, 2012.

Sakamoto, Leonardo. "Londres enxota sem-teto com pinos na calçada. São Paulo é mais professional." *Blog do Sakamoto, UOL* (6. Oct. 2014). *blogdosakamoto.blogosfera.uol.com.br/2014/06/10/londres-enxota-sem-teto-com-pinos-na-calcada-sao-paulo-e-mais-profissional/*

Saliers, Don. "Liturgy and Ethics: Some New Beginnings" and "Afterword: Liturgy and Ethics Revisited." *Liturgy and the Moral Self: Humanity at Full Stretch before God* Eds. E. Anderson and B. Morrill. Collegeville, MN: Liturgical, 1998. 15-37, 209-224.

Santos, Boaventura de Sousa. *Epistemologies of the South: Justice Against Epistemicide.* London: Routledge, 2014.

Schechner, Richard. *Essays on Performance Theory, 1970-1976.* New York: Drama Publishers, 1976.

—. *Performance Studies: An Introduction.* New York: Routledge, 2013.

Schneider, Laurel. "Promiscuous Incarnation." *The Embrace of Eros: Bodies, Desires, and Sexuality in Christianity.* Ed. M. Kamitsuka. Minneapolis: Fortress, 2010.

Schwantes, Milton. "A Teologia E O Direito Dos Pobres--Entrevista com Milton Schwantes." *Associação Rumos* (30. March 2012). *www.padrescasados.org/archives /3313/a-teologia-e-o-direito-dos-pobres-entrevista-com-milton-schwantes/?fbclid=IwAR0sH3rvqIdnkMgtE7bhpC-XaV69FtPE_0o_NqVAYHyN1ebr_R3zWO7Evnw.*

Siefert, Jeremy, dir *The Church Forests of Ethiopia.* vimeo.com/390833915, acc. 11. Feb. 2020.

Smith, Jonathan. "Religion, Religions, Religious." *Critical Terms for Religious Studies.* Ed. M. Taylor. Chicago: U Chicago P. 269-284.

—. *To Take Place: Toward Theory in Ritual.* Chicago: U Chicago P, 1992.

Soares, Afonso Maria Ligorio. "Impasses da teologia Católica diante do sincretismo religioso afro-brasileiro." *Religião & Cultura Cenas da religião no Brasil* 1.1 (2002): 66-76.

Soja, Edward W. *Thirdspace.* Malden: Blackwell, 1996.

Souza, Jr., Justino. "Mercadoria, fetichismo e discurso figurado n' O Capital." *www.unicamp.br/cemarx/ANAIS%20IV% 20COLOQUIO/comunica%E7%F5es/GT1/gt1m2c3.pdf.*

Spinks, Bryan. "Imagining the Past: Historical Methodologies and Liturgical Study." *Liturgy's Imagined Past/s: Methodologies and Materials in the Writing of Liturgical History Today,* Eds. T. Berger and B. Spinks. Collegeville, MN: Liturgical, 2016. 3-18.

Stengers, Isabelle. "Autonomy and the Intrusion of Gaia." *South Atlantic Quarterly* 116.2 (2017): 381-400. *doi.org/10.1215/00382876-3829467.*

—. *In Catastrophic Times: Resisting the Coming Barbarism.* London: Open Humanities, 2015.

Strathern, Alan. *Unearthly Powers: Interreligious Dialogue and the Whole World.* Cambridge: Cambridge UP, 2019.

Suwandi, Intan. *Value Chains, The New Imperialism.* New York: Monthly Review, 2019.

Sweet Honey in the Rock. *Twenty-Five.* CD. Rykodisc, 1998.

Tasdelen, Erdem. *The Logic of Parerga.* Studio Babak Golkar. *babakgolkar.ca/the-logic-of-parerga/.*

Teixeira, Francisco José Soares. "O Capital e suas formas de produção de mercadorias: rumo ao fim da economia política." *Crítica Marxista* 10 (2000): 67-93.

Thomas, Linda E. "The Social Sciences and Rituals of Resilience in African and African American Communities." *The Cambridge Companion to Black Theology.* Eds. D. Hopkins and E. Antonio. Cambridge: Cambridge UP, 2012. 44-57.

Tillard, J. *Flesh of the Church, Flesh of Christ: At the Source of the Ecclesiology of Communion.* Collegeville, MN: Pueblo, 2001.

Tirone. Welcome Church. *youtube.com/watch?v=48yV7ww2 l6c&index=59&list=UUTOc5PmgWWmdH_naVcNJxoQ*

Toledo, Natalia. Nación Zapoteca, México. "La Realidad," XII International Poetry Festival of Medellín, 2002. *www.youtube.com/watch?v=PcKlFJQ-q6g.*

Tsing, Anna, Andrew Matthews, and Nils Bubandt. "Patchy Anthropocene: Landscape Structure, Multispecies History, and the Retooling of Anthropology: An Introduction to Supplement 20." *Current Anthropology* 60.20 (2019): S186-S197. *www.journals.uchicago.edu/doi/full/10.1086/703391.*

Tracy, David. *The Analogical Imagination: Christian Theology and the Culture of Pluralism.* New York: Crossroad, 1981.

Tuan, Yi-Fu. *Space and Place: The Perspective of Experience.* Minneapolis: U Minnesota P, 2001.

Tutu, Desmond. *No Future Without Forgiveness.* New York: The Crown, 1999, Kindle.

Vasquez, Manuel. *More than Belief: A Materialist Theory of Religion.* Oxford: Oxford UP, 2010.

Vellem, Vuyani S. "Cracking the Skull of Racism in South Africa Post-1994." *Who Is an African: Race, Identity, and Destiny in Post-apartheid South Africa.* Eds. R. Hewitt and C. Kaunda. Lanham, MD: Lexington, 2018. 31-48.

Vigil, José M., Luiza E. Tomita, and Marcelo Barros, Organizers. *Teologia Pluralista Libertadora Intercontinental.* São Paulo: Paulinas, 2008.

von Busch, Otto. Foreword to *Artist Clothing Catalogue* (2004/ 2005). *selfpassage.info/research/Fashion%20is% 20alchemy%20ForeWord.pdf.*

Wannesnwetsch, Bernd. *Political Worship.* Trans. M. Kohl. New York: Oxford UP, 2004.

Wentz, Richard. "Introduction." In B. Lane, *The Solace of Fierce Landscapes: Exploring Desert and Mountain Spirituality.* New York: Oxford UP, 1998.

Westhelle, Vitor. *Eschatology and Space: The Lost Dimension in Theology Past and Present.* New York: Palgrave, 2012.

Wilkey, Glaucia. *Worship and Culture: Foreign Country or Homeland?* Grand Rapids: Eerdmans, 2015.

Williams, Delores. *Sisters in the Wilderness: The Challenge of Womanist God-Talk.* New York: Orbis, 2013.

Yunkaporta, Tyson. *Sand Talk: How Indigenous Thinking Can Save the World.* Sydney: HarperOne, 2020. Kindle.

Zizek, Slavoj. *Less Than Nothing: Hegel and The Shadow of Dialectical Materialism.* Brooklyn: Verso, 2013.

INDEX

Amora, 12
Animism 162, 169,349
Anthropocene, 65, 86, 92, 110, 121, 304
Appalachian Mountains, 18
Ash Wednesday, 66, 248, 286

chipmunk, 12
Chthulucene, 87, 128, 304
clown, 17, 79, 139, 140
Conodoguinet Creek, 10, 18, 19, 346
critical zone, 9

dancing, 64, 77, 78, 139, 262, 300, 344, 345
duḥkha, 219

father, 9, 17, 19, 91, 102, 108, 111, 238, 257, 363,
fruit, 56, 57, 83, 144, 188, 212, 324, 331, 351

Gaia, 84, 86, 92, 103, 128, 185, 210, 318
glaciers, 9, 142
Guaiana, 17, 18
honeyeaters, 111, 112, 113, 130

humus, 53, 86, 88, 104, 179, 184, 231, 255, 349
imago Dei, 76, 88, 149, 252, 255, 259, 265, 289, 295
Iroquois, 18, 344

James Chapel, 142, 223, 256, 260
Jurema, 40, 212, 326

Landless Movement (MST), 11, 49, 52, 67, 154, 155, 325
Lenape, 18, 344, 346

Lettuce and Tomato, 79, 365, 402

Metta Sutta, 221
minimally Brazilian religion (MBR), 327
Mooca, 17
more than humans, 31, 53, 78, 121, 173, 345
Mother/Grandmother, 8, 9, 17, 18, 64, 75, 110, 178, 256, 267, 336, 363

Nepantla, 160

Pachamama, 76, 86, 128, 139, 186, 193, 210, 256
paying attention, 10, 27, 130, 134, 244, 258, 264
plantationocene, 122, 128, 304
pluriverse, 22, 63, 79, 104, 128, 138, 347
Potawatomi, 11
public theology, 147, 161

queer theology, 16
queering, 63, 251, 252, 263, 265
Qur'an, 220, 221

reciprocity, 12, 51, 54, 119, 133, 188, 189, 346, 354

Scripture
  1 Peter 1, 161
  Acts 2, 246
  Genesis 1, 90, 166, 167
  Genesis 33, 54
  Genesis 8, 115
  Hebrews 13, 161
  Hosea 6, 220
  Isaiah 55, 299
  John 17, 161

John 18, 160
John 4, 157
Matthew 22, 157, 221
Matthew 25, 217
Matthew 5, 143
Matthew 7, 324
Matthew 8, 296
Psalm 122, 299
Psalm 137, 3
Psalm 148, 144
Psalm 159, 303
Psalm 19, 144
Psalm 22, 2
Romans 12, 183
Shawnee, 344
shoe shining, 18, 25, 216
soccer, 18
Susquehanna River, 18
Susquehannock, 18, 344

symbiosis, 12, 22, 35, 51, 64, 114,
    336, 349
syncretism, 328, 330, 340

Tamanduatei River, 17
Tiete River, 17
tradition, 13, 26, 28, 75, 185, 218,
    220, 237, 317
Tupi-Guarani Nation, 17
Tupinambá, 8, 9, 345

Ubuntu, 31, 39, 157, 212

wonder, i, 20, 57, 75, 79, 91, 92, 125,
    256
Wonder, 10, 11, 19, 346

Yanomami, 9, 140

AUTHOR

Cláudio Carvalhaes is Associate Professor of Worship at Union Theological Seminary in New York City. You can follow his work on his website, *www.claudiocarvalhaes.com.*

also by Cláudio Carvalhaes

Praying with Every Heart:
Orienting our Lives to the Wholeness of the World (2021)

Liturgies from Below:
Prayers from People at the Ends of the World (2020)

What's Worship Got to Do with It?
Interpreting Life Liturgically (2018)

Liturgy in Postcolonial Perspectives:
Only One is Holy (ed., 2015)

Eucharist and Globalization:
Redrawing the Borders of Eucharistic Hospitality (2013)

Barber's Son Press

York, Pennsylvania